Visible Spaces

Johns Hopkins Jewish Studies
Steven T. Katz and Sander Gilman, Series Editors

Visible Spaces

Hannah Arendt and the German-Jewish Experience

DAGMAR BARNOUW

THE JOHNS HOPKINS UNIVERSITY PRESS
BALTIMORE AND LONDON

The Johns Hopkins University Press
701 West 40th Street
Baltimore, MD 21211
The Johns Hopkins Press Ltd., London

The paper used in this publication meets the minimum requirements of
American National Standard for Information Sciences—Permanence of Paper
for Printed Library Materials, ANSI Z39.48–1984.

LIBRARY OF CONGRESS CATALOGING-IN-PUBLICATION DATA

Barnouw, Dagmar.
    Visible spaces : Hannah Arendt and the German-Jewish experience /
Dagmar Barnouw.
        p.   cm. — (Johns Hopkins Jewish studies)
    Includes bibliographical references.
    ISBN 0-8018-3923-8 (alk. paper)
    1. Arendt, Hannah.   2. Jews—Germany—Biography.   3. Jews—
Germany—Cultural assimilation.   4. Zionism—Controversial literature—
History and criticism.   5. Holocaust, Jewish (1939–1945)—Influence.
6. Germany—Ethnic relations.   I. Title.   II. Series.
DS135.G5A753   1990
320.5'092—dc20   89-38885
                                                              CIP

For our son, Ben

Contents

Preface

The aim of this study is to explore the influence, on the development of Arendt's political thought, of a German-Jewish history that ended in genocide. It is, then, a historical account of her political philosophy and historiography—a biography, that is, of her acts of thinking. Information about her life now easily accessible in Young-Bruehl's magisterial work or available in Arendt's unpublished correspondence with Kurt Blumenfeld (a close friend and important figure in German Zionism) and her husband, Heinrich Bluecher, are used here to situate Arendt's thought in its intersubjective and historical context. I proceed on the whole chronologically, attempting to reconstruct Arendt's historical-political philosophizing as it responded to her experience of the Jewish condition in the modern world.

Arendt has remained a controversial Jewish figure because, in all her writings about a world torn by conflict, to an exceptional degree she remained aloof to all group sympathies or affiliations. Yet it was precisely this independence that made her locate her political thought in reinterpretations of history which yielded extraordinarily concrete images of an essentially human ability to speak and act socially. In *Origins of Totalitarianism*, the book that established her as a historical-political thinker, Arendt mourned the near-total frustration of this ability. In *The Human Condition*, which, in spite of clearly utopian impulses, remains her most fully accessible, persuasive book, she celebrated its realization. But in her critical essays on political Zionism and in her notorious report on the

Eichmann trial, she drew on this independence in ways that laid these texts open to serious misunderstanding. Her insistence on seeing Jews, too, as actors in history—a view that had already informed her early biography of Rahel Varnhagen—seemed to show an intolerant disregard for the particularly difficult past of the Jewish people.

If loyal friends were disturbed by the demands Arendt made on Jews for historical agency, they reacted vehemently to her unexpectedly harsh if lucid critique of the assimilationist fallacies that adhered to certain aspects of Zionism and to the politics of the State of Israel. My aim in this study has been to show how she came to make these demands and how, in the process of making them, she developed a highly original philosophy of political history. In the cumulative intelligence of its argument for recognition of human limitations, and in the persuasive power of its pleas that we assume responsibility for human potentiality, Arendt's thought has been unique in this century. Yet I have not been interested as much in redeeming Arendt's critique of political Zionism as in trying to clear away obstacles that have obscured its implications. In this, I have been fully aware that some of her texts need such clearing away more than those of other writers dealing with the same issues. This is so because of the peculiarly independent position from which Arendt spoke, which has caused her readers to praise her brilliance but also lament her single-mindedness, even arrogance, in insisting on seeing alternative aspects of a problem, always and at any cost.

I hope to convince my readers that the cost—of having to clear away misunderstandings by pointing out the errors as well as the merits of even her most notorious arguments—will indeed be worth paying. In Arendt's political thought, errors and new insights are curiously intertwined. This reflects more clearly than most of her interpreters (especially Young-Bruehl) have been willing to see, the unsolvable, the inconsolable conflicts of her experiences as a German-Jewish woman born at the beginning of the twentieth century. She never overcame the darkness of the times she had lived through, no matter how much she was moved by— or how movingly she reconstructed—the beauties of the cultural world, especially that of antiquity. Her "love of the world" (a phrase stressed in the title of Young-Bruehl's biography) made her all the more afraid of its finite destruction, and many of her arguments in the Eichmann report are meant to shock the reader into an awareness of this danger. For the sadness that Judith Shklar finds in the poignant late portrait of Arendt (reproduced on the cover of Young-Bruehl's biography), and that she attributes to the two thousand years of Jewish suffering, reflects, I think, less the burden of the past than a fear for the future of the modern world—a fear that Jews, Arendt insisted, have to be able to share as a modern people.

Arendt's political philosophy is centered in the concept of natality, the possibility of the beginning which each generation has to renew for the next. Auschwitz, on this showing, symbolized for her not so much past crimes against the Jews as possible new crimes against humanity in general. Unlike Adorno, she did not declare a significant silence—the end of poetry—after Auschwitz: she thought it wrong to impose such silence on the men and women just entering cultural time and space, to which they would make new, unforeseen contributions. It was precisely the conflicted, dark, pessimistic aspects of her intellectual temperament, her solitariness in thought, which made her fear for the preservation of natality and insist, sometimes too forcefully, that all aspects of a situation need to be articulated and examined. She was not troubled, it seems, if such examination kept awake, or reawakened, the fully understandable anxieties of a minority with a particularly troubled history. In some cases she seems to have thought such provocation therapeutic rather than wounding—sometimes rightly, sometimes mistakenly.

Beginning with the early biographical work on Rahel Varnhagen, a Jewish woman intellectual of the Romantic period, Arendt refused to see Jews as paradisiacally innocent victims of a predestined history of persecution. In retelling Rahel's life story as it emerged from Rahel's correspondence, Arendt came to understand the individual in her historicality precisely because that meant, in Rahel's case, an attempt to write her personal history against the particularly difficult circumstances of her social and historical situation as an early nineteenth-century German Jewess, neither rich nor beautiful, but gifted with extraordinary psychological and verbal sophistication. Most important, in view of Arendt's postwar attempts to understand the problems of political modernity, Rahel's story gave Arendt the opportunity to explore Rahel's failure to accept the accidentality of her Jewish birth as a challenge rather than a catastrophe. This failure of the Jewish woman—Jaspers was very much against Arendt's stressing this rather than Rahel's marvelously articulated humanity—clarified already for the young Arendt the importance of mutual (intersubjective) dependency at the core of history as cultural achievement.

It is important to recognize the strong utopian impulses that informed Arendt's distinction between Rahel's failure and her successes—

distinctions that already contain essential elements of the political model Arendt presented twenty-five years later in *The Human Condition,* which, in turn, provided the basis on which Arendt drew the distinctions that made the report on the Eichmann trial so notorious. At the same time, it is important to recognize how these impulses are seasoned by Arendt's clearly involving concrete historical speakers and actors in her projection of an alternate history in which Eichmann would have no place or time.

Acknowledgments

For their support of the research and writing of this book I thank the University of Texas at Austin. I have had generous help from the staffs of its German Department and Library, and from the staff of the Literatur-Archiv in Marbach. I am grateful to the friends who patiently listened to my thoughts about Arendt's thoughts and helped me in my attempts to put myself in the place of the other. Very special thanks to Lotte Koehler and Rose Feitelson, and, as always, to Jeff.

Visible Spaces

Introduction

Thinking in Dark Times

In the last years of her life (after the death of her husband, Heinrich Bluecher, and her teacher, Karl Jaspers[1]) Arendt returned in a sense to the questions and interests of her intellectual beginnings—philosophy as the exploration and recording of the *vita contemplativa*. Her last, unfinished work, *The Life of the Mind*, appears to indicate a departure from more than twenty-five years of cultural and political commentary and philosophy.[2] There were exhilarating and challenging aspects to this new enterprise, to the unfamiliar focus on description and analysis of mental activities. She had, after all, always thought important the adventure, the potential of new beginnings. Yet, where she talked explicitly and exclusively about thinking—in the 1971 lecture "Thinking and Moral Considerations," in *Thinking*, the first volume of *The Life of the Mind*—she felt the need to justify her "presumptuousness,"[3] and in both cases she referred her readers to the case of Eichmann.

The lecture, in fact, immediately introduces her concept of "the banality of evil," by which she means

> no theory or doctrine but something quite factual, the phenomenon of evil deeds, committed on a gigantic scale, which could not be traced to any particularity of wickedness, pathology, or ideological conviction in the doer, whose only personal distinction was a perhaps extraordinary shallowness. However monstrous the deeds were, the doer was neither monstrous nor demonic, and the only

specific characteristic one could detect in his past as well as in his behavior during the trial and the preceding police examination was something entirely negative: it was not stupidity but a curious, quite authentic inability to think.[4]

The introduction to *Thinking*, too, promptly brings up the issue of Eichmann: the "immediate impulse" for Arendt's preoccupation with questions of thinking had its source in her experience of attending and reporting on the Eichmann trial in Jerusalem, which, for her, meant the experience of "the banality of evil."[5] She mentions here too that there was no thesis or doctrine behind her using this phrase, although she was "dimly aware" that it ran counter to traditional concepts of evil, which tend to stress the demonic, the grand scale of evil.

This phrase, used as the title for the Eichmann book, led many readers to misunderstand—or, rather, to misread—her, and caused considerable, often painful controversy.[6] It is significant that she would come back to the phrase again and again, and that so many years later she would connect it so intimately with a mental activity usually treated as marginal to the political sphere. And, indeed, the mass murderer's *"thoughtlessness"*[7] had been only one of the issues she had tried to analyze in the Eichmann book. Concentrating on the "absence of thinking" in Eichmann in the later text,[8] she now pushes aside other issues that had been very important to her argument in the Eichmann book: the staging of the trial in Jerusalem, its implications for the, to her, troubling self-presentation of the State of Israel, and, above all, the cultural-political meaning of Eichmann's acts originating in his "thoughtlessness"— namely, the violence done, through the Nazi regime's refusal to share the world with the Jews, to the community of men.

The phrase, if not the concept, of the "banality of evil" had been chosen for its shock value, intended to counteract a culturally and politically harmful demonization of Hitlerism. However, the concept, lucidly developed in the Eichmann report, seems troubling here, where she focuses not on a specific and specifically significant instance of thoughtlessness, but on the cultural-political importance of thinking in general. Because here her intention to demonstrate the unnatural completeness and exclusiveness peculiar to Eichmann's thoughtlessness has lost, with its context, its focus and appears diffuse.

This comes as somewhat of a surprise in a thinker who has been known for the forceful clarity of her argument. But there is, I think, a valid reason for Arendt's using the example of Eichmann in this context. His particular and particularly destructive inability to think has clearly been of great importance to her thinking about thinking, and her giving it such prominence in her argument serves as a signal to her readers that in her discourse on thinking she is interested in its culturally specific *function* rather than its general nature.

Arendt points out that we cannot respond at all times to the "claim on our thinking attention which all events and facts arouse by virtue of our existence";[9] it would, as she says somewhat obliquely, exhaust us. And so, in the flow of living, we protect ourselves against the shock, as it were, of being interrupted by thinking[10] with conventions in language and perception. In Eichmann, Arendt found an unusually, even absurdly, high usage of stock phrases and cultural clichés, but she asserts that Eichmann differed from the rest of us only in that he clearly knew no "claim on our thinking attention" at all, that in him the "absence of thinking" was total.

The general problem of an absence of thinking, "which is so ordinary an experience in our everyday life, where we have hardly the time, let alone the inclination, to *stop* and think," awakened Arendt's interest because it had become the specific problem of Eichmann, the unthinking common man and mass murderer. How can thinking, "in its non-cognitive, non-specialized sense as a natural need of human life," which, as she herself says, is "not a prerogative of the few but an everpresent faculty of everybody,"[11] become absent so easily? How can a dangerously high degree of thoughtlessness be such an ordinary state of affairs? And how, then, can the *total* absence of thinking, characteristic of the common man Eichmann, be usefully described as banal?

The posing of these questions indicates Arendt's focus on thinking in its specific cultural-political location: she explicitly directs her thinking about thinking to situations of crisis. She wishes to understand what it means to think in dark times, because it is then that thinking "ceases to be a marginal affair in political matters" and poses questions of political and moral significance. "When everybody is swept away unthinkingly by what everybody else does and believes in, those who think are drawn out of hiding because their refusal to join is conspicuous and thereby becomes a kind of action."[12]

In this situation, thinking requires and reflects the decisiveness of a personal, self-authored voice, not the highly mediated and qualifying authority of the professional (academic) thinker. The introduction to *Think-*

ing makes clear from the beginning—even before the reference to Eichmann—Arendt's refusal to "be numbered among what Kant, not without
irony, called *Denker von Gewerbe* (professional thinkers)." In her discussion of Socrates, Arendt shows how this arch-nonprofessional thinker participates conspicuously in thinking as "a kind of action" which will contribute to the passage from consciousness into conscience. His midwifery,
his sterility,[13] signifies for her his "expert knowledge of delivering others
of their thoughts, that is, of the implications of their opinions, and the
Greek midwife's function of deciding whether the child was fit to live or,
to use Socratic language, was a mere 'windegg,' of which the bearer must
be cleansed." Socrates' thinking, then, is an activity which does not affirm
established conventional cultural values but which, in its very negativity,
can become a cultural value in certain situations. Thinking, Socrates does
not give his fellow citizens truth but helps them to get rid of opinions,
which are an obstacle to truth—that is, purges them of their unexamined
prejudgments or prejudices, which prevent them from thinking. In its
undermining of all unexamined notions, thinking is "equally dangerous
to all creeds and, by itself, does not bring forth any new creed."[14]

Socrates, arch-intellectual, thinking in the dark times of Athens' crisis, could not but disrupt further an already precarious community.
Thinking, he dealt with invisible, remote, absent things, energized by the
"winds of thought,"[15] unconcerned about the particular, the visible, the
threatened, troubled political present. How, then, could his thinking have
been useful to the republic in crisis?

When the Athenians told him that his "wind of thought" was too
powerful, bringing with it disorder and confusion to citizens who were
unable to cope with it constructively, Socrates denied that his insistence
on an "examined life" was corrupting the young and undermining the
strength of the polis. He argued that in fact just the opposite was true: his
only expertise, his eros—that is, his need, his desire, his quest for meaning—was actively good for the polis. Thinking, philosophizing men are
in love with wisdom because they are not wise. It is this desiring love
which makes them capable of thought and therefore incapable of evil—
if, that is, thinking is understood in terms of Socrates' eros, the love for
wisdom, justice, beauty; *if* Plato's "noble nature" is accepted as a prerequisite for thinking.[16]

At this point in her argument, Arendt firmly separates the activity of
thinking from its normative Platonic context,[17] which would limit it to
the very few of a distinct cultural elite, thereby undermining her attempt

to link the absence of thinking to the capacity for doing evil in the context of a twentieth-century mass society. She tries, as it were, to find an antidote to evil in the activity of thinking itself, regardless of the quality of the thinking man's nature:

> Socrates, who, unlike Plato, thought about all subjects and talked with everybody, cannot have believed that only the few are capable of thought and that only certain objects of thought, visible to the eyes of the well-trained mind but ineffable in discourse, bestow dignity on the thinking activity. If there is anything in thinking that can prevent men from doing evil, it must be some property inherent in the activity itself, regardless of its objects.[18]

Now, there are two statements Socrates makes in the *Gorgias* which Arendt thinks she can use in her attempt to establish the potential importance of thinking for preventing evil, in the sense of violence done to the community. The first: "It is better to be wronged than to do wrong," and the second: "It would be better for me that my lyre or a chorus I directed should be out of tune and loud with discord, and that multitudes of men should disagree with me rather than that I, *being one*, should be out of harmony with myself and contradict me."[19] Her argument[20] links the two statements in an ingenious reading of mutual elucidation. "*Being one*," the phrase in which she is most interested, she understands to point to the way in which one is seen by others. A person appears to others as one. Otherwise he, she, I, would be unrecognizable: "And so long as I am together with others, barely conscious of myself, I am as I appear to others." Consciousness—she translates the concept back into the literal meaning of the term "to know with myself"—signifies the fact that I am for myself even if I do not appear to me. Being for myself in this way, I am not just one but have a difference "inserted into my Oneness." I am that "two-in-one that Socrates discovered as the essence of thought and Plato translated into conceptual language as the soundless dialogue . . . between me and myself."[21]

Thinking, then, does not constitute the unity of the person perceived by others. "Traveling through words," it relates, it is dialogical, and therefore it "heals the solitariness of thought; its inherent duality points to the infinite plurality which is the law of the earth."[22] The dialogical property of thinking, then, opens up the oneness, the identity of a person, to include others, and the capacity for evil is checked precisely by the thinking person's awareness of such plurality. Socrates, thinking, decides that given a situation in which the strong can wrong the weak with impunity, a situation in which there is no alternative to either doing or suffering wrong, it would be better to suffer than to do wrong and thus prevent[23] (or at least refrain from) contribution to the harm done to the community and plurality of men. Thus it is the activity of thinking itself to which one can attribute the dignity of cultural-political significance, regardless of the nature of the thinking person.

However, the moral side effect of thinking for the thinker is still seen as generally "marginal,"[24] or, perhaps more accurate in terms of Arendt's argument, passive. There is no getting around the fact that thinking questions rather than establishes values and dissolves rather than affirms conventions. It is only in situations of crisis that thinking enters into symbiotic relations with moral considerations and becomes active. Arendt's explanation of why and how this should be the case leads to her positing a connection between thinking and judging which, though not explicitly stated before, has been at the center of her political philosophy since the early fifties.

Thinking, Arendt argues, is intercourse with ourselves; we can have a dialogue of thought with ourselves as well as with others; the friend, in this case, is another self; the self is a friend. "The dialogue of thought can be carried out only among friends, and its basic criterion, its supreme law, as it were, says: Do not contradict yourself."[25] For situations of crisis this means that I can remain a thinking person only if I take (choose, decide on) a position in which I can be at peace with myself. Only then, Arendt implies, can I argue meaningfully with myself, which will enable me to speak to the other, be heard by the other, in my own self-authored, self-authorized voice.

While Arendt cites a number of complementary philosophical views of the "two-in-one" relation of the self, especially in the Socrates chapter,[26] she refers her readers to Jaspers' concept of a "boundary situation" for a clarification of the meanings of *crisis:*

> This term was coined by Jaspers for the general, unchanging human condition—"that I cannot live without struggling and suffering; that I cannot avoid guilt; that I must die"—to indicate an experience of something immanent which already points to "transcendence" and which, if we respond to it, will result in our "*becoming the Existenz we potentially are.*"[27]

For Arendt, the term's "suggestive plausibility" lies less in specific experiences than in the fact that life is limited, bounded by birth and death, and that it forces on us the awareness of no more and not yet, of the past and the future—in Jaspers' usage, "transcendence" of the familiar now and here. However, she makes it quite clear that she uses this term here for its *political*, not its existential-philosophical,[28] dimension. Thinking, she points out, ceases to be a politically and morally marginal activity when, transcending the limits (boundaries) of one's own lifetime, one begins to "reflect on this past, judging it, and this future, forming projects of the will." And such reflections, she maintains, "will invariably arise in political emergencies."

There is, of course, no stringent rational or emotional reason why they should do so. She seems to connect here, by implication, these reflections with the thinking person's choice of a position which would ensure the needed consistency of thought as the dialogue with oneself. But she is much less interested in a philosophically coherent analysis of such a "boundary situation" than in demonstrating effectively its cultural-political dynamics—that is, in telling the story of thinking persons as actors in times of political crisis. Significantly, she concludes the Socrates chapter with a passage that describes a "boundary situation" in which—a familiar phenomenon in totalitarian mass politics—everybody is swept away unthinkingly.[29] It is here that thinking persons, interrupting or even stemming momentarily the rapid flow of events, of what, uncontrollably, is happening, can be said to be acting:

> In such emergencies, it turns out that the purging component of thinking (Socrates' midwifery, which brings out the implications of unexamined opinions and thereby destroys them—values, doctrines, theories, and even convictions) is political by implication. For this destruction has a liberating effect on another faculty, the faculty of judgment, which one may call with some reason the most political of man's mental abilities. It is the faculty to judge *particulars* without subsuming them under general rules which can be taught and learned until they grow into habits that can be replaced by other habits and rules.[30]

Thinking undermines such habits that develop in the absence of thought. Most important for Arendt, it does so even in the situation of modern mass ideologies, which seem to impose new sets of habits and rules irresistibly—as if, Arendt says, everybody were asleep. In the absence of thought, the masses of people do not act, because they cannot judge. Thinking and judging are not the same, but interrelated—as are consciousness and conscience:

> If thinking—the two-in-one of the soundless dialogue—actualizes the difference within our identity as given in consciousness and thereby results in conscience as its by-product, the judging, the by-product of the liberating effect of thinking, realizes thinking, makes it manifest in the world of appearances, where I am never alone and always too busy to be able to think. The manifestation of the wind of thought is not knowledge; it is the ability to tell right from wrong, beautiful from ugly. And this, at the rare moments when the stakes are at the table, may indeed prevent catastrophes, at least for the self.[31]

Arendt's interest in thinking is focused on its potential political dimension—that is, its potential relevance for enabling and articulating meaningful community. But as this potential is awakened only in situations of political crisis where community has been perverted into thoughtless collectivity,[32] the political significance of thinking remains precarious in that it is confined to the culturally and politically isolated self. However, in Arendt's view, this fact by no means weakens the appeal to the responsibility of the thinking person, whose very consciousness of his isolation in dark times can become the basis for a politically active conscience.

Such thoughtfulness in times of massive thoughtlessness is extraordinary. But is the massive thoughtlessness ordinary? Is Eichmann's particular near-total version of it ordinary? The Eichmann trial had caused Arendt to think about thinking—that is, to think about the cultural-political implications of the absence of thinking as "the banality of evil." Does this mean that the *evil done* by nonthinking men and women is nothing out of the ordinary? Does Arendt refer to the *evil* done or the *doing* of it? She had tried to overcome the impasse, experienced by many observers of the Eichmann trial, of an inability to link this obviously quite normal man with his monstrous acts. She never denied these acts; rather, she clearly stressed their monstrous, if not demonic, quality in terms of their cultural meaning. Yet, the man doing the evil was, in her view, banal, ordinary. The phrase "banality of evil" was meant to point to the ordinariness of the actors in an evil play that did not have the dignity of tragedy, though it was clearly a *Zivilisationsbruch*, a cultural-political catastrophe of heretofore unseen proportions. Arendt would also, therefore, refer to Eichmann as banal *and* horrible,[33] the common man who was no common murderer.

Acts like Eichmann's, which contribute significantly to cultural catastrophe, are not banal. He acted out of a more profound, total absence of thought than did the vast majority, who were "swept away unthinkingly by what everybody else does and believes in." Arendt did not deal with the depth and purity of this absence. She brilliantly demonstrated Eichmann's cliché-ridden, literally mechanical language—in her rendering he sounds like a garbled artificial intelligence program. What she did not see or did not choose to see is the fact that in its intensity the absence had become a presence—of belief. The quality of such belief in the well-functioning, invulnerable, abstract modern system, which at the same time was presented and perceived as the body of the German folk in need of protection from the modern disease, the Jews, is one of the most difficult problems faced by the intellectual-cultural historian of Hitlerism.[34] It is one of Arendt's weaknesses as a political thinker that she was uninterested in the social psychology of modern mass societies in times of crisis.

In her report on the Eichmann trial, Arendt wanted, above all, to demonstrate the need for a secular understanding of the Holocaust as a cultural-political catastrophe, because, as she rightly saw, only then would its meaning become relevant for the future. And in that she succeeded brilliantly—for readers, that is, whose specific understanding of their cultural situation (rather than a general capacity to think) made it easier for them to approach her argument without or with relatively little prejudice.[35]

And this brings me back to the question of Arendt's attributing a political dimension or potential to the mental activity of thinking. Thinking, with its liberating energy, may very well contribute to judging; consciousness may result in conscience. However, the process is not uni- but multidirectional: thinking does not come out of nowhere, nor does the absence of thinking. Both are—in the widest sense—culturally conditioned. And it is in this cultural conditioning that thinking, willing, and judging are intimately, inseparably linked. Arendt's decision to treat them as separate mental capacities and activities first and then, having arranged the distinctions, move them together and show how they interrelate, is responsible for some of the more troubling aspects of her political thought in general and her last work in particular.

This reservation has been stated before, and I will deal with it in detail later in this study. Here, in these introductory remarks, it seems more useful to draw attention to the intensity of Arendt's desire to counteract the absence of thought, which she understood to be a cultural problem of great importance. The depth of her involvement in meeting this challenge and her curiously moving and provocative intensity in insisting on her own voice drew her to the hope that the "wind of thought" might prevent more catastrophes, "at least for the self." One should be at pains not to misunderstand her here. She is not saying that such a limited individual contribution would be a sufficient antidote in situations of general cultural crisis. Rather, thinking in dark times, she is emphasizing her desire to speak clearly from a clearly defined position. Such clarity, in her view, can be achieved only by putting the "two-in-one" intercourse, the dialogue of the self, in the service of judging. Socrates, after all, claiming not to know anything for certain, argues from a position of knowing what is wrong, or, perhaps more precisely, of knowing what it is that prevents us from knowing what is right. And so does she.

Arguably, Arendt's greatest and at the same time most controversial contribution to twentieth-century intellectual life has been the debunking of "values, doctrines, theories, and even convictions."[36] An intellectual midwife, she has felt it her professional obligation to decide whether a thought-child is fit to live. Many of her readers have been irritated by her often forceful reading of the tradition. They have been troubled by her lack of hesitation in locating, defining, and criticizing those attitudes which she thought an obstacle to political action and those concepts which undermined a fuller, truer understanding of its meaning. Her judgment has often seemed too sure; in some cases it has appeared to rely too heavily on her etymological coaxing of concepts which has then yielded eclectic if peculiarly persuasive stories told by certain words across the centuries. It is clear that in purposely rereading and reconstructing the text of the past, she has been concerned with a meaningful continuity between past and present as well as with the importance of new beginnings, the future. But admittedly this has not always protected her from prescriptive misreadings of the motivations and intentions of political speakers and actors.

Most of Arendt's critical readers, however, have acknowledged the uniqueness of her position and the originality of her perspective.[37] The provocative energy of her readings of the past has been the source of many surprising insights, and at the end of the twentieth century it seems important to understand that and how the source of this energy has been related to her thinking in the dark times of extreme cultural-political crisis. By this I do not mean that she has limited herself, as one of her irritated readers claims, to an "ultimately fruitless" "search for an historical embodiment of Jaspers' 'extreme situation' in which 'unconditional deeds' were committed."[38] On the contrary, Arendt's reaction to extreme situations has been her desire to understand their historical and cultural, not their transcendent, meanings. Her thinking about the political sphere, her attraction to utopian models of visible spaces in which politics could show itself clearly and unambiguously, has been profoundly informed by this desire. Her readers, then, need to consider her experience and the manner in which it influenced her thought. It seems to me that they are helped rather than hindered by what she thought of the activity and significance of thinking in dark times. Her dialogical concept of thought, the two-in-one discourse, is directed to the texts that she reads as well as to the readers for whom she writes her own text.

This claim may seem somewhat suspect in view of her admittedly forceful, purposely selective dealing with the past. But in fact, relatively open-minded readers will find it hard not to understand her. They may disagree with her, even strongly so. But her reasons for reading a document, an event, a person's actions in this and not in any other way, will be clear to them, because she makes accessible to them, in her discourse, the dialogue of her reasoning, which leads to her distinctions and definitions. She presents her text with the assumption that she will be understood because the intention to be understood has so clearly informed her writing based on her reading.

This intention is perhaps the single most characteristic aspect of her work, and it is supported rather than weakened by her independent perspective. Her primary motivation has been to resist a majority opinion based on inarticulate, undifferentiated collectivity rather than a community of persons speaking and acting distinctly. If she measures the quality of judgment by its capacity to enable community, the quality of thinking is measured by its disruptive energy, which liberates judgment. In Arendt's experience of the past and the present, such liberation was essential. In our experience of the present, her future, we have reasons to consider her judgment.

1

The Quality of
Judgment

Arendt and Kant

The Life of the Mind, Arendt's last and unfinished work, was to have
comprised three volumes—*Thinking, Willing*, and *Judging*—but Arendt
died less than a week after she had finished the draft of *Willing*. A sheet
of paper left in her typewriter was blank except for the heading "Judging"
and two epigraphs. She must have started the third volume sometime
between the finishing of *Willing* and her death. It was to have been, in
some ways, the culminating challenge of her political philosophy, a task
"laid on her as a vigorously thinking being—the highest she had been
called to."[1]

The two epigraphs—quotes from the Elder Cato (one of Arendt's
favorites) and from Goethe's *Faust*—are instructive, for she used epigraphs to indicate the space of the tradition in which her argument would
move and the direction it would take:

> Victrix causa diis placuit sed victa Catone

and

> Koennt ich Magie von meinem Pfad entfernen,
> Die Zaubersprueche ganz und gar verlernen,
> Stuend ich Natur vor Dir, ein Mann allein,
> Da waers der Muehe wert, ein Mensch zu sein.[2]

Arendt's identification with Cato's stubborn loyalty to the minority cause
and with the paradoxical speculative secularity of Faust is of great impor-

tance to all her work, beginning with the biography of Rahel Varnhagen. These epigraphs describe for Arendt the position from which she speaks as an intellectual, and they are essential to what she understood to be the nature of her cultural contribution. They also suggest an extraordinary *unzeitgemaess* claim to and confidence in her own voice—that is, in her right to be herself and speak as herself.[3]

Because Arendt's voice was forcefully her own in all her texts, it was controversial. Many of her Jewish readers have been particularly troubled by what she wrote on Israel's politics, especially her report on the Eichmann trial. But her writing in general is provocative because the position from which she speaks is so clearly self-authorized, distinct in the community of political scientists or historians or philosophers. Arguably, both the usefulness and the flaws of her work are located in this distinctness. It is responsible for her uncommonly realistic and sensitive perspective on the German-Jewish experience as well as her utopian[4] view of the polis and the American Revolution. By showing how the position from which she discusses the troubled history of German-Jewish assimilation is interrelated with her desire for a meaningful counterprojection to an overwhelming cultural catastrophe, I hope to contribute to a fuller understanding of her work. This does not mean that I find her utopian solutions acceptable, but rather that I find them understandable. Also, it is not only the connections between her discussion of anti-Semitism in *The Origins of Totalitarianism* and utopian communication in *The Human Condition* which need to be analyzed; between her books on the Eichmann trial and on the American Revolution; between her Rahel biography and her essays on the American republic in crisis. As important—and so far equally lacking—to an understanding of her work is serious consideration of the fact that she looked at the world, which she tried to make accessible to her readers, not as a philosopher or historian or political scientist but as a cultural-political critic with strong (if eclectic) historical interests. Her perspective on political and social issues is informed by her general sense of cultural energies, forces, and tendencies and is broader and more eclectic than many of her readers would expect from a philosopher or political scientist—the positions from which she is presumably speaking in most of her texts. Serious consideration has also to be given to a fact that is perhaps the single most important source of her readers' intellectual pleasure *and* consternation: She relates her cultural-political criticism in the shape of stories that have as their source her own cultural experience as a Jew and a woman. "Bashed on the head by history"—as she said of Rahel Varnhagen, another German Jewess, and, by implication, of herself—she could not but acknowledge the reality of historical experience, her own and others'. And such acknowledgment sustained the personal quality of her narration.

Stories, she said, "reveal the meaning of what would otherwise remain an unbearable sequence of sheer happenings." The context of this thought is an essay on Isak Dinesen in which Arendt explores the connection between the shape of a story, unfolding "in the repetition of imagination," and its meaning, which for Dinesen is the recognition, acceptance, and realization of destiny:

> To be so at one with one's own destiny that no one will be able to tell the dancer from the dance, that the answer to the question, Who are you? will be the Cardinal's answer, "Allow me . . . to answer you in the classic manner, and to tell you a story," is the only aspiration worthy of the fact that life has been given us. This is also called pride, and the true dividing line between people is whether they are capable of being "in love with [their] destiny" or whether they "accept as success what others warrant to be so . . . at the quotation of the day."[5]

Here Arendt's voice is located in the consciousness of the subject of her narration: her comment and her quotes interact and are interwoven as into a shared text; it is a method of intertextuality which she used first and most strikingly in the Rahel book. Arendt seems to consent to Dinesen's "philosophy" of storytelling as if it were her own. But, consenting, she manages both to speak in her own self-authorized voice and to let Dinesen speak in hers. Arendt grants that space to speak and be heard to any position or any person on whom she comments or whom she analyzes critically. She does not take over the other's voice. In the case of Rahel Varnhagen, Arendt explicitly attempted to write the story of Rahel's life "as she herself might have told it"[6]—regardless of the fact that she saw and approached this life story critically.

In Dinesen's case there is clearly a strong, admiring fascination with the woman and the life. But here, too, Arendt does not identify when she lends her voice to Dinesen's. She does agree

> that storytelling reveals meaning without committing the error of defining it, that it brings about consent and reconciliation with

things as they really are, and that we may even trust it to contain eventually by implication that last word which we expect from the "day of judgment."

But if the story allows meaning to be revealed without arresting it prematurely in definitions, it has its dangers for the life lived according to its shape—that is, for living mainly to make the story come true. Arendt sees this danger in Dinesen's decision, as a young girl, to act out in her life a sequel to her father's story ending in suicide which for her own story meant a disastrously wrong marriage that resisted the shape of the story. Dinesen did, however, write about the "sin" of making a story come true—that is, impatiently "interfering with life according to a preconceived pattern, instead of waiting patiently for the story to emerge, of repeating in imagination as distinguished from creating a fiction and then trying to live up to it." It was, Arendt argued, precisely the earlier part of Dinesen's life which taught her the impossibility of making life poetic, of living it as if it were a work of art—Arendt had criticized Rahel precisely for her enduring self-deception—or of using it for the realization of an idea:

> Life may contain the "essence" (what else could?); recollection, the repetition in imagination, may decipher the essence and deliver to you the "elixir"; and eventually you may even be privileged to "make" something out of it, "to compound the story." [7]

Despite all her secular caution regarding the concept of destiny, Arendt clearly embraces the idea of storytelling, not only as repetition in the imagination, but also as a deciphering of essence. Significantly, she distinguishes repeating in the imagination from "creating a fiction": Arendt's readers do not have—or are not expected to use—all the liberties inherent in fictional discourse to negotiate what they consider to be the meaning of the text.[8] The story, as Arendt understands and uses it, does not so much "present" a world that can be looked at, entered, and left at will, as it deciphers, shapes, and thereby makes accessible "things as they really are"—that is, things as they are *and* as they might be. A shared life-world, fully represented, fully entered, will control in important ways the readers' referential activity. Storytelling, then, is a serious matter for Arendt because the meanings of stories are meant to be judgments of reality, of experience.

o   2   o

Judging was the central motivating force for Arendt's work; it was what she, in her own opinion, did best. She did not live to write *Judging*, however, which she had planned would be much shorter than *Thinking* and *Willing* and "the easiest to handle."[9] This third part of *The Life of the Mind* might have led Arendt out of what she herself perceived to be a theoretical impasse at the end of *Willing*. Attempts at reconstructing what would have become *Judging* have been based on Arendt's "Lectures on Kant's Political Philosophy," delivered at the New School for Social Research in the fall of 1970.[10] The account she gives here of judging— by curious coincidence, she also argues here that she is developing ideas Kant had not lived to develop himself—can be related to her definitions of judging in previously published texts, especially *Thinking*.[11] In a "Postscriptum" to *Thinking*, Arendt tells us that in the second volume of the work she will deal with

> willing and judging, the two other mental activities. Looked at from the perspective of these time speculations, they concern matters that are absent either because they are not yet or because they are no more; but in contradistinction to the thinking activity, which deals with the invisible in all experience and always tends to generalize, they always deal with particulars and in this respect are much closer to the world of appearances.[12]

Her remarks about willing, "this paradoxical and self-contradictory faculty," point to the difficulties she will have with her argument in what turned out to be the second volume, *Willing*.[13] She proposes to follow the experience of willing into the modern primacy of the future over the present which cannot resist it, connecting this attitude with the modern tendency to understand thinking "as essentially the negation of some-thing being directly present."[14]

At this stage of the project, Arendt has not yet planned the third volume, *Judging*, but intends to end the second volume, *Willing*, with an analysis of the faculty of judgment:

> I shall conclude that my own main assumption in singling out judg-ment as a distinct capacity of our minds has been that judgments are not arrived at by either deduction or induction; in short, they have nothing in common with logical operations—as when we say: All men are mortal, Socrates is a man, hence, Socrates is mortal. We

shall be in search of the "silent sense," which—when it was dealt with at all—has always, even in Kant, been thought of as "taste" and therefore as belonging to the realm of aesthetics. In practical and moral matters it was called "conscience," and conscience did not judge; it told you, as the divine voice of either God or reason, what to do, what not to do, and what to repent of. Whatever the voice of conscience may be, it cannot be said to be "silent," and its validity depends entirely upon an authority that is above and beyond all merely human laws and rules.[15]

Setting aside here the last part of the last sentence, which leaves it open whether she speaks with or for Kant, she evidently wants to stress that judgment cannot be taught, but only practiced; the mind needs a "gift" to deal with particulars. In Arendt's scenario, the faculty of judgment interacts with but is separate from other mental faculties and it clearly has its own modus operandi.

Judging, which deals with particulars, has its field of operation in history. Arendt's concern is the historian's perspective informed by judgment and leading to judgment. *History*, she reminds us, is derived from the Greek word *historein*, the meaning of which she paraphrases as "to inquire in order to tell how it was."[16] Historical inquiry, then, is linked not only with knowing but also with telling, with Homer's *histor*. It is clear that this equation has particular significance for Arendt, who has, throughout her writing career, addressed the question of the critic's cultural responsibility, which is to present a historically mediated remembrance:

> If judgment is our faculty for dealing with the past, the historian is the inquiring man who by relating it sits in judgment over it. If that is so, we may reclaim our human dignity, win it back, as it were, from the pseudo-divinity named History of the modern age, without denying history's importance but denying its right to be the ultimate judge.[17]

And here, at the end of *Thinking*, which she had prefaced with a quote from the Elder Cato stressing the activity, in solitude, of the *vita contemplativa*,[18] she comes back to him once more: "Victrix causa deis placuit, sed victa Catoni." A curious phrase, she says, which "aptly sums up the political principle implied in the enterprise of reclamation."[19] Reclamation, however critical, has been her enterprise since the Rahel biography, and it has been intimately connected with her developing concept of the political sphere. The fact that she introduces this concept so "naturally" into what is ostensibly a discourse on questions concerning historiography points to the nature of her approach to historical inquiry: judging and retelling history, she intends to reclaim an alternate history.

I do not think that Beiner's view of a "subtle but important reorientation" in Arendt's work beginning in 1970 is borne out in the texts.[20] He sees her considering judgment from the point of view of the *vita activa* up to "Thinking and Moral Considerations" (1971),[21] but after that from the perspective of the *vita contemplativa*, the life of the mind:

> The emphasis shifts from the representative thought and enlarged mentality of political agents to spectatorship and retrospective judgment of historians and storytellers. The blind poet, at a remove from the action and therefore capable of disinterested reflection, now becomes the emblem of judging.[22]

In the twelfth session of her Kant lectures Arendt, conjuring up the blind poet, does argue that the condition of impartiality, of "disinterested delight," is the most important condition for all judgments. One becomes an "impartial, not a directly affected, spectator of visible things" by closing one's eyes. Seeing with the eyes of the mind, one is in a position to view the whole that gives meaning to the particulars. "The advantage the spectator has is that he sees the play as a whole, while each of the actors knows only his part or, if he should judge from the perspective of acting, only the part of the whole that concerns him. The actor is partial by definition."[23]

But Arendt had never been an actor; with her perspective of the whole, she had been the spectator who judges the acting of the actor from a position defined by this perspective. The provocative, irritating, and illuminating energy of Arendt's perspective on cultural and political history has been a curiously compounded partial impartiality. Her argument has always been informed by a view of the whole on which the particulars depend for meaning; but this whole has been openly and forcefully partial as a result of her acts of judging.

As a historian, Arendt tells stories that are based on and shaped by judgments. In this activity she is not motivated by Kant's "disinterested delight"—though she associates it with the impartiality of the blind poet as judge and historian (if we connect this passage to the one from her "Postscriptum" to *Thinking*). Still, shifting the different aspects of *historein* into her concept of the historian, she works with a concept of judging which importantly differs from Kant's, no matter how much it owes to him. She decides how to be guided by him according to the logic of her own work.

On the basis of Kant's text, Arendt assigns to judgment two mental operations: the operation of the imagination—we remember here her formulation of a "repetition in imagination" as the source for storytelling[24]—and the "operation of reflection." The actual activity of judgment takes place in the latter operation.[25] The operation of the imagination makes the absent present to the inner eye and leads to choosing. But in the operation of reflection, choosing is subjected to further approbation or disapprobation: "In this additional pleasure it is no longer the object that pleases but that we judge it to be pleasing." The act of approbation pleases, the act of disapprobation displeases. In the context of Arendt's argument, the highly important criterion for a choice between approbation and disapprobation is "communicability, and the standard of deciding about it is common sense." Arendt develops this point with some close paraphrasing from *Critique of Judgment*, no. 39 ("Of the Communicability of a Sensation") and no. 40 ("Of Taste as a Kind of Sensus Communis"). And it is communicability and *sensus communis* which support the "political principle implied in the enterprise of reclamation."[26]

o   3   o

Arendt's attempt to reconstruct, in her reading of the *Critique of Judgment*, Kant's political philosophy as a source of reference and support for her own reclaiming *historein* is centered in her association of judging with the public realm and of the refusal to judge with the withdrawal to the private sphere. As she put it in her 1966 Chicago lectures, "Basic Moral Propositions": "In the refusal to judge: lack of imagination, of having present before your eyes and taking into account the others whom you must represent."[27] She impresses on her students that our ability to judge, our decisions about right and wrong, are dependent on our choice of company—the importance of choosing the company with whom one wants to spend one's life (of the mind) is a frequent subject in her correspondence with Jaspers after the war. The company is chosen through thinking "in examples of persons dead or alive, and in examples of incidents, past or present."[28]

The greatest danger in the realm of morals and politics, then, is indifference, the refusal to choose between right and wrong, the withdrawal from judging as an activity supported by and supportive of community.

We relate to the other through judgment. The danger inherent in the unwillingness to do so is strongly expressed by Arendt's linking the "unwillingness or inability to choose one's examples and one's company" with "the horror and, at the same time, the banality of evil, the moral fellow-traveler as mass murderer."[29] Eichmann had been unwilling or unable to choose his company and his examples. The company into which he fell prevented him above all from relating to others through judgment. It caused him to deny the need for such relating and, in implementing the National Socialist doctrine, to focus on total separation: the refusal to "share the earth with the Jewish people and a number of other nations."[30]

Eichmann's difficulties with language, his inability to speak understandably, is closely related, in Arendt's view, to his inability to think, which she qualifies importantly as the inability to "think from the standpoint of somebody else." It was impossible to communicate with him not because he lied but because he was completely isolated from the language and presence of others, which, for her, means "reality as such."[31] Reality is language and community, or, rather, language in community. In the *Critique of Judgment*, no. 40, Kant's definition of "Taste as a Kind of Sensus Communis" does not, for Arendt, mean (mere) common sense, "a sense like our other senses—the same for everyone in his very privacy." In her reading, Kant refers here, rather, to "an extra sense—like an extra mental capacity (German: Menschenverstand)—that fits us into a community." Arendt quotes from this paragraph—the "common understanding of men . . . is the very least to be expected from anyone claiming the name of man"—and comments: "It is the capability by which men are distinguished from animals and from gods. It is the very humanity of man that is manifest in that sense."[32]

This *sensus communis*—"the specifically human sense"—is so important for her because her concept of speech as communication, that is, speech in the public sphere, depends on it. In this instance her interpretation of Kant's text is overly purposeful: she relegates "mere" common sense into the private sphere, where it does not belong, and elevates *Menschenverstand* to the level of that extra sense which the idiomatic expression *gesunder Menschenverstand* (which translates into "common sense") does not connote. Her reasons for these extrapolations are quite clear: she wants to read *judging* in the eminently political sense of putting yourself in the other's place, and of relating to the other so that it would clearly denote the public and not the private sphere.

Her lengthy quote from *Critique of Judgment*, no. 40, documents her interest in that part of Kant's definition of *sensus communis* which proposes "a faculty of judgment which, in its reflection, takes account (a priori) of the mode of representation of all other men in thought, in order, as it were, to compare its judgment with the collective reason of humanity." This can be done "by putting ourselves in the place of any other man, by abstracting from the limitations which contingently attach to our own judgment." Kant concedes that he has in mind here potential rather than actual judgments. And, anticipating objections that such an operation of reflection may seem artificial as part of the faculty called common sense, he asserts that "in itself there is nothing more natural than to abstract from charm or emotion if we are seeking a judgment that is to serve as a universal rule."[33] The *sensus communis*, then, is a *potential* expansion of common sense into *universality*. Common sense in itself does not appear to be limited, in Kant's understanding, to the private sphere, as Arendt assumes; rather, it develops in interdependence with communal standards and expectations.

∘ 4 ∘

Arendt does not deal here with the fact that Kant's *sensus communis*, starting in community, reaches into the lofty sphere of universal validity, in which the political principle, in her view, does not participate.[34] Her summary of the maxims of Kant's *sensus communis* makes it quite clear that they have largely been her guidelines in defining her position: "Think for oneself (the maxim of enlightenment); Put oneself in thought in the place of everyone else (the maxim of the enlarged mentality); and, the maxim of consistency, Be in agreement with oneself."[35] Again she points out that it is, for Kant, the "community sense" (her term) which rules worldly matters, the public realm. And the quote she selects for support serves her argument very well—with one rather significant exception:

> However small may be the area or the degree to which man's natural gifts reach, yet it indicates a man of enlarged thought if he disregards the subjective private conditions of his own judgment, by which so many others are confined, and reflects upon it from a general [*allgemein*] standpoint (which he can only determine by placing himself at the standpoint of others).[36]

The standard translations have *universal* for *allgemein*: the desirable universal standpoint in Kant's meaning is located above rather than in community.[37] Arendt chose the less explicit *general* because she explicitly wished to draw on Kant's philosophical analysis of judgment as on the essence of his political philosophy.

In her essay "The Crisis in Culture" (1960), in which she distinguishes very sharply between the realm of the political and that of the social, and has a curiously independent Moloch mass culture threaten both of them, she argues that the faculty of judgment is centrally important for a functioning culture. The first part of the essay rejects contemporary (American) mass culture in general and simplistic terms that almost echo those used in Adorno and Horkheimer's *Dialectic of Enlightenment*;[38] the second part, a counterprojection, posits the cultural interrelatedness of politics and art as phenomena of the public realm. Establishing a connection in this way, she is able to present the capacity to judge as a

> specifically political ability in exactly the sense denoted by Kant, namely, the ability to see things not only from one's own point of view but in the perspective of all those who happen to be present; even that judgment may be one of the fundamental abilities of man as a political being insofar as it enables him to orient himself in the public realm, in the common world—these are insights which are virtually as old as articulated experience.

Art belongs to this common world as the public, political realm; works of art "can fulfill their own being, which is appearance, only in a world which is common to all." Hidden in private life and private possession, they lose their "own inherent validity"—as opposed to their marketplace value—and they have to be protected from individual possessiveness by being put on display in holy places or in museums. Though culture is not defined exclusively by art, art is central to it because "culture indicates that the public realm, which is rendered politically secure by men of action, offers its space of display to those things whose essence it is to appear and to be beautiful."[39]

Art and politics, then, are not only related but interdependent,[40] because political experiences and activities, though contributing to the creation of a place in which art can appear and be visible, would not leave a trace in the world were it not for the beauty of art, which is "the very manifestation of imperishability": the greatness of speech and action would be futile, would vanish, without "the beauty, that is, the radiant glory in which potential immortality is made manifest in the human world."[41] It is not for aesthetic reasons that Arendt emphasizes the cultural centrality of beauty. Rather, she uses this centrality in her critique of mass culture by firmly locating the faculty of judging, which is crucial to the interdependence of cultural creation, visibility, and appreciation, in the political sphere. And this enables her to present the "crisis in culture" as a politically rather than socially significant phenomenon.

The work of art is so eminently dependent on the public realm and participates so importantly in establishing and articulating—making visible—the political space because it signifies most intensely, most persuasively, most durably, the world of appearances. In middle age, after she had tried to understand and explain the origins and mechanisms of processes that would lead to a heretofore unknown rupture of civilized behavior, a *Zivilisationsbruch*, Arendt came to love passionately what she saw as the civilized world of appearances.[42] Her love, as intellectual as it was sensual, made her a "disinterested"—but by no means distant or disinvolved—and fascinated spectator. She defines this attitude by referring to Cicero's description of philosophical training in its culture-supporting properties. Such a "philosophical" spectator has developed the "discriminating, discerning, judging elements of an active love of beauty" in which "culture as such expresses itself." She gives this love the name "taste," following Kant's use of the term in the "Critique of Aesthetic Judgment."[43] And it is here that she finds "perhaps the greatest and most original aspect of Kant's political philosophy"—because of the quality of judgment. It is not enough, Kant says, for rational thought to be consistent, that is, to agree with itself; nor is it enough for the thinking person to be in agreement with himself. Rather, the quality of judgment depends on the ability to "think in the place of everybody else," which Kant calls an "enlarged mentality."[44]

Both in her essay "Crisis in Culture" and her lectures on Kant, Arendt stresses that the enlarged way of thinking, which is the basis for meaningful judgment, extends beyond individual, private limitations to the presence of others, "in whose place" it is carried out. But in "Crisis in Culture," which deals explicitly with a perceived crisis in contemporary Western (American) culture, the distinctness of the visible political space is much sharper:

> Hence judgment is endowed with a certain specific validity but is never universally valid. Its claims to validity can never extend further than the others in whose place the judging person has put him-

self for his considerations. Judgment, Kant says, is valid "for every single judging person," but the emphasis in the sentence is on "judging"; it is not valid for those who do not judge or for those who are not members of the public realm where the objects of judgment appear.[45]

o   5   o

This distinctness and visibility of the political space, which, beginning with the Rahel biography, informed Arendt's critical perception of social interaction, emerged fully in her description of the "Public and the Private Realm" in *The Human Condition* and then in her very positive account of what she understood to be the grass-roots democratic elements in the American tradition.[46] It was the central importance of such a concrete, almost palpable distinctness for her cultural-political criticism that had caused her to translate Kant's *allgemein* as "general" rather than "universal." The latter meaning suggests an expanding and obscuring transcendence of the clearly visible political space, which would undermine her concept of political speech and action. The public political sphere is a community of peers who can see and hear one another and speak to one another with the expectation that, speaking as individuals with the "enlarged mentality" of judging persons, each will make him- or herself understood to the other.

Arendt's concept of the political, contained in such distinct space, excludes, in the celebration of the polis, slaves and women and, in the admiring narration of the American Revolution, the heterogeneity and diversity of temperament or style in political speech and action, and the plurality of social behavior and of cultural activities and taste. Arendt's lack of interest in analyzing, on its own terms, the modern phenomenon of mass democracy is well known: she is deeply mistrustful of political representation where the political actor does indeed think and speak in the place of "every single person" in his or her constituency, not just the "judging persons," and where the collectivity of these "single persons" appears to her to be politically indifferent, culturally passive, and connected only in instances of shared self-interest.

Such indifference, passivity, and self-chosen atomization into interest groups have had, in her experience, disastrous political and cultural consequences. She sees a modern mass society which is both anarchic in its heterogeneity and rigid in its conformity, which is simultaneously hectic and apathetic, easily led into illusions of spiritual sameness, unity, and totality, and therefore very much exploitable. Her utopian political models or stories have to be understood as counterprojections shaped by her intense concern with a realm where the reign of ideology through terror could not, would not, be possible. It is not, in itself, a justification for the obvious limitations of her concept of the political. But the specific flawedness of her political models is intimately linked to their specific effectiveness, which is based on her concrete and active, her in many ways explicitly personal, historically mediated remembrance.

Arendt's political thought is focused on situations: she sees, with the mind's eye, individuals turning toward one another in speech and action. Relating to one another through judgment, they are not the same, but are clearly articulated in their individual and cultural difference and their political equality. Distinguishing, judging, is essential to communication. Her strong intellectual fascination with conceptual demarcations has always been seasoned with suggestive images of community. In the epilogue to the 1958 edition of *The Origins of Totalitarianism*, she analyzed the totalitarian denial of political space to the individual—that is, the denial to be distinct and to share—as so palpable and desperate an absence that the paradox of the good place had to assert itself to relieve the unbearable tension. And so she searched out and focused on utopian instances of community and communal, political speech in the history of what constituted for her the civilized world. This, arguably, allowed her to diffuse important aspects or goals of political action—for instance, questions of the legitimacy, distribution, and execution of power. Her concept of power as enabling agreements on community action in unconstrained communication can appear too simple and too limited.[47] But whether she dealt with political concepts or events, she presented, coaxed into the present, thinking or speaking or acting subjects so that they could be heard and seen and remembered distinctly as contributing to political experience. In this sense she has been both a forceful and a curiously responsive reader of history as the recorded memory of these contributions, which for her constitute the continuity of culture.

Arendt's reclaiming presentation has created for her readers the peculiar accessibility and immediacy of a world expanded by the presence of others in narrated space and time. Clearly, even forcefully, she has been responsible for the decision who should be remembered and therefore present, and this decision has been based on her taste, "the chief cultural activity," and importantly connected with humanity's political abilities. Concluding her discussion of a contemporary "crisis in culture," she defines the place from which she directs her critique as that of the humanist. She attributes to herself the attitude of a person who, influenced by the *cultura animi* in the Roman sense, "knows how to take care and preserve and admire the things of the world"—that is, the things of a world shared, a public world. Precisely this attitude is threatened or absent in modern mass societies, which, as she argues, do not have mass culture, but mass entertainment, "feeding on the cultural objects of the world," consuming, destroying the world of appearances which is the public realm. For her there is no such thing as mass culture, because culture depends on taste—that is, on judgment and choice with regard to the world in which we live. The last sentence of this essay asks the reader to remember with her "what the Romans—the first people that took culture seriously the way we do—thought a cultivated person ought to be: one who knows how to choose his company among men, among things, among thoughts, in the present as well as in the past." [48]

The invocation of Rome is significant here as it shows Arendt responding to the fact that Rome—for the last time in the history of the Western World, and much more compactly than Athens—contained the need for, the seduction of, the divine in the powerful secular visibility of its political spaces. [49]

Arendt's insistence on the obligation to judge for oneself and choose one's company among men and women and their thoughts, more than anything else, has shaped her perspective on historical as well as present culture. It has been the source of many misunderstandings, many genuine misreadings of the past and questionable judgments concerning current political events. [50] It has also provided the energy for her stimulating, sometimes exhilarating illumination of large, very difficult cultural-political issues. Her perception and presentation of political spaces led her to make political models that were clearly not meant to make policy. Their utopian dimension concerns a direction, a desire to approach, not a prescribed goal. In a situation in which the argument of complexity and constant change has become the most favored cultural cliché, she was interested in a morphology of political behavior. She developed it in models built on the supposition of, as it were, frictionless social motion. But then all radical political thought—and she thought radically—works with such models, and yet it can move the social construction of reality.

Into and out of Kant's *Critique of Judgment*, Arendt read precisely that concept of the political which she needed for her historical critique

of modern culture. She used this (mis)reading in her attempt at reclaiming and restituting a cultural tradition that had been ruptured so profoundly as to be almost destroyed. In his interpretation of Arendt's reading of Kant, Beiner usefully considers some of the difficulties involved in
applying Kant's formalized, universalist concept of judging to politics,
pointing out, for instance, his explicit exclusion of prudence from practical reason. Beiner argues that Kant thought experience quite irrelevant to
political judgment because politics in his understanding is concerned not
with empirical happiness but with self-evident and indisputable rights.[51]

But Arendt, in her "Crisis in Culture," explicitly distinguishes between the different accounts of judging to be found in the *Critique of
Practical Reason*, which is usually seen as containing Kant's political philosophy, and in the *Critique of Judgment* where she chose to locate it.
The reasons for her choice are clear. In the former text, which treats reason as the lawgiving faculty, the categorical imperative—"always act in
such a manner that the principle of your action can become a general
law"—is based on the principle of rational consistency, of being in agreement with oneself, which guides thinking. It is in the latter work that
Kant focuses on the "enlarged mentality" of judging as thinking in place
of the other, which is so centrally important to Arendt's concept of the
political.

Judgment in this sense as the—for Arendt—fundamentally political
ability to see things not only from one's own perspective but also from
that of everybody else who is present, and thereby orient oneself in the
public realm, is equated by her with *phronesis*, for which the Latin term
is *prudentia*:

> The Greeks called this ability *phronesis*, or insight, and they consid-
> ered it the principal virtue or excellence of the statesman in distinc-
> tion from the wisdom of the philosopher. The difference between
> this judging insight and speculative thought lies in that the former
> has its roots in what we usually call common sense, which the latter
> constantly transcends.

Making this connection, Arendt emphasizes again Kant's concept of
judging as "one, if not the most, important activity in which this sharing-
of-the-world-with-others comes to pass." His achievement in the *Critique
of Judgment* is, for her, that he discovered "this phenomenon in all its
grandeur" through his examination of the phenomenon of taste—that is,

judgments, which have been understood to be outside the domain of the
political as well as that of reason. This enables Arendt to link culture and
politics, which, she says, belong together

> because it is not knowledge nor truth that is at stake, but rather
> judgment and decision, the judicious exchange of opinion about
> the sphere of public life and the common world, and the decision
> what manner of action is to be taken in it, as well as to how it is to
> look henceforth, what kind of things are to appear in it.[52]

Kant may exclude prudence or *phronesis* from practical reason; yet
not only does he not, in Arendt's account, exclude it from judging as
supportive of political intercourse, but he sees such acts of judging based
on prudence, almost synonymous with it. Beiner, in contrast, argues persuasively that Kant in the *Critique of Judgment* "depoliticizes" the idea
of *sensus communis*, even "aestheticizes" the faculty of taste previously
perceived as a social-moral faculty. In his view, Kant abstracts these concepts, including judging, from the experience of community.[53]

For our context, however, it has been less important to argue that
Arendt mis- or overinterpreted Kant than to explore the reasons for her
doing so and to analyze how she did it. Kant, like Jaspers, was an intellectual gestalt providing focus and continuity to balance the experience
of anarchy and rupture. This does not necessarily concern the direct intellectual influence—here Plato and Aristotle are as important, and, next
to them, Heidegger and Nietzsche. It concerns, rather, a direction for
Arendt's eros in intellectual matters. In Jaspers and Kant, Arendt found
what she needed with a characteristically active certainty: reassurance
that thinking in and about the world, no matter how troubled, could contribute to creating a space of temporary permanence in which the memory
of the past would enable men and women acting and speaking in the
present to be responsible to the promise of the future.

There is a curious statement in the first of Arendt's 1970 lectures on
Kant's political philosophy: Among the very few books on Kant's political
philosophy, she tells her students, only one is worth studying, Hans Saner's *Kants Weg vom Krieg zum Frieden*. Of all the books on the whole
of Kant's philosophy, only Jaspers' devotes considerable space to this particular aspect. And then, in parentheses: "Jaspers, the only disciple Kant
ever had; Saner, the only one Jaspers ever had."[54] She herself was not a
disciple of Jaspers or Kant in the sense of continuing in the philosophical
positions defined by their work. But she did continue in what to her had

been most significant in Jaspers' concept of philosophy: its dialogical dimension, its insistence that philosophy means a mental attitude realized in the practice of philosophizing, in relating to the other through judgment.

When Arendt resumed contact with Jaspers after the war—they were to be in close and extensive communication for more than two decades—both of them agreed on the cultural priority to inquire about and understand political events and actors of the immediate past. Taking responsibility for the future would have to be based on such historical inquiry undertaken "in order to tell how it was."[55] More clearly, more directly, *historein* was linked to judging in the wake of the German-Jewish catastrophe. Yet relating to the other through judgment had become a cultural task of enormous and eerily literal difficulties. The importance of Jaspers for Arendt's developing intellectual position emerges strongly in their recently published correspondence. Arendt is clearly better informed, more incisive, more critically focused, and much more realistic about the German-Jewish question than hopeful Jaspers; she often disagrees with him on important questions. But the reestablished continuity of a dialogue with him—that is, of her participating in his philosophizing, which included Kant's—signified to her a cultural continuity between past and future which held the promise of the quality of judgment that she sought.

2

Society, Parvenu, and Pariah

The Life Story of a German Jewess

Arendt's intellectual-cultural biography of Rahel Varnhagen, born Rahel Levin in Berlin in 1771, was begun in 1929 and completed in 1938; it appeared first, almost twenty years later, in English translation (1957), two years before its first publication in German. These years sig-nify the experience of profound cultural changes, a *Zivilisationsbruch* of heretofore unseen dimensions, an almost total rupture and reversal of longstanding agreements concerning human coexistence, a rapid rewind-ing, as it were, of the process of civilization.

In 1929 Arendt had just completed her doctoral dissertation on the concept of love in Augustine with Karl Jaspers in Heidelberg.[1] Also over-seen by Jaspers, the new project, the study of a German Jewess famous for her Berlin salon around 1800 and her strikingly original and percep-tive letters, was intended to take Arendt one step closer to a university career. Her correspondence with Jaspers between 1929 and the begin-ning of 1933 deals mainly with questions of grant support for the Rahel project and preparation of her dissertation for publication in Jaspers' se-ries, "Philosophische Forschungen." In his correspondence about the dis-sertation, Jaspers gently reminds his high-spirited student that her man-uscript had not been the neatest and that careful proofreading was of great importance because the publisher was losing money on the series, a "ser-vice to *Wissenschaft*."[2] It is not Jaspers' patient concern about practical matters which is instructive here, but the courteous informality with which he addresses the young woman student as an equal. For Arendt, the intellectual-emotional ties with Jaspers were extraordinarily important. He had been the one, she told him later, who really directed her education in the general sense of helping her toward adulthood—she uses the verb *erziehen* rather than *lehren* ("to teach") or *ausbilden* ("to educate"). What she found in her relationship with Jaspers and with her Gentile husband, Heinrich Bluecher, was the trust, all-important to her, in mutual acceptance of the other's otherness. She could be certain that, speaking in her own voice, she might be contradicted but she would not be misunderstood, and she therefore did not have to either disguise or emphasize her voice but could speak in it naturally and expect a responsible answer.[3] Such mutual acceptance would not lead to solidarity; it would not be total in the sense of unquestioning, but it would be based on an unquestioned willingness of each to understand the other according to her or his intentions.

In 1814, at the age of forty-three, Rahel Levin finally married the Gentile Karl August Varnhagen, who was fourteen years her junior and intellectually inferior to her. A Jewess who was neither rich nor beautiful and who had no talents "with which to employ her extraordinary intelligence and passionate originality,"[4] she was deeply tired from her efforts to assimilate—that is, her dissembling in order to make herself fit into the society she wanted to be a part of—and Varnhagen was prepared to admire her "as she was." In a letter accompanying her testament, she was to express her deep gratitude for this attitude toward her, the other and outsider: "As much as it was *possible*, possible for your temperament to understand one like mine, you did understand it; through a magnificent spirited acceptance; with an insight which I cannot *grasp* as it does not come from any similarity of temperament."[5]

It was all-important *and* amazing to Rahel that her husband accepted her difference and that he did so unquestioningly. (We shall see, however, that his kind of uncritical acceptance was to limit her precisely in her otherness.) She, in turn, was prepared to give her unquestioning support to his career and to declare her complete, unflagging solidarity with him. Yet her experience had persuaded her of the enduring necessity to disguise her individuality and at the same time insist on her significant uniqueness. Attempts at assimilation had undermined her ability to find stimulating the other's articulated difference if it could not be used in some way to both accentuate and mediate hers. She was grateful to Varnhagen because in his total acceptance of her uniqueness he built a permanent bridge between her and the world into which she wanted to be accepted once and for all, without further questions.

Varnhagen's acceptance of Rahel was passive and receptive: he recorded her brilliant statements and edited her letters for posterity, and in doing so served, with her encouragement, his own literary career. She spoke or wrote to him, she gave him her correspondences with others, expecting to be listened to and recorded in print. She did not expect to be answered, but she expected even less to be contradicted. It was precisely this extraordinarily intelligent Jewish woman's highly articulate monological self-centeredness which Arendt was to find so troubling—albeit instructive—and on which she decided to focus her biographical analysis.

Respect for the other's articulated individuality has to be active, mutual, dialogical, if it is to support sharing in the construction of a human reality—what Arendt would later call "worldliness." Jaspers had taught her the foundation for the concept of tolerance as the ability to accommodate the other as other which was to become the center of her political thought. But her situation as a German Jewess in the early thirties in Germany speeded up the learning process immeasurably. By late 1932 she was ready to confront and contradict Jaspers over the one issue that profoundly threatened his concept of tolerance, the question of a meaningfully shared German-Jewish history.

In early 1930 Arendt had sent Jaspers the manuscript of a lecture on Rahel about which he expressed some reservations in his letter of March 20, 1930 (no. 14). First he objected to Arendt's contrasting "Freischweben und verwurzelt-Sein" ("free floating and rootedness") as "philosophisch gar nicht geheuer" ("philosophically not at all kosher"). Arendt had read and judged negatively Mannheim's 1929 *Ideology and Utopia*. But her 1930 review essay, with its vaguely ontological assumptions, shows no attempt to understand the dangerously polarized political situation out of which Mannheim had developed his concept of a free-floating position from which the intellectual might usefully view cultural questions.[6] This should not be understood so much as the result of the enduring influence of Heidegger's existentialism: Jaspers' own indirect answer to Mannheim in his 1931 *Zur geistigen Situation der Zeit*, with its emphasis on a cultural crisis in terms of high culture rather than general culture, including social-political considerations, did not really differ all that much from the assumptions inherent in Arendt's reaction.[7] But

Jaspers is much less concerned here with Arendt's reading of Mannheim than with her use of Rahel's Jewishness, and his argument, curiously abstract and tortuous, clearly shows his uneasiness about the problem Arendt is beginning to probe:

> Jewishness is a *façon de parler*, or the appearance ("Erscheinung") of a being-in-itself ("Selbstsein") of an originally negative attitude, which cannot be based on the historical situation, but is, rather, fate which has not yet been delivered from the enchanted castle.

Shortly after the war, Jaspers' Jewish wife, Gertrud, was to complain to Arendt that Jaspers, who loyally shared her restricted life in Heidelberg during the Hitler regime, had tried to encourage her by saying, "Trude, I am Germany." She herself had found that "too easy," and Arendt had agreed with her.[8] Jaspers had done so with the best of intentions, as he explained to Arendt; and so he had.[9] But he does not seem to have really understood the quality of exclusion and isolation imposed on his wife after 1933 and the precariousness of the German-Jewish situation in the last years of the Weimar Republic. Nor was he prepared, after the war, to accept Arendt's critical and pessimistic perspective on the process of German-Jewish history as a whole.

Arendt answered immediately on March 24, 1930, reassuring Jaspers that the lecture was just a preliminary to her study of Rahel, that she was not trying to base Rahel's existence on her Jewishness, but that a "certain possibility of existence" might develop on the basis of being Jewish, to which she ascribes, if cautiously so, the dimension of fatedness, "Schicksalshaftigkeit." Such fatedness, however, is dependent precisely on rootlessness ("Bodenlosigkeit"), which means that it would develop only in separation from Judaism. Also, she seems to say that she is interested in the fact of a conflict as such between rootedness in and separation from a cultural tradition, regardless of its historical specificity, in this case Judaism.

Arendt's language in these groping explanations, which circle around what would prove to be the most difficult issues of her Rahel book, is uncharacteristically opaque and her meaning obscure. Trying to deal with Jaspers' reservations regarding her habilitation project in the field of philosophy, she uses the obfuscating self-defensive academic language intended to anticipate authoritative objections and avoid them. It is obvious, however, that she has difficulties defining her conceptual strategies in terms of her subject's social-historical existence. So far she is clear only about Rahel's peculiar, highly individual mode of self-awareness and about its potential significance for her biographer. Rahel, Arendt explains to Jaspers, did not reflect on her life from hindsight, but, from the beginning, lived her life both intensely and reflectively. Thus, the biographer's material was already formed, as it were, by such "unmediated reflection."

This indeed important insight was to have important consequences. Arendt's analysis will be in the form of a biography, she states, because, unable to deal *in abstracto* with concepts like fatedness, she has to work with concrete examples from experience. In the case of Rahel, who in her letters communicated living her life, biographical interpretation means repetition. Writing Rahel's life story, Arendt repeats it by reconstructing what Rahel had already constructed herself. And Arendt is aware of the fact that Rahel's construct—expressing and stressing her significant uniqueness—has little to do with the development of an individuality as a focus of judgment, choice, or decision, and everything to do with tracing the bewildering process of living.

Twenty-five years later, in the preface to the English edition of the Rahel book, Arendt summed up her biographical approach: "What interested me solely was to narrate the story of Rahel's life as she herself might have told it."[10] She said this partly to counter objections to her critical perspective on Rahel, for she was somewhat apprehensive about possible misunderstandings in the post-Holocaust context. But mainly she wished to stress her interest in Rahel's understanding of her own situation—that is, the question of Rahel's historical consciousness. It was not a question of Arendt's developing a narrative perspective that would merge the narrator's consciousness with that of her subject. Such merging would have prevented her from gaining precisely that clarification of the historical-political dimension of Rahel's existence which could only be achieved by distinction and differentiation. From the very beginning—Arendt's conceptual difficulties and Rahel's emphatic individuality notwithstanding—Arendt had understood that she needed to see Rahel and find ways to present her as a cultural-historical phenomenon. The subtitle of the book in the original German is "Lebensgeschichte einer deutschen Juedin aus der Romantik" (the life story of a German Jewess of the Romantic period). Its English translation, "The Life of a Jewish Woman," authorized by Arendt for an Anglo-American audience for whom "German Jewess" and "Romantic period" have little connotational value, is seriously misleading. Arendt does not tell the *life* of a *Jewish* woman; she narrates the struggles of a *German-Jewish* woman to preserve the individual spontaneity *and* the cultural meaning of living in the *story* of her life which Arendt repeats or retells in a clarifying analytical paraphrasis.

The process of working through her conceptual difficulties with the Rahel biography was to prove important for the development of Arendt's political thought, which in its characteristic striving for concreteness as enabling experiential referentiality for the reader is dependent on the historically specific phenomenon. (The fact that as a historian Arendt was highly selective—that is, "less than reliable"—is another matter.) By repeating Rahel's life story, Arendt gained insight into her historicality precisely because Rahel had told her own story against the backdrop of her social-historical situation. Most important, in view of Arendt's postwar attempts to understand the problems of political modernity, the Rahel biography taught Arendt to analyze Rahel's failures in a way that would clarify the importance of the intersubjective dependency—in cultural and political terms—that is at the core of history as the significantly ordering story of human existence. Retelling Rahel's life story, Arendt distinguished much more clearly her subject's failures from her successes, and she did so by showing that Rahel herself might have been able to risk such clarity if she had been willing to do so. The strong utopian impulse in these distinctions already contains the most important elements of the political model Arendt presented twenty-five years later in *The Human Condition*. But this impulse is seasoned, as is the body of Arendt's political thought, by her clearly involving her subject—the concrete, historical Rahel—in the projection of an alternate history.

o   2   o

Jaspers was evidently reassured by Arendt's letters, but he did not hear much more about the direction Arendt's project was taking. Over the next two years the correspondence between them dealt with grants he helped her obtain and books he sent her. On January 26, 1932, for instance, she thanks him for his three-volume *Philosophie* (1932), writing him that she is reading volume two, *Metaphysik*, and mentioning her hopes that the "Jewish grant" will be renewed.[11] But when on January 1, 1933, she thanks Jaspers for his *Max Weber: Deutsches Wesen im politischen Denken, im Forschen und Philosophieren* (1932),[12] it is clear for the first time in their correspondence that a substantial change has occurred in Arendt's view of her cultural position—and in her relationship with Jaspers as well. Going immediately to the heart of the matter, she tells him about her difficulties with the book, beginning with the introduction. She can accept Jaspers' view of Weber as "the Great German"; she cannot accept Weber as the incarnation of "deutsches Wesen," the essence of what is German, which Jaspers defines as "reason and human-ity springing from the source of passion" ("Vernuenftigkeit und Mensch-lichkeit aus dem Ursprung der Leidenschaft"). As a Jewess, her agree-ment with this, as with Weber's "impressive patriotism," would be as inappropriate, she insists, as her disagreement. For her, Germany means native language, poetry, and philosophy, but she has to keep at a distance Weber's "magnificent" statement that he would enter into an alliance with the devil to help restore Germany.[13]

Jaspers' answer is immediate, very much perplexed and concerned. Significantly, he now uses the same form of address she uses when writ-ing to him—"liebe(r) und verehrte(r)"—instead of his usual "liebe," in an attempt to equalize the positions from which they speak. In the first sentences he expresses his reservations regarding the phrase "deutsches Wesen" *and* his surprised dismay at her desire to distinguish herself from things German. ("Was ist das nur fuer eine fatale Sache mit dem deutschen Wesen! Es ist mir wunderlich, dass Sie als Juedin sich vom Deutschen unterscheiden wollen.") He explains that his motivation for using this term had been a somewhat vague historical "Totalitaetsinten-tion" of stressing for his intended audience the "ought" contained in the equation *German = reason*. This audience is Germany's nationalist youth, among whom he finds much good will and much confusion. For this reason, too, he has chosen a nationalist publisher's series, Schriften an die Nation, and has compromised on the subtitle because "Max We-ber" alone would not have been sufficiently suggestive.

Jaspers agrees that the word *German* has been misused to the point of becoming almost empty and unusable, and therefore he argues that an attempt be made to "fill it ethically" with Weber's "Gestalt." He proposes to have the success of his attempt judged by Arendt's willingness to be German. After all, she would have to add only Germany's "historical-political fate" to native language, poetry, and philosophy in order to erase the last remnant of the difference in their views. And, reasonably, he states that for the present and in political terms he sees Germany's fate linked with a unified Europe. But then he makes a highly suggestive distinction between a self-restrained "Reich *der* Deutschen" (Reich of the German people), and a "Reich *des* Deutschen" (Reich of German[ness]). The latter, in his view, links Holland to Austria, and Scandinavia to Switzer-land, thereby reinforcing his belief in the cultural expansion—a German

high culture—which was so characteristic of Weimar intellectuals, Jewish or Gentile, and across the spectrum of political sympathies and affiliations.[14]

Arendt is remarkably decisive in distancing herself from this belief in
the redemptive expansion of cultural values. In contrast to many of her
German-Jewish intellectual contemporaries, she understood the implications of the political developments for her cultural position.[15] In her answer to Jaspers dated January 6, 1933, she argues that the phrase
"deutsches Wesen" itself is identical with its misuse. She remarks on the
opacity of Jaspers' term "Totalitaetsintention," which nevertheless leaves
no doubt about its transhistorical direction. Repeating her unquestioned
and inevitable loyalty to German language, poetry, and philosophy—in
this Jaspers needed to be reassured frequently in their postwar correspondence as well—she rejects his assumption that she shares Germany's historical-political fate: Jews have come into German history as into an alien
tradition; they have been allowed to participate in it late and then only in
fragmentary ways. But this clearly stated rejection is nevertheless qualified by her awareness of the dilemma of German-Jewish history—of assimilation as historical and cultural duplicity, in all the meanings of the
term. Disassociating herself from German history, she will have to acknowledge—that is, examine critically—her part in German-Jewish history.

The difficulties of this dual history, with its attendant social-cultural
duplicity, have been caused in part by the fact that it has remained dual
in a very specific way: *assimilation* in German has meant an ongoing process in the sense of "unfinished" or "incomplete" rather than "open." And
this incompleteness, Arendt realized later in America, where this was not
a problem, made it extremely difficult to be naturally Jewish *and* German
in contributing, as a citizen, to a German culture that included politics.
Speaking about Jews in Germany, Arendt explains to Jaspers, one means
not only the few families who have been settled in Germany for generations but also the "Zustrom aus dem Osten"—the continuous influx of
Jews from the East. Her choice of term is significant in this context. It
implies the dimension of a natural event uncontrollable in cultural
terms—"Zustrom," a streaming or flowing into—and in that a certain
dissociation on her part which was very characteristic for educated assimilated German Jews, who knew from experience that tolerance for the
otherness of the other was more difficult the more it was distinct, and
even more so if it appeared to be emphasized.[16] "Germany in its old glory"

is Jaspers' past, which Arendt does not share; yet she cannot say unambiguously which is her past. In her view, every attempt to get beyond
such ambiguity—be it the Zionists', the assimilationists', or the anti-Semites'—would only obscure the real problems of the present situation.[17]

Jaspers' answer was again prompt (January 10, 1933 [no. 25]), but
it was couched in rather general terms and expressed his enthusiastic
expectations for the Rahel project. For the next five years Jaspers and
Arendt exchanged only a few short notes discussing the possibilities of
Arendt's visiting in Heidelberg and of meetings abroad. The last note was
from Arendt (September of 1938 [no.29]), who, living in Paris in a state
of statelessness, is unable to join Jaspers in Luxembourg. Then silence,
until the correspondence was resumed in the fall of 1945, acknowledging
the profound cultural rupture and desire for continuity which for Arendt
meant the continuing attempt at clarifying the historical-political meanings of the German-Jewish question.

o 3 o

The single most important influence on Arendt during the early thirties was that of the German Zionist Kurt Blumenfeld. She had met him
in 1926 on the occasion of a lecture he delivered to the Heidelberg Zionist Students' Club (arranged by her friend Hans Jonas). Blumenfeld,
who had been active in Zionist politics since the turn of the century,
was at that time chairman of the Zionistische Vereinigung fuer Deutschland (1924–1933). He referred to himself as a "Zionist by the grace of
Goethe,"[18] thereby stressing the importance of the German cultural tradition to his Zionism. It supported him, he felt, in his critical perspective
on what he saw as politically antiprogressive, oppressive aspects of international Zionism and in what Arendt experienced as his unusual ability
to tolerate the other's otherness.

Blumenfeld acquainted Arendt with the writings of Bernard Lazare,
the French-Jewish journalist and Dreyfusard[19] who had blamed the Zionist leadership for infantilizing the Jewish masses.[20] Lazare wanted a
revolution within the Jewish minority—above all, open criticism of the
role Jewish money had played in French domestic politics and of its influence on the relation between Jews and Gentiles. There was no room for
such a critical position in Herzl's static, in many ways reactionary Zionist
organization, and Lazare, elected a member of an important committee at
the 1898 second Zionist congress, withdrew from Zionist politics in

1899. Like Herzl, Lazare had reported on the first Dreyfus trial from October 1894 to January 1895 and had had to listen to the Paris mob's shouting "death to the Jews." Herzl, the Paris correspondent of the influential Vienna *Neue Freie Presse* since 1891, returned to Vienna in 1895 to become, as editor in chief of the paper's *feuilleton*, the darling of the Viennese public. His *Jewish State* (1896), an "attempt at a modern solution of the Jewish question" (subtitle: *Versuch einer modernen Loesung der Judenfrage*), had been provoked by the traumatic experience of an anti-Semitism which he thought inevitably (therefore significantly) fated and thus rationally inaccessible.

Lazare had come to Paris from his hometown in the south of France and had immediately been shocked by the anti-Semitic demonstrations on the occasion of the Panama scandal. His reaction, however, was not withdrawal in the face of massive and "fateful" prejudice, but rather the decision to understand it in terms of the motivations and dynamics of a concrete social-political conflict. In 1894, shortly before the Dreyfus affair broke, he published his two-volume *L'Antisemitisme: Son Histoire and Ses Causes*, which criticized, too, the victims of prejudice, the Jews, for their lack of social and political responsibility. Incited irresponsibly, the masses had still reacted to that fact. Lazare confronted anti-Semitism by calling on all groups, including the Jews, to share the world equitably and responsibly—a position that would be particularly accessible and attractive to Arendt's intellectual temperament. Self-confidently *and* self-consciously a French Jew, Lazare advocated using an intentional—in contrast to imposed—outsider or "pariah" position in fighting one of the most virulent cultural-racist prejudices of the nineteenth and twentieth centuries. He was able to do so because he had found his Jewish identity in confronting the challenge of anti-Semitism.[21]

Herzl, in contrast, wanted an end to the pariah existence, which he saw as imposed from without and as an existentially given transrational rather than historically developed and recognizable problem of the Jews. Where Lazare asked for the pariah's self-critical position *within* the minority group, Herzl asked for a position of unquestioning collective solidarity and affirmation, which Lazare had described as that of "the parvenu." Arendt had found this distinction very suggestive and was to use it frequently, beginning with her analysis of Rahel's attitude toward the fact that she was born Jewish.

For Herzl, there had always been anti-Semitism and there always

would be: all through history the Jews have been forced to be one people
by their enemies.[22] He is calling on them now to draw on and to use
actively the strength of such unquestionable solidarity:

> Were the founders of states which are now great states, more pow-
> erful, more prudent ["klug"], better educated, richer than today's
> Jews? . . . Our race is in all respects more able ["in allem tuech-
> tiger"] than most other peoples on this earth. This is precisely the
> source of the great hatred. We just have had no self-confidence. The
> day we believe in ourselves, our moral misery will end.[23]

Herzl was trying here to convince the old Lord Rothschild, the London
"Bank-Lord of Hosts" ("Herr der Bankheerscharen"), of the good prospects for a Jewish state. For Lazare and Arendt, however, such "self-
confidence" without self-criticism—that is, without a critical perspective
on one's own participation in history—is troubling in its social-political
implications rather than useful.

Herzl's concept of and response to expressions of anti-Semitism is
too simplistic; on February 20, 1897, he notes in his diary a Prince Friedrich von Wrede's assertion that the Jews are needed as scapegoats because
there will always be discontent. "If one couldn't go against the Jews we
would have a revolution." Herzl finds this "confession" "outright charm-
ing in its naiveté."[24] But there is naiveté, too, in his eagerness to abstract
such opportune scapegoat practice into a general scapegoat theory that
causes him to exclude the troubling question of a specifically Jewish abstention from political responsibility. Lazare and Arendt thought such an
all-embracing definition of a majority reaction to a political-cultural minority a great obstacle in the attempt to understand critically the difficult
social reality forced on the Jews. The conflicted and contradictory conditions of this reality were, after all, to influence profoundly precisely that
Jewish State which Herzl had intended to be free of them, totally and
once and for all.

In the letter to Rothschild from which I quoted above, Herzl announced the publication of his novel *Altneuland* (1902), the story of a
strictly paternalistic Zionist utopia. Working on this novel for three years,
he had tried to invalidate the reservations voiced by Rothschild and others
that "the Jewish commonwealth ["Gemeinwesen"] which I want to establish, will by needs be small, orthodox and illiberal."[25] It was not to remain
small. But it was to experience considerable and enduring difficulties of
orthodoxy and theocracy, which could, in part, be traced back to Herzl

as "Moses," "Messias," "King of the [East-] Jews."[26] Arendt came to analyze these difficulties as an important aspect of European Jewish history
and to develop her political thought in response to this analysis.

o 4 o

Arendt had not intended to write, indeed had not written, a book
about Rahel, but had retold the story of Rahel's life as she had constructed
it in the letters to her friends and lovers.[27] In the 1957 preface to the
Rahel book, Arendt accordingly stresses the fact that her criticism of
Rahel

> corresponds to Rahel's self-criticism, and since she—unburdened
> by modern inferiority feelings—could rightly say of herself that she
> did not "vainly seek applause I would not record myself" she also
> had no need "to pay flattering visits to myself." It is, of course, only
> of my intentions that I speak; I may not always carry them out suc-
> cessfully and at such times may appear to be passing judgment
> upon Rahel from some higher vantage point. If so, I have simply
> failed in what I set out to do.[28]

Arendt is speaking here about the position from which the historian views
lives lived. Her stated position is one that takes into consideration and
thereby tries to bridge temporal distance, avoiding the fallacies of an
unexamined perspective of hindsight from which so much of history has
been written. There are some serious if instructive contradictions in the
manner in which she understands and states her position. She thinks
important her deliberate avoidance of that "modern form of indiscretion
in which the writer attempts to penetrate his subject's tricks and aspires
to know more than the subject knew about himself or was willing to reveal."[29] But emphasizing this deliberately limited perspective, she seems
to wish to conceal the fact that the historian-biographer does indeed know
more than the subject knew about herself in many important ways. The
cultural task, the challenge and contribution of historiography, is precisely
the accumulation of such knowledge motivated by the desire to defeat
oblivion—of a life, but also of the process of living it. The historiographer
in her examined, reflected position of hindsight knows more than her
subject and can thus expand the subject's temporality. She also knows
less, because her reflection is informed by her own circumscribed temporality, which only historiographers after her will be able to expand.

When Arendt wrote the biography of Rahel Varnhagen from the perspective of a twentieth-century intellectual and cultural historian, she did so as a German Jewess threatened in her physical and intellectual existence by the Nazi regime. In the preface to the biography she states that her approach to the life story of the German Jewess Rahel was applied both in regard to the "Woman Problem" and, "though here with more difficulty, to the Jewish question, which in Rahel's own opinion exerted a crucial influence upon her destiny." The difficulties here have to do with the fact that in this case Rahel's life story, based on her conduct and reactions, is part of the story "of cultivated German Jewry" and has thereby acquired a "limited historical importance of which, however, this book does not treat." [30]

With this qualification Arendt shows herself to be curiously reticent about her intentions in the book and about its potential contribution. Much of the conceptual grid of "Antisemitism," the first and arguably most effective part of *The Origins of Totalitarianism*, owes its peculiar pointedness and clarity to the analysis she undertook in the Rahel book of a minority's conflicted self-perception and self-presentation. Just as Rahel understood the Jewish question to be a crucial influence on the course and shape of her life, Arendt in retelling Rahel's life story—that is, in retracing the shape Rahel had given to this life—was to highlight such influence. More, she was to present the shaping of this life by individual development and accident of birth as a historical example for the troubled social discourse of the educated, assimilated German Jews desiring assimilation. When in the early stage of her work she wrote to Jaspers about her approach to Rahel's life, she stressed more the psychological-existential dimension of Rahel's life as example; but in the process of writing the book the example clearly took on, too, historical, cultural, and political dimensions.

Looking back at that process in 1957, Arendt knew that this had happened and said as much. But she did not mention anything about the role her own self-perception and self-presentation had played in the process of retelling Rahel's story during those years. And yet Rahel, "Jewess and Schlemihl," unable to decide for the position of the pariah and, to the end, hovering "between pariah and parvenu," [31] had at that time been "truly my best friend" ("meine wirklich beste Freundin"), as Arendt wrote to Heinrich Bluecher in 1936. [32] The best friend in whom and against whom one could reflect oneself. Unlike her first husband, Bluecher was a Gentile, and Arendt found of great importance in their relationship his articulated acceptance of her articulated difference. Rahel could have written what Arendt wrote about the meaning of this attitude for her: "I have never known what it means to belong, without any conditions, to another person. And one can do so only through the other's love."[33] But Arendt differed essentially from Rahel when she expressed joy in feeling "secured" ("gesichert")—as if finally anchored—in Heinrich's love because, for the first time, she was "controlled."[34] The other's love for her restrained her in insisting too much on her own voice, because she could be certain in this relationship that she would be heard and understood—also, especially, when she spoke as a Jewess.

Even Rahel, especially with Varnhagen, and notwithstanding his unquestioning and unquestioned devotion to her, could not be certain about that. In fact, part of Arendt's motivation in writing the Rahel biography had been her wish to counteract Varnhagen's widely read, successfully falsifying presentation of Rahel. As Arendt states in the book's preface, Varnhagen's arbitrariness in the preparation and publication of Rahel's letters had been commented on frequently by critics, and yet the Rahel persona constructed by him remained largely uncontested:

> The significant fact is that almost all his omissions and misleading codings of names were intended to make Rahel's associations and circle of friends appear less Jewish and more aristocratic, and to show Rahel herself in a more conventional light, one more in keeping with the taste of the times.[35]

With this construct, Varnhagen produced, in Arendt's view, a twofold falsification by eliminating both Rahel's truly intolerable and truly lovable characteristics.[36] Rahel, of course, might not have minded, might even have desired such careful editing. Her Jewishness, which remained a painful problem to the very end because it prevented her from fitting herself into "good" society, caused her to go on with that hateful but almost instinctual "living against her inclinations,"[37] "eternal dissembling," "being reasonable," "yielding which I myself no longer notice, swallowing my own insights—I can no longer stand it; and nothing, no one, can help me."[38] As long as she did not or could not really try to help herself. In the end she even made her husband into a parvenu—if on a smaller scale and much more economical in emotional terms—because he copied her here too, as in so many other things. There is his marvelously innocent and irritating self-assessment: "I have an impulse I cannot control: to honor myself in my superiors, and to track down their good qualities in order to love them." This, Arendt points out with the satisfaction of the successful hunter for evidence, is the impulse of the arch-parvenu as ex-pariah: "By this fraud the pariah prepares society to accept his career as a parvenu."[39]

But it is not so much the rather meek and mousy persevering Varn-hagen whom Arendt wants to expose to himself: In the end, expectedly, he was recompensed for his love and veneration. For in the end, as she observes fairly, "he rescued, out of a career destroyed through no fault of his own, a considerable social influence, a degree of acknowledgment remarkable for his position and his talents and free entry into all social spheres."[40] It is Rahel who, Arendt insists, needs such exposing; Varn-hagen is just an extension of her, refining his "parvenu-ism" to perfection under her influence. And it is this perfection—strained for, pushed for, by Rahel, but not accessible to her—which incites Arendt's anger:

> Thus the intolerable cheek of his "love" for his superiors actually derived from her. His natural Prussian subordinate's temperament would not, of its own accord, have spawned such repulsive close-ness and audacity; without Rahel, his ambition would rather have remained that of the petty official. Rahel, however, wanted decid-edly more; she wanted to be esteemed as a peer; indeed, she ought to have been a "princess."[41] And since she was not that, after all, she conceived how she would act if she were—and then used Varn-hagen to enthrone her. Like all parvenus, she never dreamt of a radical alteration of bad conditions but rather of a shift of personnel that would work out in her favor, so that the situation would im-prove as if by the stroke of a magic wand.[42]

Wilhelm von Humboldt, commenting on the Levin-Varnhagen mar-riage in 1814, observed that now at last Rahel can become "an Excellency and Ambassador's wife. There is nothing the Jews cannot achieve." Here, as elsewhere, Arendt remarks, generalizing somewhat unfairly, Humboldt was "the best, keenest and most malicious gossip of his age," hitting the nail right on the head. But she also supplies one—not *the*—explanation of Rahel's self-centeredness and Humboldt's malice in the context of the Jewish question: If nineteenth-century Jews wanted to play a part in so-ciety, they "had no choice but to become parvenus par excellence, and certainly in those decades of reaction they were the choicest examples of parvenus."[43] She points out the lack of Jewish involvement in the political struggle for equal rights—Humboldt disliked individual Jews in Berlin society and fought for the civic emancipation of Jews as a group—and their entanglement in the struggle for social betterment. In Arendt's words, Jews in the late eighteenth and early nineteenth centuries "did not even want to be emancipated as a whole; all they wanted was to escape from Jewishness, as individuals if possible. Their urge was secretly and silently to settle what seemed to them a personal problem."[44] She found troubling precisely that secrecy and silence about their Judaism which she observed, too, in Rahel, notwithstanding, even underlining, her highly self-conscious articulateness.[45]

Arendt's critical understanding of Rahel's dilemma is centrally informed by her experiences as a German Jewess more than a century later. The precariousness of Jewish existence had suddenly increased immeasurably, and so had, though over a longer period, the anonymity of mass society. From this perspective, the distinction between parvenu and pariah which she had borrowed from Lazare was now apparently meaningless. "Society" as the distinct cultural-political elite so attractive to the ambitious outsider had been largely dissolved, especially in Germany after World War I, making the phenomenon of the parvenu obsolete. But above all, the Jew's choice had again been eliminated; there was no way of escaping, within the modern mass society that had imposed it, the now literally life-threatening status of pariah. Why, then, was Arendt, who had distanced and then exiled herself from that mass society, so intent on clarifying Rahel's difficulties in choosing between the status of the pariah and that of the parvenu?

Rahel, the most self-centered, self-conscious self-observer, was unable to admit, fully and critically, the meaning of her Jewishness into her exhaustive discourse of the self. In her never-ending, never-stilled desire to assimilate, she was unable to examine the conflict experienced in her desire to hide *and* to assert the "real" self. Desiring too much, too unquestioningly, the world of the other, she compromised the possibility of making it her own. *Assimilating* in this sense means the inability to choose one's company, to relate to the other through informed and considered judgment.[46] Having grown up in late-eighteenth-century Berlin "like the children of savage tribes," uneducated both culturally and socially, she had to make do with what came her way.[47] All her life she complained bitterly of being an ignoramus, in spite of her boundless intellectual curiosity and sensitivity. And she seized on people—to explain herself to them and to use them, especially Gentile men of nobility who might marry her—in her attempts to escape from what made these explanations necessary: the personal misfortune of having been born a Jewess, the essential outsider. Yet, notwithstanding all her efforts in self-expression and self-presentation, all her grasping at relationships and suffering over their inadequacy, she found her *"Uremigrantentum"* irreversible.[48] In the company that she had desired too intensely and accepted too eagerly, she did not meet with any encouragement to examine, much less to confront, her Jewishness; and her state of being in exile endured precisely because she was unable to do so on her own.

Arendt, a German Jewess in exile in France, was sharply aware of the outsider's difficulties in choosing her or his company, but this awareness did not prevent her from demanding that the outsider, herself and Rahel, confront them openly and thereby begin to cope with them.[49] In this she was helped by Bluecher, another exile and pariah by choice, who supported her in her trying to deal with her Jewishness, which meant, too, overcoming her need for such support. In the late summer of 1936, when they did not yet know each other very well, Arendt quoted to Bluecher Rahel's insight into Jews' difficulties with social relations—that is, her lament that Jews always had to legitimate themselves—and she stressed the fact that it is *"always* the others who do the legitimizing" ("Legitimieren tun *immer* nur die anderen").[50] But in her letters to Bluecher during that time Arendt also resisted instances of his too unquestioning perspective on the Jewish tradition. She was skeptical of such total affirmation, which she understood to be potentially exclusionary rather than sharing. And so she chose, in disagreeing with him about troubling aspects of Jewish history, to speak from the position of the *pariah* as self-critical outsider in her own group.[51]

This is in sharp contrast to Rahel's lamentations about the influence of that unquestioned history on her life. The Jews, Arendt writes to Bluecher, "the craziest of all peoples," have been content for two thousand years to "hold the past in the present" ("das Vergangene in der Gegenwart zu halten") because—and here she quotes Herder—"the ruins of Jerusalem for them have their foundation in the heart of time."[52] She does not with this critique reject her Jewishness or express "Jewish self-hatred." On the contrary, from this critical perspective she explicitly accepts the accident of her—and Rahel's—birth as the challenge to understand, by questioning, its influence on their lives. It is only in such considered acceptance, signified by the term *pariah*, that the accident of birth, so crucial to the individual's development, can become a personally meaningful fact and a contribution to cultural development.

Arendt was arguably in a much better position to choose such acceptance than was Rahel. But her critical analysis of Rahel's difficulties can be read as an attempt to reclaim and release the enabling power of the past: not the past as a pile of ruins or as a bloodstained road leading inexorably from prejudice to destruction, but the past as a source of energy for the always possible new beginning.[53] In contributing to the writing of history, she is motivated by the guiding idea of an alternate history based on the hope rather than despair of sharing the world. Such an alternate history sustains promises only if past failures to realize them have been analyzed and understood. In her 1957 introduction to *Rahel Varnhagen*, Arendt repeatedly stresses the fact that the history of German Jews and also their specific complex of problems "are a matter of the past." Now, "after the history of the German Jews has come to an end," it is time to investigate fully the "altogether unique phenomenon," in the general context of Jewish assimilation, "which among other things found expression in a literally astonishing wealth of talent and of scientific and intellectual productivity."[54]

The biography of the astonishingly gifted nineteenth-century intellectual Rahel was intended to be part of that troubled history which Arendt herself shared in her "awareness of the doom of German Judaism." There is a curious and revealing statement of reservation in her asking her readers to remember that this historical biography treats only "one aspect of the complex problems of assimilation": "the manner in which assimilation to the intellectual and social life of the environment works out concretely in the history of an individual's life, thus shaping a personal destiny."[55] This is hardly one aspect among others of the history of assimilation. Rather, it goes to the heart of it—and to the heart of Arendt's political-philosophical historiography, which poses questions of political communication and community in terms of the individual's realized— that is, articulated—potential through responsible speech and action within the group. And in this sense, too, the Rahel biography is an important part of Arendt's work.[56]

o 5 o

Arendt's retelling of Rahel's unedited life story brings to the surface the secretiveness and silence of the subtext, which signify the troubled history of Jews and women. Historically informed and perceptive female readers like Lotte Koehler, impressed by Rahel's subtle social intelligence and sympathetic to her claims to unique individuality, have understandably judged Arendt's perspective to be too one-sided in its conceptual emphasis on the Jewish question.[57] In her review "Emancipation and Destiny," Sybille Bedford, too, is critical of Arendt's tendencies to "abstract" from the real life story—this is how she sees Arendt's reclaiming its, as it were, deleted part. Bedford argues that Arendt misses the "factual bones," which would presumably structure the story of a life by drawing attention to its important events as markers in the flow of lifetime. And she regrets that Arendt does not "break her subject's mood":

> In a sense it is a tour de force. The result is a relentlessly abstract book—slow, cluttered, static, curiously oppressive; reading it feels like sitting in a hothouse with no watch. One is made to feel the subject, the waiting distraught woman; one is made aware, almost physically, of her intense femininity, her frustration.[58]

And then, as if with a great sense of relief at her release from that prison of relentless inactivity, Bedford tells, in the shrewd and comfortably detached manner of British biography, the story of Rahel's life as it was edited by Varnhagen. But in her rewriting of this story, Arendt was motivated by her insight that it had not been the true one, because it did not, as do true stories, reveal the cultural meaning of living.

Rahel herself proves Arendt to be right. Her letters to her friend Pauline Wiesel, the mistress of Prince Louis Ferdinand of Prussia, express precisely the almost physically oppressive "mood" of the "waiting distraught woman" which Arendt, to Bedford's dismay, forces on the reader.[59] Whereas Pauline Wiesel, one of the extraordinary, independent women of the Romantic period, "*lives* everything" ("Sie *leben* alles") because she has had courage and luck, Rahel "*imagines* most of it" ("ich *denke* mir das meiste") because she has had no luck and thus has been unable to gain courage, Rahel wrote to her friend in 1810.[60] For our context it is important to note how Rahel distinguishes herself from the friend to whom she felt so essentially akin: she and Pauline share a position which is so explosively asocial that "only once could nature permit two like us simultaneously. In this age." ("Nur einmal konnte die Natur zwei solche zugleich leben lassen. In diesem Zeitalter.") They have been created to "live truth in this world" and they have come to their significant outsider's position ("Wir sind *neben* der menschlichen Gesellschaft") by different roads. There is no place, no office, no vain title, for their truth; these are occupied by lies. Rahel congratulates both Pauline and herself on being emphatic outsiders: Pauline, because she has been excluded from society by intentionally offending it; herself, "because I cannot sin and lie with it [society]."[61]

This, however, signifies a misrepresentation of the meaning of the outsider position for Rahel. She has been painfully aware of her "dissembling," her silence, her secretiveness, and she has not been able to share in Pauline's straightforward offensive. Separated from her, Rahel can do nothing but repeat Pauline's "every word, every small deed." Her own "greatness" is that of forbearance in contrast to Pauline's greatness of being decisive, active.[62] Because she has not had Pauline's luck, Rahel reasons, she has not been able to develop her courage. But Arendt, in her critique of Rahel's attempts at assimilating herself to the social sphere, does not allow such excuse-making or self-consolation. There is no greatness in Rahel's highly articulate passivity and secretiveness; there is the accident of her birth, which she, in contrast to Pauline, has not been able to see as a challenge.

But then, though both were born as women, Pauline was Gentile and, by all accounts, beautiful, and Rahel was, in her own words, "unpleasantly unprepossessing, without there being immediately apparent any striking deformities."[63] Rahel's phrasing here is highly perceptive, because it stresses the social aspect of physical beauty or attractiveness. Her plainness, the absence of beauty, is more than just neutral, nonattracting. It is unattractive, unpleasant, a negative quality; it signifies the lack of social power that beauty can give to women. Arendt immediately seizes on the fact of Rahel's physical plainness: "Jewish girls were frequently not married for their dowries alone," she states. And, significantly, she describes the power of beauty in a woman as creating "a perspective from which she can judge and choose. Neither intelligence nor experience can make up for the lack of that natural perspective." Arendt is again concerned with the social consequences of the natural, accidental fact: the beautiful woman can actively use her beauty to control social intercourse and thereby overcome a culturally developed and enforced female passivity and lack of control. Because it was more difficult for Jews to gain a measure of control in social intercourse, lack of beauty would be more important to the Jewess Rahel than to the Gentile Pauline. Unlike her friend, Rahel was not born into a world that she could reject offensively. It was not hers to reject; she first had to struggle to gain access:

> Not rich, not cultivated and not beautiful—that meant that she was entirely without weapons with which to begin the great struggle for

recognition in society, for social existence, for a morsel of happiness, for security and an established position in the bourgeois world.[64]

Does Arendt, then, grant Rahel the dilemma—that is, the personal significance—of these cultural handicaps? Not really. She immediately suggests, as a possible remedy, that Rahel could have engaged in the political struggle for equal rights—if educated Jews of her generation, as a group, had wanted such an open struggle.[65] On the whole, however, Jews struggled into society as individuals on terms that were secretly and silently negotiable, never clearly stated, never fully comprehensible. The success of the struggle could be measured only by having secured that place, office, vain title, which Rahel understood to be occupied by lies. And because Rahel never gave up struggling for social acceptance, they were her lies too. It is these lies—that is, the troubled conditions of social intercourse—which Arendt judges to be the most important among the forces shaping Rahel's life and which, therefore, she wishes to explore in detail. Beauty—or the lack of it—is just one, albeit important, ameliorating or aggravating factor; it does not go to the heart of the matter, which for Arendt is the obscurity, confusion, and exclusiveness of the social sphere as it presents itself to the outsider.

In Arendt's view, Rahel's "woman problem" is intimately connected with and interdependent upon the Jewish condition. The subtitle of the Rahel biography draws attention to this fact—importantly, the original German subtitle also points to the German aspect of the problem. In her critical discussion of the impact of cultural exclusion on personal development, Arendt analyzes the outsider's position primarily and most consistently in terms of the minority existence of German Jews. Here the mechanisms of social exclusion and the discrepancies between cultural contribution and social position can be perceived and analyzed most clearly.

Arendt's personal situation, imposed as it was by social developments, was, of course, a crucial influence on her perspective in this matter. She lived in the dark times of Hitlerism, when the most profound and most painful self-consciousness of being excluded from understanding, and thereby from achieving the meaning of one's personal history in its cultural context, was connected with the accident of being born a Jew rather than that of being born a woman. Arendt set out to confront her Jewishness under extreme circumstances (stateless and in exile), and her experience informed the unforgiving clarity with which she saw her best friend, Rahel, trying to avoid such confrontation and falling victim to the temptations of parvenuism—that is, trying to gain access and acceptance at all costs. She saw how the social exclusion of women and Jews encouraged the endlessly complicated evasions, hesitations, and modifications with which they sought to manipulate social (rather than political) intercourse, their literally indirect discourse, their reluctance to speak in their own voice for fear they would be misunderstood or punished for the others' misunderstanding of them. The historical-political relevance of this reluctance, which was to become the focus of Arendt's political thought, is for her more clearly posed in the Jewish situation than in the woman problem. Arguably, however, much of her peculiarly sharp and consistent concreteness in perceiving, analyzing, and presenting the destructive mechanisms underlying the Jewish experience of assimilation and anti-Semitism was informed by the fact that she analyzed it first in the life story of a woman to whom she, as a woman, was particularly close and of whom she, as a woman, was particularly critical. Rahel's subtext was immediately accessible to her. Bringing it to the surface was not an act of indiscretion, imposition, or hindsight falsification; rather, it was, in peculiarly personal, unmediated terms, a historical reclamation of deleted parts of a life story by one articulate woman relating, through judgment, to another in expressing kinship *and* difference. In this sense, Arendt's collating of the Jewish situation and the "Woman Question" in its emphasis on the pariah's self-critical perspective contributes significantly to an understanding of the cultural-historical meaning of both issues.

It was not, then, from the hindsight of twenty years that Arendt pointed out, in the 1957 preface to her biography of Rahel, the Romantic error in Rahel's seeing her life as her greatest artistic "assignment":[66]

> To live life as if it were a work of art, to believe that by "cultivation" one can make a work of art of one's own life, was the great error that Rahel shared with her contemporaries; or rather, it was the misconception of self which was inevitable so long as she wished to understand and express within the categories of her time her sense of life: the resolve to consider life and the history it imposes on the individual as more important and more serious than her own person.[67]

Underlying this important and, for some readers, unclear or even misleading distinction is Arendt's analysis of the individual's responsibility for relating to others in her own voice—that is, as a historically articulated judging person. This analysis was fully developed in the model of ideal political (rather than social) intercourse in *The Human Condition*, on which Arendt was working when she wrote the 1957 preface to the Rahel biography. But the seeds of this crucial distinction between history as mere happening imposed on the individual and history as challenge to the individual to make sense of the flow of events—that is, to understand their personal and cultural meanings—are clearly present in the Rahel biography and provide its structural basis.

In accepting life itself as her assignment, Rahel saw herself as both unique—as unique as the greatest phenomenon on this earth—and equal, in essence and achievement, to the greatest artists, philosophers, and poets.[68] But it was, as the young Hannah Arendt already understood, precisely Rahel's insistence on her uniqueness in these terms which prevented her from achieving concrete and satisfying personal distinction in her cultural environment. The projected cloudy community in which all distinctions and differences between specifically talented, specifically articulate, individuals were dissolved, provided neither cultural nurture for personal development nor contributions to the well-being of culture. Rahel, the unwilling outsider, insisted on her uniqueness and her originality as *her* truth, which by definition could not be related to others, because they, the insiders, by definition were all caught up in the lies of social intercourse.

At the same time, Rahel was firmly convinced that somehow she could also make her truth precious to "them," her many Gentile, mostly aristocratic, correspondents—as precious as the truth of the poets and philosophers—because she could make them admire and love her. She was deeply convinced as well that her letters were her "Originalgeschichte," and therefore needed to be collected.[69] What she had written could not be allowed to be lost, she told La Motte-Fouqué in 1810, because it contained jewels.[70] Habitually she quoted her own brilliant utterances, together with the admiring reaction of her listeners, in her letters to the ever-attentive, receptive Varnhagen.[71] She encouraged and supported him eagerly in his enterprise of collecting all her remarks, made in writing or orally, and of recording their effect on the circle of her (respectable, arrivés) friends for posterity. Her observations were indeed highly original and witty, often stunningly perceptive, and they gave the impression of having been made and communicated spontaneously. Yet, for Rahel, the spontaneity had become, over time, a rhetorical device in the service of impressing on the other *her* needs and desires: opening herself to the other, she, above all, wanted the other to be open to *her*.

Indeed, in this needy other-directedness, which left no or little space for mutuality, Rahel's "Originalgeschichte" emerged most clearly as one of profound frustration. Her friends' love and admiration, imagined or real, did not bring her the secure acceptance she desired. The letter to Pauline Wiesel which celebrates and affirms her and Pauline's uniqueness and truth, in contrast to everybody else's ordinariness and lies, ends with Rahel's bitter complaints about her isolation in the spring of 1810, when she is still very uncertain about Varnhagen. Her brother, Moritz, who has lived with her through the winter and spring—she did not enjoy his company much—will get married soon: "Then I will, again, be totally alone on this earth." She has decided not to see anymore her friend Rebecca Friedlaender (who, like Rahel, has been preoccupied with assimilating herself to good society): "She is too intolerable, unnaturally *pauvre* in character, and pretentious." Of the young Alexander von der Marwitz, whom she met a year after Varnhagen in the spring of 1809, currently the last male friend left to her, she writes that he loves her the way one loves the ocean, a constellation of clouds, a gorge: "That is *not* enough for me. *Not any longer*. The person I love must want to live with me, to stay with me."[72] She has maneuvered herself into a position where she has no choice left but that of marrying Varnhagen, the only one willing to do so. But such a choice, based on sheer necessity, is no choice. Moreover, in Arendt's judgment, such restricting necessity not only signified Rahel's bad fortune of having been born a Jew and a woman but had to be considered, too, the result of her having made ill-considered choices before. Notwithstanding the difficulties caused by her birth, it would have been part of Rahel's personal responsibility to herself and to others to develop, like Pauline, the courage of the willing outsider.

And yet Rahel herself, with all her protestations and lamentations about her misfortune, was able to locate the pain it caused her in the difficulties she encountered in confronting her Jewishness. This, at any rate, was how Arendt read Rahel's letters, and was an important reason why she had been attracted to Rahel as her "truly best friend," whose life story she could narrate "as she herself might have told it." As I have argued above, this assumption is in some ways troubling, because it gives Arendt the license to judge Rahel by that "might" which then, on occasion, is turned into too rigid an "ought." Yet Arendt's retelling of Rahel's life story, which undeniably reshapes it by shifting the emphasis, does enable her reader to see important aspects of the German-Jewish experience in more complex, conflicted, and nevertheless greater clarity. Most significant in this context is Arendt's refusal to tell the story of victimization by social exclusion solely from the impossibly passive perspective of the victim to whom everything just happens and who then, in her unexamined experience of exclusion, maintains an impossible-because-paradisical personal innocence.

Arendt's attempts to understand German-Jewish history from the perspective of the social-political interaction between minority and majority were continued in the forties in her critique of the concept of exile and, after the war, in her analysis of anti-Semitism. They have met with many reservations and often with great hostility. And given the dimensions of the German-Jewish catastrophe, this is understandable to a degree. It is also, however, regrettable, because her forceful and critical reading of that interaction, her understanding as a cultural-political historian, flawed as it may be, has been the opposite of "one-sided," "arbitrary," or "perversely original"—the labels critics have attached to her interpretations, especially in the case of her report on the Eichmann trial.

◦ 6 ◦

Arendt's perspective on the "Jewish question" is indeed original, but it is rooted in her understanding of the historical reality of lives lived under its impact. This is one of the reasons why the Rahel biography has held such an important place in Arendt's development as a political thinker. It was no accident that she chose as the subject of her analysis of victimization Rahel, a Jewish woman of the Romantic period who "was neither beautiful nor attractive" and "who possessed no talents with which to employ her extraordinary intelligence and passionate originality."[73] Rahel experienced great difficulties in participating, as an adult, in social intercourse, because she seemed to have no means of control—that is, she had not been able to come of age and speak for herself. Her passive and innocent receptiveness to life—"What are you doing? Nothing. I am letting life rain on me"—was the source of her verbal imagination and inventiveness and her great charm.[74] It was also the reason for her refusal to confront her own adult life through considered choices. In this articulated refusal, the conflicts of the existence of a German Jewess appeared to Arendt with a lucid intensity that she thought illuminated her own and other twentieth-century Jews' conflicts.

Rahel's contemporaries did indeed love and admire her originality, which was both "typically" Romantic in sensibility and uncommonly sophisticated in its social perceptiveness.[75] But in many cases they also felt an ambivalence, which, though naturally present in all relations (also in loving human relationships), was much aggravated by the German-Jewish social situation. Rahel's relationship with the diplomat Friedrich von Gentz is a good case in point. The beginning of their erotic friendship went back to the days of her famous *Dachstuben* (attic) salon in turn-of-the-century Berlin, when the social intercourse between extraordinary Jews and Gentiles, willing, or, rather, self-styled Romantic outsiders, was much easier than in the period of Restoration after 1815, with its attendant more narrowly religious patriotism. One could say that everybody who was young and "coming" in cultured Berlin society around 1800 gathered under Rahel's roof: aristocrat and bourgeois, Gentile and Jew, diplomats, officers, scholars, students, actors—among them the brothers Humboldt, Tieck, Schleiermacher, Friedrich Schlegel, Jean Paul, Pauline, and her lover, Prince Louis Ferdinand of Prussia, the "most human prince of his time."[76]

But the place where they came together was outside of society—namely, in Rahel's and other Jewish salons. Significantly, the association was not transferred to the young Gentiles' family homes. From the beginning it was clear, albeit not to Rahel and other young educated Jews, that their Gentile friends had the unquestioned choice of being temporary outsiders, allowing themselves to be befriended by Jews in the social no man's land of *their* houses; that in fact they had never given up their citizenship in the majority. Rahel had come to understand this situation a decade later when she lamented her "eternal and profound" awareness of the fact that she was not a citizen, but she still waited for Varnhagen and baptism to make her one: as Antonie Friederike von Varnhagen, baptized on the day of her wedding, September 27, 1814, she could begin to work through Varnhagen toward acceptance into Restoration society. From 1819 to 1833, the year of her death, she again held a salon in Berlin, the salon of now-established Frau von Varnhagen, who, with her husband's skillful literary editorial help, was an active leader in the cult of Goethe.

Gentz's and Rahel's friendship had lasted, in spite of his highly ambivalent feelings about Jews and his frequent betrayals of Rahel. Gentz, the highly intelligent, versatile "secretary of Europe" during the years of Restoration and a thoroughly political animal in the Machiavellian sense, had been, as Poliakov puts it, an "assiduous guest" at Jewish salons in Berlin and Vienna before he became the official speaker for the Rothschilds in his article on them for Brockhaus's encyclopedia. Here he praised the Rothschilds for their spiritual qualities, which he singled out as one of the important sources of their huge financial success. In the privacy of letters, however, Gentz expressed his mixed feelings quite exuberantly and in ways that say as much about his Romantic self-perception and self-stylization as about his views on "the Jews":

> Intelligence—that is the mortal sin of the Jews. All of them are more or less intelligent; but only let one be born in which a spark of heart, a spark of true feeling can be found. The curse pronounced on them, and it pursues them to the ten-thousandth generation, is that they can never leave the sphere of intelligence, in the narrower meaning of the word, to their own detriment and that of the world, but must make endless circles in it until their black souls descend into hell. That is why the monsters are at home everywhere where intelligence, stupid and criminal intelligence, arrogates the right to govern alone; born representatives of atheism, Jacobinism, Enlightenment and so on. No Jew has yet believed seriously in God! No Jewess—I make no exception—has ever known real love! All the misfortune of the modern world, if it is traced to its furthest roots, comes manifestly from the Jews, they alone made Bonaparte emperor.[77]

Now Gentz, who had followed Rahel's turbulent relationships, did know that she had indeed "known real love."[78] Toward the end of their lives—both died within a year—they became, again, emotionally very close, supporting each other in their religious feelings toward life and living.[79] And all his life Gentz adored Rahel's "Goetteraussprueche,"[80] her "divine" surprising connections between the most diverse experiences, those often marvelously fitting descriptions of emotional states and social relations. He would have adored, too, what Rahel wrote after his death to Leopold Ranke about her admiration for his great talents and her love for his luck (like Pauline's, one may assume), the lightness, in fortune, of his being:

> He glided, soared in Fortune's toboggan, down a track that he alone followed; and no one can rightly compare himself with him. . . . But now, in sum, there remains to me only pure living love. Let this be his epitaph: he always stirred me to love; he was *always* receptive to what struck him as true. He seized upon untruth with a passion for truth. Many people must be praised item by item; and they do not arouse love in our hearts; others, a few, can be reproached for much,

but they always open our hearts, move them to love. Gentz did that for me: and he will never die in me.[81]

When Gentz's fortune left him, he demanded help and comfort, which Rahel gave him. But he gave none back, and for this she punished him, she wrote Ranke. She also wrote that she knew about Gentz's many "Perfidien" against her. But what she understood, and therefore loved, in this complex, uniquely and typically Romantic diplomatic ideologue, was much more important to her than his betrayals. There may of course be consoling self-deception in her assessment of this troubled relationship. But the very fact of her articulating in such splendid images Gentz's individuality as the worth of his life to her may persuade her reader otherwise. And yet Arendt, in her account of the relationship, is not so certain. She stresses, rather, the limitation of Rahel's life compared to Gentz's, which importantly—and here I agree with her—is a limitation of understanding. Rahel may have held Gentz in the end, when he was old and vulnerable in his last great passion for the famously beautiful young dancer Fanny Elssler. But she could not hold him when they were both young, because she demanded too much of his life in the world in order to secure her own. Gentz was more than charmed by Rahel; he was fascinated and threatened by her, in his words, *"infinitely productive"* intellectuality.[82] He betrays her with beautiful mistresses. Were these really betrayals of a potential reality he and Rahel could have shared? Arendt does not seem to think so. She thinks, rather, that it was "intelligent" of Gentz not to insist on Rahel's giving herself to him totally—that is, also physically (Rahel had refused him "that trifle")—"and to remain 'stupidly dazzled by the physical charms of an insignificant creature' (Gentz)."

When Rahel tried to imitate Gentz and fell violently in love with the handsome secretary of the Spanish legation, Don Raphael d'Urquijo, the relationship turned out to be a disaster that nearly paralyzed her emotionally for three years, 1801/2 to 1804. Early in 1800 she had had to break her engagement with the young count Karl von Finckenstein, whom she had met in 1795/96 at the opera—another neutral place where Jews and Gentiles could meet—and whose sisters had continued to oppose the relationship. Rahel called the pain caused by this severing "a kind of death," a deep shame: "one is ashamed of real misfortune," she wrote in her diary about the break.[83]

The "real misfortune" was Rahel's Jewish birth, combined with the fact that she was neither beautiful nor rich, which had caused the rather

weak and dependent young man to give in to his family's resistance. Falling in love with a young aristocrat, who was to open for her the world of
society, and a young Spaniard, who was to take her into the world of
pleasure, she was too needy in her exclusion to fully understand and be
able to capture, as were Gentz and Pauline, the reality of the things of the
world.[84] Yet in her magnificent summing up of the beauty of Gentz's life,
she stressed precisely his fortune, his exhilarating worldliness. Did she
adore him in spite of or because of her own inability to share it?

I think it is here, in this uncertainty of motivation, that Arendt centers her critique of Rahel as "Jewess and Shlemihl"—the title of the first
chapter of the biography. Admiring Rahel's extraordinary psychological
and verbal intelligence, Arendt also recognizes its profound frustration
under the circumstances brought about by the fact that Rahel was born a
Jewess. But she still insists on the need to recognize the depth of Rahel's
grieving over incomplete comprehension and therefore incomplete meaning, for which she also holds her partly responsible. The meaning of such
a life cannot be located in the consolations of its closure, Frau von Varnhagen's beautiful resignation. It has to be searched for, from its beginnings, in the whole painful life story of Rahel Levin.

Immediately, in the first chapter, Arendt confronts the reader with
the historicality of Rahel's life: it is a text woven of the interconnecting
accidentality of birth with cultural environment and personal development, of nature with nurture. In this interconnection are located the difficulties of understanding "our own history when we are born in 1771 in
Berlin and that history has already begun seventeen hundred years earlier
in Jerusalem." "But if we do not understand it," Arendt warns, "and if we
are not outright opportunists who always accept the here-and-now, who
circumvent unpleasantness by lies and forget the good, our history will
take its revenge, will exert its superiority and become our personal destiny."[85] Arendt, living four generations after her friend Rahel, during the
last and most calamitous crisis of German-Jewish history, understands
and accepts such historicality. Rahel, who has experienced it again and
again without learning from the experience, pretends that she need not
accept it.

In 1793, the twenty-one-year-old Rahel wrote to the trusted friend of
her youth, David Veit, that she would never be convinced that she was "a
Shlemihl and a Jewess; since in all these years and after so much thinking
about it, it has not dawned upon me, I shall never really grasp it. That is
why 'the clang of the murderous axe does not nibble at my root'; that is

why I am still living."[86] Two years later she laments that her Jewishness
is at the root of all her suffering, that it makes her whole life a bleeding-
to-death, "eine Verblutung."[87] In 1809 she wrote to La Motte-Fouqué
how much pain had been caused by the "misfortune" of her "wrong
birth," but the same year she could also admit to Varnhagen: "My history
starts earlier than with my life."[88]

Arendt's statement that the full force of history is unleashed to im-
press "something of its significance upon the hapless being, the *shlemihl*,
who anticipated nothing," does not so much deny Rahel such insight as
explain her predicament: "Whoever wants aid and protection from History, in which our insignificant birth is almost lost, must be able to know
and understand it." Rahel was largely unable to do so, and thus her development was stopped—a serious matter in view of the fact that development "is the sole continuity in time that nature recognizes. Then the
pain, the grief is overwhelming. And the person who has no recourse but
nature is destroyed by his own inexperience, by his inability to comprehend more than himself."[89]

Arendt is fully aware of the intensity of this grief and of her responsibility, as Rahel's biographer, to articulate it. But she also feels it is her
responsibility to show and analyze Rahel's abdicating her own responsibility to herself. The learning process that is life had not gone far enough
when, toward the end of her life, Rahel still stressed its limitation as the
paradoxically ultimate value of individuality: "All my life I have taken
myself for Rahel and for nothing else."[90] Not even Rahel's words on her
deathbed—which were reported by the ever-faithful Varnhagen and
prominently quoted by Arendt as introduction to the first chapter of her
biography, "Jewess and Shlemihl"—can persuade Arendt otherwise:

> What a history!—A fugitive from Egypt and Palestine, here I am
> and find help, love, fostering in you people. With real rapture I
> think of these origins of mine and this whole nexus of destiny,
> through which the oldest memories of the human race stand side
> by side with the latest developments. The greatest distances in time
> and space are bridged. The thing which all my life seemed to me
> the greatest shame, which was the misery and misfortune of my
> life—having been born a Jewess—this I should on no account now
> wish to have missed.

Rahel's unedited life story tells us quite clearly that and why it had taken
her so long to confront the historical and personal meaning of her Jewish

birth, and Arendt, thinking the late insight too late, refuses to succumb to the seduction of a consoling closure. She insists that Rahel's biographer needs to analyze and show exactly how the Romantic shlemihl's "struggle against the facts, above all against the fact of having been born a Jew, very rapidly became a struggle against herself. She herself refused to consent to herself; she, born to so many disadvantages, had to deny, change, reshape by lies this self of hers, since she could not very well deny her existence out of hand."[91]

o 7 o

After the critical success of *The Origins of Totalitarianism*, Arendt sent the manuscript of *Rahel Varnhagen* to Jaspers, asking him to advise her what to do with it. Jaspers reported his impressions on August 23, 1952, and indeed his letter is an instructive demonstration of the difficulties experienced by even the most enlightened German-Gentile and male reader of Arendt's biography of Rahel.[92] It seems almost impossible for him to understand the realism underlying the conceptual intentions and narrative strategies in the biography of Rahel as an analysis of the troubled German-Jewish history. Pedagogically, he starts with praises: he could not put *Rahel* down; the text is deeply affecting and significant, large parts are extremely well written, there are pages of extraordinary depth. Then he shrewdly suggests ways in which the reader could be helped to find his way through Rahel's life more smoothly, suggestions that were implemented when Lotte Koehler prepared the manuscript for publication four years later. (Jaspers' critique also informed the 1957 preface, which anticipated readers' reservations).

But then he comes directly to the point of their central and indeed serious disagreement: Arendt's text reflects her attempt at coming to terms with basic questions of Jewish existence, *using* Rahel's life to help her (Arendt) clarify these problems and, in doing so, to disentangle herself from them. At the same time, he carefully stresses the "objective" ("sachlich") quality of Arendt's analysis, but also his impression of an all-pervasive "strange mood"—Sybille Bedford was to describe it as oppressive—caused by the absence of love for, even interest in, "Rahel as Rahel." Jaspers is a very perceptive reader of Arendt's narrative strategies vis-à-vis her subject; he criticizes them because he objects strongly to her conceptual intentions. A serious shortcoming of her approach is the fact that there is no *"image of Rahel herself"*; there are only images of events that are located in this individual. And he connects the selection of and focus on these events directly with Arendt's personal experience. It seems probable to him that she might be fairer to Rahel now, looking at her from a perspective shaped by her own different life situation: no longer in exile, recognized, happily married. *Now* she might be able to see Rahel not only under the aspect of the "Jewish question" but, according to Rahel's intentions, as an individual in whose life the Jewish problem had played an important but by no means the only role.

Jaspers comes back to this point repeatedly, and it is, of course, true that Arendt had read Rahel through her own experiences. He does not understand, however, that Arendt's different perspective *then* had enabled her to see particularly clearly the social-psychological mechanisms that dominated Rahel's and other German Jews' relationships with Gentiles. He does not understand, that is, that her comparative harshness vis-à-vis the nineteenth-century Jewish woman, from whom she needed to distance herself and with whom she also identified, had distinct historiographical advantages. He cannot control his instinctive negative reaction to that perspective, which seems to him above all loveless—Scholem was to make the same accusation concerning Arendt's perspective on Jewish history in the context of the controversy over her report on the Eichmann trial.[93] Looking at Rahel "without love," he complains, Arendt does not admit the reader to her real depth, the life of her soul ("Seelentiefe"). Trying, as always, to be fair, he does grant Arendt a few exceptions, noticing her sympathy with Rahel in narrating her relationship with Gentz, her distancing herself from Marwitz,[94] her ties to Pauline. But when he delivers his eloquent counterprojection to Arendt's (in his eyes all-too-human) Rahel, he stresses a true, essential greatness in her loneliness and suffering—trembling and bleeding without home, world, without being anchored in that unique love—and in her honest self-reflection. Arendt, he objects, does not let Rahel speak from the "center," from her "humanity itself," which is not essentially Jewish even if she experiences the world as a Jew.

There is, in Jaspers' argument, a neo-Platonic split between the real, true, essential Rahel and her Jewish "Kleid," the dress, the surface of her existence. The metaphors he uses in this context are quite instructive. Arendt does move the reader in her description of Rahel's difficulties, but she suppresses the brightness in all the obscurity of Rahel's experience, the fact that Rahel remains true to herself, that she affected others greatly, that, notwithstanding her confusions, she had knowledge of what was hidden in appearance and timeless in temporary experience. And then he makes a very revealing complaint: the analysis suggests that a Jew could not really live a human life. In the early fifties, this is the worst possible suggestion for a German intellectual like Jaspers, to whom, understandably, some remnant of belief in the successful aspects of German-Jewish interaction is profoundly important. There is, he points out, Spinoza, who rejected both Jewish and Christian dogma; there is the Enlightenment. In Lessing, too, "thank God," reason is "transhistorical" ("uebergeschichtlich"). And the way Arendt presents Humboldt seems "almost grotesque" to him. (He is right, however, in correcting her lumping together the liberal anti-anti-Semitic Bettina von Arnim with her illiberal Christian Nationalist husband, Achim).

Because Jaspers' argument is communicated in the comparatively informal medium of a letter, it is quite easy to sort out in his discussion of Arendt's perspective on the German-Jewish question several conflicting aspects of his view of German-Jewish history. On the one hand, he thinks that she does not give enough credit to Enlightenment efforts to better the civil situation of the German-Jewish minority. There is a passage in *Rahel* to which Jaspers refers, and which he tries to reverse, with his "thank God." In the context of criticizing Rahel for her "struggle against the facts, above all against the fact of having been born a Jew," Arendt distinguishes Lessing's concept of history from that of his friend Mendelssohn. For Lessing history can be the teacher of mankind precisely because the mature individual recognizes historical truth by virtue of his reason. But for Mendelssohn there is a separation between historical and rational truths so total and final that man, seeking for truth, has to withdraw from history:

> Mendelssohn expressly opposes Lessing's philosophy of history, referring slightingly to "the Education of the Human Race, of which my late friend Lessing allowed himself to be persuaded by I do not know what historian." Mendelssohn held that all realities such as environment, history and society could not—thank God—be warranted by Reason.[95]

Jaspers rejects the distinction Arendt makes here. Lessing's concept of reason, he insists, is founded on a more permanent basis than that of (only) historicality, and Mendelssohn, though less deep and more naive than Lessing, shares with his friend a truth which cannot be lost. Both developed their thought before the later (Romantic) "bewitchment by a deified history." Arendt's insistence on the need to consider the accidentality of historical facts a challenge to human reason is disturbing to Jaspers because it has made her hold Jews like Rahel and Mendelssohn responsible for their reactions to facts and events over which they had no control and no matter how difficult it might have been to cope with them. He wants to make it clear that he objects to the harshness of Arendt's perspective on Rahel *and* that he is very much aware of the intense disappointments Jews had been subjected to in their dealings with the Christian majority and the consequences of this experience for their social behavior—for instance Rahel's.

Instructively, Jaspers sees a connection between Arendt's analysis of and Dilthey's reaction to Rahel's letters, which he quotes: "One is frightened by the passion with which Rahel, in her intimate correspondence, reacts to her fate to be a Jewess; she feels like an outcast." In parentheses he adds that Lujo Brentano had told him, Jaspers, about the heated arguments he had had with Dilthey when the latter did not want to let his daughter marry the Jew Misch and how he had finally given in. Jaspers does not see that he shares, in important ways, Dilthey's reaction, which he clearly rejects as inadequate. Dilthey had, in his judgment, "typically" pushed away Rahel's passion with his comment about her letters—which arguably he had not done—and in not wanting the Jew Misch for a son-in-law, he had behaved in a contemptibly bigoted fashion. At the same time, Jaspers insists that the individual Rahel was essentially liberated in her humanity (that is, from her Jewishness) by the Enlightenment, and that Arendt should have made this transhistorical and therefore particularly meaningful fact, and not the accidental fact of Rahel's having been born a Jew, the center of her biography.

Both Dilthey's and Rahel's reactions to the troubled German-Jewish interaction were motivated by the conditions of social exclusion, which, in the case of the Jewish minority in the nineteenth century, was a particularly complex issue that labels like "anti-Semitism" and "Jewish self-hatred" often obscure rather than clarify. Arendt's analysis could have explained to readers like Dilthey why Rahel resented so passionately the fact of her Jewishness and how her feeling like an outcast—whether "objectively" justified or unjustified—had in important ways frustrated her considerable intellect and hindered her emotional development. Readers of Arendt's *Rahel* would come away frightened not so much by the outbursts of Rahel's passion but by the enduring consequences of its causes for the life of a brilliantly gifted individual who found it impossible to "rise above" her historicality—that is, the social, cultural, and political conditions of her life.

For Arendt, such "rising above" is naturally impossible: no individual can do so; no individual should be expected to do so—neither for his own good nor for society's. All Arendt had asked of Rahel was that she acknowledge the fact of her Jewishness and meet it as a challenge. But where Arendt had shown, by no means without sympathy, the self-destructive energies of Rahel's passion, she had done so with the expectation, passionate and frustrated, that Rahel would learn to turn them into something other than the spiritually beautiful, socially acceptable Frau von Varnhagen. It is the intensity of this expectation, directed at another life whose conditions she shared and did not share, which makes for the consistency of the analysis her readers have found disturbing.

Such disturbance can prove very effective, both in creating and denying accessibility to the reader. An intelligent and skilled biographer like Sybille Bedford, who was not particularly sensitive to either the "Jewish question" or the "Woman Problem," responded to Arendt's passionate frustration with Rahel's arrest in the social sphere. And yet she went back to the more harmless *Rahel* edited by Varnhagen. For Jaspers, highly sensitive to the "Jewish question," Rahel's life had been significantly fulfilled, no matter how passionate her laments that it had not, and he was only made uneasy by Arendt's insistence on Rahel's very serious failures.

For Arendt these failures mark the center in Rahel's life, they have been caused by her flawed way of dealing with her own historicality, and they are therefore historically important. I think it is significant that Arendt did not quote in full Rahel's deathbed statement, with which she starts the biography. It is significant because the last sentences of that statement modify Rahel's final reconciliation with her fate as a Jewess suggested by the preceding part: "Will the same thing [Rahel's being content that she had not missed what caused her such great misery in her life, her Jewishness] happen to me with this bed of suffering, will I not rise once again in the same way and not to wish to miss it for anything? Dear August, what a consoling idea, what a significant comparison."[96] August Varnhagen, recording and publishing these deathbed words, did not act so much out of character after all. It is quite clear that Rahel, at this significant moment of taking stock of her life, still connects Judaism with sickness and suffering—more, that the motivation for the "significant comparison" is her enduring capacity to deny the conditions of her existence, the facts. Second-guessing Arendt's motivations in cutting these important sentences from this important quote, I find praiseworthy both her narrative tact—one can hardly use a dying person's hope for recovery against her—and her conceptual determination—she takes off from this quote in her efforts at documenting and proving the illusory nature of such late reconciliation, namely, Rahel's enduring struggles against the fact of her Jewishness.

Answering Jaspers' letter on September 7, 1952, Arendt thanks him for his "clear illuminating patience," tells him that she had expected his reservations, that the book, almost completed in 1933, had been quite distant to her for years, and that she had finished it in 1938 because Bluecher and Benjamin insisted that she do so.[97] She agrees with Jaspers that she should not publish it immediately—at the end of his letter, Jaspers had stressed that this "important work" ought to be published but needed to be thoroughly reworked. He connected this recommendation with his wish for her to speak publicly to the Jewish question in ways that would guarantee the permanent validity of the printed text.

Arendt, though emphasizing as always the importance of Jaspers' judgment for her decisions, asserts that much of her argument in the Rahel book might have been useful had it been published before 1933 and perhaps even before 1938, and might be useful again after the last (her) generation of German Jews is gone. She concedes that the present situation might not be a good time for publication: she is afraid not so much of anti-Semites using her arguments as of well-meaning readers seeing a connection between her analysis of Rahel's difficulties and the destruction of European Jewry which de facto does not exist. In this context Arendt refers to her distinction between social and political anti-Semitism. The situation experienced by Rahel led to social anti-Semitism on the one hand and Zionism on the other; it is political anti-Semitism which has to be linked with the phenomenon of political totalitarianism.

This distinction, which provided the conceptual grid for "Antisemitism," Part One of her Origins of Totalitarianism (1951), had not been clear to her when she worked on the Rahel biography. At that time, she reminds Jaspers, she was still under the influence of the Zionist critique of social assimilation. It is true that she thinks this critique essentially justified now, though politically as naive as assimilation itself. (This evaluation has to be placed in the context of her distinguishing between social and political anti-Semitism.) She agrees with Jaspers that the book is indeed very personal in tone and mode of reflection, and therefore alien to

her now. But she insists that it is not personal in terms of Jewish experience, in which she had to educate herself ("die ich mir mit Muehe und
Not anerzogen habe") with the help of Kurt Blumenfeld, who as a young
man around the turn of century had been as "naively assimilated as she
had been in the late twenties."[98] This does not contradict the fact that
such "education in the Jewish experience" was accelerated immeasurably
in the early thirties and did indeed have a profound influence on her
perspective on Rahel.

But more than anything else, Arendt wanted to correct Jaspers' image
of Rahel. The insight that Jews could not really live like human beings
under the conditions of legal emancipation and social assimilation is central to the book's argument, and Arendt is still convinced of its validity.
Rahel's life is proof positive precisely because she experimented with herself in this social situation without sparing herself and without lying to
herself. What had always intrigued Arendt about Rahel was just this
openness to life, her letting life rain on her without an umbrella. It is the
reason why she presented herself so clearly and accessibly to the observer,
but it is also why she was "so absolutely intolerable."

Jaspers' different image of Rahel is based on Varnhagen's falsifica-
tions and on his own understanding of the role the Enlightenment played
in the emancipation of Jews (with which Arendt very much disagrees).
In Arendt's view, this role was decisively shaped by Mendelssohn and his
enthusiastic, wealthy follower David Friedlaender, rather than by Lessing,
whom she wants clearly distinguished from Mendelssohn's, as she sees
it, shallowness and opportunism in these matters. Now, Lessing had
based his wise and humane Jew Nathan on his friend Mendelssohn; and
the nonconformist yearning he expressed at the end of his life for a land
where there would be neither Christian nor Jew seems to find support in
Mendelssohn's *Jerusalem oder ueber religioese Macht und Judentum*.
Also, could one not expect Arendt to appreciate Mendelssohn's plea in
this text for a separation of church and state? Like his friend the Prussian
official Christian-Wilhelm Dohm in his *Ueber die buergerliche Verbesser-
ung der Juden* (1781), Mendelssohn had aimed here for the granting of
civic rights to Jews. But where the Gentile Dohm argued from the political and judicial point of view and assumed Jewish cultural assimilation
(language, customs, values) to the Christian majority as basis for their
gradual "civic betterment," Mendelssohn projected a secular state—that
is, abolition of the political and judicial rights of churches which would
distinctly modify the concept of assimilation to a Christian environment.

There would be a secular German-Jewish symbiosis in some ways not unlike that envisioned three generations later by Hermann Cohen.[99] It is true that Mendelssohn's projection, extending the principle of separation, also called for abolition of the Jewish "church"—that is, of the judicial autonomy of Jewish communities, including rabbinical excommunication. Such a conclusion on the grounds of reason may have suggested to Arendt a "denial" or "abolition" of historical facts which, like Rahel's denial, could support Mendelssohn's desire to be accepted into (at that time Gentile) society. And indeed in her letter to Jaspers, Arendt links Rahel and Mendelssohn through this "primary" impulse, for which, she writes, one cannot blame them. Only Heine, the poet and revolutionary, and Spinoza, the philosopher, could exist outside society. Not Mendelssohn, whom Arendt does not take seriously as a philosopher, and certainly not the "Jewish girl" Rahel, whose extraordinary intelligence needed the social medium. But did not Heine's too? And was not Rahel in many ways as "creative" in language as Heine, a poet in her own right?[100] Does not Arendt really blame Rahel, or Mendelssohn for that matter, because, not being able to live humanly within society, she still wished to join it rather than change it? Because she did not, as Arendt had done, choose the position of the pariah?

Jaspers had accused Arendt of "moralizing" about Rahel. However, Arendt's intention had been to reason with her within the categories of parvenu and pariah, which she thought accessible and "somehow" acceptable to Rahel herself. She had tried, she explains, to "measure and correct" the parvenu by the standards of the pariah because she thought that Rahel herself was doing that—often, perhaps, without knowing it. Yet, second-guessing Rahel in measuring her in terms of these standards *and* finding her wanting, Arendt had indeed moralized about Rahel— more, she had reshaped her life story by applying an "ought" that was too consistently informed by hindsight. From her pariah perspective as a twentieth-century German Jewess, a perspective from which the history of German-Jewish coexistence seemed so troubled as to be doomed, she had judged Rahel for having contributed to that history. For Jaspers, it was even more difficult now, after the political-cultural catastrophe of the Hitler regime, to consider Arendt's perspective on that history than it had been twenty years earlier, when he had argued with his young student about the meaning, for her, of German high culture, which had meant so much to Jews in their struggle for social assimilation and to which Jewish Germans had contributed so significantly.

What Arendt had learned from Blumenfeld's "Zionism by the Grace of Goethe"—it would have been "Zionism by the Grace of Lessing" for her—was the clarity with which she saw the problem of tolerance as active and mutual acceptance of the other in his otherness. It is significant that in her letter to Jaspers she mentions Blumenfeld's unconstrained, natural acceptance of Bluecher, which was not so common among her Jewish friends, at least not in the beginning. Whether intended or not, this information was an effective answer to Jaspers' suggestion that her all-too-harsh view of Rahel would at any rate have been changed by her different situation now, above all by her contentment in her relationship with Bluecher. In reality, Arendt wrote the last two chapters, which are most directly critical of Rahel's passionate desire to assimilate herself to the world of the other, when she was already living with Bluecher and was urged by him to complete her work on the book.

Arendt's historical understanding of anti-Semitism, so important for the development of her political thought, is distinguished by her indeed quite original emphasis on the concrete social-psychological consequences of exclusion for the minority's ability to consider with tolerance its own and the other's otherness. This essentially civilized ability to accept actively the plurality of human existence is essentially human, but has been profoundly threatened in the experience of German-Jewish assimilation. Mendelssohn's concept of Enlightenment tolerance, which appeals to fraternity but is critical of unquestioned (especially religious) solidarity,[101] does take into consideration this problem, all his striving for social acceptance notwithstanding; and Arendt did not give him enough credit for it.

The Rahel biography is important in this context precisely because, as a detailed case history, it enabled Arendt to show how such a threat to mutual acceptance of the other in her otherness shaped the life of an individual who seems so eminently predisposed to appreciate, to embrace human plurality. Rahel, highly intelligent and imaginative, never learned to put herself, temporarily or in the imagination, in the other's place. She either coveted it or rejected it; she either too eagerly, too unquestioningly, too unreflectedly assimilated herself to the other or insisted on her own unique and therefore *eo ipso* meaningful otherness. In any case she was unable to mediate, to develop a relationship of mutual acceptance, and this prevented her from comprehending herself in a world shared with others—namely, with persons whom she perceived as different from her and who thought her different.

Such sharing has to be learned culturally, and assimilation undermined rather than encouraged the learning process. It is not that Arendt
puts all the burden of learning on the minority member, the victim of
exclusion. It is rather that she wishes to stress the considerable difficulties
experienced by Rahel, the victim of exclusion, in her understanding of
exactly what harm has been done to her own ability to achieve mutuality.
She is concerned, that is, about the victim's ability to understand the other
in his otherness and not as an instrument of her desire to be (become)
like him or be not (no longer) like him. This is particularly clear in the
case of Rahel's generation of German Jews, for whom assimilation is still
concretely difficult in political terms and not at all as widespread an option in social terms. In this situation, the victim of exclusion, desiring so
fervently inclusion by assimilation, strives quite naturally for a new kind
of solidarity. The "naively assimilated" Arendt shows how such unquestioning solidarity with the majority group can be more self-limiting than
the often rigid solidarity within the minority group itself, which was to
continue into the twentieth century in many cases, in spite of political
emancipation and social assimilation, and which was so alien to her.[104]
Readers disturbed by her later critical analyses of the exclusionary mechanisms controlling the self-perception and politics of the State of Israel
might usefully keep this in mind to avoid misunderstanding Arendt's intentions.

Arendt was not right when, trying to neutralize the disagreement
with Jaspers, she withdrew the Rahel book with the argument that the
problem of German-Jewish assimilation, ending as it did in 1933, was no
longer very important, at least not to her, especially since the relevant
historical insights, she argued, could be found more economically and
"without all that psychology" in the anti-Semitism part of *The Origins of
Totalitarianism*. It is arguable, however, that it had been precisely "all that
psychology" which had made the historical insights particularly useful
because particularly concrete, and that it had been her own situation, her
own perspective, which had contributed significantly to the energy of her
social-psychological analysis.

Arendt clearly disagrees with Rahel to the very end, forcefully strip-
ping her of all illusions about greatness and uniqueness in the face of
failures. She imposes on Rahel her own strength, that of the young
woman who can still do without the consolations of closure because she
does not yet herself have to confront the experience of life just ending.
She is cruelly perceptive in not letting Rahel forget the exact turning point

after which she is too old and too tired to do without the echo of Varnhagen, and she is ungenerously shrewd about the soulful emptiness and
lifelessness of the social climber Varnhagen.[103] She does not allow Rahel
to forget or to gloss over what happened to her, because this depended,
too, on her having made wrong choices. Never for one moment does she
allow Rahel to escape from the self shaped by these choices. Noble sentiments in the end do not right the wrongs of a life; semireligious resignation is too easy and too much of the moment in whose significance,
Goethean or otherwise, Arendt does not believe.

But Arendt does all these things to Rahel because she is profoundly
angry with her out of a concrete sympathy with her life as a woman and
a Jew. Putting herself in Rahel's place, seeing her so clearly, understanding her so well, she wishes passionately that the other Jewish woman,
living more than a century before her, could have had the courage and
the encouragement to change. No male, no Gentile, would have been so
angry with Rahel, nor would they have seen so clearly the waste of her
life and the flaws in her life story. Arendt's anger, not so extraordinary in
a young observer, is so effective in this historical biography because it is
informed by a social-psychological shrewdness that is indeed extraordinary. She has lent her voice to Rahel, whom she thinks intolerable in her
other-directed pushing, wanting, needing, scheming, lamenting fixation
on herself, and lovable in her lack of prejudice, her articulated emotional
and intellectual generosity, her infectious exhilaration by the "true realities of life," "love, trees, children, music,"[104] to Rahel the parvenu *and* the
pariah.

Arendt understands how Rahel's choices have thrown her life out of
its natural temporal balance and rhythm: childless, married to a much
younger man who admires and records an unchanging persona, she is
accepted as Frau von Varnhagen and lonely as Rahel, who can no longer
afford to grieve, but who also cannot grow old:

> I should really like to present myself as just as old as I am; I cannot
> do that . . . because I have a young husband who loves me dearly.
> There is nothing more comical. The upside-down crown upon my
> fate; still I am *grateful*.[105]

August Varnhagen did not or refused to understand the pariah in Rahel.
When shortly after their marriage she asked him to find Pauline Wiesel
in Paris, where he was attending the peace conferences, he did so dutifully and was properly scandalized, both by the state of Pauline's financial

and love affairs and by her attempts to seduce him. She would be the only person Varnhagen objected to during Rahel's lifetime and whom after her death he did his best to erase from her life. But Rahel, amused by Pauline's trying to "taste Rahel's husband—like iced punch," because she understood it to be proof of her friend's interest in her,[106] continued to think of Pauline as her alter ego and to stay in contact with her.[107] This was, in Arendt's eyes, one of the assertions of Rahel's enduring pariahism which constituted her "salvage from the *great* bankruptcy of life"— "great" in the sense of total.[108]

The Rahel biography may be structured too clearly as a case history of German-Jewish assimilation. But as a case history it explores the gray areas of social interaction where the voice and actions of the victim are not without ambiguities, because they are human. Arendt's inclusion of this gray area in the task of cultural anamnesis was crucially influenced by the fact that she herself was a Jew *and* a woman. Her intellectual temperament, shaped by these facts, enabled her to put herself in the place of the other and to refuse to limit her observation to one group's perspective. The experience of victimization had taught her to consider very carefully the victim's history—that is, Rahel's responsibility, in experience, to herself and others. Such a concept of responsibility has nothing to do with allegations of the victim's share in the victimizer's guilt, but it does question assumptions of the victim's total, that is, paradisical, ahistorical innocence.

3

The Silence of Exile

Arendt's Critique of Political Zionism

One of the first essays Arendt wrote in America concerned the para-doxically difficult situation of the German-Jewish refugee from Hitlerism who had reached the relative safety of the United States.[1] Her intention is to make clear to the American reader the difficulties, on many levels of experience, confronting the exiles. But the main interest and focus of the article is her analysis of the refugees' attempt at repressing awareness of their exile status, both in relation to others and in relation to themselves. In Arendt's view, this repression is a symptomatic phenomenon with far-reaching social-psychological implications. Having almost despaired of escaping from Hitlerism, the exiles desperately want to hide the fact that they had to escape, that they are refugees.

> We ourselves call each other "newcomers" or "immigrants." Our newspapers are papers for "Americans of German language"; and, as far as I know, there is not and never was any club founded by Hitler-persecuted people whose name indicated that its members were refugees.[2]

Arendt points out that before the outbreak of World War II, exiled Jews were even more sensitive about being called refugees, declaring that they had departed of their own free will to countries of their choice and denying that their situation was connected in any way with the "so-called Jewish problems." They wanted to be seen—like everybody else—as im-migrants who had come to America for economic reasons, strong and future-oriented in their determination to rebuild their lives. Optimistic newcomers, they learned English and unlearned German and with it both the norms and values of their old world-view and their traumatic memories. Yet, in some cases, the still-unexamined trauma of their past drove them beyond the hectic optimism of their new life toward suicide.

What is the meaning of these suicides committed by assimilated Jews who continue to react in this way to the experience of persecution in cities like New York and Los Angeles, where, in contrast to Berlin, Vienna, and Paris, they can expect to be safe? For a religious Jew, suicide is blasphemy, an instance of man's interfering with creation by destroying what is not his to destroy because he did not create it. Taking one's own life in this case means asserting against the Creator that the life He gave is not worth living and that the world He created is not good enough—an act of hubris with which the young Arendt would have been able to identify, at least temperamentally. In the case of the assimilated nonreligious Jew, however, suicide signifies the acknowledgment of defeat. To that individual nothing is left but to leave a world—quietly, secretively—which has robbed him of the possibility to maintain a sense of self and with it a sense of trust in himself in his world, of self-assertion. Suicide, then, is the final gesture in conceding that the progressive loss of self could not be stopped.

There have been many cases of such self-loss, though they have not all ended in suicide. Arendt charts one "typical" (composite) case of Jewish emigration from Germany: Mr. Cohn from Berlin, a super-German patriot, flees to Prague in 1933 and becomes a fervent Czech patriot, is expelled from Prague and flees to Vienna, where he quickly becomes an Austrian patriot, has to leave in 1938 and flees to Paris, where he never acquires a regular residence permit, but prepares himself for eventual French citizenship by identifying immediately with the *gloire* of France. Now, in France he is literally a refracted being: a *Boche* for French Gentiles, a *Polak* for the French Jews, a *Jaecke* for the first-generation Eastern Jews in France.[3] The attempt to maintain a functioning Jewish self under these circumstances seems hopelessly impossible and is replaced by the attempt to construct a non-Jewish self:

> Whatever we do, whatever we pretend to be, we reveal nothing but our insane desire to be changed, not to be Jews. All our activities are directed to attain this aim: we don't want to be refugees, since we don't want to be Jews; we pretend to be English-speaking

people, since German-speaking immigrants of recent years are marked as Jews; we don't call ourselves stateless, since the majority of stateless people in the world are Jews; we are willing to become loyal Hottentots, only to hide the fact that we are Jews. We don't succeed and we can't succeed; under the cover of our "optimism" you can easily detect the hopeless sadness of assimilationists.[4]

In their majority, German Jews have accepted assimilation as a solution to the problems caused by their minority status. Arendt recounts her experience with a compatriot who, shortly after his arrival in France, formed a group devoted to self-help in adjustment—one of many—where Jews learned to be French by asserting to themselves that they would, by necessity, be good French people. Under his direction they would repeat the magic formula: "We have been good Germans in Germany and therefore we shall be good Frenchmen in France." Nobody in the group laughed; they were presumably happy to know how to prove their loyalty.[5]

Arendt is both incredulous and sympathetic toward the group, for this sentence aptly sums up their situation, which is desperate and has been desperate for a long time. The assimilated Jews' existence for the previous one hundred fifty years had, after all, been founded on the paradox that they were intent on getting rid of their Jewishness, that they were always trying to prove that it did not exist, and that somehow they always remained Jews. They seemed to have had no choice to either be or not be Jewish. And it is the question of choice—that is, of choices not made—rather than the question of a threatened, unwanted, and paradoxically preserved identity, which underlies Arendt's analysis of the Jewish refugees' dilemma. They are eternal wanderers like their ancestor-prototype, but unlike Ahasver, they do not know who they are. Worse, in their confusion they not only desist from asserting, they actively refuse to hold on to, their identity. Arendt's conclusion, then, is that the Hitler regime did not create, it only cruelly brought to the surface, the desperate absurdity of this situation.

Beginning with the Rahel biography, the question of choice had been central to Arendt's political thought. But in the context of the German-Jewish experience it was not only a troubling question but also a painfully controversial one. Describing so well the plight of the German-Jewish refugees in the dispersion of exile, Arendt does not even stop to ask whether they had any realistic alternative to rapid assimilation to their new environments. In France, for instance, they were caught in the vicious circle of no work—no regular residence permit—no work, with only a slight chance of breaking through the circle by obtaining work as a refugee. French language skills and a general cultural assimilation were of the greatest importance in this situation, which for many exiles was literally a desperate one, as Arendt knows very well as she explains the mechanisms of these difficulties. Why, then, does she focus so emphatically on the negative aspects of the willingness and ability to assimilate in a situation in which, for many refugees, survival depended on that very ability? Why does she stress the importance of making a choice in a situation in which there was no or very little choice?

In "We Refugees," Arendt does not answer these questions, does not seem to have anticipated them, and the argument remains conflicted to the very end. On the one hand, she acknowledges the extreme precariousness of the refugee's situation if he does indeed "naively," unselfconsciously insist on his Jewishness. Such insistence, under the circumstances, would mean exposure to the "fate of human beings who, unprotected by any specific law or political convention, are nothing but human beings."[6] Implied is the equation between the status of the exile and that of the outlaw, who in German is called *vogelfrei* (free as a bird), that is, in the state of nature, unprotected, in his exclusion from the group, by social constraints. It is important, then, she seems to admit, for the refugee to strive for inclusion because we all depend on social standards for survival. But here her argument shifts, drawing attention to a few individuals who are sufficiently independent to look at the mechanisms of social inclusion and exclusion from the distance of the "conscious pariah." Like the parvenus, the Mr. Cohns who desperately want to be included, they are sons and daughters of the nineteenth century, the century of German-Jewish assimilation. But in contrast to the assimilationists, they joined "the tradition of Heine, Rahel Varnhagen, Sholom Aleichem, of Bernard Lazare, Franz Kafka or even Charlie Chaplin," rather than that of the rich court Jews or the millionaire bankers:

> All vaunted Jewish qualities—the "Jewish heart," humanity, humor, disinterested intelligence—are pariah qualities. All Jewish shortcomings—tactlessness, political stupidity, inferiority complexes and money-grubbing—are characteristic of upstarts. There have always been Jews who did not think it worthwhile to change their

humane attitude and their natural insight into reality for the narrowness of caste spirit or the essential unreality of financial transactions.[7]

This passage must have been deeply troubling to many of Arendt's
readers because it is blatantly unfair to the Mr. Cohns in exile. Arguably
it was less Mr. Cohn's love for socially upward mobility than the perceived
need of sheer, barest survival which made him try to suppress his refugee
status in dealing with an ever-changing, unfamiliar, threatening environment over which he had little or no control. Arendt's contrasting "humane
attitude" and "natural insight into reality" with "narrowness of caste
spirit" and "the essential unreality of financial transactions" seems to
place her in the company of German-Jewish intellectual contemporaries
like Lukacs, Adorno, or Benjamin. But if she was not then (and never
was to be) a bourgeois liberal, she also was not a Marxist; and though
certain tenets of Zionism continued to be important to her political
thought, she was no longer—if indeed she had ever been—a Zionist in
any conventional sense. What she had taken or, rather, extrapolated from
the secular Zionism of Blumenfeld and his group—in some cases to
Blumenfeld's deep chagrin[8]—was her analysis of the crucial connection
between recognition and acceptance of minority identity and the ability
to participate fully and naturally in "the world"—that is, for her, in the
public sphere.
    The most urgent problem of German-Jewish refugees in exile, then,
was not the loss of identity through the loss of language, work, and social
situation. It was, rather, the loss of an identity defined by the acceptance
of political responsibility. This may be considered a moot distinction,
given the many pressing day-to-day difficulties encountered by the refugees. But it is central to Arendt's developing understanding of the meanings of political experience, which moved her to question rather than accept as a given the impact of those difficulties on political participation.
And her reflections on the assimilationism of the exiles, notwithstanding
the text's unresolved contradictions, belong to a group of essays concerned with the problem of exile and political responsibility which Arendt
wrote in the forties in reaction to Jewish political behavior in Palestine
and which became the starting point from which she pursued the questions most important to her political philosophy.
    Responsibility, as Michael Denneny points out in his essay "The

Privilege of Ourselves: Hannah Arendt on Judgment," has three distinct but interdependent components of meaning: "to declare the presence of that which is present; to declare oneself present; and to declare a bond between oneself and that which is."[9] Unable to declare himself fully present, the exile is unable to act responsibly in the public sphere, which for Arendt means that he cannot participate humanly in the world. Exile, then, is a political, not a religious or existential, concept. Arendt is interested in the Jewish cultural tension of a lost and regained homeland, a lost and regained state of nonalienation in terms of its—in her view— dangerous political potential.[10] As a state of fragmentation and estrangement, the Galut, the dispersion of the Jews (also in the United States), is not in itself a meaningful concept to her. Like many socially and politically engaged German-Jewish intellectuals, including German Zionists, she did not share in a Jewish imagination preoccupied with exile rather than paradise.[11] As Eisen points out, it "has always had both a *political* dimension—the perils of statelessness, the disabilities of the alien—and a *metaphysical* dimension: a function of our brief sojourn as human beings on God's earth."[12] In Arendt's secular view, this earth is not God's but ours, our responsibility. Nor is our temporary sojourn here all that transitory—or rather it need not and ought not be. But it was the failure of German-Jewish assimilation—namely, the wrong kind of cultural secularization—which created her interest in political spaces of temporary permanence and visibility. They would be defined by a community of peers into which the individual would be admitted. And in such a space, established in and for the duration of political speech and action, the individual could find her voice and use it responsibly in support of a construct achieved by women and men before her and intended to be useful to women and men after her.[13]

Responsible speech and action in this world require the effort to comprehend a social and political reality, no matter how difficult, conflicted, or painful. In the preface to the first edition of *The Origins of Totalitarianism*, Arendt explicitly tells the reader that

> comprehension does not mean denying the outrageous, deducing the unprecedented from precedents, or explaining phenomena by such analogies and generalizations that the impact of reality and the shock of reality are no longer felt. It means, rather, examining and bearing consciously the burden which our century has placed on

us—neither denying its existence, nor submitting meekly to its weight. Comprehension, in short, means the unpremeditated, attentive facing up to, and resisting of reality—whatever it may be.[14]

Or, as she wrote two years later: "If we want to be at home on this earth, even at the price of being at home in this century, we must try to take part in the interminable dialogue with its essence."[15] Being at home on this earth is synonymous not with final redemptive homecoming but with accepting the challenge of being—for a time—in the only home there is, which means facing up to the social and political reality of this century of mass human destruction.

o 2 o

The provocation and usefulness of Arendt's political thought lie in her insistence on confronting reality, a process which breaks up encrusted ideological certainties. Her analysis of contemporary Jewish history has often put her in the position of the dissenter, and her dissent has been deeply resented—not only in the case of her report on the Eichmann trial but also in the case of her critical interpretation of assimilationism in Germany, the United States, and Palestine. The Jewish-American political scientist Shklar thinks Arendt's perception of herself as a nonassimilated Jew "a bizarre notion." How can Arendt be so naive as to understand nonassimilation as an "act of personal defiance and not a matter of actively maintaining a cultural and religious tradition with its own rites and patterns of speech."[16] Shklar judges Arendt from the perspective of a member of a Jewish minority in the United States which is one minority among others, and she is very much uninformed with regard to the history of German-Jewish assimilation. Thus she misunderstands Arendt's concept of "the Jew as Pariah" as referring to "outcasts who develop an intense sense of honor and pride in their status as aliens" and is offended by Arendt's treatment of Rahel:

> That she should have used that word [parvenu] for assimilated Jews tells us a good deal about Arendt. The pariah is so sure of her superiority that she no longer wishes to make efforts to join the larger society. She has, in fact, absorbed the attitudes of its upper class so completely that there is no impulse for her to rise from her actual position. Who, after all, goes back further than "the people of the book"?[17]

But this is precisely not Arendt's point. The pariah is the outsider who, in acknowledging and accepting this position rather than disguising and denying it, will be able to develop, with her Jewish identity, the necessary critical distance to her own group. The pariah is not proud of her Jewishness—it is, after all, nothing but an accident of birth and not her merit. Rather, the pariah accepts this accident as a challenge. And the energy released by this acceptance is essential for overcoming what Arendt understood to be, in the German-Jewish context, a specifically Jewish apolitical inwardness or worldlessness (curiously analogous to what Marx had called "die deutsche Misere").

This worldlessness—in Jacob Katz's words, "The outside world did not overly occupy the Jewish mind" [18]—had been imposed on the Jewish minority with the occupational restrictions to moneylending and trade, "a variety of peddling, of endless buying and selling—and always in an atmosphere of suspicion between lender and buyer, Jew and Gentile" [19]—which did anything but encourage inclusion and participation. After the emancipation legislation of 1812, the restrictions were gradually removed. However, it was not political emancipation but "the modernization of society, the sudden possibilities of obtaining eminence through education and wealth (Besitz und Bildung) that gave the Jews the unanticipated chance of leaping ahead." [20] As court Jews, German Jews had historically been in personal alliance with governments and states that had limited their political experience and tradition. For helping to make possible, through financing, political events like wars, their rewards had always been social—case in point, the permission granted the court jeweler of Frederick II, Veitel Ephraim, who had financed the Seven Years' War, to build the much-admired rococo Ephraim Palais in Berlin's Nicolai Viertel.

Stern points out that the rapid advancement of Jews as a group came at a time of rapid industrialization and modernization in which many other groups experienced rootlessness, fragmentation, and estrangement from a once securely anchored, familiar lifeworld. This difficult experience gave rise to feelings of hostility toward the Jews, who were perceived as operators of a process of change that seemed to be too sudden and too far-reaching. One should add to this the observation that highly successful—that is, socially visible—Jewish businessmen and bankers did not just seem to be responsible in a general and somewhat opaque way for political events connected with certain highly important aspects of social change; they were indeed partly responsible by reason of making them possible financially. Yet they did so without being visible in the political sphere—that is, without admitting or declaring their responsibility.

The negative consequences of this situation for Jews were considerable and complex: Powerful financiers like Bismarck's banker, Bleichroeder, who in spite of political interests, saw their power in social rather than political terms, experienced the painful dilemma of being sought after, famous, and honored on the one hand and distinctly excluded on the other.[21] Especially Jews in high finance met with a confusing mixture of hospitality and hostility. Their political influence was potentially very great, even if not explicitly used. They were valued because of this influence and because of their cultural buying power—Bleichroeder was a philanthropist on the level of the Rothschilds. But the political elites never accepted them as social equals. This made it easier to see Jews as allegories of the social problems connected with modernity, especially increasing urban alienation, labor mechanization, and abstraction in money exchange:

> The Jews were disproportionately active in large cities, in commerce, and in professions that generally assured them an income and an influence far greater than those of the German population at large. Bleichroeder was merely the visible exemplar of this new role, and after his sojourn in Versailles and his ennoblement in 1872, he symbolized as well the link between the new plutocracy and power.[22]

Jews, then, became objects of hatred for all those who felt both driven out of a familiar, manageable world and excluded from the new plutocratic industrialist society. At the same time, they were objects of contempt for many in the ruling elite who used Jews to support their position but did not approve of the Jews' struggle for real—that is, unquestioned, unquestionable—inclusion. Indeed, Jews were victimized by their very success. Moreover, their victimization, from hindsight, seems overdetermined: they were doomed to lose, no matter what they did, and all that is left for the historian to explain is the process of their inevitable defeat. Arendt disagreed, and the fact that she included Jews, too, in her critical perspective on the history of German-Jewish assimilation has been as shocking as it has been useful. She developed this perspective in the interest of understanding the sociopolitical-historical reasons for a failure that contributed to what seemed and still seems to many historians a metahistorical catastrophe. In its insistence on the accessible historicality

of this failure and its consequences, this perspective presupposes the accessible specificity of the people who were involved in it.

In the beginning of the first chapter of *Origins of Totalitarianism*,
"Antisemitism as an Outrage to Common Sense," Arendt forcefully rejected the scapegoat theory precisely because it prevents the historian
from asking certain culturally important questions:

> The theory that the Jews are always the scapegoat implies that the
> scapegoat might have been anyone else as well. It upholds the per-
> fect innocence of the victim, an innocence which insinuates not
> only that no evil was done but that nothing at all was done which
> might possibly have a connection with the issue at stake. It is true
> that the scapegoat theory in its purely arbitrary form[23] never ap-
> pears in print. Whenever, however, its adherents painstakingly try
> to explain why a specific scapegoat was so well suited to his role,
> they show that they have left the theory behind them and have got
> themselves involved in the usual historical research—where noth-
> ing is ever discovered except that history is made by many groups
> and that for certain reasons one group was singled out. The so-
> called scapegoat necessarily ceases to be the innocent victim whom
> the world blames for all its sins and through whom it wishes to
> escape punishment; it becomes one group of people among other
> groups, all of which are involved in the business of this world. And
> it does not simply cease to be co-responsible because it became the
> victim of the world's injustice and cruelty.[24]

To reject as useless for the task of historical understanding the notion
of the victims' paradisical, worldless innocence, which does not permit
any consideration of co-responsibility, is the opposite of "Jewish self-
hatred" as the minority's internalization of majority prejudice. (Arendt,
however, has been accused of both Jewish self-hatred and Jewish anti-
Semitism, most explicitly in connection with the Eichmann book.) The
argument for co-responsibility is, rather, the result of the relational perspective of the pariah, the voluntarily temporary outsider who escapes the
epistemological distortions inherent in the by definition unquestioned
perspective of solidarity. This perspective does not deny the power of the
mechanism controlling the internalization of imposed prejudice. The
Jews'

> self-disdain reflected and reinforced their own sense of inferiority
> vis-à-vis the Germans. Ludwig Bamberger, next to Lasker, Ger-

many's chief parliamentarian, thought "Jewish characteristics comprised: pushiness and tactlessness, greed, insolence, vanity and title-chasing, intellectual parvenuism and servility." The Jews were boastful even in their self-criticism.[25]

But why were they? Out of self-hatred? Jewish anti-Semitism? And do these labels suggest anything other than a general problem of minority self-consciousness? Stern points out that "perhaps never before in Europe had a minority risen as fast or gone as far as did German Jews in the nineteenth century." And having done so they found themselves in a situation of general political and social instability. It was not their fault that they had no political tradition or experience, but it caused them to be "as little aware of the tensions between society and state as they were of the obvious risks and power-possibilities of their new role."[26] In Arendt's view, this lack of political experience and maturity caused Jews to conceive their Jewish identity too narrowly—that is, to focus too much on success or failure in the social sphere. The sons of successful Jewish businessmen and bankers turned to the liberal professions, German high culture, the arts, and intellectual pursuits, leaving to others the responsibility for political affairs—that is, for the execution of power.

This does not mean that such participation would have been easy or, in many situations, even possible. But it is through the analysis of a specifically Jewish "worldlessness," an (however understandable) unwillingness to deal as a group with the challenges of the political sphere, that Arendt anchors the questions of Jewish victimization and social and political anti-Semitism in history.[27]

In her essay "On Humanity in Dark Times: Thoughts about Lessing,"[28] originally her acceptance speech for the 1959 Lessing Prize of the City of Hamburg,[29] Arendt distinguishes between Lessing's concept of friendship[30] and Rousseau's concept of compassion and fraternity.[31] For Lessing, the political man, "truth can exist only where it is humanized by discourse,"[32] and thus his concept of friendship is selective, differentiating, and judicious in terms of the relations between individuals and groups. Rousseau's concept of fraternity, however, is simply and all-embracingly the "fulfillment of humanity." Arendt's understanding of the ideological implications of Rousseau's insistence on unanimous fraternity—what Lessing called "philanthropic feelings," springing from a shared hatred of a world in which men are not treated according to their humanity—is clarified by this distinction and instructive for our context. Humanity, Arendt argues,

> manifests itself in such brotherhood most frequently in "dark times." This kind of humanity actually becomes inevitable when the times become so extremely dark for certain groups of people that it is no longer up to them, their insight or choice, to withdraw from the world. Humanity in the form of fraternité invariably appears historically among persecuted peoples and enslaved groups; and in eighteenth-century Europe it must have been quite natural to detect it among the Jews, who were then newcomers in literary circles. This kind of humanity is the great privilege of pariah peoples; it is the advantage that the pariahs of this world always and in all circumstances can have over others. The privilege is dearly bought; it is often accompanied by so radical a loss of the world, so fearful an atrophy of all the organs with which we respond to it—starting with the common sense with which we orient ourselves in a world common to ourselves and others and going on to the sense of beauty, or taste, with which we love the world—that in extreme cases, in which pariahdom has persisted for centuries, we can speak of real worldlessness. And worldlessness, alas, is always a form of barbarism.[33]

It was this uncritical togetherness, this unquestioned fraternity and solidarity of the minority group, which Arendt connected with the development of assimilationism leading to parvenuism: the outsider struggling too single-mindedly to be the insider, without the benefits of a critical, judging perspective on the majority's *and* his own group's exclusionary and inclusionary practices. The failure of assimilation (with the help of her Zionist friends, Arendt realized by the late twenties that it had failed) was the co-responsibility of the Jews because, like most Germans, herself included, they had been excellent Germans and mediocre citizens.

The question is not blame or guilt but responsibility, which in Arendt's grid of distinctions is a political concept. It was her effort to be clear in a fantastically entangled, complex, and obscure area of inquiry which caused much misunderstanding, but which also proved to be very helpful for many readers. At issue is not a model of explanation to be accepted and applied; at issue is the belief that where the catastrophic results of failed German-Jewish assimilation are concerned, differentiating speech is better than total silence, and the attempted, partial clarity of speech is better than the uncontrolled suggestiveness of paradox. Arendt's argument implies that the refugee trying too hard to assimilate, the refugee as parvenu, will understand only the imposition on her of the status of the ultimate pariah, the outlawed. She will be unable to acknowledge—and thereby at least partly understand—her partaking (in the sense of the German *teilhaben* rather than *teilnehmen*) in the historical developments which led to her being outlawed. She is the refugee as conscious pariah to whom "history is no longer a closed book" and politics no longer "the privilege of Gentiles." She knows, as Arendt says at the end of "We Refugees,"

> that the outlawing of the Jewish people in Europe has been followed
> closely by the outlawing of most European nations. Refugees driven
> from country to country represent the vanguard of their peoples—
> if they keep their identity. For the first time Jewish history is not
> separate but tied up with that of all other nations. The comity of
> European peoples went to pieces when, and because, it allowed its
> weakest member to be excluded and persecuted.[34]

Historical events, especially in the recent past, have in the eyes of many Jews supported the idea of a unique Jewish history resulting in a metahistorical state of separation and exile. This idea is in Arendt's view dangerously a- or anti-political, and it has caused her to stress the fact that of course Jews, too, have been partaking in European and world history and that their reaction to the past should be not a withdrawal but a more active, more judicious, more political participation in history. Now, at the end of the failed process of assimilation, which is an important part of European history, such partaking can be seen more clearly, acknowledged more openly, and interpreted more constructively. It is significant that Arendt emphasizes such involvement from the perspective of the Jewish intellectual in America, where, as she pointed out repeatedly, one could be an American citizen as a Jew and a Jew as an American citizen. In a country where the political sphere was fully accessible to Jews, the concept of exile was meaningless. I assume that she would have attributed Jewish underrepresentation in high political office to social-cultural reasons—both within and outside the control of members of a minority. As in the case of other minorities, these could be solved, or at least ameliorated, through political action. Clearly, she is interested in plurality not so much as a cultural as a political value. She continues to be rooted in a, by comparison to the American situation, homogeneous German-European (high) culture. Nonassimilation in the United States does not, in her view, mean preserving Jewish traditions and speech patterns. It means, rather, a critical awareness of Jewish partaking in European history and participation in American history, which she understands to be, on the whole, a history of compromise rather than conformism, inclusion rather than exclusion.[35]

○ 3 ○

When Arendt later tried to explain to a bewildered American audience the conflictedness and ambiguity of her friend Walter Benjamin's life and work,[36] she said that the two schools of thought in which her male German-Jewish contemporaries could articulate their rebellion against their fathers had been Marxism and Zionism. This is a shrewd observation if one adds "Hegelian" to the first term and "German" to the latter. Arendt herself had never assumed a Marxist position, and as a Zionist, she had often been in a position of dissent. But she shared with both Marxism and Zionism the aversion to a hierarchically structured, economically based class society, with its temptations of inclusion and social climbing, which is directly connected with personal wealth. It is necessary to remember here that German Zionism has never been a homogeneous movement, not even within generationally distinct groups. A second-generation Zionist like Richard Lichtheim, speaking about his assimilated parents' attitude toward their minority situation, pointed out that for them it was a naturally given fact that "Jews in Berlin were materially well off; there could be no doubt." They were also fully aware that the "rigid stratification of the 'class state' protected them more effectively than even the law."[37] These assimilated middle- and upper-middle-class Jews, then, shared the views Herzl expressed in *The Jewish State*. Attempting to shape the Eastern Jewish masses in the image of the assimilated Western Jews, he spoke out strongly in favor of modern business and high-finance practices and a rigidly hierarchic social stratification.[38]

But many first-generation German Zionists from a bourgeois background, too, were not much troubled by Herzl's utopian cementing of social-economic inequality. And like assimilated Jews, they disagreed with him in regard to the meaning of Diaspora. Whereas Herzl thought it impossible for Zionists to lead an authentically Jewish life outside a Jewish state, they stressed their loyalty to the German nation and supported, for the sake of their children, a Jewish national identity.[39] The founding members of Zionistische Vereinigung fuer Deutschland (ZVfD) saw their personal future in Germany and their Zionist ideology in the service of their efforts to harmonize their Jewish identity with German culture. In this they were not so far removed from the position of the religiously liberal Centralverein deutscher Staatsbuerger juedischen Glaubens (CV), in spite of its opposition to their assertion that a spirit of Jewish nationalism was developing among Jews dispersed all over the world.

Now, the second generation of Zionists differed profoundly in this respect. The change was brought about shortly before the outbreak of World War I by developments in the World Zionist Organization, which called for concentration on practical and cultural work in Palestine; by the influence of Martin Buber and Achad Ha'am; and, most importantly, by the fact that this generation did not share the older generation's bourgeois stability and secure belief in emancipation. The product of a liberal age, that belief in progress—and with it the belief in emancipation—was rapidly losing its validity and power of persuasion in the prewar period of national conflict and social tension.[40] This younger generation of Zionist Jews distanced themselves from their fathers' generation by criticizing, like the children of the Western European bourgeoisie in general, the fragmentation, mechanization, and alienation of their contemporary bourgeois world and stressing the importance, for their humanity, of nature, community, wholeness, and simplicity. Influenced by the German *Wandervoegel*, they founded Jewish *Wanderbuende*, where Jewish young people came together to realize their Jewish identity in "the spiritual and moral health of youth and the awakening of a natural and idealistic world view" in preparation for a later "decision to meet the challenge and claims of a Jewish nationalism."[41]

The most effective spokesman for this young generation was Kurt Blumenfeld, who was largely responsible for the change in the ideological direction of the ZVfD from 1910 to 1914. From his position as a "post-assimilationist" Zionist, Blumenfeld developed his concept of *Palaestino-zentrismus*, a stronger emphasis on Jewish nationalism, which was accepted as the basic ZVfD ideology in 1912 and affirmed at the Leipzig Zionist meeting in July 1914. German Jews, in the Zionist view, could no longer entertain the illusion of a successful German-Jewish synthesis or symbiosis. They could not honestly claim loyalty to both Jewish and German nationalism, but had to make a choice. Forty years later Blum-

enfeld was to sum up the significance of German Zionism as the realization that Jews are not Germans.[42]

For Blumenfeld and the second generation of German Zionists, recognition of the fact that Jews are German citizens but not part of the
German nation had a positive meaning: the possibility of a choice. Zionists could decide to reject the assimilationist illusion that complete politi-
cal-social emancipation could be achieved and with it a merging of the
Jewish with the German people. This decision enabled them to work
toward a true understanding of the reality of Jewish existence. The resolution of a *"palaestinozentrisch* Zionism," accepted at the 1912 Zionist
delegates' meeting in Posen, was to direct the course taken by the ZVfD,
even though the document seemed unrealistically radical in its assertion
that the duty of every Zionist was to plan to resettle in Palestine, an un-
developed country then under Turkish rule. Notwithstanding the generational conflict with their bourgeois parents, the second-generation Zionists were thoroughly bourgeois themselves in their cultural, if not their
social, expectations. Critics therefore viewed the resolution as an empty
demonstration, and indeed it did not have much credibility. But Blumenfeld stood by his concept, and in retrospect pointed out that almost
two thousand German Jews had settled in Palestine before 1933—he
himself moved there in August 1933—and that in terms of percentages,
a large number of these, men and women, had contributed significantly
to the development of the country. The main impact of Blumenfeld's
Palaestinozentrism, however, had been the disquieting, unsettling effect of
its continuous probing of the Jewish question as a question of Jewish
consciousness and conscience.[43] Zionism for Blumenfeld meant a readiness to challenge the *status quo* and expect the unexpected.

It was precisely the mixture of realism and idealism, flexibility and
firmness, openness and direction, in Blumenfeld's Zionism which attracted Arendt at the end of the Weimar Republic. Blumenfeld had
shown himself to be a political realist during the very difficult war years
when the majority of Zionists felt that they had to support Germany's war
effort. Zionists and anti-Zionists suspended their animosities and their
ideological struggle for the duration of the war, but Blumenfeld went beyond such efficacious "armistice." In October 1916 the Ministry of War
ordered a census of Jews in the German army, a decision that was deeply
disturbing to both assimilationists and Zionists. In reaction, Blumenfeld
published an article, "Innere Politik," in the February 1917 issue of Bu-

ber's recently founded journal *Der Jude,* suggesting a politics of limited alliance between Zionists and non-Zionists for specific purposes and goals. This idea was realized in 1920 by the establishment of Keren Ha-jessod, a fund for financing Jewish construction work in Eretz Israel. It also influenced the decision in 1929 to open the Jewish Agency for Palestine to representatives of non-Zionists.

Blumenfeld, chairman of the ZVfD since 1924, proved the maturity of his political vision and his talents as a negotiator again during the bloody disturbances in Palestine in August 1929. German Zionists, who had learned from their experience of right-extremist German nationalism, reacted most intensely to these events, questioning the role of Zionism in the difficult situation of Arab-Jewish sharing of Palestine. Members of the ZVfD engaged in heated debates provoked by a series of articles Robert Weltsch had published in *Juedische Rundschau.*[44] Here Weltsch protested the murder of more than one hundred Jewish men, women, and children, demanding from the British government punishment of the Arab leaders of the revolt and protection of Jewish lives and property. But he also acknowledged a lack of concrete efforts toward Jewish-Arab understanding on the part of the Zionist movement, which he accused of being content with statements of general goodwill. Zionists, forced to coexist with Arabs in Palestine, had to learn how to do so peacefully. Such a learning process involved concrete plans for bringing about and supporting an Arab-Jewish reconciliation, and in Weltsch's view this goal would be best served in a binational state. He categorically rejected all use of violence—in whatever form—in the attempt at solving the conflict. Similar views were stated in a memorandum that was sent to the Zionist Executive in London on September 16, 1929, bearing, among others, the signatures of Weltsch, Blumenfeld, Georg Landauer, Moritz Bileski, and Fritz Naphtali. This memorandum did not explicitly affirm the idea of a binational state, but it did emphasize the demand for Jewish-Arab understanding. It also acknowledged that such a demand was in many ways alien to traditional Zionist assumptions and necessitated a completely new orientation of the Zionist movement.[45]

The leaders were right to expect difficulties. ZVfD delegates met in December 1929 in Jena to discuss the position of ZVfD with regard to the Arab question. Chaim Weizmann, who served as president of the World Zionist Organization from 1920 to 1931 and who valued German Zionist leaders like Blumenfeld and Weltsch, spoke at the meeting but did not take a position. Blumenfeld, on the other hand, who had expressed reservations in private, publicly supported Weltsch. His and Weltsch's memorandum, which stressed peaceful coexistence with the Arabs on the basis of mutual understanding and respect and demanded from the Zionist Executive an active politics of reconciliation, was accepted by the meeting delegates, and Blumenfeld was reelected as chairman of the ZVfD.

Blumenfeld traveled to Palestine in the spring of 1930, after new immigration regulations had been put into effect. Radically revised along the lines of Arab demands, they were the result of the report published by a British commission charged with investigating the 1929 disturbances in Palestine. Blumenfeld, who had feared that these revisions would be difficult for the Jewish settlement to accept, found the mood there optimistic and was greatly impressed by its vitality and energy. The reality of life in Jewish Palestine as he experienced it contrasted sharply with the political fears for its future. He did not, however, share the optimism of Jews in Germany after the September 1930 election that some kind of negotiation or compromise might be reached with the Nazi party, which had just shown its increased power, winning 107 seats in the Reichstag. Blumenfeld understood that the political and social irrationalism reflected in the National Socialists' gains placed in jeopardy the Enlightenment foundation of Jewish emancipation—it was to be annulled by the 1935 Nuremberg laws—and that in this situation the only option for Jews was Jewish nationalism.

An excellent summary of the potential significance of German political Zionism on the eve of the Nazis' seizure of power—and, for the historian, a testimony to its impressively rational motivations for hope, even if it proved illusory—can be found in Blumenfeld's Frankfurt address to the ZVfD delegates in September 1932.[46] It was an important text for German Zionists, and there are clear reverberations of its argument, almost twenty years later, in Arendt's Origins of Totalitarianism, especially the important Part One, "Antisemitism," but also Part Two, "Imperialism," chapter 9, "The Decline of the Nation-State and the End of the Rights of Man."[47]

In an attempt to help his Jewish audience distinguish between different kinds of nationalism, the modern (right-wing) German kind and Zionism, Blumenfeld emphasized the fact that the origin of nineteenth-century national liberation movements had to be located both in their opposition to nineteenth-century liberal rejection of the ties of tradition and in their embracing a variation of the liberal idea of a limited state.

These movements, including Zionism, replaced the misunderstood idea of the political freedom of the individual with the demand that every historically developed group of people be allowed political freedom and participation as a group. While the Liberals wanted to secure a sphere free of the influence of the state—*staatsfrei*—the national liberation movements were struggling to establish a sphere that would be—to use Blumenfeld's coinage—*nationsfrei*. Minority nationalisms, which recognized the power of the state and which consequently often aimed for statehood, wanted the state to guarantee equal rights for the group (instead of the individual), arguing that majority nationalities should not be allowed to exclude minority nationalities living within the borders of the same state. Early German Zionist nationalism—as Blumenfeld's analysis implied—had been based on the demand that the Jewish people should be allowed to retain their identity as Jews *and* be fully participating citizens of the German State.

Modern nationalist movements, however, particularly the New-German nationalism, come from very different sources. Blumenfeld drew attention to the fact that rapid technological (and with them social-cultural) changes have produced a new understanding of state and nation. Historically, democracy has never been based on the concept of equality for all, but rather on equality for the equal, that is, the rule of one particular group. The political situation brought about by the modern experience of change has caused democracy to self-destruct: "And thus the desire for dictatorship, shared by a majority of the people, evolved democratically."[48] This development is based on and supports the absence of reasoned thought—after all, thought, according to the new nationalist irrationalism, destroys reality and life. In the modern nationalist view the true state is the total state, in which society, culture, and state are identical and which allows no cultural, much less national, pluralism.

But cultural pluralism is a reality in Germany: Germany's population is not uniform, nor do all Germans live within the borders of the German State, nor do all leaders of German minorities outside Germany, who support the idea of a German folk, sympathize with the demands to take civil rights away from national minorities living within Germany. As a timely example, Blumenfeld used the 1932 *Saengerfest* in Frankfurt. On this occasion Minister of the Interior von Gayl acknowledged his responsibility for the unity of Germans inside and outside the German Reich. Blumenfeld quoted, with approval, from the resolution to uphold Germany as the cultural homeland of all Germans within and outside the borders of the state. He saw—and pointed out—the analogy to the German-Jewish situation in such an acceptance of a German fate of dispersal over many countries *and* the challenge of a community of the German people. The importance of the community of Jews as centered in the Jewish homeland for the German-Jewish minority underscores the necessity to distinguish, on principle, between state and nation—that is, to insist that civil rights not be dependent on national identity.

With this argumentation Blumenfeld wished to demonstrate that Zionism was a significant contribution toward a better understanding of the Jews' position in the nation-state and toward a solution of the difficulties inherent in this situation. Political Zionism in Germany had the advantages of a young movement unburdened by the eighteenth- and nineteenth-century political entanglements of German Jews who equated emancipation with assimilation. It was unburdened, too, by the religious-cultural aspirations of Jews in dispersion, in the Galut. The "Rabbiner-Verband in Deutschland" had rejected Herzl's proposals on July 6, 1897, because "the aspirations of the Zionists are opposed to the messianic hopes of Judaism." This proclamation, issued in Berlin and signed by the Executive Committee of the Verband, was released for publication by the newspapers. It stated clearly that the rabbis directed their opposition only against the political-national aspect of Zionism and not against "those lofty aspirations of Jewish workers of the soil to establish a settlement in Palestine."[49] The call of the land, after all, had to be acknowledged.[50] Like the Liberals of the Centralverein, the rabbis were afraid that political Zionism might endanger or limit the social-cultural existence of Jews in Germany, and for this reason they wanted to keep the issues of religion and nationality separate.[51]

The rabbis' efforts were attacked by German Conservatives, who, like Herzl, used the argument of anti-Semitism as the most natural reason for Zionist political—that is, national—aspirations. The conservative *Kreuz-zeitung*, in a report on "Der Widerspruch gegen den Zionisten-Kongress," called the rabbis' declaration of complete Jewish loyalty to the German nation "hypocritical," pointing out complaints in the Jewish press that the rights granted to Jews by the state "are recognized only grudgingly, and that the Jews continue to be exposed to many further insults."[52] The article claimed that there were reasons for these insults. In an era of nationalism, when the idea/reality of the nation-state is of extremely high cultural value and has become an important factor in the community of nations, the citizens of a nation-state cannot be expected to trust those who deny their (Jewish) nationality. The article also asserted that the Chief Rabbi of England was not realistic in his fear that Jewish support of political Zionism might create the impression that Jews were not loyal to the state in which they lived. Those who were loyal to their country of origin were esteemed, and in Judaism, national identity was inseparable from religion. The implication was that the Chief Rabbi should logically support political Zionism because it was the only possible and credible Jewish nationalism and because its goal was to establish a nation whose cultural-political identity was based on religious Judaism.

> Whoever is imbued with the hope for the future of his fatherland or his religion and refuses to do what is required of him to realize this hope is a fool or a traitor who has forgotten his duty. If the Jew wishes to think as a German national, then he must also be open to this form of thinking. If we and other nations permit the Jewish people to live within our borders as guests, does this mean that we wish to erase from the hearts of these guests the memory of their nationality [*Volksthum*]? On the contrary, it is precisely here that anti-Semitism finds the nourishment on which it thrives. . . . the Jews alone in the Christian states claim that they wish to preserve their religious but not their national separateness . . . and from this fraud against the people that grant them the rights of the fatherland they derive their means of subsistence . . . pretending to belong to a foreign nationality but without in fact relinquishing their peculiar stubborn character.[53]

In the Christian German national state there was no room for the religious Jew who wanted to be a citizen. But there was also in many cases no room for the Jew who had converted, because the redeeming effect of baptism could be and was widely questioned by Christian Germans on the grounds that the decision for it had been based not on religious belief but on social opportunism.[54] The dilemma of the Jew who wished to live as a loyal citizen of the German state was unsolvable as long as this state understood its nationality to be German *and* Christian and as long as state and nationality went together. There was no way in which Jews could speak or act unambiguously—that is, without taking the risk of being seriously misunderstood and punished as a result.

Political Zionism removes this risk by distinguishing clearly who is a Jew. At the end of the process of failed assimilation, Blumenfeld argued too hopefully that Jews can show their value only as Jews because it is only then that they can articulate clearly their demands for a separation between state and nation. He reminded his audience that it is the majority environment which forces the minority to develop its identity in majority terms—that is, to internalize an imposed exclusion. (Rahel had made this observation in the beginning stage of assimilation.) But it is important to understand that Blumenfeld's placing the Jewish question in the context of other minorities enabled him to go beyond the assertion of a significantly fated, inevitable rejection of German Jews by German Gentiles. No matter how German Jews feel, no matter how much they contribute to German culture, they will be confronted with the German majority's feeling that they are un-German. But the reason for this is not so much a specifically and inevitably Jewish fate of millennia of persecution; it is, rather, a specifically twentieth-century national minority position in the context of New-German pan-nationalism. This argument was especially persuasive to Arendt, as can be seen in her critique, in the forties, of Zionist politics in Palestine, in which she focused on the Jews' preoccupation with one-nation statehood and later the State of Israel's pan-nationalism. She understood these preoccupations to be a degeneration of the original potential of the Zionist concept of nationhood to signify for its people the end of apolitical migration, the homecoming as the constitution of the body politic.[55] However, Blumenfeld in Palestine, speaking from the perspective of and also for the beleaguered Yishuv, felt for a time profoundly betrayed by Arendt, unable, during these difficult years, to see the connectedness and consistency of her argument.[56]

His analysis of the "deutsch-juedischer Kulturkonflikt," too, helped Arendt redefine her position within a German cultural tradition that had, until the late twenties, been unquestioned and had seemed to her unquestionable. From Blumenfeld's Zionist perspective, which revealed as illusionary the social-political security Jews hoped to gain through assimilation, it appeared that crossing the borders in the area of culture would provoke the sharpest reaction:

> But *then* it was clear to us that it was neither within *our* rights nor was it *our* task to form the German world which obeys its own laws. In the past Jews thought that the world would become what they desired and needed. We recognized the supreme importance of standing our ground in this world. The most recent developments most certainly have supported the realization that we cannot point the way in the German world.[57]

Active Jewish participation in German cultural life had caused problems precisely because the cultural contributions of a talented minority
had been so considerable and significant. The subtext of Blumenfeld's
remarks was the argument of cultural overrepresentation, one of the most
difficult issues to discuss openly and reasonably in a situation where the
distinction between nationhood and statehood was not sufficiently clear
and where, in defense, majority and minority solidarity was overempha-
sized. Explicitly, Blumenfeld appealed to the German people to work for
a humane German nationalism for the reason, too, that there had before
been a German nationalism which, placing high value on German
achievement, had respected the achievement of the other—German ideas
which Jews had thought highly valuable.

In the precarious situation of 1932, Blumenfeld called for a reasonable assessment of German-Jewish difficulties, a task which seems impossible from hindsight and must have seemed very unlikely then. But Blumenfeld did not so much hope to reach a German audience; his real goal
was to address openly the problems of German-Jewish symbiosis so that
assimilated Jews could understand their position and start weaning themselves from a German cultural tradition in which, despite the ambiguities
of their political position, they had felt so much at home. He argued that
the Zionist who was certain of his Jewish identity had the "tact"—that
is, the natural distance—necessary for successful political coexistence in
the German State. Conceding the fact of great Jewish intimacy with German culture, Blumenfeld insisted that the Jews who had penetrated this
culture most deeply had always felt most sharply their otherness. In Arendt's terms assimilation had been a failure because this otherness could
not be acknowledged—that is, it could not present itself and be present
in the public sphere.

o   4   o

The seemingly unsolvable paradox of German-Jewish closeness and
distance, identity and nonidentity, similarity and otherness, familiarity
and strangeness, as Blumenfeld saw it, was a profound challenge to Arendt, a student of German literature and philosophy, and it was to influence her development as a political thinker and as a historian of political
ideas. However, most immediately and concretely, Blumenfeld's leadership in the ZVfD guided her reaction to her personal experience of increasing anti-Semitism. She was in close intellectual and political contact

with him and other Zionist leaders like Weltsch during these years, lec-
turing under their auspices on Zionism and the history of German anti-
Semitism in various German cities.[58] The ZVfD grew rapidly after Hitler
became *Reichskanzler* in January 1933; its official journal, *Die Juedische
Rundschau*, increased its circulation from 15,000 to almost 40,000 in
1935. The ZVfD continued to work effectively through groups like
Hechalutz (The Pioneer), a youth association that had been founded in
1918 to prepare its members for settlement in Eretz Israel, and Youth
Aliyah, which organized the transportation of children to Palestine and
for which Arendt worked in Paris.

Arendt visited Palestine for the first time in 1935, when she accom-
panied a group of Youth Aliyah trainees. The boat from Marseilles to
Haifa stopped over in Sicily, where she saw her first Greek temple and
introduced her young charges to Greek culture. In Palestine she visited
members of her own family who had arrived there only very recently and
met with some of Blumenfeld's associates. On her return, she spoke to
groups who supported Youth Aliyah, admiring the political experiments
of the new communities, especially the kibbutzim. She shared with the
third-generation Zionists the interest in the antibourgeois ideal of the
Chalutz, the pioneer, and in new forms of community. But she also had
private reservations, which she expressed to her friends in Paris. Many
years later, remembering that first trip to Palestine, she wrote to Mary
McCarthy about her reaction to the kibbutzim:

> I thought: a new aristocracy. I knew even then . . . that one could
> not live there. "Rule by your neighbors," that is of course what it
> finally amounts to. Still, if one honestly believes in equality, Israel
> is very impressive.[59]

Arendt was never to have much trust in the possibility of social equality; her interest had always been focused on the meaning and the potential
of political equality, and in this respect she was to find Israel highly problematic. The single most important aspect of Blumenfeld's Zionism for
her had been his insistence on the importance and the possibility of political choice. Such choice had meant, in the German situation, the reasoned decision for Zionism. In the situation in Palestine she expected it
to mean the reasoned decision to coexist, in political equality and with
political tolerance for the other's otherness, with the Arabs—a goal best
achieved by a bi- or multinational Palestinian state. But both British im-

perialist attitudes and Arab revolts made it difficult even for Zionist leaders sympathetic to this idea to pursue it seriously as a concrete political
goal.

The group Brit Shalom, organized in Jerusalem in 1925 by intellectuals of mostly Central and West European origin to propose a binational
state in Palestine in which Jews and Arabs would have equal rights, was
considered by many Zionists to be severely lacking in political realism
and national feeling. Especially after the 1929 disturbances, its proposal
was ignored. (In contrast, the German Zionist Executive had adopted
Weltsch's and Blumenfeld's 1929 memorandum calling for peaceful political coexistence between Jews and Arabs.) And when another Arab
revolt began in 1936, most of the Brit Shalom members gave up hope of
reaching a Jewish-Arab rapprochement. Yet, as late as 1942, Judah L.
Magnes, the president of Hebrew University, founded a party called
Ihud (Unity) with the intention of furthering Jewish-Arab understanding
and calling again and more urgently for a binational state. Magnes, with
whom Arendt was to cooperate politically under very difficult and dramatic circumstances in 1948, had come to Eretz Israel "not as a leader
. . . but simply as a Jew . . . bound to it not through any political program,
but through Judaism, which I cannot conceive of without its roots
planted there." [60]

Importantly, for Magnes the decision to settle in Israel did not mean
negation of the life in the Diaspora. In an address, "Eretz Israel and the
Galut," delivered in May 1923 shortly after his arrival in Jerusalem, he
spoke explicitly in support of the integrity of Judaism in the Diaspora:

> Everyone who lives here in Eretz Israel and works is helping the
> Jewish people creating spiritual values and is thus aiding the Jewish
> people to carry out its work in the world. The same is true of those
> who live and work in the galut. Where a man can do best for his
> people is an individual and private matter. But whatever happens to
> the individual, may Eretz Israel give the Jewish people new forms
> of beauty and speech, and may it see created ways of life and a
> society based upon human freedom and filled with knowledge as
> the waters cover the sea. [61]

Magnes had "converted" to Zionism during his studies at the Berlin
Lehranstalt fuer die Wissenschaft des Judentums at the turn of century.
As he wrote to his family in California in the fall of 1901, Zionism was
now his "whole philosophy," his "Lebensprogramm." "My Zionism

makes me more than a preacher or community leader. It makes me a worker for the preservation of the Jewish people as a whole and for their greater glory and better life in their own land."[62] From 1925 to 1935 he was Chancellor of Hebrew University—after that its president—trying to shape an institution that would represent Judaism, humanism, and internationalism, and be a forum for uninhibited intellectual discourse.

In his understanding of the relation between Eretz Israel and the Galut and of the cultural mission of Judaism, Magnes was very much influenced and inspired by the conflicted spiritual-cultural Zionism of Ahad Ha'am, who had proposed a complicated synthesis between rejuvenation of the Jewish spirit and reestablishment of the Jewish body politic. (Ha'am was proved wrong in thinking the latter more difficult to achieve.) In his 1923 lecture Magnes speculated about the kind of (political) nationalism Jews would develop in Eretz Israel. Would they, in their efforts to create a political organism, embrace the use of brute force and militarism, as did some of the later Hasmoneans? (In their territorial expansion to the ancient biblical frontiers of Israel, these power-minded kings did not create the hoped-for "dominion of the Saints of the Most High.")[63] Would they, like the Edomite Herod the Great, who ruled Judea by the grace of Rome, be subservient to economic and militaristic imperialism?

> Is it among the possibilities that some day it may become political treason for someone sincerely to repeat in the streets of Jerusalem Isaiah's teaching that swords are to be beaten into ploughshares and men are to learn war no more? Or will the Jews of Eretz Israel be true to the teaching of the Prophets of Israel and attempt to work out their ideal society so that Israel may be restored and Zion redeemed through righteousness and peace?[64]

Magnes, too, asks about the negative influence of dispersion in exile on the Jewish mind: will not a life of conflict and strife in the Galut have ill-prepared him for this redemptive utopia? But following Ha'am, Magnes stresses potentially positive consequences of the experience of Galut—for instance, a hatred of war and of the use of brute force (something positive that the Galut has *given*, not taken away).[65]

For Ha'am—and Magnes followed him in this—the spiritual center in Eretz Israel was to unify and give meaning to the lives of Jews both in Palestine and on the periphery, in the Diaspora. But this cultural Zionism did not, as did political Zionism, clearly privilege one choice over the other. Moreover, in Ha'am's view the spiritual center was to serve the periphery until Jews were ready "to aspire to freedom in their own home-land."[66] Freedom had to be learned in any case; it could not simply be seized. And "Auto-Emancipation" would have to be developed slowly through the love for cultural—rather than religious—Judaism and the land.

Ha'am's secular concept of Zionism stressed the need for cultural-national rather than political-national unity: the land and Judaism did not in themselves represent values, but in the service they rendered to the Jewish people they became valuable. It was for this reason that Magnes saw, as he wrote in his journal in 1906, Ha'am as representative of "mod-ern Judaism"—in contrast to the Judaism of the senior rabbi at the Temple Emanu-El, the cathedral temple of Reform Judaism in New York, where Magnes had become associate rabbi in 1906.[67] Two decades later, on the occasion of the politically difficult 1925 inauguration of Hebrew University, Magnes appealed to Ahad Ha'am as "one of the moral guides of our generation." Describing to him the difficulties connected with the presence of Lord Balfour at the inauguration ceremony and the Arab demonstrations it provoked, Magnes expressed both his being deeply moved by the absence of violence and his disappointment that the uni-versity had not avoided the provocation:

> It was to have been expected that the University of all enterprises would be that agency which upon the plane of pure scholarship, would in the course of time, bring about a spiritual reconciliation between the two most gifted races of Semitic stock. But the Uni-versity has become the instrument of the very reverse. It may take us long years of hard work to overcome this disadvantage.

In contrast to the prevailing Jewish opinion that the Arab demonstra-tions had no meaning because fortunately there had not been any ex-cesses, Magnes preferred to think that this restraint had been due not so much to the presence of government forces as to the conviction

> that is growing in the Moslem world as elsewhere that understand-ing and reconciliation between peoples can come only through pac-ifist and nonviolent methods. It is a good augury for the future.
>
> All that we Jews here have a right to ask, is peace and the open door for our immigrants, and the opportunity without let or hin-drance to live our spiritual and cultural life. This is all the Arabs have a right to ask for themselves, or any other people in this inter-

national land. Thus the country can be developed and forms of life created upon the basis of free field and no favors. Our University should be the highest of our spiritual endeavors, preaching peace and practising it, devoted to the passionate pursuit of truth, to the ideals of righteousness and brotherhood.

I am writing you in order to solicit an answer from you as our great ethical teacher. The inauguration of the University is, I hope and believe, one of the great moments of our history, and we should be unworthy of this great great hour were we not to seek out its deeper spiritual meaning.[68]

Practicing peace, Magnes realized, was infinitely more difficult than preaching it. The extension of spiritual-cultural Zionism into political praxis required setting up political structures. Magnes became increasingly aware of the need to make self-government of Arabs and Jews a priority and to pay close attention to concrete political arrangements and institutions. In his 1930 essay "Like All the Nations?" he emphasized the fact that the "Jewish conscience" must realize "that the inhabitants of this country, both Arabs and Jews, have not only the right but the duty to participate, in equitable and practical ways, in the government of their common Home-land." And in this context he stressed, again and again, the political sphere as the focus for solutions: "The life of this unhappy country will be much saner and much less hysterical the sooner its population can exercise its political energies in legitimate and practical and constructive ways."[69]

Magnes's work for peace in Palestine was based on his understanding the meaning of history to be the establishing of community. Like Arendt, he did not believe in a unique or uniquely Jewish fate among the peoples of the earth. There were historical reasons for the separateness of the Jewish people—all the more reason to learn how to live in the comity of other peoples:

The anti-Semite has accused us of being democrats and liberals and radicals everywhere on the ground that we are not deeply rooted in any soil. He has charged us with having no conservative instincts because we have no real hearth and home, boundaries and property of our ancestors to defend. We are spectators, onlookers, bystanders, he says. We have always answered that, should we have the opportunity of exercising statecraft on our own soil, we would as participants and not as bystanders uphold our prophetic traditions.[70]

Magnes was appealing here to the democratic tradition of Judaism. He continued this appeal in the policies of Ihud, which he introduced to Americans in his article "Towards Peace in Palestine," published in the January 1943 issue of *Foreign Affairs*. In contrast to many American-Jewish readers, Arendt respected the Ihud position as it was stated. She approved of the association's political opposition to the Jewish Agency, but thought that the proposal, supported by Buber and Ernst Simon, of an Arab Federation connected with an Anglo-American Alliance was not workable and was too close to Chaim Weizmann's pro-British policies. Three years later, when Magnes, Buber, and Moses Smilanski gave their "Testimony before the Anglo-American Inquiry Commission for the Ihud (Union) Association" in August 1946, the goals of Ihud were much more clearly stated in political terms and were to be reflected in the development of Arendt's critique of political Zionism.

In his preface to the printed text,[71] Magnes stated both the pressing need to move the 100,000 displaced persons to Palestine—this had been the suggested first stage in a limited and gradated Jewish immigration process[72]—and Ihud's disappointment that the movement had not yet begun. He also expressed intense disappointment that the commission had not recommended an immediate increase of self-government for Palestine, an issue he deemed as important as the recommendation to move the 100,000 refugees:

> There must be a policy whose main objective is Jewish-Arab cooperation. Jews and Arabs will not be gotten to cooperate by keeping them apart. Nor can the situation wait till the Jews and Arabs "agree" to cooperate. Conditions—economic, social, political—must be *created* which will require them to cooperate, and there is no part of life more important for this than full participation together in government.[73] Jews and Arabs should not be treated as children, but as mature communities, and imagination and courage and faith are required of those in America and Britain, in whose hands fateful decisions rest.
>
> If these conditions are not created, if Jews and Arabs are not helped to become adults in political terms there will be increasing use of violence and the results will be disastrous.

In his address "A Solution Through Force?" given in New York on July 17, 1946, Magnes posed the question of goals with respect to the relation between ends and means: Idealistic Jewish youth, taught that

Jewish spirit, religion, culture are all in grave danger of deterioration, even extinction, without a Jewish State, is driven to the "logical" conclusion that this State is absolutely necessary and therefore has to be gotten by force, by acts of terrorism.[74] He appealed to his audience to be clear, in this complex and emotional context, about the issue of domination: to the Arabs a Jewish State means "the rule by Jews of others who live in that Jewish State."[75] And again he expressed his disappointment with the Anglo-American Commission, which otherwise had adopted much from the report of Ihud:

> But they overlooked a primary consideration, namely that the process of self-government be begun at once, expedited. Why do we think that that is so important? Because in that way Jews and Arabs would come together in one of the most important concerns of life, government.[76]

Magnes's utopian impulses, which were shared by Arendt, did not have their source in a radical suspension of the experienced reality of human nature and natural laws—as so much twentieth-century utopian thought has been.[77] Rather, he was fully aware of the need to negotiate a compromise between (unlimited) fears and desires and (limited) reassurance and satisfaction. This compromise, this cooperation, would not come by itself; it would have to be supported by the coming together of adult people as political agents who, in the act and for the period of coming together in the political sphere, are seen by and see one another as equals. It was out of this insight into the nature of political cooperation that Magnes arrived at the conclusion of his argument, a conclusion that was central to Arendt's political thought: neither a Jewish state nor a binational state nor a Yishuv in Palestine could be maintained "if the whole surrounding world be our enemies."[78] If there is any significance in being in the world, it is in sharing it. Such sharing can be achieved most reliably and most enduringly through participation and cooperation in government, through political speech and action. The answer to the question "Like All the Nations?" is "yes." Magnes had posed the question and given the answer in 1930, when German Zionists were trying to wean German assimilated Jews from their dependence on both the fated uniqueness of their people and their symbiosis with uniquely significant German (high) culture. The only realistic position the Jewish people could take was to see themselves as part of a community of peoples and only as a part.[79] In the continuing, extraordinarily difficult political situ-

ation in Palestine, the implications of this position remained unacceptable
to the large majority of even the most flexible, open-minded Zionists.

o   5   o

Ironically, Arendt's acceptance of them caused the serious, and to her
painful, disagreements with her friend Blumenfeld, to whom, as she
wrote him after their reconciliation in 1951, she owed so much in her
efforts to understand the Jewish condition.[80] Blumenfeld had participated
in the Biltmore conference in New York in May 1942, which in view of
the refugee problem and British politics in Palestine, had adopted a resolution calling for a Jewish state. He was surprised at this outcome of the
conference, because founding a Jewish state in a country where the Arab
population was in the majority seemed to him to be asking for grave political trouble. At the same time, he received news of a new political movement in Palestine, the Aliyah Hadasha (New Immigration), founded by
German Zionists in opposition to the Biltmore program and headed by
his friends Felix Rosenblueth and Georg Landauer. It had developed out
of the Hitachdut Olej Germania (HOG), an organization of immigrants
from Central Europe which had been founded in 1932 and had played
an important role in helping German Jews adapt culturally, socially, and
economically to life in Palestine.

HOG had represented the rights and interests of the new immigrants
in their fight for reforms in the outdated administrative system of the Yishuv. But since the beginning of the war, proponents of the core questions
of Zionist politics had asserted themselves more forcefully, leading in October 1942 to the founding of the Aliyah Hadasha, which was organiza-
tionally separate from HOG, but in many ways identical to it, and whose
position was close to that of Magnes's Ihud. The Aliyah Hadasha emphatically opposed the Biltmore program because it undermined, in the
association's view, all attempts at Arab-Jewish reconciliation. The Aliyah
Hadasha's rather optimistic prognosis of future developments was based
on a postwar new world order of progress, reconciliation, and cooperation
enabling Arabs and Jews to coexist peacefully and to develop to the fullest
their societies in a Palestine under British administration. It denounced
all acts of terrorism and demanded that the Jewish Agency distance itself
unambiguously and forcefully from Jewish terrorists and their acts. Arendt, in her May 1948 essay "To Save the Jewish Homeland: There Is
Still Time," mentioned with approval that the "small Aliyah Hadasha,
mostly composed of recent immigrants from Central Europe, still retains

some of its old moderation"—in a situation in which both moderation and difference of opinion regarding Zionist nationalism had disappeared.[81] It was this essay which caused Magnes to enlist Arendt's active help in the fight for peace in Palestine. (In December 1948, together with Albert Einstein and other intellectuals, Arendt signed a letter, which she herself may have drafted, protesting the Jewish terrorist Menachem Begin's visit to America, during which he tried to gain support for his Revisionist Herut party. The letter compared the Revisionist position to that of the "Nazi and Fascist parties" and rejected Revisionist ideology as a blend of "ultranationalism, religious mysticism and racial superiority."[82])

Blumenfeld had at first declared his support for the program of Aliyah Hadasha. After his return to Israel in 1945, however, confronted with the now fully disclosed horror of the destruction of European Jewry, the urgent problem of large numbers of displaced persons and the newly elected British Labor government's attitude toward the situation in Palestine, he changed his mind. As Arendt noted in "To Save the Jewish Homeland," Aliyah Hadasha continued in its pro-British position and Blumenfeld began to criticize the views of Landauer and Weltsch. As the German-language weekly *Mitteilungsblatt* (published by HOG) complained in October 1945, Aliyah Hadasha refused to believe that England would close the door to the remnant of European Jewry, whose only hope for rescue lay in Palestine.[83] There seemed to be some reason for hope when the Anglo-American Commission, responding to the suggestions made in the Ihud report, recommended the immediate immigration of 100,000 refugees and United Nations trusteeship for Palestine in preparation for a binational state.

But England rejected the recommendation, and Blumenfeld returned to his old conviction that the country had to be divided. Aliyah Hadasha split over this issue. A resolution in June 1947, supported by the majority of its Central Committee, including Blumenfeld and Felix Rosenblueth, approved the plan for division as the best solution under the circumstances. Landauer, leader of a minority in the Aliyah Hadasha, opposed the resolution. In the midst of nationalist enthusiasm over the United Nations' decision to divide Palestine into a Jewish and an Arab state and England's withdrawal from Palestine, he was deeply apprehensive about the possibility of a permanent Jewish-Arab war. For Blumenfeld the break with Landauer was painful, but he had come to believe in the necessity of creating a State of Israel of "blood and iron."[84] Yet, in spite of his initial wholehearted affirmation of the new state, he did not participate in the political life of Israel, partly for personal reasons, but also because he was fearful of the political results of unexamined, unrestrained nationalism.

Arendt had articulated her forceful critique of Zionist politics in the article "Zionism Reconsidered," which she submitted to *Commentary* in 1944, but which the editors found too disturbing to publish. It contained, in their opinion, "too many anti-Semitic implications—not in the sense that you intend them as such implications, but that the unfriendly reader might intend them as such." [85] At issue was Arendt's claim of a close affinity between Revisionists and General Zionists:

> The end result of fifty years of Zionist politics was embodied in the recent resolution of the largest and most influential section of the World Zionist Organisation. American Zionists from left to right adopted unanimously, at their last annual convention held in Atlantic City in October, 1944, the demand for a "free and democratic Jewish commonwealth . . . [which] shall embrace the whole of Palestine, undivided and undiminished." This is a turning point in Zionist history; for it means that the Revisionist program, so long bitterly repudiated, has proved finally victorious. [86]

Arendt did acknowledge the tremendous pressures under which the Zionist leadership had had to operate. The nationalism of Ben-Gurion's majority group, which negated all the efforts of those Jewish parties in Palestine which, like Magnes's group, have "tirelessly preached the necessity of an understanding between the Arab and Jewish peoples," [87] had been greatly intensified by the experience of many injustices in Palestine and by the German catastrophe. Yet, Arendt insisted, nationalism was not the answer, particularly not in the case of the Jewish question. In this context Jewish nationalism not only trusted in "nothing but the rude force of the nation" but, decidedly worse, "admittedly depends on the force of a foreign nation." Like Magnes, Arendt argued for the practical need to coexist with the Arabs as well as the other Mediterranean peoples. Unlike Magnes, she alerted her readers emphatically to the dangerous mechanism of anti-Semitism inherent in a situation of understandably resented interference by big outside powers:

> Jews who know their own history should be aware that such a state of affairs will inevitably lead to a new wave of Jew-hatred; the anti-Semitism of tomorrow will assert that Jews not only profiteered from the presence of the foreign big powers in that region but had actually plotted it and hence are guilty of the consequences. [88]

Did the editors of *Commentary* anticipate that statements like this could be misunderstood or misconstrued? Arendt, of course, was not speaking here from any position even remotely related to (Jewish) anti-Semitism, but she did refer to Jewish experience as located firmly in the realm of history rather than metahistory. Like all peoples', the historical experience of Jews, Zionists, and assimilationists had been one of active and passive participation and therefore not inevitably or significantly fated in its direction and outcome. Notwithstanding the disproportion-ately large share of persecution and suffering in Jewish history, it could be appealed to as a learning experience which might lead to a more thoughtfully responsive and flexible reaction to the situation in Palestine than the increasing, ever more intense Jewish nationalism.

What Arendt missed in contemporary Zionist politics was a sober and detailed realistic analysis of the Palestine question which extended beyond the Jewish question, though it was interdependent with it. In fact, she missed the realistic assessment of such interdependencies in general. The "double-loyalty conflict," for instance, which was never, as she pointed out, clearly answered, was an "unavoidable problem of every na-tional movement of a people living within the boundaries of other States and unwilling to resign their civil and political rights therein." And it was a problem for both Zionists and assimilationists. The fact that the presi-dent of the World Zionist Organization and of the Jewish Agency for Palestine had been a loyal, patriotic British subject who therefore had been forced "into a theory of predestined harmony of Jewish and British interests," reminded Arendt of assimilationist theories in Europe. On the other hand, the American Revisionist notion of a Hebrew nation in Pal-estine and a Jewish people in the Diaspora, which was meant to provide a neat solution to the problem of an obviously thriving Jewish existence in the Galut—that is, to the double-loyalty conflict of American Jews—seemed to her a mere abstraction that skirted the real issues and under-scored the affinities between the general Zionist and Revisionist posi-tions.[89]

The important and dangerously apolitical nature of Zionism and Zi-onist politics had its roots in the history of Zionism, which Arendt traced to its nineteenth-century sources, socialism and nationalism. These sources were never amalgamated in the Zionist movement, which was split between the social-revolutionary energies of the East European masses and Herzl's and his followers' aspiration for national emancipa-tion:

The paradox of this split was that, whereas the former was actually a people's movement, caused by national oppression, the latter, created by social discrimination, became the political creed of intellectuals.[90]

Arendt's distinction here between political and social anti-Semitism may or may not be useful for an understanding of the situation of the Eastern Jewish masses. But it does support her attempt to trace the development of the less than politically realistic "political creed" of Zionist intellectuals. Socialist Zionists, she argued, seeing their national aspirations fulfilled by settlement in the promised land of Palestine, did not foresee any possible national conflict with the already present inhabitants of the land:

> Nothing could better prove the entirely unpolitical character of the new movement than this innocent obliviousness. True, those Jews were rebels; but they rebelled not so much against the oppressions of their people as against the crippling, stifling atmosphere of Jewish ghetto-life, on the one hand, and the injustices of social life in general, on the other. From both they hoped to have escaped when once established in Palestine, whose very name was still holy as well as familiar to them, emancipated though they were from Jewish orthodoxy. They escaped to Palestine as one might wish to escape to the moon, to a region beyond the wickedness of the world. True to their ideals, they established themselves on the moon; and with the extraordinary strength of their faith they were able to create small islands of perfection.[91]

Arendt clearly admired the achievements of these idealistic Zionists, the "new kind of aristocracy" created by the *chalutz* and *kibbutz* movements. There is strong implicit agreement, even celebration of their values, in her description of their rigorously examined lives:

> their genuine contempt for material wealth, exploitation, and bourgeois life; their unique combination of culture and labor; their rigorous realization of social justice within their small circle; and their loving pride in the fertile soil, the work of their hands, together with an utter and surprising lack of any wish for personal possession.[92]

But though these achievements had contributed greatly to the creation of a "new type of Jew," their political influence had been negligible. And here Arendt's remarks on these "sectarians"—their self-contented concern with the realization of lofty ideas, their admirable decency, which kept them away from politics, their social and cultural provinciality with respect to Jewish life outside Palestine,[93] and their missionary attitude toward immigration to Palestine and guidance of youth according to their values—strongly suggest an analogy to the politically dangerous self-limitation of assimilationist Jews to the social and cultural sphere in nine-teenth-century Germany. Where the latter had focused their energies too exclusively on social acceptance and participation in German high cul-ture, the "aristocracy of Palestine Jewry," even after 1933, focused their attention too single-mindedly on the existing and future Yishuv, the Jew-ish settlement, to the exclusion of a worldwide Jewish national movement. In spite of their great social influence, their creation of social values in Palestine, they did not leave any mark on narrowly nationalist Zionist politics. They made no attempt to develop a considered position on polit-ical anti-Semitism; rather, they were content with repeating "the old so-cialist or the new nationalist banalities, as though the whole affair did not concern them." So they did not provide any fresh ideas concerning the Arab-Jewish conflict, notwithstanding their revolutionary background and ideology, and they did not articulate any critique of Jewish bourgeoi-sie outside Palestine or "attack the role of finance in the political structure of Jewish life." In short, they did not assume the role of the critical outsider-insider, the role of the pariah.

> Thus the social-revolutionary Jewish national movement, which
> started half a century ago with ideals so lofty that it overlooked the
> particular realities of the Near East and the general wickedness of
> the world, has ended—as do most such movements—with the un-
> equivocal support not only of national but of chauvinist claims—
> not against the foes of the Jewish people but against its possible
> friends and neighbors.[94]

As the assimilationists tried to survive by escaping from the particu-larly Jewish conflict of double loyalty into an imaginary, illusionary uni-versal history, so the Zionists circumvented dealing with actual and press-ing political conflicts in Palestine by settling into a doctrine of a fated anti-Semitism which had, from the beginning to the end of history—that is, at all times and everywhere—controlled Jewish-Gentile relations.[95] It was, then, the ahistorical, apolitical, irrational substance of this concept of anti-Semitism which made it so attractive. So conceived, anti-Semitism explained something which, in terms of the argument, could not be explained, and thus it did not have to meet the admittedly considerable challenge of explaining a phenomenon that, by its very historical-political nature, would have been accessible to attempts at explanation.[96] Arendt was to analyze the same problem in her report on the Eichmann trial, in which she argued against a metahistorical discussion of evil and the German catastrophe. The motivation for her argument in both cases was recognition of the potential political damage that could be caused by such an escape from historical-political reality, leading to a serious misappraisal of political conditions, which vary from country to country, from period to period. The ancient tradition of the Jewish people to distinguish so sharply between Jews and non-Jews tended to unanimously support rather than pose questions to such concepts of anti-Semitism, and thus it fortified "the dangerous, time-honored, deep-seated distrust of Jews for Gentiles."[97]

Herzl's view of the crucial role of anti-Semitism in the preservation of the Jewish people as a nation is dangerous because, as corroborated by many Zionists' personal experiences—they had become (aware of being) Jews through the perceived hostility of Gentiles toward Jews—it led to the conclusion that "antisemites will be our most reliable friends, the anti-semitic countries our allies."[98] Such an assumption creates a situation in which the open enemy is seen as the hidden friend and the declared friend as the hidden enemy, a situation in which political speech and action cannot but be seriously impeded. And, indeed, in *The Jewish State*, Theodor Herzl's analysis of the role played by anti-Semitic pressure in the formation of a Jewish national consciousness is contradictory in its emphasis on both the identity-preserving historical fame of the Jewish national character and the ease with which Jews would assimilate were they only allowed to do so. Herzl claims, then, both the innate historical uniqueness of the Jewish people and their enemies' imposition of such uniqueness on them, and bases on this claim his appeal to the unquestionable, "unmistakable solidarity" of the Jewish people.[99]

Arendt does not refer to this passage, but her argument is centered in a critique of the general Jewish feeling, strengthened by the Zionist concept of a nation held together and defined by its enemies, that "we are all in the same boat." Not only did this feeling not correspond to the historical-political realities; equally dangerous, in her view, it prevented the necessary self-criticism of Jews as a group which would, if anything, be the opposite of Jewish self-hatred. Presenting the upbuilding of Palestine as *the* answer to anti-Semitism[100] presupposed both an unquestioned solidarity of Jewish settlers in Palestine (who would not be expected to analyze the political situation in which they acted) *and* the assumption that anti-Semitism, a corollary of nationalism, would not be directed against an established Jewish nation. Not only would Palestine be the place and the only place where Jews could be safe from the attacks of their enemies, "nay, their very enemies would miraculously change into their friends." [101]

Arendt links this concept of Palestine as the ultimate and only haven for a desperate people fleeing from persecution and the unreal state of statelessness to the Zionist doctrine of the inevitable decline of Jewish life in the Galut, which enabled the Yishuv to set itself apart from the life and destiny of Jews all over the world. It is clear that she neglected here to deal with or even refer to a complex, articulate Judaic tradition of reflecting on the meanings of Galut, about which she knew little. What interested her was the political rather than the spiritual aspect of the relation between Yishuv and Galut, and while her focus on this aspect may seem to impoverish her vision and flatten her argument, it does lend to her analysis a useful sharpness and clarity. She is concerned with the political interdependence of peoples and nations—more, with the fact that the destruction of European Jewry called for a greater Jewish awareness of such interdependency rather than greater isolationism. Palestine Jewry, she wrote in this context, "instead of making itself the political vanguard of the whole Jewish people, developed a spirit of self-centeredness, though its preoccupation with its own affairs was veiled by its readiness to welcome refugees who would help it become a stronger factor in Palestine." [102] Even worse, in her view, was the Zionist-nationalist solution for Jews remaining temporarily in the Galut for insurmountable practical reasons—Palestine could not possibly take them all in: "Pan-Semitism is the best answer to anti-Semitism." [103]

What, then, were her suggestions for a reasonable perspective on the situation in Palestine? Certainly it included a realistic—that is, historically informed—view of anti-Semitism. Zionism had based much of its argument on eternal outbursts of popular Jew-hatred, which, Arendt pointed out, "fitted well with its general mistrust of the peoples and overconfidence in Governments." Not only did these outbursts not take place, but they were replaced by far deadlier government actions. [104] In terms of political organization, she suggested a federation, because the proposal of a Jewish commonwealth or a Jewish state would result in Jews establishing themselves from the very beginning as a "'sphere of interest' under

the delusion of nationhood." She drew attention, too, to the fact that the
Yishuv had not only been an asylum for persecuted Jews from Diaspora
countries but had also needed the support of other Diaspora Jewries, especially the American Jews. And here she predicted exactly the troubled
future of a Jewish commonwealth established with the help of the political
influence of American Jews against the will of the Arabs and without the
support of the Mediterranean peoples.[105] But in 1944 this painful future
had not yet been brought about by the kind of Zionism she wanted reconsidered, and so she ended her appeal with a hopeful reference to the
"small chances that small peoples still have in this none too beautiful
world of ours"—provided they opted for historically informed, future-
oriented political practice rather than political ideologies arrested in the
past.

o 6 o

In Arendt's view, political practice was motivated by the experience
of historical change. Looking at Herzl's The Jewish State after five decades, she observed that, curiously, those aspects of Herzl's projection
which had been considered utopian at the turn of the century were determining Zionist ideology and policies in the mid-forties. However, Herzl's
practical proposals for the building of a Jewish homeland as a rigorously,
oppressively stratified class society, the authoritarian paternalism of the
"Jewish Company" which had once seemed quite contemporary, had not
had any influence:

> And it is altogether to the honor of the Jewish people that nobody—
> as far as I know—ever discussed these "realistic" proposals seri-
> ously, and that Palestinian reality has turned out to be almost the
> opposite of what Herzl dreamt.[106]

Mid-century Palestinian social reality was in Arendt's view deeply
influenced by the positive ideal of the "new Jew" shaped by the kibbutz
and chalutz movements. Not so, Palestinian political reality, which she
found troubling because it still reflected in many ways Herzl's political
Zionism. Now, Herzl, in his proposal to look at the Jewish people
through the eyes of the other nations—that is, relationally—had posed
the question of anti-Semitism in political terms. This was a fresh approach to the Jewish question, and as Arendt stated explicitly, it was decidedly better than the apolitical and highly precarious "solutions" of assimilationism.[107] The merits of Herzl's movement, in its historical

situation, were its political perspective and its actionism, which supported the Jews' determination to solve their problems by their own efforts. As Arendt summed it up, Zionism around the turn of the century
proposed a "comparatively sound nationalism"—a Jewish nation like all
other nations—in contrast to the "hidden chauvinism of assimilationism"
and "a relatively sound realism" in contrast to the "obvious utopianism of
Jewish radicals."[108]

But that had been half a century ago. Moreover, Herzl's motivation
for political action toward a Jewish state had been based on a concept of
anti-Semitism which called for an arrangement of "eternally established
nation-states arrayed compactly against the Jews on one side, and on the
other side the Jews themselves, in dispersion and eternally persecuted."[109]
This concept, as Arendt was to argue in *The Origins of Totalitarianism*,
was already outdated by the end of the nineteenth century, when a new
brand of racist anti-Semitism developed which did not stop at national
boundaries.[110]

Herzl's concept of the nation-state, on the other hand, was very much
contemporary at the turn of the century, and the demand for national self-
determination was as natural for the Jewish people as for the other op-
pressed peoples of Europe. Half a century later, however, the concept of
national sovereignty had changed dramatically. Arendt seems to be suggesting a connection between the static nature of Herzl's concept of political anti-Semitism—all Gentiles eternally against all Jews outside the
boundaries of the Jewish nation-state—and the energetic stubbornness
of mid-century Zionist demands for a sovereign Jewish state in a country
where they are the minority. But though her argument is not entirely clear
here, she is very clear in her assessment of the contemporary Palestinian
question: Jews cannot live in isolation in Palestine; nor can they expect
to be safe there, finally and forever, from anti-Semitism.

But they do; and understandably so. The experience of catastrophic
persecution bred the urgent need for such an illusionary concept of safety
and for being exclusively among Jews. The dilemma is a political one.
Half a century after Herzl, Zionist politics are determined by a situation
which demands complete concentration on and solidarity with the remnants of European Jewry. This situation, Arendt agrees, cannot be dealt
with in any other way; yet it supports assumptions central to Herzl's Zionism, which she finds politically troubling. Jews who have fled to Palestine from Hitlerism and "displaced" survivors of the camps who are
trying to find in Palestine, finally, a place where they can come to rest

believe, even more strongly than the early Zionists, in the omnipresence and omnipotence of anti-Semitism, in all countries, at all times. Struggle against such an enemy must then seem hopeless, but it is also all-consuming. If established, a Jewish state would become the fortress from which to fight off the enemy, a fortress in which to be permanently safe in permanent struggle.

It is this situation of feeling and acting embattled which poses such a grave threat to attempts at finding a political solution to the Arab-Jewish question in Palestine:

> Some of the Zionist leaders pretend to believe that the Jews can maintain themselves in Palestine against the whole world and that they themselves can persevere in claiming everything or nothing against everybody and everything. However, behind this spurious optimism lurks a despair of everything and a genuine readiness for suicide that can become extremely dangerous should they grow to be the mood and atmosphere of Palestinian politics.[111]

There is, in Arendt's view, nothing in Herzl's Zionism that would act as a check on this double seduction by politically unrealistic optimism *and* despair; rather, it is precisely its enduring influence on contemporary Zionism in Palestine which threatens "to lead the Jews out of reality once more and out of the sphere of political action."[112]

This is a harsh judgment of the political reality in Palestine, delivered by a female German-Jewish intellectual from a position of political safety and stability in America, speaking, moreover, not with the circumspect caution of the outsider, but with the passion of the insider as dissenter. Even an old and close friend like Blumenfeld reacted with bitter anger to Arendt's critique of political Zionism. In a letter of January 17, 1946, to Martin Rosenblueth[113] he accused Arendt's "Zionism Reconsidered," which Scholem had brought him the previous evening, of "journalistic superficiality," lamenting the "horrible baseness" ("Minderwertigkeit") of her evaluations of human behavior. The fact that she judged the situation from outside the fortress Palestine and that she understood it to be a political-historical rather than metaphysical-existential problem made her position in his eyes "totally indifferent" ("voellig unbeteiligt") and "heartless."[114] These accusations have recurred, most intensely and most forcefully in the context of Arendt's report on the Eichmann trial. But the fact that they are used here by Blumenfeld, a friend of long standing who himself had been critical of many trends in Zionist politics in the thirties, is significant.

Blumenfeld was outraged by what he viewed as Arendt's betrayal of Zionism in its hour of need. There was indeed, as she had been pointing out in essay after essay, no room for dissent in the embattled Yishuv. In a letter written to her two weeks earlier, on January 4, 1946, before he read "Zionism Reconsidered," Blumenfeld had playfully reassured her that to him and their friendship their occasional political disagreements did not matter at all. Expressing his admiration for her charm and her schooled intellect, he had also asserted that politics is an art rather than a science, gladly attesting to her considerable knowledge regarding the science of politics. (This personal but important passage was cut from the published text of the letter.)[115]

The reservation regarding Arendt's political analyses implied here is new. In a letter written immediately after his return to Palestine from the United States in June 1945, he had expressed enthusiastic, optimistic feelings about the country and discussed the possibility of Arendt's and Bluecher's coming to Palestine.[116] Soon, however, he started to share with Arendt certain doubts, speaking openly about serious difficulties with the new immigration of the remnants of European Jewry in Palestine. (He mentioned in this context that Palestine was probably the only country in the world where money did not buy respect—an observation that would have been tempting to Arendt.) Stressing the importance, in this difficult situation, of good educators, he remarked that in the United States Arendt would hear only the optimistic, official version, not the truth. He noted that people swept up in the chaos after the Thirty Years' War in Germany must have been similar to many of the new immigrants to Palestine. He saw cultural problems, too, in the superman ideal and in the hostility of Oriental Jews toward all Gentiles.[117]

Arendt answered both letters on August 2, 1945, expressing her great interest in Blumenfeld's political activities and observations and her conviction that there would not be all that many disagreements between them, especially not in the immediate future, for which she foresaw a situation of clearly outlined issues and positions reminiscent of the thirties: this time not pro and contra fascism but pro and contra statehood. Arendt clearly expected Blumenfeld to be against the idea of a Jewish state. In his letter of September 19, 1945, he did not respond to her assessment of political developments, but expressed his enthusiastic admiration for the young people in Palestine, both Jews and Arabs, praising their lack of prejudice. He again stressed the need for and importance of teachers as leaders for the rebellious young, and the general insufficiency in this respect of his and even Arendt's contemporaries.[118] Arendt does not seem to have answered this letter, and Blumenfeld's next letter dates from January 4, 1946, showing a changed position.

The introductory passage from which I quoted is not really related to the rest of the letter, which is even less optimistic than the previous ones, though, Blumenfeld assumes, more hopeful about the situation in Palestine than she. He reminds her that when he left for Palestine she had expressed her hope that he would continue the fight not only for the Jews' taking root in this country but also for the de-rooting of Jews in other countries—that is, "the fight against assimilation which is highly unpopular in Zionism." "I will try to do my best," he had promised. The effect of Palestine on the Jews, he now explains, has been to split them into groups, which are becoming more and more separate: the Jewish people in Palestine, often misguided in their actions, but ready to risk everything; and the Jews in America and England, who watch the fight as if from a theater stall, unwilling to risk their lives or any serious interests. The Jewish people in Palestine are and feel beleaguered, and Blumenfeld, though in many ways an outsider (increasingly so after 1948) in the country that he has come to love, is one of them in this feeling of "us" against "them." No one in the Galut can speak with authority to the situation in Palestine, he writes, certainly not critically.

Arendt answered this letter, which must have alarmed her, immediately, on January 14, 1946;[119] her letter crossed Blumenfeld's complaint to Rosenblueth. Apologizing for not having written earlier, she informs Blumenfeld that she had sent off several articles before the arrival of his letter, including "Zionism Reconsidered," and pleads with him not to be annoyed by this piece. But she evidently knew that he probably would be, especially after his last letter, and so she takes great care to be gentle in leading up to this piece of information and to her attempts at explaining her reasons for her argument—namely, her deep fears about the situation in Palestine.

In her correspondence with Blumenfeld, Arendt was usually spontaneous, emotional, playfully flirtatious—as he was too. She was not in the habit of writing carefully planned, strategic letters to her friends, though she often discussed political issues. Up to this time she had relied, it seems, on being understood by him, even if they disagreed on details.

Here, anticipating misunderstanding, she is uncharacteristically careful. Significantly, she begins by relating her missing Blumenfeld since his departure from the United States with the resumption of contact with Jaspers: "a great joy which I must not hide." She is relieved that the continuity of her life and her emotions could be reestablished, first by connecting again with Blumenfeld in New York, and now in correspondence with Jaspers. Blumenfeld and Jaspers marked the boundaries of her German-Jewish identity, and Jaspers was to become the more important, more enduring influence after the war. This is not to say that her Jewishness was to become less important to her in emotional and intellectual terms; but her perception of her responsibility to a European-American cultural tradition was to change. The question of the cultural (in contradistinction to the political) contribution of Judaism to this tradition, its significance for it, became less problematic as she developed her political thought in the United States, where she was unquestionably a Jew and an American citizen and therefore unquestionably not in exile.

Now, Arendt either misremembered or misrepresented her relationship with Jaspers when she wrote Blumenfeld that she had always secretly expected that such a reconnection would take place one day, even though she had not written to Jaspers once since 1933. She *had* written—her last note is from 1938—always discussing possible meetings. And it was not Jaspers who had taken the first step to contact her, though he was the first to write in October 1945, thanking her for a message sent through a friend and for gifts of food. She may not have wanted Blumenfeld to think her too eager to resume contact with her German intellectual past. But she did want to see the reestablished continuity of this past as a gift—if not of Jaspers, then of life. Trust, she commented to Blumenfeld, "is not an empty illusion and [is] finally the only thing which prevents the private world from becoming a hell, too."

It is after this appeal to trust that she rejects the idea of mass immigration to Israel from the United States and pleads for a different attitude toward the immediate evacuation of roughly a million Jews from Europe to Israel: "With all due respect for political reasons, this is a matter of life and death. At least I am afraid that the situation is that desperate. I just read in the paper a declaration by Silver[120] that the Jews do not want to accept immigration without a state. My god, these people are really out of their mind." Her implied rejection of this Zionist political concept of exclusion—her interpretation of the overriding insistence on nation-statehood—is clear. In this context, too, she writes of a conversation with

Leo Baeck which suggested to her a troubling cultural exclusiveness. On one level she found him very impressive because he had remained fearless and untouched. But his arguments, too, were still the same as in 1932: "Hitler persecuted the Jews—why? Because of their great talents. And no Jew would ever be as base as other people. In short, the usual chauvinistic assimilationist stuff. Also, we are immediately the heart of mankind again etc."

But she responded very positively to a representative from Bergen-Belsen because of his and the camp committee's self-reliance. Her comment: "These are no longer schnorrers, these are human beings." It is a remark that could easily be misunderstood as being grotesquely inadequate to the situation: why would the fact that this man had come to inform American Jews about the situation in the camps without ostensibly asking for financial help be so important in view of the desperate situation of large numbers of displaced persons about which she is so concerned, too? Because a group's attempt at self-help and self-reliance is central to her concept of community. Always looking first for help from the outside, even in desperate situations, may build up the group's unquestioned solidarity, but it does not build a self-reliant, that is, also self-critical, community. That is why she is so interested in information about the democratic administration, the political structure, of the camps.

She may have been overly (and idiosyncratically) hopeful in her interpretation of this information. However, her comments on the traumatized condition of these survivors are shrewd and compassionate, no less so because she sees it in terms of potential political danger. And this leads her to her argument in "Zionism Reconsidered." The general feeling of these "displaced" survivors about their situation is that they are "dead persons on leave," preoccupied with dying rather than living in dignity. Their most profound experience has been not the fact of the death of six million but rather the way in which they died. They are motivated not so much by hatred for the Germans as by their experience of the indifference of everyone, including Jews. Because they cannot turn anywhere else but to the Jewish people, they tend to see all other peoples as hostile non-Jews. In Arendt's opinion, formed by a number of reports, they lost all belief in any kind of international connection, a comity of nations, and they are easily seduced by a racist version of Jewish nationalism. She believes strongly in the need to reassure every one of them of the importance of their individual survival.

The connection of these experiences to Arendt's argument in "Zion-

ism Reconsidered" is quite clear.[121] She had been apprehensive about
Blumenfeld's reaction to her critical remarks because she had been aware
of his solidarity with the beleaguered Yishuv. A group so hard-pressed by
the events of the immediate past and present is too easily swayed by either
unrealistic, uninformed hope for and reliance on help from the outside—
here Arendt expresses her fear that the Yishuv has not been fully aware
of how little consideration Great Powers show for small peoples—or total
despair of help and understanding from anyone but their own. Such pressure, such tension, makes it especially difficult for them to develop a politically responsible attitude.

Arendt reminds Blumenfeld how he used to say "suicide is no policy." Political decisions should not have their source in despair as the total
absence of trust in the other. In "Zionism Reconsidered" she quoted his
interpretation of anti-Semitism as "'a feeling of peripheral tension' com-
parable to 'the tension between nations . . . at the national boundaries
where the constant human contacts of national elements at variance with
each other tend constantly to renew the international conflict' (Kurt
Blumenfeld)." She clearly disagreed with "this most advanced interpretation, in which at least one aspect of Jew-hatred is correctly attributed to
the national organization of peoples," because it

> still presupposes the eternity of antisemitism in an eternal world of
> nations and, moreover, denies the Jewish part of responsibility for
> existing conditions. Thereby it not only cuts off Jewish history from
> European history and even from the rest of mankind; it ignores the
> role that European Jewry played in the construction and the func-
> tioning of the national state; and thus it is reduced to the assump-
> tion, as arbitrary as it is absurd, that every Gentile living with Jews
> must become a conscious or subconscious Jew-hater.[122]

Blumenfeld had not lived by this assumption but had been naturally
tolerant and accepting, in friendship, of the otherness of the other.[123] He
had also, following Lazare, to whom he introduced Arendt, been able to
develop a critical perspective on his own group. In his 1932 lecture on
the challenge of right-wing political anti-Semitism to Zionism, he had
stated explicitly that a strong enduring nationalism—in contrast to the
new nationalism of National Socialism—could not afford to be only self-
affirmative but had to be capable of self-criticism. If this were not the case,
it would collapse.[124] To extrapolate from this statement in Arendt's sense:
politically responsible nationalism is strong enough to be relational; it is

capable of looking at itself in the context of other nationalisms.

In her exchange with Scholem over her report on the Eichmann trial, Arendt questioned Scholem's making an issue of her Jewishness.[125] To his "I regard you wholly as a daughter of our people and in no other way," she answered that her Jewishness was a given. But having left Germany behind, living in America in the sixties, she did not see any need to stress this fact as the center and essence of her existence. To clarify for Scholem her attitude toward her Judaism, she reminded him how Ben-Gurion in his obituary of Kurt Blumenfeld had stated his regret over Blumenfeld's failure to change his name when he settled in Israel. Is it not obvious, she asked Scholem (who had changed his name), "that Blumenfeld did not do so for exactly the same reasons that had led him in his youth to become a Zionist?"[126] What she meant was that the young Blumenfeld had rejected assimilation—that is, the unquestioned, uncritical desire for acceptance, with its concomitant need of solidarity. Now, as an old man, he would not give in to insufficiently examined group pressures that he had come to see as politically problematic and that had driven him, increasingly, into personal and political isolation.[127] It is unlikely that Scholem, angered by Arendt's "betrayal" of the Jewish cause, even considered her argument. His solidarity with the Jewish people in Palestine and later with the State of Israel was considerably less reflected, less questioned, than Blumenfeld's.

But writing to Martin Rosenblueth in early January 1946, troubled by the controversy over Jewish statehood, Blumenfeld, too, was for a time unable to maintain a flexible perspective. In this difficult situation the truth, and the only truth, was with the Yishuv in Palestine, and no one but an insider, affirming solidarity, had the right to speak about it. He even excluded, excommunicated really, Arendt retroactively: he had never believed in her Zionism,[128] though he had been her teacher; he had felt their disagreements to be extreme ("ein Kampf auf Tod und Leben"). The article revealed to him a "psychopathic" component of her mind, a "ressentiment intensified into madness." It was for personal reasons—he implied here her marriage to a Gentile—that she projected with such violence the disappearance of anti-Semitism (she had never argued such a disappearance); Jew-hatred in the Galut did not play a decisive role in Palestine (this had not been her point in the discussion of the role of anti-Semitism in Zionist politics). Finally, he made the distinction, so common in the attacks on the Eichmann book, between the (disturbing) substance of her argument and her (hateful) mode of discourse, which "somehow" always, *eo ipso*, discredits the argument: he could face her anti-Zionism, but he could not bear the "spitefulness and baseness of her presentation." [129]

Blumenfeld was temperamental—as was Arendt, especially in her younger years. But his response to her article was more than that; it was profoundly irrational, provoked by the extremely difficult situation in Palestine, which encouraged political irrationalism, as Arendt (and Magnes) had argued repeatedly. Arendt's critical analyses of Zionist politics in the forties were motivated by her fears, which were intensified when thoughtful Zionists like Blumenfeld reacted so violently to the pariah perspective[130] they had once thought useful, even essential. There is a curious coincidence which brings into sharp focus the different development of student and teacher, especially since the mid-forties: Arendt concluded her 1946 critical assessment, "*The Jewish State* Fifty Years After," with a warning that the parallels between contemporary Zionism, so much influenced by the Revisionist minority, and the Sabbatai Zevi episode had "become terribly close." Blumenfeld, arguing in support of Weizmann for political realism and sanity at the Seventeenth Zionist Congress in 1931, accused the Revisionists of creating a new pseudo-messianism: "We are not, after all, a Sabbatai Zwi-movement. We are the serious political movement of contemporary Jewry." [131] This was the movement Arendt had joined; she left it when, in her view, it was in danger of becoming reactionary and an impediment to international comity.

o   7   o

Arendt's article "To Save the Jewish Homeland: There Is Still Time," which was published in *Commentary* in May 1948, the birth month of the Jewish State, established her personal connection with Magnes. After his long advocacy of binationalism ended with the proclamation of the State of Israel on May 15, 1948, Magnes set out to find a political formula that would both recognize the Jewish State and calm Arab fears. From June until his death at the end of October, he worked, with Arendt's help, on the concept of a confederation of Jewish and Arab states with Jerusalem as the capital. Magnes had come to America on April 21 with the goal of bringing about a cease-fire in Jerusalem which could then be extended to the whole country. He also wanted to get support for a temporary United Nations trusteeship for Palestine which Warren Austin, America's chief U.N. delegate, had announced on March 19 as the plan the United States favored over the immediate implementation of partition.

Magnes saw President Truman on May 6, and in his talks with him and State Department officials, he emphasized his Jerusalem strategy. He had arrived in New York at a climactic moment in the battle for and against Jewish statehood, wanting above all to bring about peace "at nearly any price, surely at the price of statehood." [132] Magnes continued his diplomatic efforts in the United States all through May and into June, and although the Jewish Agency was opposed to his activities, it maintained contact with him. On June 10 he suffered a stroke, which necessitated hospitalization for three weeks; on June 14 he dictated a letter to Robert McClintock of the U.S. State Department in which he outlined a plan for a confederation of a Jewish and an Arab state, both sovereign, but allied in defense and foreign policy. "The plan was, in a sense, a compromise between binationalism and statehood, between partitioning Palestine and maintaining its unity." [133]

Magnes, whom Arendt met in June, was a man who deeply appealed to her sense of political integrity and rationality. She knew that he was seriously ill and she admired his gallantry in continuing to fight for his political convictions, which she shared. [134] He had been impressed by the fierce clarity of Arendt's dissection of an ominous Jewish unanimity on the Palestine issue and her agreement with him on the proposition of a confederation of states as the only possible, that is, realistic, solution.

Arendt's essay was written exactly at the time when Magnes was negotiating patiently for a peaceful solution to the conflict, but though she, too, desired such a solution above all, she did not do so patiently. At first glance it seems that she still had not learned anything from the many critical, often hostile reactions to her previous essays on the problems of political Zionism. However, her appeal here to political relationism and perspectivism, which was the message of her critique of the politics of solidarity, was informed by a slightly increased awareness on her part that in the current explosive situation this was a very difficult position to propose to her Jewish readers in Palestine.

Since her analysis of the mechanics of assimilationism in the Rahel book, Arendt had been convinced that unanimity of opinion

> destroys social and personal life, which is based on the fact that we are different by nature and by conviction. To hold different opinions and to be aware that different people think differently on the same issues shields us from that god-like certainty which stops all discussion and reduces social relationships to those of an ant heap. A

unanimous public opinion tends to eliminate bodily those who differ, for mass unanimity is not the result of agreement, but an expression of fanaticism and hysteria. In contrast to agreement, unanimity
does not stop at certain well-defined objects, but spreads like an
infection into every related issue.[135]

Arendt had always argued against such unanimity and had shaped
her arguments accordingly. But in those texts which addressed the Jewish
question directly—that is, without historical mediation—she had encountered much resistance from readers who, in the context of this difficult complex of problems, found troubling the intellectual—if not quite
godlike—certainty of her discourse. In May 1948 she sensed that she
needed not only to analyze the gravely serious situation in Palestine but
also to admit, if critically, its inherent logic, which would make it so very
difficult for those caught in the situation to see it with the degree of distance she proposed.

The fact that Arendt spoke from a position that was already defined
by such distance, and then with a certain tone of pedagogical impatience,
would of course have irritated readers who felt pushed too forcefully to
see things her way in a situation where this implied a concrete and rather
immediate rethinking and reevaluation of complex and troubling issues.
The often-criticized "coldness" or remoteness of Arendt's discourse, her
crisp conceptual arrangements, her rapid and sharp distinctions, her un-
gentle irony, all had their source in this impatience. It would be particularly important, in this situation of crisis, where the fate of the homeland
seemed suspended in a balance no longer open to rational decision, to
temper her appeals to political sanity. Analyzing the "sheer irrationality"
of both the Arab and the Jewish peoples' desire "to fight it out at any
price," she needed to find ways that would make it easier for readers hostile to her argument to at least consider her criticism. In this, of course,
she did not succeed. But "To Save the Jewish Homeland" is distinguished from her previous critiques of political Zionism in that it stresses
the admirable achievements of the homeland, it ends on a note of hope
rather than one of warning, and it contains a list of concrete and detailed
suggestions to ameliorate the situation.

Arendt started the essay with a short historical outline of the decision
to partition Palestine and create a Jewish state—that is, the "cooperation"
of the United Nations, the Arab Higher Committee, and the Jewish
Agency[136] in creating an untenable situation that Arendt believed would

lead to guerrilla warfare. In this warfare the Arabs, as demonstrated by their behavior, their refusal to compromise, would rely on time and superior numerical strength. The Jews, in view of their military situation, "might well be expected to jump at the chance to exploit their present advantage by offering a negotiated peace."[137] That they did not do so— in Arendt's view an "unnatural," "tragic" development—was connected with a change in Jewish opinion both in the Galut and the Yishuv which had come about concomitantly with the indeed confusing politics of the Great Powers. In the Galut, opinion had become nearly unanimous in support of Zionism; in Palestine, opinion had become nearly unanimous in support of a Jewish state. Moreover, there was a general mood of tolerance for terrorism and totalitarian methods in the Yishuv which had to be taken into consideration by anyone wishing to appeal to the Yishuv. Most upsetting to Arendt was the growing unanimity of opinion among both American and Palestinian Jews regarding the conflict of Arab and Jewish claims. They were in agreement on a series of politically dangerous propositions:

> The moment has now come to get everything or nothing, victory or death; Arab and Jewish claims are irreconcilable and only a military decision can settle the issue; the Arabs—all Arabs—are our enemies and we accept this fact; only outmoded liberals believe in compromises, only philistines believe in justice, and only *schlemiels* prefer truth and negotiation to propaganda and machine guns; Jewish experience in the last decades—or over the last centuries, or over the last two thousand years—has finally awakened us and taught us to look out for ourselves; this alone is reality, everything else is stupid sentimentality; everybody is against us, Great Britain is anti-Semitic, the United States is imperialist—but Russia might be our ally for a certain period because her interests happen to coincide with ours;[138] yet, in the final analysis we count upon nobody except ourselves; in sum—we are ready to go down fighting, and we will consider anybody who stands in our way a traitor, anything done to hinder us a stab in the back.[139]

This list of propositions stated "more or less roughly" is not, of course, what I had in mind when I drew attention to certain modifications in Arendt's presentation of her critical argument here. It is true that she immediately pointed out the connection of these propositions to the recent catastrophic events in Europe and "the subsequent fantastic injustice and callousness toward the surviving remnant [of European Jewry] that were thereby so ruthlessly transformed into displaced persons."[140] It is also likely that the unmistakable reference to the myth of a "stab in the back"—*Dolchstosslegende*—which allegedly brought about the defeat and destruction of an otherwise undefeated Germany, made it more difficult for many of her readers to give serious consideration to her argument. And yet the reference was important, because it underscored her fears regarding the cultural consequences of a racist Jewish chauvinism inherent in the contemporary Zionist understanding of "Israel's mission."[141] This mission could not be realized through playing up the "despair and resoluteness" of the Yishuv or by suicide threats of Jewish leaders, precisely because there was too much to lose if the Yishuv failed.

Above all, Arendt did not want to lose the contributions made to the homeland by the collective settlements, the kibbutzim, "which constitute perhaps the most promising of all social experiments made in the twentieth century."[142] The Palestinian Jews' paranoid rejection of all differing opinions or critiques as a "stab in the back" was associated, for the reader, with the politically dangerous—and exploitable—German cultural mood of being besieged on all sides after the Great War, a mood which played an important part in the destruction of the Weimar Republic. In contrast, the achievements of the kibbutzim pointed to a fresh, positive perspective on centrally important cultural conflicts which, unresolved, had been both socially explosive and politically manipulable during the Weimar period in Germany, but problematic in all developing Western mass societies:

> Here, in complete freedom and unhampered by any government, a new form of ownership, a new type of farmer, a new way of family life and child education, and new approaches to the troublesome conflicts between city and country, between rural and industrial labor, have been created.[143]

She pointed out that in effecting their "quiet and effective revolution," the people of the kibbutzim had not made "their voices sufficiently heard in Zionist politics"—they had not offered serious obstacles to terrorism. However, she dwelt not so much on the fact that their achievement was politically flawed as on the fact that its destruction would be a serious, an irreparable loss to Jews and non-Jews alike. To both groups the "new type of man"[144] emerging from the kibbutz movements could suggest, in his questioning of the status quo, a possible solution to the "pressures of modern life and its unsolved problems." [145]

Arendt wanted the Jews in Palestine to react to their recent traumatic history by looking at old conflicts and dilemmas in new ways because in her view that was the only way in which, coping with the past, they could have a future. In this they might even serve as a model for other peoples. But Arendt, who did not think much of the concept of Jewish uniqueness and distinctness from other peoples, put much more emphasis on their learning to live as one people among others. Arguing against partition (in which, she conceded, "many non-fanatical Jews of sincere good will have believed") because it would both petrify the conflict and mean preparation for further war, she concluded with an alternative proposition for a federated state as endorsed by Magnes. Propositions like these must not, in a situation ruled by panic, be dismissed as "stabs in the back," she argued (this was the second time she used this expression in this essay), or as unrealistic, because they are the only way to save "the reality of the Jewish homeland." Her five propositions followed closely those made by Magnes and Buber to the Anglo-American Inquiry Commission for the Ihud Association in August 1946. [146]

Arendt's essay "Peace or Armistice in the Near East?"—published in the January 1950 issue of the *Review of Politics*—was written in 1948 on the suggestion of Magnes, with whom Arendt collaborated in the summer of 1948 in refining proposals for Arab-Jewish reconciliation. [147] It is dedicated to the memory of the man who, in Arendt's words, "from the close of World War I to the day of his death in October, 1948, had been the outstanding Jewish spokesman for Arab-Jewish understanding in Palestine." [148] Into this long, important article, which presents the sum of her thought on the Jewish-Arab question, Arendt integrated arguments she had developed in her exchanges with Magnes, which, in their consensus regarding the main goals, left room for diverging opinions on the best (most feasible) routes to be taken. [149] The text reflects the openness and circumspection gained or strengthened by her involvement with the political thought and activities of a man like Magnes. Conceptually clearer and surer, more concise, more incisively realistic than he, she had learned from him—as she had learned before, and was to learn again, from Jaspers—not what questions to ask of the world, nor how to ask them, but how to present them so that they could be shared and thereby become more meaningful. Shortly before Magnes's death, Arendt wrote him about the significance of their relation for her: "Politics in our century is almost a business of despair and I have always been tempted to run away from it. I wanted you to know that your example prevented me from despairing and will prevent me for many years to come." [150]

In a short piece, "The Mission of Bernadotte," published in the *New Leader* after the assassination of Bernadotte by Jewish extremists in September 1948,[151] Arendt attempted to present a persuasive concept of "loyal opposition" to politics in Israel among American Jews.[152] Magnes, in a postscript added to his *Commentary* response to Abba Eban on September 20, after the assassination, had stressed the importance of Bernadotte's role for peace and reconciliation between Arabs and Jews in the Holy Land: "His murder is a tragedy of historic importance for both peoples" because "at a crucial moment, this great task of peace-making has been deprived of Bernadotte's integrity of heart and mind and the great store of insight he had accumulated regarding personalities and other important factors involved." Magnes extended responsibility for that crime from the Jewish terrorists to "those official circles in Israel who at one time and another carried on joint activities with terrorist groups, and instead of suppressing them, came to an understanding with them, incorporating them into their armed forces." But in Magnes's view, responsibility also rested with large numbers of American supporters of terror in Palestine: "the senators and congressmen, the newspaper publishers and the large number of Jews and others who have supported terrorists morally and financially." [153]

Arendt's article argued that there were two possible ways out of the Palestinian dilemma—Bernadotte's second proposal for a U.N. trusteeship, or a Jewish-Arab confederation as envisioned by Magnes; she thought the first one more feasible under the circumstances. Magnes, whether he agreed with her or not, had high praise for the piece, which he had seen in manuscript form, in his letter of October 7, less than three weeks before his own death:

> Your article for the *New Leader* is not only a rarely penetrating analysis, it might also be called a momentous article, i.e., it might have serious practical consequences if it were studied and taken to heart by anyone in whose hands decisions lay. You seem to have laid bare the inner meanings of Bernadotte's efforts and proposals; I very much doubt if that has been done in many places. Your story may be called tragic. Here was a great and good man who started full of hope and ended almost in despair. Suppose Secretary Marshall saw your article, with its alternatives of another form of UN

trusteeship, or a continuation of the Jewish-Arab war, what would his conclusion be? In any event, it ought to help clarify his mind and help him to a realistic conclusion. It is a grave choice, this way or that. Your article has depressed me, and I am asking myself, is there really no way out? I think every effort should be made to bring the article to the attention of those making decisions at Paris.[154]

There is a poignant analogy in Arendt's comment on the meaning of Magnes's death in a letter to his friend Hans Kohn, a historian at Smith College who before the war had worked for the Zionist Organization in London and in Jerusalem and who had resigned in 1929, protesting Zionist policy on the Arab question:

> Magnes' death is a real tragedy at this moment. Nobody has his moral authority. I don't see anybody, moreover, who lives really in the Jewish world and who is prominent in a Jewish institution who would have the courage to speak up against what is going on now.[155]

Arendt supported the Judah Magnes Foundation, but she did not want to be directly involved in political activities, especially not after her experience of being shouted down by a hostile audience in Massachusetts to whom she had spoken about Magnes's goals and proposals at the request of Hans Kohn.[156] Nevertheless, her writing was to remain political both in a figurative and a literal sense.

o   8   o

The article "Peace or Armistice in the Near East?" begins with the important distinction that peace cannot, as can armistice, be imposed from the outside, but can only result from negotiation and mutual compromise leading to eventual agreement between Jews and Arabs. In Arendt's view, this goal is the only realistic one in terms of the long-term coexistence of Arabs and Jews, but the obstacles are powerful: the Jewish settlement in Palestine is a potentially important factor in the development of the Near East, but it will always remain very small compared to the surrounding Arab populations, and they have been consistently hostile to it. The declaration of a Jewish state and Jewish victories over Arab armies have not influenced Arab politics: "All hopes to the contrary notwithstanding, it seems as though the *one* argument the Arabs are incapable of understanding is force."[157]

This statement implies that a learning process in consideration of self-interest—that is, peace reached by mutual compromise—is needed. It is in the self-interest of the Arabs to make possible, through negotiation, close economic and political cooperation with the Jews, the "most advanced and Westernized people of the region"; it is in the self-interest of the Jews to seriously seek such cooperation and to change their handling of the Arab refugee problem.[158] But it is the Jews who have more to lose by a "no-peace/no-war" situation following an armistice: especially in the current mood of reaction against Hitler's slaughterhouses, preparing for war would mean an impossible drain on the country's economy, an end to social experiments, and increasing dependence of the whole Jewish population on support from American Jewry. This situation, in the short run, will be easier to bear for the economically and socially underdeveloped Arabs. Yet, in order to deal constructively with this situation and overcome a politically dangerous power vacuum, the Arabs need Jewish cooperation. The world's political pace will not allow them to grow, as some of their leaders envision, slowly and "organically," without the influence of "foreign" Western ideas. "If they continue to be anti-Western, to spend their energies fighting the tiny Jewish state and indulging their sterile pride in keeping the national character intact, they are threatened with something far worse, and much more real, than the bogey of Jewish domination."[159]

Again and again Arendt warns of the danger that the Great Powers will intervene in this situation—the result of and a further reason for the small peoples' abdication of political responsibility. In this context she analyzes a mood of messianism with regard to Jewish victories, which, she says, are not

> judged in the light of present realities in the Near East but in the light of a very distant past; the present war fills every Jew with "such satisfaction as we have not had for centuries, perhaps not since the days of the Maccabees" (Ben-Gurion).[160]

But the underlying mood is apocalyptic, even if success in battle has strengthened the determination to see the current conflict in terms of a final verdict of history. Arendt is clearly troubled by the "spirit of Massadah" with which the Jewish troops fought against the British occupation troops and the Arab soldiers: a mood of "or else we shall go down" poses, above all, a horrendous obstacle to all compromise. The clearest indication is the change in Jewish political vocabulary:

Today the Israeli government speaks of accomplished facts, of Might is Right, of military necessities, of the law of conquest, whereas two years ago, the same people in the Jewish Agency spoke of justice and the desperate needs of the Jewish people. Palestinian Jewry bet on one card—and won.[161]

The lack of political prudence or realism in Israel—the determination to regard the chancy outcome of the armed conflict as final, as having solved, once and for all, the social and political conflict—has a parallel in the Arabs' determination to see their defeat as merely an interlude and not to draw any conclusions from it. And it is precisely this shared refusal to take the other and the other's position seriously which points to the seriousness of the situation, because it implies that both sides are working with an ideological, unrealistic concept of history. History is a combination of accident and human action which has to be responsible to the future precisely because it is not known. Both teleological messianic yearning and fatalism transcend and thereby close off historical experience. Arendt's insistence on the cultural importance of new beginnings, natality, which plays such an important role in *The Human Condition* and *On Revolution* (and which caused some of the painful misunderstandings concerning her position vis-à-vis the State of Israel in her report on the Eichmann trial), can be traced to her critical analysis of the Arab-Jewish question. In posing this question, which was central to their existence as a people, Palestinian Jews were too much influenced by an incompletely understood German-Jewish history. Arendt rejects as politically counterproductive the Jewish claims

that the world—or history or higher morality—owes them a righting of the wrongs of two thousand years and, more specifically, a compensation for the catastrophe of European Jewry which, in their opinion, was not simply a crime of Nazi Germany but of the whole civilized world. The Arabs, on the other hand, reply that two wrongs do not make a right and that "no code of morals can justify the persecution of one people in an attempt to relieve the persecution of the other." The point of this kind of argumentation is that it is unanswerable. Both claims are nationalistic because they make sense only in the closed framework of one's own people and history, and legalistic because they discount the concrete factors of the situation.[162]

The Jews, in defending their state, which had been established against the wishes of the Arab majority in Palestine and had caused a very serious refugee problem, rationalize their wronging the Arabs by pointing to the history of their people's persecution—an argument which the Arabs can neither deny in general nor accept in particular terms. The Arabs, in their resistance to the Jewish State, use an argument which, as a general statement, the Jews cannot deny, but which detracts from the fact that the Arabs had also resisted the building of the Jewish homeland in Palestine, in spite of the historical significance of this enterprise. In both cases the arguments do not constitute political speech, which is intended to be understandable and answerable. Such intention would have to be supported by an awareness that the world extends beyond the confused, conflicted present. This is the meaning of Arendt's stressing natality, which to her signifies only one of the boundaries of life, the other being mortality. There will be new life, new possibilities, after us, and in political speech and action we express our willingness to be responsible for their potential. That is, we speak and act politically so that we can be a future's past that will not have imposed the silence of the inevitable, the fated, the inexplicable: a past that cannot be used, as has been the Jews' and the Arabs' past, as the final, inarticulate, unremovable obstacle to communication.

Linking the Jewish-Arab conflict to the German-Jewish catastrophe, Arendt stresses the openness of the future over the closedness of the past. But in her analysis of the genesis of the Palestinian conflict, she also demonstrates that both past and future need to be questioned more rigorously: neither is the past fully known nor is the future fully unknowable. The current impasse has historical reasons that bear examination. One is the incompatibility of claims made by Arabs and Jews on each other, the social and economic separation that made it very difficult for both Jews and Arabs to "visualize a close neighbor as a concrete human being."[163] Arendt's focus on the issue of Jewish responsibility for this situation does not imply that the Arabs should not also be held responsible. She was speaking to a Jewish audience, hoping that their attitudes toward the conflicts in which they were involved might be changed by her arguments.

For this reason she concentrated on certain fallacies in the Zionist position, most importantly, the fact that the Zionist concept of Yishuv, a homeland for a homeless people, as if by definition tended to disregard native inhabitants of that land. And the economic situation in Palestine added to the tendency of Jewish settlers to just neglect the Arab problem because of the very great difficulties involved in settling a largely urban population in a poor, arid country and educating it in making this country livable. What could not be neglected so smoothly was the question of cheap Arab labor. The unaccustomed hardship of working the land made easily available labor a serious temptation that needed to be rigorously resisted in view of the unmediated cultural significance of the land for every single Jew who worked it because it brought deliverance from dispersion and rootlessness in the Galut. The Zionist achievement of in-gathering could not be allowed to degenerate into another imperialist colonial enterprise. And so the bitter struggle of organized Jewish labor against cheap Arab labor appealed not just to the desire to protect the rights and higher wages of Jewish workers but also to the broad cultural, moral foundations of Zionism.

Not only, then, was an anticapitalist position equated with an anti-Arab position, but this experience also affirmed the notion of the Yishuv, the home that had been built up for and by a people without a country in a country without a people.[164] Caught in this circle that had affirmed rather then probed the notion of Jewish uniqueness, it was easy for Jews to overlook the fact that Arabs were neither "primitive," that is, subhuman, nor picturesque remnants of an old civilization, but were human beings with desires similar to theirs, human beings who wished to settle down, felt the need for agricultural machines, wanted a higher standard of living—precisely because of the example of Jewish achievements.

There was, of course, as Arendt was the first to admit, a unique quality to the Jewish achievement in Palestine. Its artificiality has often been remarked on and is expressive of the unambiguously admirable aspects of the experiment:

> The collective rural settlements, the backbone of Palestinian society and the expression of pioneerdom, can certainly not be explained by utilitarian reasons. The development of the soil, the erection of a Hebrew university, the establishment of great health centers, were all "artificial" developments, supported from abroad and initiated by a spirit of enterprise which paid no heed to calculations of profit and loss.[165]

Zionists, stressing the "natural," inevitable logic of the achievement, tended to emphasize the argument of blind and urgent necessity rather than that of challenges met creatively. Building the homeland, Jews had to work against eternal anti-Semitism, against a difficult labor situation (the collective settlements), for certain important national interests (health centers, Hebrew University). Arendt thought it more helpful to understand the "human significance" of the Yishuv in terms of the *kind* of response with which the challenges were met.[166] As a human creation, the experiment of building up a Jewish homeland provided a new, in important ways spontaneous, unpredictable answer to past experience. Zionist "ideology," stressing eternal necessity—above all, the need to escape the oppression of anti-Semitism—did not understand sufficiently the implications, for the future, of this experiment and thereby endangered rather than protected it.

These implications concerned the quality of the learning experience provided by the experiment. The proof of its (partial) success would be the ability to change that attitude toward the past which had originally motivated the enterprise of building the homeland. Means—the experiences made in the process of building—should change attitudes not only toward the goal, the future, but also toward the effort of understanding the past. These were the unstated assumptions in which Arendt's argument was centered. She focused on the ideological arrest of the Zionist position as politically counterproductive or even destructive in a situation where profound social and economic change had been brought about by human action. This action in response to certain challenges had been responsible for unforeseen, unpredictable developments which, in order to be understood and handled responsibly, had to be analyzed on their own terms. And it was precisely such an analysis that would open, as it were, the past to a different, more questioning, more reflected, more conflicted understanding.

It is significant that, as an example, Arendt chose here the establishment of political structures by the Palestinian trade unions in which the great majority of Jewish labor was organized and which covered many more areas of social activities—immigration, defense, education, health, public works, communication—than trade unions would do in the "normal" situation of statehood. Under the "not too sympathetic eye of the British trustee," something like a state-within-a-nonexistent-state, and a very modern one, was constructed. And this, for Arendt, explained "the miraculous fact that a mere proclamation of Jewish self-government eventually sufficed to bring a state machine into being."[167]

This "miraculous fact" did indeed make the Palestinian experiment unique, but it was a uniqueness that Arendt believed should provide a new perspective on the argument of Jewish uniqueness in the past. She observed that the Jewish farmers and workers responsible for building up the homeland were aware and proud of their achievements. In this essay, too, she stressed the creation of a new type of man, a new social elite or aristocracy in the rural collective settlements where the "age-old Jewish dream of a society based on justice, formed in complete equality, indifferent to all profit motives, was realized, even if on a small scale"[168]—anticipating her model of the polis in *The Human Condition*. But neither the Jewish people in Palestine nor the Zionist leadership understood the political meaning of such a unique achievement. The leadership's assertions to the contrary, the country "could not possibly fit into the political scheme of imperialism because it was neither a master nor a subject nation." The fact and manner of change—transforming deserts into fertile land, designing political structures that would ensure equality in heterogeneous groups—could have been understood as a reaffirmation of the possibility of change in the world in general. The uniqueness of the achievement could have supported the desire of the Jewish people to be one nation among other nations in a world shared. But the conclusions drawn by the Israeli leadership were, in Arendt's view, just the opposite. Their nationalist aggressiveness projected, and fed on, an unrealistic need to fight for everything against everyone.[169]

It was in the context of the failure of the ideological Zionist leadership to take seriously the question of Jewish-Arab cooperation that the "true stature" of the few representatives of the "non-nationalist tradition" revealed itself:

> So few in number that they can hardly be called a real opposition force, so isolated from the masses and mass propaganda media that they were frequently ignored or suffocated by that peculiar praise which discredits a man as impractical by calling him an "idealist" or a "prophet," they nevertheless created, on the Jewish as well as the Arab side, an articulate tradition. At least their approach to the Palestinian problem begins in the objective realities of the situation.[170]

Arendt's political thought has often been viewed as "idealist," implying reservations about the adequacy of her models.[171] Here she explicitly linked the implied reproach of an "idealist" perspective or position to its actual realism. In Magnes's work she admired precisely the broad political vision based on detailed information about actual policies and political activities. He had set her an example which, as she wrote to him shortly before his death, had prevented her from despairing of ever finding a responsible political solution and would prevent her from doing so "for many years to come."[172] Her outline of the history of attempts at Arab-Jewish cooperation made in good faith yet seemingly always doomed to fail because of the "insuperable" difficulties of the situation[173] provides enough reasons for despairing of even the possibility of success. Yet she saw hopeful signs in the fact that the *fait accompli* of the Jewish State did not prevent the representative of Lebanon to the United Nations, Charles Malik, from insisting before the Security Council on the priority of an agreement between Arabs and Jews. Speaking about the need for peace and for recognizing the realities of the Near East situation, he echoed statements made earlier by Buber and Magnes which had pointed out both the central importance and the possibility of Jewish-Arab cooperation in view of the alternative, war.[174]

The emphasis, for Arendt, was quite clearly on the concept of possibility in this extremely difficult political situation. The necessity for cooperation could be "proved by objective factors," but she acknowledged the difficulty of accepting the proof. ("Necessity, based on economic, military and geographic considerations, will make itself felt in the long run only, or possibly, at a time when it is too late.") Possibility depends on decisions made in the immediate present by leaders on both sides who are able "to anticipate the direction of long-range necessary trends and channel them into constructive political institutions."[175]

Arguing for peace in a confederated Palestine, Magnes had presented possible political solutions. Arendt was clearly intent on separating the political from the economic questions. There was no economic necessity to support the arguments for peace instead of armistice, she argued in the last part of her essay, which opposed "Federation" to "Balkanization."[176] And the same was true for the argument for confederation, where Arendt insisted, somewhat in contrast to Magnes, that political implementation would have to come before economic cooperation. The alternative to Balkanization—that is, turning the whole region into a battlefield of conflicting Great Power interests in disregard of authentic national interests—was the *political* solution of federation, which would keep in check nationalistic aggressiveness and its misuse of the *religious* concept of the chosen people.

In the absence of this political solution, the Yishuv as identical with the State of Israel—that is, as the result of successful manipulation of international machinery—meant permanent alienation of Jews from Arabs.[177] The refusal to speak as one nation among other nations—in the Mediterranean, in the world as a whole—may be psychologically understandable. But in its insistence on group solidarity and unanimity, this refusal prevented the Jewish people in Palestine from international political participation and responsibility. It prolonged for Jews in Palestine not only the status but also the silence of exile—a silence which, in Arendt's experience, had long been broken by Jews in America.

4

The Quality of Guilt

The Trial of the Germans

Arendt finally heard of Blumenfeld's bitterly angry reaction to her critical assessment of political Zionism in January 1946, and of his serious illness in the spring of that year. On July 17, 1946, when she wrote to him of her anxiety about his illness, she pointed out the importance of loyalty in friendship in spite of political disagreements—that is, the opposite of uncritical solidarity, namely, tolerance in friendship for the otherness of the other, which she saw threatened or undermined by the situation in Palestine.[1] She also sent him Hermann Broch's *Death of Virgil*, for which he thanked her on December 12, 1946, emphasizing how sought-after the book was ("belagert") in Jerusalem and how much it had occupied him. The significance of the book immediately after the war—it was published first in English translation—was centered in its poetic-historical presentation of death as personally and culturally significant rather than meaningless and accidental. Arendt deemed the *Death of Virgil* by far the greatest of Broch's achievements, and in the first postwar years was very much impressed by it.[2]

Neither Arendt nor Blumenfeld, however, projected their own preoccupation with the experience of death—of friends and relations, of their people, of Jewish-German culture—into the future, which would hold new, unforeseen challenges to new generations signifying new, not-yet-charted ways of dealing with the consequences of the present cultural experience of chaos and destruction. On September 16, 1946, writing to the young Jona Wolff in Sweden (Wolff later became a member of the

Kibbutz Maos Chaim, where he was killed during the 1948 Jewish-Arab war), Blumenfeld pointed out that no politician who led his people to their collective death has ever found an honorable place in history. Implying that the Biltmore program with its covert goal of partition might result in the ruin of the Yishuv, Blumenfeld lamented the fact that a very large number of young Jews growing up in the shadow of the politics of desperate self-assertion had substituted the ideal of the political activist (terrorist) for that of the pioneer. His argument was close to Arendt's in her critical essays on political Zionism: the Yishuv would have no chance to be heard in the age of Great Nations unless it began to insist on freedom (of speech) within. Small peoples live by virtue of natality, by nurturing new men and women with new ideas, not by imitating the bad qualities of Great Powers.[3] Arendt, too, was sharply aware of the self-destructive potential of the Biltmore program. This awareness was deepened by her inability to deal with the *Vernichtungsfabriken*, the destruction factories, "on that level of the brutal factual, on which the question of this latest development in production (*Fabrikationsart*) is no longer connected to Jews or to Germans."[4] Trying to understand the mass destruction of European Jewry as a sociopolitical-historical fact, Arendt was particularly sensitive to the suicidal mood of the Yishuv, especially among the young, who were strongly inclined—as Blumenfeld, too, points out in his letter—to substitute a (charismatic) leader for their own individual political responsibility.

In her January 1945 article, "Organized Guilt and Universal Responsibility," Arendt described totalitarian[5] policy, with its "destruction of the neutral zone in which the daily life of human beings is ordinarily lived as seeking to make the existence of each individual German depend either on committing crimes or on complicity with crimes." This policy, in the deepest sense a- and antinational, recognized a German people only if they were totally in its power. Thinking about the postwar situation, when it would again be necessary to judge human behavior outside this totalitarian closed circle, Arendt warned of certain fallacies:

> The true problem, however, is not to prove what is self-evident, namely that Germans have not been potential Nazis ever since Tacitus' times, nor what is impossible, that all Germans harbor Nazi views. It is rather to consider how to conduct ourselves and how to bear the trial of confronting a people among whom the boundaries dividing criminals from normal persons, the guilty from the inno-

cent, have been so completely effaced that nobody will be able to tell in Germany whether in any case he is dealing with a secret hero or with a former mass murderer. . . . The number of those who are responsible *and* guilty will be relatively small. There are many who share responsibility without any visible proof of guilt. There are many more who have become guilty without being in the least re-sponsible.[6]

This distinction between "guilty" and "responsible" has problematic aspects as far as it concerns a concept of responsibility as "fully," "really" knowing what it is one is doing or with whom one is dealing in situations which, by their very nature, present serious impediments to such knowl-edge. What does, what can, "guilty" mean in this context? It is, indeed, an extraordinarily difficult question, both for the person who has to judge and for the person who is to be judged. Just how difficult it is, is clearly demonstrated in Jaspers' important, though in many ways inconclusive, too loosely constructed essay *The Question of German Guilt*,[7] which was influenced to a degree by Arendt's article, but avoided, on the whole, posing the question of German guilt in political terms.[8] In Jaspers' scheme the concept of responsibility as full consciousness of one's acts is removed explicitly and exclusively to the domain of "moral guilt," which he distinguishes clearly from "criminal guilt," "political guilt," and "meta-physical guilt." Criminal guilt is for him purely legal guilt, a violation of unequivocal laws, and jurisdiction lies with the courts. Political guilt in-volves at least (passive) co-responsibility in the case of every citizen of a state; each has to "bear the consequences for the deeds of the state under whose order" he lives. "Everybody is co-responsible for the way in which he is governed." Jurisdiction is with the "power and the will of the victor, in both domestic and foreign politics. Success decides." Moral guilt ap-plies to the individual who is morally responsible for all, including the execution of military and political orders, and for whom, by virtue of such responsibility (which is central to his individual existence), it "is never simply true that 'orders are orders.'" There may be mitigating circum-stances, but every deed remains "subject to moral judgment"; jurisdiction is "with my conscience, and in communication with my friends and inti-mates who are lovingly concerned about my soul." Metaphysical guilt, finally, concerns the "solidarity among men as human beings which makes each co-responsible for every wrong and every injustice in the world, especially for crimes committed in his presence or with his knowledge. . . . If I was present at the murder of others without risking my life to prevent it, I would feel guilty in a way not adequately conceivable either legally, politically or morally." In contrast to moral guilt in Jaspers' sense, metaphysical guilt seems to extend a priori beyond the capability and therefore the culpability of the individual:

> That somewhere among men the unconditioned prevails—the capacity to live only together or not at all, if crimes are committed against the one or the other, or if physical living requirements have to be shared—therein consists the substance of their being. But that this does not extend to the solidarity of all men, nor to that of fellow-citizens or even of smaller groups, but remains confined to the closest human ties—therein lies the guilt of us all. Jurisdiction lies with God alone.[9]

The attempt to clarify the question of political guilt was highly important to Arendt, but she was wary of the notion of a collective German co-responsibility if it was to be used in support of the verdict of a collective "guilty." The question of guilt, in her view, needed to be put clearly and concretely so that the issue of responsibility could be discussed in terms that would have some bearing on concrete projections for a better political future. Categories of moral and metaphysical guilt as separated from political guilt did not interest her, for she worked with a concept of the political which includes the question of personal moral responsibility.

It is true that the issue of a general human solidarity was very much Arendt's concern, especially in situations in which "crimes against humanity" had to be judged. But she did not think useful the apodictic declaration of a collective metaphysical guilt, which implies—as Jaspers indeed suggested—an a priori collective inability to judge and act from a position of shared humanity. One would be dealing, then, with a concept of original sin which, if acknowledged, could excuse one from acknowledging the need to change and from trying to act accordingly. In this painful and extraordinarily difficult, entangled moral political situation, too, Arendt was centrally interested in using its potential for political education. It was important to her to examine and judge the possible criteria for judging in order not to pass judgment too promptly, too exclusively, and too irrevocably. She anticipated correctly the great temptation on the part of the rest of the world to pass judgment on Germans indiscriminately, and the even greater temptation on the part of Germans to escape or reject such judgment. But both indiscriminate judgment, which rejects out of hand all attempts at explanation as nothing but irresponsible excuses, and indiscriminate avoidance of being judged, which denies out of hand all responsibility for what has happened, would only contribute to an even greater obfuscation of culturally central issues.

o   2   o

Arendt's examination of German guilt deals with the difficult question of responsibility in situations that were often physically and emotionally extreme, culturally unprecedented, and (therefore) morally perplexing. Avoiding a discussion of these difficulties leads to the ease with which the judgment "guilty" is both passed and avoided. However, these difficulties are by no means easy to deal with, as is richly documented in the literature on the legal and moral questions raised by the concept of war crimes in modern warfare. Though the situations discussed and judged in this context are less entangled than many of the deeds constituting German crimes against humanity, they can still help us focus on the most important issues. They tend to be the most elusive, too, because they have to do with knowledge, intention, and decision as components of the deed rather than the fact of the deed. The question of culpability as a serious liability where it concerns the violation of internationally agreed-on laws of war "ought not attach unless the actor had a certain conception of what he was doing—unless he knew or should have known that what he was doing was wrong." This statement is self-evident if we understand the body of laws of war as being essentially related to legal systems in democratic societies. But as Richard A. Wasserstrom points out in his "Conduct and Responsibility in War," we should not carry this narrowly legal analogy too far:

> The principle that the actor must know that what he is doing is wrong can be the principle that the actor must know that what he is doing is legally wrong—that it is forbidden by the legal system. Or it can be the very different principle that the actor must know that what he was doing is morally wrong—that he is doing what one who is concerned to be moral ought surely not do.[10]

The cultural assumption has been that soldiering does not annihilate such concern, as Francis Lieber stated in his 1863 army regulations: "Men who take up arms against one another in public war do not cease on this account to be moral beings, responsible to one another and to God."[11]

But how can such concern, such responsibility, be measured,

counted on, or even expected? Still, the question of German guilt cannot be asked without asking about this concern; it has to be considered in the judgment of the deed. In the attempt to do so, Arendt came to develop her provocative and controversial concept of totalitarianism and her (unfortunately misnamed) concept of "a banality of evil"—a specifically modern cultural obscurity concerning the question of what is immoral. Under Nazi totalitarian rule, Germany's legal system had become so perverted that conforming to the laws of the land was synonymous with immoral behavior. There is, in this situation of enforced totalitarian solidarity of the *Volk*, a certain structural analogy to the situation of (total) war, when all judgment of behavior is subjected to the measure of military necessity in the interest of group survival. Here, too, normal standards of civilized behavior are "inverted"; even the most "humane" (in intention) laws of war as international agreements meant to regulate behavior in the extraordinary situation of war clearly contradict what is approved as decent, moral social behavior in peacetime. These laws are also—and for much same reason—on a very basic level imprecise and confusing.[12] Modern warfare can undermine to an extraordinary degree the capacity to make moral judgments—that is, to measure the interpretive flexibility of "military necessity" against the firmer rules of acceptable, permissible peacetime behavior:

> If the distinctions between what is obligatory, what is permissible, and what is prohibited appear to rest on no intelligible grounds or persuasive principles, if one is encouraged in war to neglect as morally uninteresting many of those distinctions which in any other context are of utmost moral importance, and if one has no reasonable assurance (as one cannot in time of war) that others will behave with a careful regard for the moral point of view, then it is not surprising that persons lose interest in and concern for even the minimum demands of morality. They are somewhat excusable even when they do terrible things, because war has, in some important ways, the very strong tendency to make a kind of psychopathic view of matters appear reasonable.[13]

Wasserstrom is explicitly not interested in finding excuses for soldiers who do things that are morally impermissible though they may be legal in terms of a possible interpretation of the laws of war. He is interested, rather, in understanding how soldiers came to behave the way they did in certain situations. This leads him to point out certain difficulties involved in judging and passing judgment on such behavior—namely, "that the illegal would be confused with the impermissible and the legal with the permissible."[14] What seems impermissible and therefore illegal to the observer and judge who looks from the outside at the moral corruption of combat engendered, too, by the confusion and lack of consistency regarding the laws of war, could have been legal in terms of the possible interpretation of the laws of war and would, then, have seemed permissible to the soldier.[15]

The difficulties of judging apply also to the soldier's attempts to justify—rather than excuse[16]—his action, especially the action of a soldier of subordinate rank who has been found in violation of the laws even though he thought that he could not, in principle, be in violation, because he had done nothing but obey an order.[17] To obey an order without questioning is part of the overruling principle of military necessity with regard to group preservation to which these laws defer and the violation of which would have meant, in many cases, going against the instinct of self-preservation—an act which requires an independent (that is, absolute rather than relative) moral strength that cannot reasonably be expected. However, from the victor's perspective, military necessity is not an argument to be used by the defeated opponent who waged war aggressively and, at least on the eastern front, with an unprecedented disregard for minimally civilized standards. To follow an order that, though legal in terms of a possible interpretation of the laws of war in the situation in which the soldier acted, leads to acts that in a different situation would appear impermissible and therefore illegal, can in itself be considered an illegal act—regardless of the consequences for the soldier of a refusal to follow that order.

More important to this refusal to accept the defense of having obeyed an order is the old distinction between lawful and unlawful orders, which, though more easily made from the perspective of the victor, has been seen as generally valid:

It is an issue that must be as old as the laws of war themselves, and it emerged in legal guise over three centuries ago when, after the Stuart restoration in 1660, the commander of the guards at the trial and execution of Charles I was put on trial for treason and murder. The officer defended himself on the ground "that all he did was as a soldier, by the command of his superior officer whom he must obey or die," but the court gave him short shrift, saying that "when the command is traitorous, then the obedience to that command is also traitorous."[18]

Under the law of the United States, soldiers of all ranks have been expected to disobey unlawful orders. In 1804 Chief Justice John Marshall declared that a subordinate can refer to a superior's order for justification of his conduct only if the order did not concern a "prohibited act." And, more rigidly, Chief Justice Taney stated in 1851 that no military officer could ever justify an unlawful act "by producing the order of his superior."[19] The rule, enacted at the Nuremberg trial, that under some circumstances military orders should be disobeyed, then, was by no means unprecedented. However, it is true that there are difficulties with this rule, one being the already touched-on question of military necessity,[20] another one being the question of knowledge.[21] The earliest statement of a general governing rule concerning disobedience of unlawful orders made by the military—in contrast to the judiciary—is found in Article 47 of the 1872 German Military Penal Code, which also contains an explicit reference to the fact and condition of knowledge:

> If execution of an order given in line of duty violates a statute of the penal code, the superior giving the order is alone responsible. However, the subordinate obeying the order is liable to punishment as an accomplice if . . . he knew that the order involved an act the commission of which constituted a civil or military crime or offense.[22]

The 1914 British and American manuals explicitly did not assign liability in those cases in which violations of laws of war were committed under orders of the respective "governments" or "commanders." Taylor points out that these provisions raised questions as to whether anyone could ever be held liable if the commanders were very high up in the chain of command, and that consequently military law in Britain and the United States was in a state of confusion at the outbreak of World War II.[23] The 1944 revision of the British manual on this question adopted the principle of the German law of 1872, though the language was more conditional. The 1944 American revision, on the other hand, did not provide any guiding principle.[24] Neither manual dealt with the issue of knowledge or (less surprisingly) with the question of fear.

Where the question of German guilt was posed mainly in terms of war crimes,[25] it did not, in most cases, concern the German as a subordinate (including an officer) in the field; rather, it pertained to military leaders who could, presumably, have disobeyed without imminently endangering their lives in modifying the orders they gave and expected to be followed. Because these leaders were not immersed in the immediate confusion of combat, they should have been better prepared to distinguish between the morally permissible and impermissible. Where the question of guilt was posed explicitly in terms of crimes against humanity, it concerned the German as a subordinate of the criminal Hitler regime. And though distinctions—very important distinctions—were made between political leaders and followers in terms of punishment, the question of German guilt was indeed, as Arendt feared it would be, posed in general, comprehensive, collective terms. Followers of a criminal regime could not expect to be able to use as justification or defense their having done just that: followed/obeyed orders. Because the civilian is not ordinarily involved with the literal connection between the hierarchy of orders and group and individual survival, he is expected to use his judgment as to the kind of order he follows—quite apart from the fact that he is seen as co-responsible in bringing the criminal regime to power. On the other hand, there is the situation of a totalitarian regime which from the beginning had stressed, in very literal, physical terms, the ideological importance of total solidarity to an allegedly beleaguered community,[26] and it is arguable that here the distinction between civilian and soldier is in certain important ways obscured. This was even more true once total war had been declared and the civilians' daily experience, too, began to be determined by total warfare.[27]

o   3   o

Arendt also posed the question of German guilt in terms of crimes against humanity when she used the term *war criminals*. But her argument concerning the nature of this guilt and the possibility of judgment touched on the issues of morality and responsibility in the extreme situation of a totalitarian regime, which in some important ways refracts dilemmas experienced in front-line and combat situations. Distinguishing between some individuals' co-responsibility for the Nazis' rise to power but lack of active, conscious involvement in Nazi crimes, it did not seem difficult to Arendt to conclude that in contrast to the Nazi leaders, some of their early accomplices and effective aides, certain members of the German and European high society, "truly did not know what they were

doing nor with whom they were dealing." Though very much blamewor-
thy, they were not war criminals.[28] The question of guilt was more difficult
to pose in the case of the mass of German civilians, who, whether know-
ingly or not, made it possible for the criminal regime to function—though
after the war Arendt often strongly criticized the professional elites. They
kept going "that vast machine of administrative mass murder in whose
service not only thousands of persons, nor even scores of thousands of
selected murderers, but a whole people could be and was employed." Prepared by Himmler against defeat, this machine reduced everyone to

> either an executioner, a victim, or an automaton, marching onward
> over the corpses of his comrades—chosen at first out of the various
> storm-troop formations and later from any army unit or other mass
> organization. That everyone, whether or not he is directly active in
> a murder camp, is forced to take part in one way or another in the
> workings of this machine of mass murder—that is the horrible
> thing. For systematic mass murder—the true consequence of all
> race theories and other modern ideologies which preach that might
> is right—strains not only the imagination of human beings, but also
> the framework and categories of our political thought and action.[29]

In the attempt to establish such a framework, the charter provisions
of the International Tribunal at Nuremberg distinguished between (1)
"Crimes against peace," (2) "War crimes," and (3) "Crimes against humanity," defining the latter as:

> Namely, murder, extermination, enslavement, deportation, and
> other inhumane acts committed against any civilian population, be-
> fore or during the war, or persecutions on political, racial, or reli-
> gious grounds in execution of or in connection with any crime
> within the jurisdiction of the Tribunal, whether or not in violation
> of the domestic law of the country where perpetrated.[30]

Arendt wrote "Organized Guilt and Universal Responsibility" when
World War II was not yet quite over. But she foresaw very clearly the
victors' refusal to make allowances for an alleged legality—under the circumstances of warfare—of deeds which after the lost war they judged
impermissible, including the forced execution of orders leading to such
deeds. She also anticipated the profound and general lack of comprehension—of their situation, of the consequences of their deeds—on the part
of the defeated. To illustrate what she thought would be a general German

political-cultural dilemma after the war, she used a dialogue reported by an American correspondent which, characteristically, she declared "worthy of the imagination and creative power of a great poet":

Q. Did you kill people in the camp?
A. Yes.
Q. Did you poison them with gas?
A. Yes.
Q. Did you bury them alive?
A. It sometimes happened.
Q. Were the victims picked from all over Europe?
A. I suppose so.
Q. Did you personally help kill people?
A. Absolutely not. I was only paymaster in the camp.
Q. What did you think of what was going on?
A. It was bad at first but we got used to it.
Q. Do you know the Russians will hang you?
A. (Bursting into tears) Why should they? *What have I done?*[31]

Arendt affirmed the justification of these answers by asking questions of her own: "He had only carried out orders and since when has it been a crime to carry out orders? Since when has it been a virtue to rebel? Since when could one only be decent by welcoming death? What then had he done?" She reminded her readers that Karl Kraus, after World War I, had made Wilhelm II cry out "I did not want this" at the end of *Last Days of Mankind,* and that horribly and comically, this was indeed factually true. After this war, the second world war begun by the Germans, she predicted, there would be a chorus shouting "We did not do this," and horribly that would be true, too.[32] Obeying orders, the Germans had not known that by following them they had committed, or at least contributed to, "acts which both violate unchallenged rules of warfare and outrage the general sentiment of humanity."[33]

"Organized Guilt and Universal Responsibility" contained, in rudimentary form, Arendt's argumentation in *The Origins of Totalitarianism;* moreover, its strategies of presentation illustrated certain important and often-misunderstood intentions of her concept of political analysis and historiography. Readers have reacted most forcefully against them in particular controversial contexts—her critique of political Zionism, for instance, and especially her report on the Eichmann trial. Yet these intentions have indeed informed all of her texts, beginning with the Rahel biography. Political historiography, in Arendt's view, is based on *historein* as historical inquiry in order to tell how it was—that is, to relate human experience of the past.[34] In historiography, knowledge is intimately linked to the telling of stories that depend on "recollection, the repetition in imagination."[35] Such recollection will enable the historiographer as story-teller to focus, in the imagination, on what it was like to live at another time, in another place, in very different cultural-political situations. More than other cultural activities, historiography depends on memory, which includes the other. And, consciously or not, it also gives shape to the remembered past experience of the self in the retrieved experience of the other.[36] Arendt's political historiography is characterized by a peculiarly literal openness of the process of memory—that is, her self-conscious attempt to put herself temporarily in the place of the other. Such temporary and functional merging of experiences serves historical inquiry—to tell what it was like—and has nothing to do with apology, justification, acceptance, or partisanship. This has sometimes, and then painfully, been misunderstood as an eagerness on Arendt's part to distance herself from her own people in situations in which declarations of complete solidarity seemed to be of particular cultural significance, importantly in the case of the Eichmann trial. In her report on this trial, Arendt tried to help her readers understand Eichmann—that is, the quality of his guilt—and for that reason she used a narrative perspective and the device of narrated monologue to show what it had been like to be Eichmann. This approach to *historein* made her vulnerable to accusations that her solidarity was with the Nazi criminal Eichmann rather than the Jewish people. From a certain cultural and temporal distance, such misunderstandings of the intention of her perspectivist narration seem irrational, though they may have been understandable in the situation. She had always acknowledged her Jewishness as a given and had shown nothing but contempt for Eich-mann, yet her report on his trial in Israel was indeed not meant to reaffirm Jewish solidarity. Rather, it was precisely such unquestioned solidarity which seemed to her an impediment to the understanding of the quality of Eichmann's guilt, because she wished the quality of the judgment of Eichmann to fit his crime, which in her view had been, above all, a crime against humanity.[37]

In 1945 Arendt feared that there would be "no political method" for dealing with German mass murder, mass crime, unless all Germans were eradicated, which would only have meant the final, complete victory of Nazi ideology. Hitler and other Nazi leaders had certainly seen such total destruction as the fitting end for a people who, drawn into the crime against humanity, had not shown themselves sufficiently strong to base their self-preservation on active, consciously affirmative, and perpetual participation in this crime.[38] There was no political method because there was no way of making distinctions on which judging could be based: "Where all are guilty, nobody in the last analysis can be judged," Arendt argued. This argument does not imply that where all are guilty, nobody is guilty. The implication is, rather, that in a situation in which all are guilty, there cannot be the consciousness of guilt without which there is no responsibility[39] and therefore no sense of justice and right: *What have I done?* I just obeyed the orders of my lawful superiors. How can I be punished for that? For Arendt, the question "What have I done?" is not as horribly silly and automatically self-indicting as it has often been perceived to be. It is, rather, a question deserving a considered, responsible answer; it is justified, though not to be used as a justification. But the many who made possible the crimes against humanity without being conscious of, without understanding, their participation and contribution cannot be answered unless the question of their guilt is seen in the context of the "domestic law of the country"—the situation created by a totalitarian regime—where these crimes were perpetrated. The origin of Arendt's inquiry into the genesis and nature of totalitarianism, the source for "organized guilt," was the question "What have I done?"

○ 4 ○

The crimes against humanity perpetrated by the Nazi regime with the help, active or passive, of the German people may have exploded the frame of political thought, but they have remained a challenge to the understanding of how they could have happened. In her 1953 essay "Understanding and Politics," Arendt distinguishes "correct information and scientific knowledge" from understanding as a

> complicated process which never produces unequivocal results. It is an unending activity by which, in constant change and variation, we come to terms with, reconcile ourselves to reality, that is, try to be at home in the world.[40]

The concept of reconciliation with reality as a challenge to accept things as they are now is central to Arendt's political thought, and so is her distinction between understanding and forgiving. One does well to keep in mind that her usage of these concepts is decidedly not psycholog-

ical, and especially in the case of forgiving, her description is too limiting.
Forgiving, though sometimes linked with understanding, is neither its
condition nor its consequence, and it is, in her view, "perhaps the boldest
of human actions" in its attempt to "undo" the other's action. For Arendt,
the importance of forgiving lies precisely in its conquest, so to speak, of
inexorable chronological time: it means to take back the event in the
imagination, to rewind the act, as it were, and thus prepare for "making
a new beginning where everything seemed to have come to an end." The
act of forgiving, a single, (too) clearly defined act, signifies the rejection
of inevitability, of fatedness, where human interaction is concerned. In
contrast, understanding as an "unending activity" makes possible the individual's coming to terms with her strangeness in this world:

> Understanding begins with birth and ends with death. To the ex-
> tent that the rise of totalitarian governments is the central event of
> our world, to understand totalitarianism is not to condone anything,
> but to reconcile ourselves to a world in which these things are pos-
> sible at all.[41]

Not being the same, knowledge and understanding are interrelated,
knowledge being part of the process of understanding. What has been
learned about the reality of the Nazi regime seems to defy understanding
in the conventional sense of the word. Arendt pointed to the fact that
usage of the term *totalitarianism* "for the purpose of denouncing some
supreme political evil" was quite new in 1953.[42] She was ostensibly
speaking about the contemporary response to the phenomenon as an evil
(almost) transcending human comprehension. But the essay about the
connection between understanding and politics was in effect a guide to a
better understanding of her attempt, in the 1951 *Origins of Totalitarianism*, to understand the genesis and nature of totalitarian regimes—because she had observed their reality.

More than any other of Arendt's works, *Origins of Totalitarianism*
draws on a wealth of sociopolitical-historical information, precisely because she wanted and needed to understand the present reality—the
aftermath of the Nazi regime[43]—as a process extending into the past and
the future. The new term *totalitarianism* signified a new event, not just a
new term, and it could be understood "only as the end and culmination
of everything that happened before." But the effect of such an understanding of a new event on (political) action is motivation toward the future:
we will proceed "from the changed set of circumstances that the event has

created, that is, treat it as a beginning." Significantly, the perspective of the historian is presented here to include the view of the end as the beginning:

> It is the task of the historian to detect this . . . new [event] with all its implications in any given period and to bring out the full power of its significance. He must know that though his story has a beginning and an end, it occurs within a larger frame, history itself. And History is a story which has many endings but no end. The end in any strict and final sense of the word, could only be the disappearance of man from the earth. For whatever the historian calls an end, the end of a period or a tradition or a whole civilization, is a new beginning for those who are alive. The fallacy of all prophecies of doom lies in the disregard of this simple but fundamental fact.[44]

Arendt always acknowledged that Nazi crimes created situations which have defeated human understanding, as do historians today, half a century after the events. But to ensure the possibility of a new beginning after the catastrophic end, whose importance for her political thought cannot be overestimated,[45] Arendt always insisted that understanding had to precede judgment of the crimes perpetrated by the Nazi regime with the help, unknowing or knowing, of many Germans. She also made it clear that such understanding required a perspective that was based not on a position of solidarity with one particular group,[46] but rather on "common sense, the political sense par excellence"—later she was to refer to it as *sensus communis*[47]—because it sustains the "common realm *between* men."[48] She came to stress so strongly the importance of communality for political-historical understanding because under the rule of totalitarian terror[49] both common sense and the common realm between men were destroyed and their experience of such destruction was rendered mute. The often-remarked-on passionate eloquence in Arendt's descriptions of the silencing, freezing, shrinking effects of totalitarian terror was put in the service of understanding and articulating how they were experienced:

> By pressing men against each other, total terror destroys the space between them; compared to the condition within its iron band, even the desert of tyranny, insofar as it is still some kind of space, appears like a guarantee of freedom. Totalitarian government does not just curtail liberties or abolish essential freedoms; nor does it, at least to our limited knowledge, succeed in eradicating the love for freedom from the hearts of man. It destroys the one essential prerequisite of

all freedom which is simply the capacity of motion which cannot exist without space.[50]

Common sense as the "political sense par excellence" cannot exist even in rudimentary form under the conditions of totalitarian terror. Allowed to develop, it would permit the space and motion for a critical community in which it is possible to put oneself judiciously in the place of others and judiciously let others speak in their own voices—no matter how disturbing or alien. Speaking from such a position, the political historian as witness[51] to the complexities of others' experiences, too, would be able to ask disturbing questions about guilt and responsibility without being misunderstood as condoning or apologizing for the crime.[52] In "Understanding and Politics," Arendt justified her own approach to the entangled problems of German guilt by stressing common sense, common interests, as conditions which nurture understanding, and referring, by implication, to her analysis of the effects of their absence in *The Origins of Totalitarianism*. As a political historian responsible to a critical community, she had allowed passive contributors to the Nazi crimes against humanity to speak in their own desperate and ineffective voices: What have I done? Her answer had been that, on their own terms, as subjects of the Nazi regime of organized terror, they had indeed done nothing. Judged on the terms of others who had no share in their experience, they had done a great deal. But in order to achieve a judgment to fit the crime, these terms had to be mediated. There had to be an attempt to understand the reality of their experience—namely, the conditions under which they acted.

The achievement of "Organized Guilt and Universal Responsibility," Arendt's first attempt at dealing with these painfully entangled questions, lay in her accepting the challenge of putting herself in the place of persons who were so totally alien to her in almost every respect. In spite of their distance, she allowed them, too, their own voices, and was willing to begin searching for answers to the questions these voices posed. But because she was interested in their political meanings, she was reticent about penetrating and making accessible the psychological, the private, dimension of these persons' experiences under totalitarian rule. In her *Origins of Totalitarianism*, published six years later, she told the most provocatively complete interlinked stories of anti-Semitism, imperialism, and totalitarianism, yet she allowed the answers to retain contradictions and lacunae, and to remain incomplete.

Arendt did not show contempt for the subjects of totalitarian rule, but she also did not show sympathy for their predicament; rather, she explained why and how it had happened to them. Part of the reason was to be found in the economically desperate situation at the end of the Weimar Republic and in the cultural nature of the average German. It was, in Arendt's words, the "satanic genius" of the arch-bourgeois Himmler which led him to discover that responsible family men were literally willing to do anything when the bare existence of their families was threatened, provided they should not be held responsible for their acts.

> Thus that very person, the average German, whom the Nazis not-withstanding years of the most furious propaganda could not induce to kill a Jew on his own account (not even when they made it quite clear that such a murder would go unpunished) now serves the machine of destruction without opposition. In contrast to the earlier units of the SS men and Gestapo, Himmler's over-all organization relies not on fanatics, nor on congenital murderers, nor on sadists; it relies entirely upon the normality of jobholders and family-men.[53]

Chaotic[54] economic conditions fostered this "modern type of man" with whom one could do anything, who was "the exact opposite of the 'citoyen'"—namely, the "bourgeois." But though this bourgeois, with his vulnerability to totalitarian rule, was a phenomenon that had resulted from modern European developments, Arendt pointed out the special role played by German history and culture—namely, the absence, in Germany, of a developed political sphere. This absence was responsible for the emphasis on "private life and private calculations"; for the substitution of chauvinism, the opposite of loyalty and courage, for patriotism; for stressing solidarity rather than critical community—in short (though she does not use the term here), for the negative aspects of assimilation to the larger, dominant group. Still, she insisted, this "mob-man" was a dangerous international phenomenon rather than a purely German one, and for this reason, too, needed to be studied.[55]

Arendt was to trace the genesis of this "mob-man" or "mass man" in *The Origins of Totalitarianism*. But the question "What have I done?" was not laid to rest in that exhaustive study. Rather, it showed her that for the mass of ordinary people caught up in the destructive mechanics of totalitarian rule, the question had to be restated: "What have I not done? What have I failed to do?" The answers to these questions were given most fully in her 1958 *The Human Condition*, and in works of the sixties like *On Revolution* (1963) and "Civil Disobedience" (1970). The direction these answers were to take was suggested at the end of her early essay "Organized Guilt and Universal Responsibility," and it indicated the symbiosis of utopianism and realism which had been characteristic of her concept of the political: If, in 1945, Germans felt ashamed of being Germans, she felt ashamed of being human. "This elemental shame, which many people of the most various nationalities share with one another today, is what finally is left of our sense of international solidarity, and it has not yet found an adequate political expression." [56]

Arendt never invoked the idea of humanity lightly. It meant for her the political obligation of a *general* responsibility, which is different, in kind, from the nonpolitical, individual shame at being human. If the idea of humanity is inclusive, it is so, too, in terms of guilt. Not to assign a monopoly of guilt to one people would signal an important step in the direction of a future goal of nonimperialistic, nonracist policies, because it would indicate a more realistic acknowledgment of "how great a burden mankind is for man"[57]—how difficult it is for many men and women in many situations to act as persons whose concern it is to be moral. George Kateb, in his excellent study of politics, conscience, and evil in Arendt's work, does not fully understand the utopian thrust and scope of her concept of the political when he excludes from it the dimension of morality. "Arendt's exploration of the evil of totalitarianism," he says,

> does not lead her to look for refuge in a public realm where the moral opposites of totalitarianism would reign. To the contrary, she is eager to conceptualize a realm that either is not charged with moral purposes (politics as imagined in the light of the polis) or is made moral only from an indissociable connection to a political artifice, a constitution (modern politics).[58]

This is precisely what Arendt had learned from her experience of the Nazi regime. The paymaster's case had been an extreme one, as was the case of totalitarian rule in modern politics. It had been impossibly difficult for the bourgeois family man, whose guilt was organized by a totalitarian rule of terror, to act responsibly—that is, in this instance, to question authority. Was it, then, impossible to declare him guilty? But was it possible to declare him innocent? Arendt had argued from the beginning the very great difficulties involved in separating clearly the really innocent from the not really innocent and not really guilty. She focused, instead, on the political meaning of the observed fact that for an overwhelming majority of ordinary people, individual responsibility can be expected only in a cultural environment of general responsibility. In the notable and, in certain situations, near-total absence of that general sense of "fundamental standards of morality" in support of a shared humanity, crimes against it have been committed by many anonymous common men rather than by easily distinguishable socio- and psychopathic monsters. They may not be guiltless; but the quality of their guilt has too often eluded a fitting, completing judgment.

To understand is not to condone anything; it is "to reconcile ourselves to a world in which these things are possible."[59] In "Organized Guilt and Universal Responsibility" and *The Origins of Totalitarianism*, Arendt tried to do just that. Yet, such reconciliation did not mean acceptance. In its inconsolableness and intensity, Arendt's description of totalitarian rule brought about and supported by the common inability to act responsibly cries out for radical change of the political-cultural environment so that men and women might act differently. Too optimistically, as she herself later realized, she expected dramatic changes for the better, once the Germans were liberated from the rule of terror. In her analysis "The Aftermath of Nazi Rule," published in 1950 in *Commentary*, she showed her intense disappointment with what she had seen and heard in Germany during her six-month European visit—she represented Jewish Cultural Reconstruction from August 1949 to March 1950.[60] The essay contains a harsh critique of the Germans for their attempts at escaping from the reality of the destruction they had wrought, moral and physical; their too easy acceptance of the profound rupture of their (high) culture; their lack of community and communication; and the isolation of the mass of individuals who were frantically constructing a new physical, but not a new moral, environment. And even worse, in her view, was their rapid reestablishment of the old elites. It was out of deep frustration that she began her report on Germany with a juxtaposition of (collective) guilt and the near-total destruction of a thousand of years of cultural achievements:

> In less than six years Germany laid waste the moral structure of Western society, committing crimes that nobody would have believed possible, while her conquerors buried in rubble the visible marks of more than a thousand years of German history.[61]

And she ended the report with this prognosis:

The German example shows that help from the outside is not likely to set free the indigenous forces of self-help, and that totalitarian rule is something more than merely the worst kind of tyranny. Totalitarianism kills the roots.[62]

Arendt's American biographer, Young-Bruehl, did not understand the profound bitterness of her subject's disappointment:

Arendt wrote with compassion about the Germans' inability either to face the reality of the destruction of their country or to think about the events that brought it about, but she underestimated how much, be it ever so precarious, can be reconstructed without new roots. The economic miracle of postwar Germany lay ahead.[63]

Indeed, Arendt was alarmed precisely by the foreshadowing of that economic miracle in the still-fragmentary reconstruction and ruins of Germany. Together with Germany's rearmament following Adenauer's controversial ratification of the European Defense Community treaty in 1952, the economic miracle would put a premature seal on a painful past that had not been sufficiently understood and reflected upon. There was in Arendt's analysis little if any "compassion" or even empathy with the Germans' situation. She noted a "general lack of emotion," an "apparent heartlessness, sometimes covered up with cheap sentimentality"—symptoms of "a deep-rooted, stubborn, and at times vicious refusal to face and come to terms with what really happened."[64] Such an escape from reality was an escape from responsibility for their past *and* their future.

Characteristically (and under the circumstances rather harshly), Arendt even pointed out the cheapness of much of the reconstruction, the incipient consumerism.[65] In Germany, she generalized, people felt less sadness about the extraordinarily severe destruction of their cultural treasures than did people in France and England about the loss of relatively few landmarks. Wanting to be modern and forward-looking at all costs, denying its continuity with, its responsibility to, its past, Germany was heavily mortgaging its future. With all the craving for the new, there was no new beginning.

Arendt's analysis of the developments toward social and political normalization in postwar Germany seemed to show relatively little willingness to understand the difficulties faced in the processes of cultural witnessing and cultural memory. But the often-invoked German "inability to mourn"[66] had been a very serious cultural problem, and indeed, as Arendt noted, was not helped much by social-political developments in Germany after 1948. Arendt, looking at this Germany, seemed oddly unsure of her judgment, though sure of her verdict. Curiously, in the general moral confusion, she singled out for praise Ernst Juenger's war diaries, which

> offer perhaps the best and most honest evidence of the tremendous difficulties the individual encounters in keeping himself and his standards of truth and morality intact in a world where truth and morality have lost all visible expression. Despite the undeniable influence of Juenger's earlier writings on certain members of the Nazi intelligentsia, he was an active anti-Nazi from the first to the last day of the regime, proving that the somewhat oldfashioned notion of honor, once current in the Prussian officer corps, was quite sufficient for individual resistance.[67]

Juenger, whose anti-Nazi stance (not to mention activities) are greatly exaggerated here, and whose postwar texts show a distinct continuity rather than break with his prewar texts,[68] seems indeed an ill-considered choice. Arendt was groping for some sort of moral standard in a Germany that seemed to her changed beyond recognition, as if lobotomized into a new, terrible innocence through the trauma of moral and physical destruction. Germany's "rebirth," *Erneuerung,* signifying its moving toward an in many ways successfully equitable modern democracy, did not correspond to Arendt's more radically healing vision of a German new beginning born out of a full recognition of the meanings of the old ending. She wrote explicitly about such new beginnings in *The Human Condition,* which followed *The Origins of Totalitarianism,* and in *On Revolution,* which was published the same year as the book version of her report on the Eichmann trial. Here, in the most misunderstood and most provocatively utopian of her books, she brought the question of understanding German guilt to bear on the question of Israel's responsibility toward the Jewish people's past and future.

o   5   o

How could post–World War II Germany have been less disappointing to Arendt? The concept of a German collective guilt was and has been as pervasive as it is abstract; for this reason, too, popular fascination with the Nazi leadership has been great. The number of active participants in Nazi crimes who were actually tried and sentenced was comparatively very small.[69] The Nuremberg psychologist Gilbert reports that after viewing an American documentary film on Nazi concentration camps, Speer, asked about his reactions, said that he "was all the more resolved to acknowledge a collective responsibility of the party leadership and absolve the German people of the guilt."[70] But Hans Fritzsche, Chief of German Broadcasting, who while viewing the film "really seem[ed] in agony"[71] and who got more and more desperate over the evidence as the trial[72] progressed, complained to Gilbert that even if some Nazi leaders were partially exonerated,

> "Germany is *not* exonerated. It is a chain of partial responsibility that extended into every sphere of German government.—I just cannot stand it any longer." He mentioned that not one of the defendants had had the courage to come out and put the blame where it properly belongs—on Hitler.[73]

In its simplicity, Fritzsche's reaction—he was used to treating the concept of responsibility as a many-sided interpretive abstraction—proved to be common: all good things had come from the charismatic leader,[74] and now that they had turned bad, they could be redirected against him. Blaming Hitler would exonerate the people, including Fritzsche, and yet the need to blame Hitler would also indicate the feeling that the people were not, could not really be, exonerated. The chief American prosecutor at Nuremberg, Justice Robert H. Jackson, made it clear in his opening speech that the intent of the tribunal was not to incriminate the whole German people, who had not in their majority voted for the Nazi party. And indeed, the German people themselves were not formally indicted.[75] They did, of course contribute in large numbers:

> A total of 80,000 technicians of slaughter had been involved in the extermination process, it was calculated, but to make their operations possible in the wide reaches of the empire of the Great German Reich, a well-trained bureaucracy and a superb army had been required too, as well as the cooperation, willing and unwilling, of millions of people in Germany and the occupied territories.[76]

Mass murder is not new in history, but such a bureaucratic, well-functioning mass-murder machine—*sine ira et studio*, adds one scholar to emphasize the disturbing singularity of the Holocaust[77]—is indeed something new. The Nazi state was distinguished from other totalitarian systems by the "efficiency of its inversion of every value"; the "efficiency of the process of extermination—its careful records, the turning of science and technology to pseudoresearch and inflicting horrors—was unique."[78] And it was this always-remarked-upon combination of bureaucratic competence and horror, the smoothly organized surrealistic brutality, which claimed the shadowy presence of the German people in the deeds done in their name, albeit in most cases without their conscious knowledge.[79]

The evidence itself, as it was brought to the first Nuremberg trial, was perceived as a kind of collective indictment, regardless of the individuals' manner of participation. Testimony to the 1943 razing of the Warsaw ghetto made one of the defense lawyers speak of the "indelible besmirching of the German name." The former governor general of Poland, Hans Frank, commented on the evidence accumulated in the trial, that a thousand years would not erase "this guilt of Germany." There was the sense, and not only on the part of the defendants at this first trial, that they had all awakened from a fantastic dream. The reaction of the defendants has been recorded by several observers as disbelief and horror: "They confessed and squirmed and alternately blamed themselves and even more readily the men and creeds they had served."[80] Photos documenting the liberation of the concentration camps show the "German population" filing by the trenchlike graves they had had to dig for the victims, or standing in front of the piles of bodies that were kept around longer than hygienically advisable for the sake of documentation. They sullenly, dutifully look, unseeing, unbelieving. Only the children seem to be shocked, retreating; women, adolescents, and some old men move slowly or stand as they have been told to, turned toward the horrible sight, enveloped in the unique, horrible stench, which the GI's found defied description.[81] The liberators, enraged by what they had had to see, hear, and smell, wanted the Germans to witness the horrors they had helped create. But these faces show us that, unlike punishment, witnessing cannot be imposed. Even if reluctant or unwilling, it has to be, to a certain degree, the spontaneous response of the survivor to the voicelessness of the dead. The survivor has to be willing to assume responsibility for that voicelessness.

It is this responsibility which is central to Arendt's approach to the question of German guilt and which she had hoped to find in postwar Germany. It was not that Germans on the whole rejected the idea that they, as a people, had somehow shared in the Nazi crimes. Davidson points out quite rightly that outside the courts of law, where the question of collective guilt was avoided, many Germans felt it a burden they had somehow to cope with. Christians met "in solemn sessions to confess their responsibility for what had happened." Collective guilt, though mostly rejected by the victors, "clung to millions of Germans despite the philosophical and historical demonstrations that it could scarcely exist."[82] Jaspers, writing on the "Differentiation of German Guilt," introduced his discussion of the first Nuremberg trial with the psychologically shrewd move of distinguishing the situation after World War II from that after World War I. He also presented the victors' court, "something entirely new in world history,"[83] as potentially very helpful for the Germans' attempts to come to terms with their recent past. Pointing out that "individual, criminally accused Germans," all leaders of the Nazi regime, were on trial, he quoted Justice Jackson: "We do not intend to accuse the whole German people. . . . Indeed the Germans—as much as the outside world—have an account to settle with the defendants."[84]

Intent on helping his readers face the issue of moral responsibility, Jaspers, discussing the question of German guilt, put himself in the place of the many Germans whose position vis-à-vis the Nazi regime had not been as unambiguous as his, and he explicitly made allowances for experiences of danger and destruction which he personally had not had. Moreover, he did so in full awareness of the fact that such a temporary shifting of position would mean a learning process for him, too. Even if he had not participated in most of the evasions and illusions of Germans living under the Hitler regime, the German question was his question too, and he identified with the fall of Germany—into the hands of the Nazis, into the chaos of mass destruction—as a cultural catastrophe. His perspective on this catastrophe had an immediacy which Arendt's did not, and it provoked her to redirect some of her questions. The fact that he did not exclude himself from moral guilt impressed on her even more strongly the difficulty of determining the quality of German guilt.

Jaspers meant for the acceptance of moral guilt to be an important motivation in the, under the circumstances, most necessary search for a common ground in the current situation of "common non-community."[85] His appeal addressed two of the most important conditioning aspects of totalitarian rule which enable the moral inversion to spread: the paralysis of thought through corrupted language, and the destruction or prevention of articulated critical community through the enforced (shouted) silence of collective solidarity. The common ground is the position from which it will be possible to acknowledge that no one is guiltless—this was the most important, much-repeated message of the essay. Yet, perhaps even

more critical for Jaspers was his insistence—realized in his discourse—
on the supreme importance of talking to one another about the immediate
past, and on breaking the twelve-year interregnum of silence.[86] Speaking
about sharing moral guilt, Jaspers made it clear to his readers that he was
speaking *to* them,[87] not *for* them:

> Morally man can condemn only himself, not another—or, if an-
> other, then only in the solidarity of charitable struggle. No one can
> morally judge another. It is only where the other seems to me like
> myself that the closeness reigns which in free communication can
> make a common cause of what finally each does in solitude.[88]

In this by no means ineffective respect for the other's individuality
even where the question of guilt was concerned, Jaspers differed sharply
from Arendt's position. But the cleansing process, as he proposed it, was
in danger of remaining not only too private but also too exclusively German. When he stressed the need to analyze and clarify the question of
German guilt "independent of outside charges, however much we may
hear and use them as questions and mirrors,"[89] he stressed the separateness and inwardness of German guilt. With the (overly) clear distinction
between moral guilt and political liability, Jaspers removed the whole
question of German guilt into the personal sphere, where it became in
many ways a less disturbing psychological category. In effect, he shifted
the emphasis from understanding the issue of political responsibility to
healing the minds torn and soiled in the chaotic political sphere.

Also, and more important in the immediate postwar situation, Jaspers worked with a concept of spiritual Germanness which was bound to
defy his efforts at clarification. No doubt he himself felt such an essential
link to his people;[90] and up to a point this fact was useful for his perspective, because it allowed him direct access to the general experience of
cultural confusion and conflictedness. However, he then attempted to
present collective guilt as both inescapable and deeply meaningful: our
spiritual Germanness somehow made us both susceptible to this kind of
regime *and* will now, if acknowledged, enable us to contribute more significantly than other people to the "entire task of renewing human existence from its origin."[91] Such transhistorical redirecting of an important
political cultural issue was in many ways problematic, even though it
seemed to have helped Jaspers' readers to at least approach it. But Jaspers
had remained open to learning processes. The confrontation with Arendt's critical comments in this respect was to have some impact on his

perspective of the German question—as were his comments on her own presentation of the Jewish question.

o 6 o

In November 1945, when Arendt resumed contact with Jaspers, it was apparent that she had been changed, not only by the years spent in exile in France, but also by her experiences in the United States. In fact, reading together Arendt's and Jaspers' letters from the years immediately following the war, one is struck by the older man's relative innocence and optimism—relative, that is, to Arendt's shrewdness and darkly conflicted hope. When Arendt writes about her own loyalty, during all these years of silence, to what Jaspers had taught her, she points to his importance to her as a kind of symbol, a guarantee of enduring cultural continuity in a continuing dialogue—a continuity that she perceived as accommodating the changes she had undergone.

The United States had provided for her the new and extremely important experience of citizenship obtainable without paying the price of assimilation. In her second letter to Jaspers on January 29, 1946, thanking him for his offer to have her write on contemporary postwar issues for the journal *Die Wandlung*, she tried to help him understand that she could do so only as a Jew writing about Jewish questions: the only way for her to go back to Germany was as a Jew. Jaspers' naiveté with respect to this issue is both touching and irritating in its insistence on the surviving continuity of a good Germany, of which Arendt, of course, would be a citizen. He never fully understood the quality of her judgment of the German-Jewish past, or the extent of her sensitivity to the quality of guilt. While she very much needed—as she always acknowledged—continuity in her personal relations, she was able to articulate the profound cultural rupture and yet remain loyal to what was—without positing the fiction of an easily accessible continuity. The flexibility of her historical perspective in the context of the German-Jewish question was informed by her acceptance of change and her insistence on anamnesis, on not forgetting.

Arendt's experience in America, with its (to a European) curious mixture of diversity and conformity, otherness and sameness, and especially its tolerance for the relational and the temporary, had certainly contributed to the development of this "mixed" position. There are no clear distinctions between the alien and the familiar: in (the flux of) time, every alien becomes (more) familiar. Arendt pointed out to Jaspers the American intellectuals' usefully argumentative opposition to the reigning social

conformism, mentioning as an example the welcoming attitude of a Jewish journal to her article "Organized Guilt and Universal Responsibility."

This secular tolerance for temporality made it easier for the American
intellectual to take or leave the perspective of the outsider for a time, depending on the social-political situation—that is, without elevating it into
an existential decision. The U.S. experience, then, supported Arendt's
sense of needing to choose, as an individual Jewish woman, the challenge
to her responsibility of dealing with a painfully difficult complex of questions. The choice was helped by the fact that she was able to speak from
a position informed by distance and solitariness rather than closeness and
solidarity. And it was precisely the fact of speaking from this particular
position of a German Jewess in the United States which helped her
understand how problematic it is to speak about the other's responsibility
in normative terms—especially in the context of those proverbially dark
times. Looking into the past from the distance of another life in another
country, Arendt became more sharply aware of the temporariness of her
historical understanding, that is, of her own historicality.

And from this position she questioned Jaspers' approach to the issue
of German guilt and accepted his questioning of hers. She disagreed, for
instance, with his definition of Nazi politics—that is, the leaders' guilt—
as "criminal." These crimes, she argued, go beyond existing legal definitions and are therefore monstrous and not adequately punishable. But she
was not so much interested in stressing a demonic dimension of this political guilt as she was troubled by the fact that this total, monstrous guilt
of the victimizers is as impossible to deal with as is the innocence of the
victims. No human being, she pointed out to Jaspers, can be as innocent
as were all Jews in front of the gas ovens. In human-political terms a guilt
beyond crime, an innocence beyond kindness or virtue, is meaningless
("man kann nichts damit anfangen"). The Germans would have to carry
the burden of a large number of people who cannot be punished adequately within the confines of conventional legal systems; the Jews would
have to carry the burden of the millions of innocents who make every Jew
today feel like innocence personified.[92]

On the other hand, as Arendt wrote in the same letter, a reinterpre-
tation was needed of Jaspers' concept of metaphysical guilt. She was right
to notice his emphasis, in this concept, on a transcendent, transhistorical
sphere of the "Unbedingtes," where, indeed, no human judge has authority. She, in contrast, wanted to stress, above all, the need to include in the
question of German guilt the question of a general human solidarity. In

his answer to her suggestion, Jaspers objected that in her definition guilt assumed a quality of diabolical greatness ("satanische Groesse") and that in his experience nothing was less true with respect to the Nazis.[93] He was afraid of mythmaking in this respect, he wrote, reminding her that bacteria can be the source of catastrophic epidemics and yet remain just that, bacteria. Counseling sobriety, he asked her to consider the reality of the "events in their banality." Whether or not this passus directly influenced Arendt's choice of the notorious subtitle for her controversial and illuminating report on the Eichmann trial,[94] it certainly affirmed the direction her inquiry into the political-historical reasons for the catastrophic "solution" of the German-Jewish question was taking. In her letter of December 17, 1946 (no. 50), Arendt agreed that she had indeed come close to "satanische Groesse" in her argument, asserting that she very much objected to all myths of terror or horror. In her critique of Jaspers' category, she had sought to articulate the fact, centrally important to her understanding of the meaning of the Holocaust, that this kind of genocide had been an organized attempt to annihilate the concept of man. She had argued, that is, from a position she would develop in *The Origins of Totalitarianism* (the book that established her stature as a political thinker) and present most consistently in her report on the Eichmann trial (the book that created the most painful notoriety and controversy).

The dialogue with Jaspers—a man, a Gentile, a generation older, less decisive in his distinctions, less clear in his judgments—contributed to the genesis of these books, which may turn out to be her most important achievements. It was a dialogue in which both could rely on being asked freely and answered responsibly. In their sharing of a German cultural, but not political, tradition—a distinction that is quintessentially German and that has contributed much to the failure of the German-Jewish symbiosis—they communicated with a particular kind of ease or trust. This, curiously, is a situation that Arendt tended to reconstruct in her models of the political sphere. But whereas these models stressed self-articulation in a critical community of peers, Arendt, in her dialogue with Jaspers, was also helped to develop self-questioning, always a highly important ingredient in the historiographer's perspective, but especially so with respect to the entangled question of German guilt. As her reader, Jaspers praised her for her passion, clarity, and forcefulness, and warned her of possible misunderstandings. This, too, helped Arendt develop a perspective that was sufficiently broad, flexible, and self-questioning to focus her political-historical inquiry sharply, to risk certain misunderstandings, and to speak, as a German Jewess, in her own voice.

In the introduction to her first book published in postwar Germany, *Sechs Essays*,[95] she alerted her readers to the position from which she spoke in a passage which Jaspers, again, found admirable and perhaps too difficult of access for the normal reader in 1948 Germany. She had written all the essays collected in this volume, she said, in full consciousness of the facts of our time and of the fate of Jews in our century. In none of them had she accepted the world created by these facts as necessary and irreversible. German-Jewish and a woman, she had resumed, after the war and the genocide, what she had started with her biography of another German Jewess: in her empathetically critical view of social-political relations as they had and should not have been, the vision of a world as it might have been and therefore might yet become.

◦   7   ◦

For Arendt, the German-Jewish past was over but not completed; moreover, the concept of such completion suggested by the concept of an "uncompleted" past, *unbewaeltigte Vergangenheit*, seemed illusionary from the beginning. Not that she wished to argue from a position of trans-historicality, a position of "we will never know." She did proceed from the assumption that gradually we will indeed know more and understand better. But implicit in her postwar discussion of German guilt was the sense that already the distance to the most recent past was too great; the rupture had been too profound, the temporary absence of thought too total and too alien.[96] There was the danger that questions asked from the other side of that *Zivilisationsbruch* might miss the quality of guilt even if they were accepted as judgment.

What concerned Arendt most in the late forties was the issue of anamnesis. For the living, the voicelessness of the dead[97] meant the challenge to speak responsibly of not forgetting.[98] She came to see that shame—if it is to be a meaningful concept in the context of a general indirect, rather than individual direct, responsibility—could not be limited to Germans, but had to be shared by all humans.

This broadness of perspective can be misunderstood—as can so many arguments where questions of German guilt, responsibility, and shame are concerned. The bitterness, the both heated and awkward publicity, with which the current *Historikerstreit*[99] about the historical singularity of National Socialist genocide has been conducted, is a good case in point. For Arendt it was not a question of admitting or not admitting such singularity, but of understanding events that seemed to transcend human understanding and therefore appeared to be unique. In this perspective, questions of guilt and shame were not to be taken lightly: if they could not be dismissed easily, they also should not be appropriated easily. Jaspers, of course, had taken on the burden of moral guilt in full awareness of its conflicted meanings and had been willing to pay the price for it. In one of his first letters after the war, he wrote to Arendt about his "Germanness" in a way that particularly touched her, because it repeated and thereby affirmed her husband's reaction to the painful dilemma, at the end of the war, of being German:[100] Now that Germany had been destroyed, literally, and to an extent and with a finality that no one had really quite understood yet, Bluecher and Jaspers thought it possible to again be unselfconsciously German.[101] But the book on the question "in what sense are we German," *in welchem Sinne wir Deutsche sind,* which Jaspers was hoping to write out of this experience, was never written— and it is hard to imagine how it could have been. The experience of that fantastic destruction, physical and moral, had been too ambiguous, too overwhelmed by the profound cultural rupture. Jaspers, notwithstanding all his optimism regarding human potential for change and therefore the meaningful continuity of a cultural tradition, could not but be deeply shaken by it.

Arendt was by no means so optimistic about the chances for serious self-questioning in postwar Germany, especially in the case of the academic establishment.[102] She wrote to Jaspers very critically about the thoughtless career opportunism of German professors in general, even if they had not been serious Nazis—and Heidegger's in particular— troubled by the historian Gerhard Ritter's analysis of their role in his "The German Professor in the Third Reich."[103] In her 1946 article "What is Existenz Philosophy?" she stated in strongly critical terms that

> Heidegger's Self is an ideal which has been working mischief in German philosophy and literature since Romanticism. In Heidegger this arrogant passion to will to be a Self has contradicted itself; for never before was it so clear as in his philosophy that this is probably the one being which man cannot be.[104]

In its "absolute egotism," its "radical separation from all its fellows," this concept of the self has to be seen as the polar opposite of the political[105] and of natality. Death, the end of human reality, affirms the absolute *principium individuationis:* "With the experience of death as nothingness I have the chance of devoting myself exclusively to being a Self, and once and for all freeing myself from the surrounding world."[106] The political-historical implications of this philosophy are clear: a particular, politically destructive vulnerability to illusionary, totally affirmative community and charismatic leadership. As Arendt wrote:

> Heidegger has therefore attempted in later lectures to bring in by way of afterthought, such mythologizing confusions as Folk and Earth as a social foundation for his isolated Selves. It is evident that such conceptions can lead one only out of philosophy into some naturalistic superstition. If it is not part of the concept of Man that he inhabits the world with his fellows, then there remains only a mechanical reconciliation by which the atomized self is given a substratum essentially discordant with its own concept. This can only serve to organize the Selves engaged in willing themselves into an Over-self, in order to make a transition from the fundamental guilt, grasped through resoluteness, to action.[107]

Heidegger's *Existenz Philosophy* tends toward a decisionism[108] which rejects the social existence and destroys the temporality and historicality of the self. Arendt had learned to understand the political implications of that position and unambiguously rejected it.[109]

Heidegger's stylization of the modern experience of atomization and isolation into the meaningful singularity and separateness of the self may have appealed to the young Arendt, as it did to many bright young students in Weimar Germany (for instance, Herbert Marcuse). But Arendt had long since come to see it as the symptomatic failure of the German elites to cope with modern social developments. The classless society as a result of the breakdown of the old class system, she explains in *The Origins of Totalitarianism,* only brought to light the apolitical character of the nation-state's populations: membership in a class, with its "limited group obligations and traditional attitudes toward government," had prevented the growth of "a citizenry that felt individually and personally responsible for the rule of the country."[110] Class membership had prevented the growth of a critical, diversified community of values, and thus had contributed to a situation the Nazi movement could exploit. Arendt quotes the Nazi political theorist Reinhard Hoehn, who commented in his *Reichsgemeinschaft und Volksgemeinschaft:* "From the point of view of a folk community, every community of values is destructive."[111] Such community admits inequality at the basis of social order and supports the social (or, in Arendt's scheme, political) nature of identity. In their "self-centered bitterness," both modern elites and mass men were attracted to the idea of folk community, in which inequality and (a troublesome) identity would be eliminated by the merging of all into the one body of the folk. This community did not, however, as Arendt pointed out, establish

> a common bond despite its tendency to extinguish individual differences, because it was based on no common interest, economic, or social, or political. Self-centeredness, therefore, went hand in hand with a decisive weakening of the instinct for self-preservation. Selflessness in the sense that oneself does not matter, the feeling of being expendable, was no longer the expression of individual idealism but a mass phenomenon.[112]

The "desocialized" sense of the individual self and the "decommunalized" concept of society[113] led to a "new terrifying negative solidarity" across the whole political and social spectrum and prepared the field for the attraction of more and more extreme, emotional politics.[114] Of course, the attraction worked differently for the masses, who adored the charismatic leader, and the (intellectual) elites, who not only did not believe in such leadership but had contempt for "genius."[115] The intellectuals, who thought they could use the totalitarian movement, were attracted by its negativity—in relation to the bourgeois world of respectable established order—and its actionism.[116] If this negativity and actionism became the basis of their (negative) value system, it supported rather than kept in check their opportunism, which destroyed the last vestiges of common sense and community. On their unwillingness to assume, as citizens, individual and personal responsibility for the rule of their country was based their modern ability to respond with what has to be called "profound" moral indifference to the fate of their fellow men.[117]

Does this profound moral indifference constitute collective guilt? Even if Arendt did not think this concept useful, her analysis of how the elites and the masses prepared the ground for the reign of terror can be read as an indirect but compelling indictment that allows few if any excuses, much less justifications. Even though she understood how the paymaster in the camp, the lawyer and industrialist at their desks in the city, could have looked the other way, she not only did not condone such moral indifference, she quite clearly expressed her contempt for it. And she did so without allowing them the excuse of having been caught in a situation of totalitarian rule and total war which they had allowed to overcome them. Consequently, she complained to Jaspers about the reactions from Germany to her article "Organized Guilt": people are so happy to be "understood," *die Leute fuehlen sich alle so "verstanden."* No one seemed to have noticed her antipathy against the philistines, *Spiesser.* Most unfortunate, in her view, was the fact that one newspaper had declared her to be "Germany in a beautiful sense."[118]

Jaspers reaffirmed Arendt in her attempts to understand but not be understanding if Germans, faced with the catastrophe they had allowed to happen, were now grasping for excuses.[119] His own approach to the German question was, however, largely informed by diagnostic and therapeutic empathy with the psychological difficulties faced by Germans, who, trying to deal with the fact that they were collectively accused of a uniquely aggressive militarism and anti-Semitism, had ended up resenting the accusers. These difficulties were to be expected, he sensibly told his readers: "Whoever has not yet found himself guilty in spontaneous self-analysis will tend to accuse his accusers."[120] But if they were recognized and explained, they could be overcome. In order to help in this process, Jaspers allowed the post-Nazi German to bring up examples of the unfortunate, unjust, or unhelpful political behavior of the accusers.[121] But he used this therapeutic position to make easier for his readers the acknowledgment that as a nation the Germans alone were guilty of starting the war, even if as individuals they had not wanted it, and of committing unparalleled atrocities against humanity, even if they had not been really aware of it.

Jaspers followed a similar pattern in his discussion of anti-Semitism. He affirmed his readers' opinion that anti-Semitism had never been a popular movement in Germany, that the German population did not willingly cooperate in the Nazi pogroms in Germany, that there had been no spontaneous acts of cruelty against Jews, that the criminally guilty were a "small group (plus an indefinite number of others capable of cooperating under orders)." These assertions were unquestionably unacceptable to some German Jews, but they fit the experience of many Germans whose perspective Jaspers seemed to share. Arguably, this shared perspective gave more authority to another observation, which also fit his audience's experience but was difficult to acknowledge: Even if the mass of the German people had not been actively anti-Semitic, there had been only an occasional, feeble demonstration of resentment of Nazi policies; mostly there had been silence and withdrawal. Jaspers did reassure his readers that they would not have to accept the both unique and collective accusation of being "the evil people, the guilty people as such."[122] Yet his explicit intention in doing so was to better "penetrate the meaning" of German guilt.[123]

Discussing the absence of substantial anti-Semitism in Germany and the national and international failure to recognize the terrorist, murderous nature of the Hitler regime, Jaspers laid himself open to accusations of apologism. It did not matter that he did so in order to support his diagnostic reading of a symptomatic German lack of active responsibility and tendency to blame others; nor that he insisted throughout on "the particular present truth of our own guilt."[124] Ironically, the most easily misunderstood, "incriminating" part of this portion of his argument was probably a statement he quoted from the German version, published in Switzerland in 1945, of Roepke's *Solution of the German Problem:*[125]

> Everyone should realize by now that the Germans were the first victims of the barbaric invasion which swamped them from below, that they were the first to succumb to terror and mass hypnosis, and that whatever had to be suffered later in occupied countries was first inflicted on the Germans themselves—including the worst of fates: to be forced or tricked into serving as tools of further conquest and oppression.[126]

Blumenfeld, for one, was highly critical of Jaspers' argument in *The Question of German Guilt.* He had visited him and upon leaving had been presented with a copy of the German text, he wrote to Arendt in the fall of 1954; it had been Jaspers who had introduced the Jewish question into their conversation. Troubled by Jaspers' gravely distorted view of German anti-Semitism, Blumenfeld charged that Jaspers had used apologetically Arendt's correct assertion that terror had enforced the German people's participation in the leaders' crimes. Jaspers, he complained, "will not understand that Hannah Arendt can explain the question of German guilt in an analysis of the totalitarian regime where a German will have to say: 'Forgive me my guilt.'"[127]

Arendt did not think useful such insistence on collective contrition, because it reintroduced the issue of collective guilt; and she rightly did not think Jaspers' arguments apologetic. But then she was remarkably circumspect about the meanings of anti-Semitism and she appreciated—even if she did not share—Jaspers' optimistically explanatory, therapeutic approach to the German question. Blumenfeld, however, with the sharper perception of ambivalence toward Arendt's revered German Gentile friend, rightly pointed to Jaspers' lack of political-historical realism.[128] Jaspers' making so central the individual acceptance of moral guilt—no matter how much that might have helped a cultural "mourning"[129]—may indeed have prevented rather than encouraged a more rigorous inquiry into its social-political genesis. In contrast, Roepke's *The Solution of the German Problem*, an analysis which Jaspers frequently drew on, is on the one hand most emphatic on the uselessness of a concept like collective guilt;[130] on the other hand, however, it insists strongly on specifying and defining the guilt incurred by certain groups. While only a minority of Germans could claim to have lived up to their responsibility to disassociate themselves from the regime, another, much larger minority, consisting of political, financial, industrial, and civil service groups, had indeed become guilty in specific, concrete terms. And in his own comparatively large group, the intellectuals—"professors, journalists, artists and authors"—Roepke found an unpardonable abdication of responsibility.[131]

Jaspers did not discuss the connection between abdication of responsibility on the part of specific groups and the issue of guilt. The categories "legal responsibility" (which he took over from Roepke), and "criminal guilt" separated those few who were guilty beyond the shadow of a doubt and all those who accepted moral guilt on a personal basis. For Arendt, who sought to understand what had happened, this distinction was not helpful. Yet the dialogue with Jaspers undoubtedly contributed both to her composite perspective on the German question[132] and to her attempt to develop, in *The Origins of Totalitarianism*, a definition of the particular, singular quality of Nazi domination and genocide.

o   8   o

In contrast to Jaspers, Arendt was decidedly not interested in "being understanding"—that is, in anticipating and sorting out the conflicted, often ambivalent, and highly emotional postwar reactions of many Germans to the German question. If they seemed indifferent, she reacted critically, even with frustration, but she did not probe the possible meanings of that attitude. When she put herself in their place temporarily, she focused on the social and political dynamics that had been largely responsible for their situation. She tried to locate herself, that is, in that political situation created by a totalitarian regime which had undermined, or at least made very much more difficult, the development of individual and personal responsibility. There is, in the behavioral analyses of the elites and the masses in *The Origins of Totalitarianism*, often the sense of an inexorable motion toward the nightmare scenarios of totalitarianism, and an exhausted resignation that "this is how it was and, given certain modern developments, it (almost? perhaps?) could not have been otherwise." This sense of futility forms a subtext to her explicit message of political-historical analysis as a warning and as preparation for prevention, even for a new cultural beginning. And yet, this subtext, with its realistic resignation to the limited endurance of human nature, no matter how great its riches, most motivated Arendt to locate the human condition as the good place. Consider the two essays with which she concluded the 1958 edition of *Origins*—the 1953 "Ideology and Terror: A Novel Form of Government" and the 1958 "Totalitarian Imperialism: Reflections on the Hungarian Revolution." [133] In these analyses of ideological power and terror, the space in which the individual would be able to move, and which is denied her under a totalitarian regime, becomes so palpable and desperate an absence that the paradox of the good place has to assert itself to relieve the unbearable tension. Total domination totally remakes historically evolved social reality and therefore radically changes human nature—a change that occurred and that Arendt understood, acknowledged, and could not accept. The provocative, powerful concreteness of her political thought, as well as its controversial thrust, is centered in her vision of possible radical change toward the good or the bad: Against the totalitarian annihilation of the time and space in which the individual's potential might richly unfold, against the real, the acknowledged, the unacceptable changing of humans into shadows and slaves, she needed to pose a political realm as the good place where individual responsibility, freedom, even heroism, were possible—because there they could be nurtured.

Questioning Arendt's total concept of totalitarianism in August 1949, David Riesman commented on the manuscript of *Origins* that her critique of the bourgeois was just as harsh as that of the "elite" and the "mob"—groups which hated the bourgeoisie as much as they hated the Jews. Perhaps, he noted perceptively,

> what leads you to this position is your contempt for the cowardice of too many of the people you describe. It seems to me, however, that you cannot ask of people that they be heroes, but only that they

recognize heroism, and know a little more than they do about what
they are doing.[134]

Arendt knew this very well, and yet in important ways she did ask.
Her own experiences, especially the exile in France, had quite clearly
taught her not to expect or demand too much, and so had Jaspers' discussion of the German question, with its acknowledgment of intellectual
and emotional paralysis during the Nazi regime and enduring postwar
confusion. But asking nevertheless for the possibility of heroism and freedom, she also saw more sharply and concretely than did many of her male
intellectual contemporaries how profoundly ordinary people changed
when this possibility was denied them totally. She understood better, too,
how such change caused the all-pervasive radically apolitical, the inhuman indifference to the fate of their fellow man.

Eric Voegelin, in his partly laudatory and largely—though instructively—misunderstanding review of Origins,[135] took issue precisely with
Arendt's notion of (possible and factual) radical change. He quoted and
agreed with her observation that totalitarian ideologies aim not at "the
transformation of the outside world or the revolutionizing transmutation
of society, but the transformation of human nature itself."[136] This is indeed, he comments,

> the essence of totalitarianism as an immanentist creed movement.
> Totalitarian movements do not intend to remedy social evils by in-
> dustrial changes, but want to create a millennium in the eschatolog-
> ical sense through transformation of human nature itself. The
> Christian faith in transcendental perfection through the grace of
> god has been converted—and perverted—into the idea of imma-
> nent perfection through an act of man.

Arendt has, then, grasped the "spiritual and intellectual breakdown"
caused by totalitarian rule and experimentation. But the conclusions she
has drawn from her observations of such breakdown, which he quotes,
are deeply disturbing, indeed unacceptable to him:

> Human nature as such is at stake, and even though it seems that
> these experiments succeed not in changing man but only in destroy-
> ing him, by creating a society in which the nihilistic banality of
> homo homini lupus is consistently realized, one should bear in mind

the necessary limitations to an experiment which requires global
control in order to show conclusive results.[137]

To think this possible, Voegelin protests vehemently, "is a symptom of the
intellectual breakdown of Western civilization. Arendt, in fact, has
adopted the "immanentist" ideology; her conclusions reflect a "typically
liberal, progressive, pragmatist attitude toward philosophical problems,"
which is itself close to that of totalitarianism:

> The true dividing line in the contemporary crisis does not run be-
> tween liberals and totalitarians, but between the religious and phil-
> osophical transcendentalists on the one side and the liberal and to-
> talitarian immanentist sectarians on the other side.[138]

Voegelin accused Arendt of having produced, from a position of lib-
eralism/totalitarianism, a "nihilistic nightmare" in which there is no place
for "the philosophers of Greece, the prophets of Israel, Christ, not to
mention the Patres and Scholastics."[139] It was as if her realistic, frightened
recognition of the radical dehumanization caused by totalitarian terror
were itself responsible for the nightmare; as if she had not clearly branded
as inhumanly "nihilistic"[140] the attitude, central to the totalitarian belief,
that everything is possible, meaning that everything can be destroyed.[141]
Evidently she had seen more clearly than he the realization of this belief
in the realized superfluity of humans who had become vermin and then
were destroyed.[142] If not as a philosophical concept, but certainly as a
shared reality, the nature of man can be changed radically because it has
been observed to have become so. For Voegelin, such an observation is
sacrilegious, considering the stature of man—that is, Western high culture. For Arendt, such an observation is inevitably real, profoundly sad-
dening, and incomprehensible in terms of cultural norms and expectations.

> It is inherent in our entire philosophical tradition that we cannot
> conceive of a "radical evil." . . . Therefore, we actually have nothing
> to fall back on in order to understand a phenomenon that neverthe-
> less confronts us with its overpowering reality and breaks down all
> standards we know. There is only one thing that seems to be dis-
> cernible: we may say that radical evil has emerged in connection
> with a system in which all men have become equally superflu-
> ous. . . . The danger of the corpse factories and holes of oblivion is
> that today, with populations and homelessness everywhere on the

increase, masses of people are continuously rendered superfluous if we continue to think of our world in utilitarian terms.[143]

Arendt did share with Voegelin an extraordinarily strong (almost religious) belief in the significance of high culture; but she did not think it capable of shielding humans against the imposition of changes that were so radical that their humanity could not be reconstituted. It was not the victims alone who had become superfluous. Their torturers, too, totalitarian ideologues, had believed in their own superfluity, not caring "if they themselves are alive or dead, if they ever lived or never were born."[144] While such an extreme attitude toward individual survival was not literally true for the great majority of National Socialists, the dichotomous tension of survival and destruction at the core of Nazi ideology did produce a notable indifference to self-destruction.[145] Not caring "if they ever lived or never were born"—imposed, finally, on victims and torturers alike—was the most terrible achievement of total domination through terror. Against it, Arendt insisted, in the conclusion of her analysis of totalitarianism, on the possibility of bridging the end and the new beginning:

> But there remains also the truth that every end in history necessarily contains a new beginning; this beginning is the promise, the only "message" which the end can ever produce. Beginning, before it becomes a historical event, is the supreme capacity of man; politically, it is identical with man's freedom. *Initium ut esset homo creatus est*—"that a beginning be made man was created" said Augustine. This beginning is guaranteed by each new birth; it is indeed every man.[146]

This was the message Arendt explored in *The Human Condition* and tested in *On Revolution*. She had found it in the superfluity and final destruction of humans through the rule of totalitarian terror, which could not be safe unless man's great resources—for diversity, plurality, spontaneity, for common interest and natality—had been totally depleted.[147] In her 1953 reply to Voegelin's critique, she stressed both the historical factuality of this loss and the historian's inability to be consoled. She also, in this context, explained her historiographical approach as not a history of totalitarianism but rather an "analysis in terms of history." This distinction is important for a clearer understanding of both the appeal and the controversial nature of this approach. What she said here about historiography in general reveals the particular focus of her specific position:

All historiography is necessarily salvation and frequently justification; it is due to man's fear that he may forget and to his striving for something which is even more than remembrance.[148]

How could she write historically about totalitarianism, "which I did not want to conserve but on the contrary felt engaged to destroy"? As she explained to Voegelin, by giving "a historical account of the elements which crystallized into totalitarianism, this account is followed by an analysis of the elemental structure of totalitarian movements and domination itself."[149] Such historical investigation is motivated and helped by the imagination[150] to focus "on the distinct quality of what was actually happening." Where Voegelin saw "phenomenal differences" obscuring the "essential sameness" of totalitarian ideology, Arendt stressed, in her rejoinder, that it is precisely these phenomena which "can alone help us in finding its essence":

> What is unprecedented in totalitarianism is not primarily its ideological content, but the *event* of totalitarian domination itself. This can be seen clearly if we have to admit that the deeds of its considered policies have exploded our traditional categories of political thought (totalitarian domination is unlike all forms of tyranny and despotism we know of) and the standards of our moral judgment (totalitarian crimes are very inadequately described as "murder" and totalitarian criminals can hardly be punished as "murderers").[151]

Arendt had used this argument before to show Jaspers the novel aspect of Nazi crime, though unlike Voegelin, Jaspers did not have to be shown that she proceeded from "facts and events"—in contrast to Voegelin's approach through "intellectual affinities and influences."[152] Even if he did not grasp in full the complexity of Arendt's perspective on the German-Jewish question, Jaspers had understood—and valued—the reality of her personal experience in the power of her observation. Voegelin, as a reader of *Origins*, was not able, it seems, to respond to that power. He insisted on bringing ideational structures and developments to bear on the phenomenon of National Socialist totalitarianism, which consequently remained curiously indistinct in his review. In her rejoinder, Arendt therefore sought to reestablish important distinctions which would counteract Voegelin's reading into her argument a gradual emergence of the "essence of totalitarianism" since the eighteenth century, and with that a sameness of political structures and movements which she did not accept.[153] The essence of totalitarianism, she reiterated, did not exist before it came into being; it was not the "spiritual disease" which distinguished modern masses from those of earlier centuries, but rather the observable social-political fact that they now were "'masses' in a strict sense of the word." Individuals as parts of these modern masses, as Arendt described them in *Origins*, have literally had no self, because they have had no common *inter-est*, no common ground between them, which "fulfills the double function of binding men together and separating them in an articulate way."[154]

Large numbers of lonely, atomized, isolated, politically indifferent individuals, without common interest and without defined obtainable goals, were pressed together into the one collective body of the modern mass.[155] Their organization was predicated on demands for the "total, unrestricted, unconditional, and unalterable loyalty" of the individual member to the totalitarian movement. Such demands, as Arendt observed, were made by the leaders even before they seized power: "It usually[156] precedes the total organization of the country under their actual rule and it follows from the claim of their ideologies that their organization will encompass, in due course, the entire human race."[157] Sworn to loyalty, the individual members will literally be incorporated into the totalitarian movement, become literally one with its force and momentum—or be swept away by it like meaningless particles. In this sense, the concentration and extermination camps of totalitarian regimes could indeed be seen as laboratories for the total application of that force and momentum:

> Total domination, which strives to organize the infinite plurality and differentiation of human beings as if all of humanity were just one individual, is possible only if each and every person can be reduced to a never-changing identity of reactions, so that each of these bundles of reactions can be exchanged at random for any other. . . . Totalitarian domination attempts to achieve this goal both through ideological indoctrination of the elite formations and through absolute terror in the camps; and the atrocities for which the elite formations are ruthlessly used become, as it were, the practical application of the ideological indoctrination—the testing ground in which the latter must prove itself—while the appalling spectacle of the camps themselves is supposed to furnish the "theoretical" verification of the ideology.[158]

Totalitarianism, Arendt asserted against Voegelin's argument, was not caused by some otherwise unfulfilled need for religion—unless the term *religion* was used metaphorically: "the metaphysical place for God has remained empty." She conceded a connection between totalitarianism and atheism, but a purely negative one which, besides, she did not think exclusively characteristic of the rise of totalitarianism. The secularization of morality could at most be considered a *conditio sine qua non;* it did not explain totalitarian domination and genocide.[159]

Reminding Voegelin of his statement, in the 1952 *New Science of Politics,* that "one might almost say that before the discovery of psyche man had no soul," Arendt pointed out that she did not propose a more radical change of nature than did he—albeit in the opposite direction: "In Mr. Voegelin's terms, I could have said that after the discoveries of totalitarian domination and its experiments we have reason to fear that man may lose his soul."[160] In view of the radical liquidation by totalitarian rule of freedom "as a political and as a human reality," it did not make much sense, she reasoned, to insist on the

> unchangeable nature of man and conclude that either man is being destroyed or that freedom does not belong to man's essential capabilities. Historically we know of man's nature only insofar as it has existence and no realm of eternal essences will ever console us if man loses his essential capabilities.[161]

There was, for Arendt, no consolation if the human capability for freedom—that is, the human being's natural diversity, plurality, spontaneity, and natality—were lost. Both the factual destruction of this capability and its potential realization required radical change: in the first case, of human nature; in the second case, of human politics. The question of German guilt could not be posed—much less answered—intelligibly, because the quality of this guilt, which was essentially linked with the total liquidation of human freedom as Arendt understood it, could not be located in her concept of the political. Yet it was this question which reinforced her resolution to present realizations of the political as synonymous with the human condition, which meant for Arendt, above all, the capability for the new beginning.

5

Visible Spaces

Good Men and Good Citizens

Arendt prefaced *The Origins of Totalitarianism* with a quote from Jaspers which pleads the priority of the present over the past and the future.[1] To Jaspers she wrote on March 4, 1951, how much this sentence had helped her accept the completion of the book, its being ready to be sent out into the world.[2] She also responded to a question he had posed in his last letter, when, praising the concluding chapter of *Origins*, he had asked whether Yahweh had not been too noticeably absent from her argument.[3] In her answer she linked her lack of interest in all established religion, Jewish or Christian, to the experience of "radical evil"—namely, a delusion of omnipotence which resulted in making man (*Mensch*) superfluous as man, seeking to destroy, as she had argued in *Origins*, human diversity, plurality, spontaneity, and natality. Whereas Jaspers in his discussion of genocide had relegated the incomprehensible dimension of such mass destruction to the realm of the metaphysical and metaphysical guilt, she located it in the experienced reality of a radically evil superfluity of man. But to end her analysis of totalitarian rule and mass destruction with such total negation of the human potential was intolerable. In the second edition of *Origins* (1958) she added, as an epilogue, her 1958 essay "Reflections on the Hungarian Revolution." The "amazing," the highly positive and encouraging quality of this revolution was, in her view, the absence of a civil war. It was carried by the

sheer momentum of acting-together of the whole people whose demands were so obvious that they hardly needed elaborate formulation: Russian troops should leave the territory and free elections
should determine a new government. . . . No group, no class in the
nation opposed the will of the people once it had become known
and its voice had been heard in the market place.[4]

But even more enthusiastically than to this "acting-together" of the
whole people, their making themselves heard in one voice, Arendt responded to the constitution (almost simultaneously with the uprising) of
the revolutionary and workers' councils. These councils were of the ut-
most importance for the admirably sane course of the revolution, which
saw no mob rule, no crimes against property and life, in spite of the
people's deep frustration over the scarcity of goods and the irrationality of
Russian domination. Arendt's description of the emergence and functioning of these councils stressed precisely that essentially human potential
for diversity, plurality, and spontaneity: the councils emerged in many
different situations, from many different affiliations, bringing together
Communists and non-Communists, workers, students, civil servants, artists. Perhaps even more important, the new councils immediately began
to associate freely among themselves, choosing from among themselves
representatives to the higher councils, all the way up to the Supreme National Council. In its responsive mobility and flexibility, the system of
representation itself retained the "grass roots" quality which Arendt
thought sorely lacking in the party systems of modern (mass) democracies.[5]
    There is in her description admiration for the people who, having
been allowed "to follow their own political devices without a government
(or a party program) imposed on them from above," will support such
councils, which is reminiscent of many German intellectuals' belief in the
spontaneous wisdom of the people during the aborted 1918/1919 revolution. But there is also admiration for the concept of "direct" representation and the demonstrated political responsibility of the elected. The
choice of the voters is prompted not by a program or ideology,

    but exclusively by his estimation of a man, in whose personal integ-
    rity, courage and judgment he is supposed to have enough confi-
    dence to entrust him with his representation. The elected, therefore,
    is not bound by anything except trust in his personal qualities, and
    his pride is "to have been elected by the workers, and not by the

government" or a party, that is, by his peers and from neither above nor below.[6]

The essay on the Hungarian revolution had come out the same year as *The Human Condition* and, with its emphasis on the significant political potential of the councils, it reflected the argument of chapter 2 of that work, "The Public and the Private Realm."[7] In her 1963 study of the American Revolution, she discussed in very positive terms the *covenants*, which preceded the Constitution and were so important to it, and the Jeffersonian concept of "wards" or councils. These books and the essays collected in *Between Past and Future* (1961) are the fruits of Arendt's search for historically realized instances of community and communal speech—as if she was trying to balance what had happened in the immediate past. She found them in the Western tradition of political thought, mainly in Greek and Roman antiquity, and then in eighteenth-century North America. But the message she extracted from these utopian examples, that history had not always been ruled by necessity, was meant for the future.

In the fall of 1951, Arendt expressed her regrets that Jaspers had declined an invitation from Princeton. She had very much wanted him to have the experience of the United States—that is, the American political tradition. She was herself looking forward to obtaining her citizenship soon and had studied, in celebration of this occasion, some aspects of American constitutional history: "Quite magnificent. Down to every single formulation." And it was, she thought, still very much alive in contemporary Americans.[8] More than ten years later her study of the American Revolution was to show how deeply she had been impressed by the concrete power of political language, the common-sensical sentiments, the clear distinctions, the articulated accessibility, the visibility of the new beginning and its enduring energy. It was important for her, too, that the United States had its beginning in history, that the Revolution and Constitution were not a foundation myth, but a story which made sense.

It is tempting to speculate why Arendt did not begin her study of the American Revolution in 1951, when she was reading the history of the American Constitution. While she had never shared Bluecher's—albeit short-lived—uncritical pro-Americanism,[9] she was, in 1951, very positive about her life in the United States, writing to Jaspers, "I am really grateful that I have landed here."[10] But the growing McCarthyism, on which she reported to her friends in Europe, changed the American experience in some important ways—it also changed, though more subtly, her attitude toward communism, or, rather, Communists. To Jaspers[11] she stressed the role of ex-Communists in these attacks on American political life,[12] taking care to explain that they were not motivated by anti-Semitism or any other kind of racism and that Jews as victims played a large part in the witch hunt simply because they constituted a large percentage of the intelligentsia. In this letter, Arendt's analysis of McCarthyism focused on the role of public opinion, the psychological pressure of the conformist social sphere brought to bear on the millions of good "job-holders" who, unlike good citizens, had not developed the capability to resist such pressure. In this context she drew an instructive parallel to Weimar Germany—instructive, that is, for her rather too pure concept of the role of the citizen and the political sphere rather than for the situation: "In this situation, where everybody has the most magnificent prospects and just has to get up there because they are all getting richer and richer by the minute, prosperity plays the same role as did unemployment in Germany." In October 1954 she wrote Jaspers that it looked as if McCarthy was finished, but she very much regretted the losses to American political life. Complaining that Jews were currently too quick to see anti-Semitism everywhere and hold it responsible for everything, she reiterated her belief that the persecution of left-wing intellectuals had nothing to do with anti-Semitism. Rather, she saw "totalitarian developments rising out of society, mass society itself, without a 'movement' and without a firm ideology."[13]

Important in these observations are Arendt's rejection of a beleaguered Jewish solidarity of victimization which excludes the possibility of other political motivations for persecution, and her own in many ways "beleaguered" intellectual-political rejection of mass society. Mid-twentieth-century America had become a politically less-satisfying place, and Arendt went back into the past to understand more fully the present. From St. Moritz, where she stayed with the Jaspers—she was in Europe for almost five months in the summer of 1952—Arendt wrote to Blumenfeld how much she enjoyed life, in spite of the discouraging picture of American and world politics and the "mostly unpleasant" situation in Germany. The Guggenheim Fellowship would enable her, for the first time since 1933, to "only work," and Bluecher had "now really become a professor of philosophy" at Bard College. Happy in her intellectual and spatial closeness to Jaspers and the, as she always described it, "brightness" (*Helle*) of their conversations, she was trying to find her way into a new "real" project, reading the *Republic* in Greek.[14]

Her next letter to Blumenfeld, written in New York in the fall of 1952, sounded much less happy. She was afraid that Stevenson, if elected, might not be able to stop Nixon and McCarthy, and, most disturbing, she could see no reasons for this extremism in a situation of full prosperity. To Blumenfeld, too, she complained about the portentous role of ex-Communists in this affair and the absurd demands made on everyone to prove that neither they nor anyone in their family were or had ever been Communists. Pointing out that the Nazis had already used anti-Semitism that way in support of totalitarian organization, "not by attacking Jews, but by demanding of everyone to prove that he was *not* a Jew," Arendt commented: "Fantastic, absurd, but it works!" In all this she was, as usual, sitting in between chairs, observing the growing cracks in the foundations and "reading philosophy from Plato to Nietzsche to find out why it is that the Western world has never had a proper political philosophy; or, the other way round, why the great tradition falls silent when we pose our questions." Again, as if for a consoling contrast, she mentions the happiness of the past summer, the peculiarly illuminating and clarifying discussions with Jaspers, and the great security, which she needed in the emotional and intellectual private sphere and which she had found in her marriage to Bluecher.[15]

Later that year, she received an invitation to deliver a series of lectures at Princeton University in connection with the Gauss Seminars in Criticism. She wrote to Blumenfeld in February 1953 how much she enjoyed her complete freedom in her work, which seemed to be going well, and noted that she was writing "so slowly and cautiously that I hardly recognize myself." She needed this pleasure in her work because the situation in the United States looked darker and darker: "By the way, Jews behave particularly badly; they contribute the largest percentage of ex-Communists and bring even more fanaticism to the whole affair. . . . Our friend Elliot Cohen plays a particularly unpleasant role and Sidney Hook is absolutely insufferable."[16] Whether or not she was right about the relative over-representation of Jews among the active and articulate group of ex-Communists, it was significant for the direction her work was taking that she saw it that way. She told Blumenfeld, too, that recently she and several American friends—a history professor, two well-known journalists, and a woman novelist, none of them Jews, but all of them with many close

Jewish friends—had been putting together a list of reliable fighters for civil liberties. "Suddenly one of them said: 'Isn't it funny, only Hannah of all those Jews is with us. I had not realized that myself before.'" She was to experience a similar division along Jewish and non-Jewish lines with the reactions to her Eichmann book. It is possible that the Nazi persecution of Jews had contributed to the eagerness of Jewish ex-Communists to declare their solidarity with McCarthy's attacks on left-wing intellectuals, many of them Jews, and that the overwhelmingly negative, bitterly hostile reception of the Eichmann book in New York's Jewish intellectual circles a decade later reflected, too, the still-remembered anxieties caused by these attacks. Arendt was disturbed by the connection between the fears shared by a group of people and their politically and intellectually stifling solidarity.

At Princeton she experienced another kind of questionable solidarity. In November 1953 she wrote to Blumenfeld about her initial apprehensiveness regarding her preparation and performance in the rarefied, snobbish men's club atmosphere of the Institute for Advanced Studies and her later attempts at subversiveness: At a reception at the end of the lecture series, slightly tipsy, she had explained to the "dignified gentlemen" [17] the phenomenon of the "exception Jew" (Ausnahmejude), to make it clear to them that the situation in Princeton, by necessity, had made her feel like an "exception woman." On the whole, however, she had liked the experience and the fact that she had been "what one calls a success." "I believe, above all," she wrote, "also for the whole female sex. In any case, they are thinking about inviting another woman for 1955 and, imagine, are even willing to tolerate her and myself among the audience of another series. All this is meant to amuse you." [18]

In spite of the light tone of her description, Arendt was not amused. The remark about the importance of her success for "the whole female sex" is most uncharacteristic, as is the comparison between the "exception Jew" and the "exception woman." The experience of exclusiveness at this all-male elite institution, even though it included her, must have reminded her sharply of the ambiguities inherent in relations based on privilege rather than right. She had always refuted easy accusations of anti-Semitism,[19] and in spite of her impulsive temperament, she had been remarkably shrewd about the psychological dynamics at work in emotionally charged questions of minority politics. But the unquestioned, naive[20] majority attitude of solidarity, in this case toward the woman rather than the Jew, had brought up the old problem of selective assimilation and made her wary.

The lectures at Princeton were based on Arendt's work on a study of the totalitarian elements of Marxism, which was conceived, as she explained in her 1952 grant proposal to the Guggenheim Foundation, as a necessary complement to *Origins*. The unprecedentedness of totalitarian rule, she had argued in *Origins*, was not, in her view, connected with specific flaws of the "great" Western cultural tradition. Rather, it was linked to the breakdown of social and political structures, structures which she felt needed to be studied more closely—for instance, political Marxism as the ideological background of Bolshevism.[21] In her progress report of January 19, 1953, she described her research on the history and

> theory of labor, philosophically considered, as distinguished from work. By this I mean the distinction between man as *homo faber* and man as *animal laborans*; between man as a craftsman and artist (in the Greek sense) and man as submitted to the curse of earning his daily bread in the sweat of his brow. A clear conceptual distinction as well as precise historical knowledge in this field seemed to me important in view of the fact that Marx' dignification of labor as essentially creative activity constitutes a precise break with the entire Western tradition for which labor had presented the animal, not the human, part of man.[22]

In order to understand Marx's break with the tradition, she had gone back to its beginnings, reading Plato's *Republic* in Greek. But broadening her area of inquiry, she began to see Marx's indebtedness to the tradition, too, and her critical focus on his concept of labor, which she contrasted with the concept of work, moved the Marx project in the direction of an inquiry into the *vita activa*.

Early in 1953, at the time of the Guggenheim report, Arendt still thought of her work in progress as a study of Marxism. She described the first four chapters, of which only "Ideology and Terror," published in the *Review of Politics* in July 1953 and added to the second, enlarged edition of *Origins* as the last chapter,[23] retained its original shape. There were to be two more chapters and finally a "Marx analysis itself" (intended for the Princeton lectures in the fall of 1953 but not finished in time to be delivered).[24] Arendt called the lectures based on the first four chapters "Karl Marx and the Great Tradition." The material in the "Marx analysis itself" went into the Walgreen Foundation Lectures at the University of Chicago which she delivered in the spring of 1956, and by this time the study of Marxism had turned into a first version of *The Human Condition*. The beginnings of Western political-philosophical thought in Greek and Roman antiquity, with their attempts at defining, through distinctions, cultural activities in their relation to the human condition, had proved to be profoundly appealing to her. What she had written to Blumenfeld in October 1952 about the silence of the "great tradition" when we pose our questions was no longer true.[25] There were answers for listeners like herself, and they addressed precisely the questions most important to her: how to overcome the waste of life-time by mere unmitigated necessity, how to preserve human plurality and diversity in freedom, how to create spaces for human intercourse so that it can be seen and heard and leave traces, how to share a world which houses the individual between birth and death, how to remember such sharing in (political) speech and action, and how to be remembered.

◦ 2 ◦

Marx's presence in *The Human Condition* was most distinct in the important chapter "Labor,"[26] which shows clearly that Arendt had thought her way through and past him. This chapter, too, reflects most directly her concern with the precariousness and limitations of human life and her inconsolable remembrance of its mass destruction. The first signpost on the way to the book was an essay drawn from the Princeton lectures and published in the January 1954 issue of *Partisan Review*, "Tradition and the Modern Age," which in 1961 was included, as the first piece, in *Between Past and Future*. This essay presented a somewhat conflicted attempt to view simultaneously the beginning of the Western tradition of political thought in the teachings of Plato and Aristotle and its ending in the theories of Karl Marx.[27] Marx's philosophy, like Nietzsche's, subversive in the grand style of the nineteenth century, had not so much turned Hegel upside down as it had "inverted" the whole traditional "hierarchy of thought and action, of contemplation and labor, and of philosophy and politics."[28] If Marx had done so from a position of conscious rebellion against this tradition, he had also been—and remained—very much tied to it, especially in his utopian projection of a "stateless (apolitical) and almost laborless society," with its "traditional connotation of leisure as *skhole* and *otium*, that is, a life devoted to aims higher than work or politics."[29]

However, Arendt was mainly interested in Marx's rupture of the tradition. It was this rupture which attracted her as a possibility and yet would continue to engage her ambivalence and finally her efforts at reestablishing a continuity. After the completion of *Origins*, titled more aptly *The Burden of Our Time* in the British edition, she thought it necessary to study political thought and political structures in the time *before* political and moral inversion were brought about by twentieth-century totalitarian rule. In the beginning stage of this enterprise, reflected in an essay like "Tradition and the Modern Age," she was still inclined to see this tradition, which had deteriorated and then ended, as a burden that threatened to obscure the past. In contrast to her own position, she thought Marx's position was informed by the greater hold the tradition had over him. To support her argument, she brought together three key Marxian statements: on labor, "labor created man"; on violence, "violence is the midwife of history"; and on Feuerbach, "The philosophers have only interpreted the world differently; the point is, however, to change it." In her translation this last statement reads, "The philosophers have interpreted the world long enough; the time has come to change it,"[30] and motivates an arresting, if problematic, assessment: "Marx' theory of ideological superstructures ultimately rests on his anti-traditional hostility to speech and the concomitant glorification of violence."[31]

This statement was meant to shock Arendt's readers as Marx's statements had been meant to shock his. She drew attention, in this context, to Marx's intention to shock, but she held him to the consequences of his position—namely, several fundamental and insoluble contradictions. If labor is the most human and productive of man's activities, if violence is "the most dignified form of all human action," what will human existence be like when man has been emancipated from both labor and violence? Finally, and to her most importantly, "When philosophy has been both realized and abolished in the future society, what kind of thought will be left?"[32] These contradictions, which lead to the center of Marx's work, arose out of his ending—without freeing himself from it—the Western tradition of political thought. It began

> when Plato discovered that it is somehow inherent in the philosophical experience to turn away from the common world of human affairs; it ended when nothing was left of this experience but the opposition of thinking and acting, which, depriving thought of reality and action of sense, makes both meaningless.[33]

It was time, Arendt thought, to acknowledge the need for a new beginning—post-Marxian, post-totalitarian—in the tradition of political thought. For the beginning, as Plato said in *Laws*, "is like a god which as long as it dwells among men saves all things." As long as the beginning of the tradition was alive, it could balance and stabilize. The tradition became destructive as it neared its end, and "confusion and helplessness" have reigned since it ended.[34] Arendt's descriptions of this ending are clearly informed by what she saw as the division between the modern age[35] and the "world of the twentieth century which came into existence through the chain of catastrophes touched off by the First World War."[36] The division was brought about by the twentieth-century phenomenon of totalitarian domination through the reign of terror and ideology. Unprecedented, incomprehensible, and unpunishable within the established frame of political and legal thought, it ended "the continuity of Occidental history. The break in our tradition is now an accomplished fact. It is neither the result of anyone's deliberate choice nor subject to further decision."[37]

This break, however, is itself an aspect of the modern age. It is the result of certain tendencies inherent in the experience of modernity as an ongoing process. To acknowledge the "accomplished fact" of the break does not mean to be done with the past but rather to acknowledge the challenge of giving it a new meaning for a new cultural beginning, in order to show a way out of the present confusion in political thought and action.

Arendt's acknowledgment here of the great *Zivilisationsbruch* is indeed radical—that is, it matches the completeness of the break. Our "guideposts" to the past, which has lost its authority for us, are Kierkegaard, Marx, and Nietzsche in their revolt against this authority *and* in their continuing rootedness in the tradition.[38] But in our position after the break, no matter how precarious or confused, we, in contrast to these great thinkers, have "the great chance to look upon the past with eyes undistracted by any tradition, with a directness which has disappeared from Occidental reading and hearing ever since Roman civilization submitted to the authority of Greek thought."[39]

What will this direct, unmediated gaze yield? We are not told in this essay, which marks the beginning of Arendt's consciously new, fresh approach to the tradition of political thought. We are told, however, about the impediments to such direct vision caused by Marx's, Nietzsche's, and Kierkegaard's rebellion against the tradition. Completely independent of one another, they saw their enterprise in similar terms or images of leaps, inversions, turning things upside down:

> Kierkegaard speaks of his leap from doubt into belief; Marx turns Hegel, or rather "Plato and the whole Platonic tradition" (Sidney Hook), "right side up again," leaping "from the realm of necessity into the realm of freedom"; and Nietzsche understands his philosophy as "inverted Platonism" and "transformation of all values."[40]

These nineteenth-century thinkers, whom Arendt in no way holds responsible for the event of the break, marked the ending, in poverty and obscurity, of the tradition. There are, in her essay, no conceptually unambiguous statements that would support the reader's sense of her sadness about this ending. But as in Plato's and Heidegger's texts, which she approached with suspicion and, at the same time, unstinting fascination, her "meaning" asserts itself, as elsewhere, in her very way of speaking to her reader. We cannot but respond to its descriptive flow and suggestive power—for instance, in the concluding sentence of the essay:

> Turning the tradition upside down within its own framework, he [Marx] did not actually get rid of Plato's ideas, though he did record the darkening of the clear sky where those ideas, as well as many other presences, had once become visible to the eyes of men.[41]

o 3 o

In its ending, the Western tradition of political thought became so impoverished because, in its beginning, it had been so rich. Arendt's 1958 essay "What Was Authority?" communicated, now unmistakably, the sense of an impoverished contemporary experience[42]—in spite of the acknowledged ending of the old political tradition and the potentially liberating energy of such an acknowledgment. The loss of political authority, it is true, was only the final, albeit highly important, stage of a development that for centuries had undermined mainly religion and (a general cultural) tradition. "With the loss of authority, however, the general doubt of the modern age also invaded the political realm, where things not only assume a more radical expression but become endowed with a reality peculiar to the political realm alone."[43]

Arendt led into her argument with a distinction between the loss of tradition, so often associated with the contemporary sense of crisis, and the loss of the past, suggesting, as she had in "Tradition and the Modern Age," that the loss of tradition might indeed be seen as liberating: "It

could be that only now will the past open up to us with unexpected freshness and tell us things no one has yet had ears to hear." But in contrast to
the earlier essay, this statement is now followed by an assessment of the
dangers of cultural forgetting, which leaves the reader little choice but to
appreciate her concern:

> But it cannot be denied that without a securely anchored tradi-
> tion—and the loss of this security occurred several hundred years
> ago—the whole dimension of the past has also been endangered.
> We are in danger of forgetting, and such an oblivion—quite apart
> from the contents themselves that could be lost—would mean that,
> humanly speaking, we would deprive ourselves of one dimension,
> the dimension of depth in human existence. For memory and depth
> are the same, or rather, depth cannot be reached by man except
> through remembrance.[44]

Trying to establish a new beginning of the tradition in readings of
the past which would yield fresh messages, Arendt had come to see the
past as the medium for understanding the potential of the present,
whereas in *Origins* she had questioned the past in order to understand
the catastrophic denial of such potential. "What Was Authority?"[45] came
out of her work on *The Human Condition*, and it could be read, in part,
as a commentary on the uses here of her perspective on the past: going
toward the present rather than coming from the present. This perspective
had provided her with the capacity to search out and appreciate distinctions, lost in the confusion of the aftermath of twentieth-century political
and moral inversions. She was aware of the possibility that her insistence
on distinctions might be misunderstood to be prescriptive in a neocon-
servative sense. Distinguishing between mortality and natality, labor and
work, the private and the public realm, the *vita activa* and the *vita contemplativa*, in an attempt to define the meanings of the human condition, she
had suggested a possible authority of the past which could be used for
understanding and articulating the present.

The essay "What Was Authority?" ostensibly approached the question of authority in the political realm; it explicitly did not attempt to
define "the nature or essence of 'authority in general.'" We have not lost
authority in general, Arendt asserted; we have lost "a very specific form
which has been valid throughout the Western World over a long period
of time."[46] Part of the loss has been the lack of a distinct concept of authority in liberal and conservative views on authority and freedom in the

realm of politics. Liberal political thinkers, interested in the progress of freedom rather than in forms of government, tend to equate totalitarianism with authoritarianism, illegitimate with legitimate power, and legitimate power with violence. But in contrast to tyranny or, in the twentieth century, totalitarian rule, the source of authority in authoritarian rule has always been external and superior to its own power. The "most draconic" authoritarian government was controlled by laws from which it derived its "authority"—that is, its legitimacy. Its exercise of power could always be checked against these laws.

Conservative political thinkers, on the other hand, tend to see a process of doom, "which started with the dwindling of authority, so that freedom, after it lost the restricting limitations which protected its boundaries, became helpless, defenseless, and bound to be destroyed."[47] In parentheses Arendt adds the observation that, even though the concept varies, both liberal and conservative political thought are centered around the idea of freedom, the only important exception being the political philosophy of Thomas Hobbes, "who, of course, was anything but a conservative."[48] This is an important observation in view of the development of her own political thought as it informed her analyses of contemporary political issues in the sixties and early seventies—the Eichmann trial, the Vietnam war, student unrest, political corruption, and cultural corruption in a consumers' society. The quality of freedom changed when she attempted to articulate, in distinctions, the human condition.

The truth about the threats to liberty and authority—though they are seen in opposing terms—is equally divided between liberals and conservatives: "[We are] in fact confronted with a simultaneous recession of both freedom and authority in the modern world."[49] This recession is linked, by implication, to the growing inability of both groups to make theoretical distinctions in the human and social sciences, an inability caused by their peculiarly history-conscious progressivism and their concept of functionalism.[50]

The blurring of distinctions in one area of cultural activity—politics—carries over into another and produces the conceptual and emotional confusion characteristic of our contemporary situation. Arguing against the tendency to equate and substitute unthinkingly,[51] Arendt in fact favored the adoption of a different historical perspective, which she developed in *The Human Condition* and *On Revolution*. The distinctions that she proposed between tyrannical, authoritarian, and totalitarian systems are indeed unhistorical

if one understands by history not the historical space in which certain forms of government appeared as recognizable entities, but the
historical process in which everything can always change into something else; and they are anti-functional insofar as the content of the
phenomenon is taken to determine both the nature of the political
body and its function in society, and not vice-versa. Politically
speaking, they [the distinctions] have a tendency to assume that in
the modern world authority has disappeared almost to the vanishing
point, and this in the so-called authoritarian systems no less than in
the free world, and that freedom—that is, the freedom of movement
of human beings—is threatened everywhere, even in free societies,
but abolished radically only in totalitarian systems, and not in tyr-
annies and dictatorships.[52]

Insisting on distinctions and clear definitions in the realm of the political,
Arendt's main concern was to point out the precariousness, in the contemporary world, of that essentially human freedom to keep spaces in which
to move, interact, and develop common interests. In *Origins* she had argued the unprecedented nature of totalitarian rule by demonstrating how
it had eliminated such spaces and such movement.[53] Now she wished to
claim her readers' responsibility to understand the preciousness and vulnerability of this freedom, leading them back to "the political experiences
that corresponded to the concept of authority and from which it
sprang."[54]

o   4   o

The Western concept of authority sprang from the experience of one-
man rule, a tyranny that threatened to destroy the polis. This rule was
bound by no law and therefore destroyed everyone's freedom, including
the ruler's. Just as the despot, the head and uncontested master of the
household, was not free when he moved among his slaves, so the tyrant
was not free when he moved among his subjects. In contrast to the tyrant,
however, the despot could leave the private sphere of the household and
move among his equals in the public sphere, where he and his peers were
free in obedience to the rules that regulated political interaction. This is
why Plato, in his last work, sought to establish laws as indisputably governing the political sphere and giving men the illusion of freedom, for in
their obedience to these laws, they were not dependent on other men. But
as Arendt saw, too, Plato's laws were conceived in terms of coercion—
that is, in "despotic" rather than authoritative terms; they were informed

by the private sphere of the household rather than by the public sphere of political interaction. In the *Republic*, where he sought to deal with the conflict between philosophy and the polis by making the philosopher king, Plato wanted to coerce through reason. (Aristotle seems to have recognized the "fatal resemblance" between the philosopher-king and the Greek tyrant.)[55] Plato's problem was that such coercion—without resorting to other means, like violence—would be effective only for the few, not for the many who make up the general body politic. He tried to solve it with the concluding myth, meant for those many, of rewards and punishments in an afterlife. In contrast, the cave allegory, intended for the few—the philosophers—tells

> of the philosopher's loss of orientation in human affairs, of the blindness striking the eyes, of the predicament of not being able to communicate what he has seen, and of the actual danger to his life which thereby arises. It is in this predicament that the philosopher resorts to what he has seen, the ideas, as standards and measures, and finally, in fear of his life, uses them as instruments of domination.[56]

Responding to the suggestive power of the cave allegory, Arendt was fully aware of the temptation on the part of the philosophers to use doctrine or ideology as a means of domination. But if she appreciated the cultural precariousness of their situation, she was also suspicious of the claims to domination made by philosophy.[57] Plato's defensive attack on the world of human affairs, imposing norms on "the varied multitude of things [and humans] measurable," explicitly so in the political realm, has had too great an influence on the Western tradition.[58] And Aristotle, too, in Arendt's reading—though he accepted neither Plato's doctrinal concept of ideas nor his ideal state—distinguished hierarchically between a "theoretical way of life" (*bios theoretikos*) and a life involved in human affairs (*bios politikos*).

In political terms this distinction gave rise to the need for rulership, and the irony of this development for Arendt lay in the fact that the political philosophy of the Socratic school came to be based on precisely the dichotomy between thinking and acting which Socrates had tried to overcome. She made this observation here only in passing, but it was important because it foreshadowed her later analysis of the potentially disastrous consequences, for the political sphere, of the inability to relate thinking and acting.[59]

Aristotle's political philosophy introduced a concept of authority as relation between the ruler and the ruled. The polis, enabling men to lead the "good life" (*bios politikos*), is "a community of equals" or "composed of many rulers"—namely, the household heads.[60] But in Arendt's understanding of the political sphere, ruling itself, as well as the distinction between rulers and ruled, belongs to the prepolitical sphere of the household. What distinguishes the political from the "economic" sphere is its foundation on the principle of equality: it is the nature of the polis that it "knows no differentiation between rulers and ruled."[61] Every citizen participates in two spheres, the public and the private, but because the private sphere of the household is involved with the preservation of life, both individual and species, it is controlled by necessity, which must be mastered through controlled labor. From this it follows that the equality and freedom of the "good life" of the polis rests, by necessity, on domination in the household:

> The opinion that labor and work were despised in antiquity because only slaves were engaged in them is a prejudice of modern historians. The ancients reasoned the other way around and felt it necessary to possess slaves because of the slavish nature of all occupations that served the needs for the maintenance of life. It was precisely on these grounds that the institution of slavery was defended and justified. To labor meant to be enslaved by necessity, and this enslavement was inherent in the conditions of human life. Because men were dominated by the necessities of life, they could win their freedom only through the domination of those whom they subjected to necessity by force. The slave's degradation was a blow of fate and a fate worse than death, because it carried with it a metamorphosis of man into something akin to a tame animal.[62]

It was only against this dark background, then, that the "good life" as *bios politikos* could unfold.[63] Even a sympathetic reader will find it hard to reconcile Arendt's passionately engaged analysis of mass enslavement under totalitarian rule with her evident tolerance for such domination as the necessary precondition for the *bios politikos*.[64] However, it is important to note the way in which she presented, in the quoted passage, the dichotomy of enslavement and freedom, which emphasized both the preciousness of freedom and the horror of enslavement—the metamorphosis of the human into a lesser being. This double emphasis as double perspective is characteristic of her exploration of the human condition.

All her distinctions are meant to reveal in speech and thereby celebrate what is uniquely human—"only man can . . ."—imploring that this uniqueness not be wasted again in mass destruction.

The acceptance of slavery by Plato and Aristotle was culturally conditioned in its assumption that "without forced labor there might have been no *polis*, and hence no basis for virtue and wisdom." They lived in a society which was more and more intent on keeping culture and public service free from the taint of manual labor, and so they saw slavery as "a necessary means of supplying the wants of life":

> In an apparent admission, seized upon by nineteenth-century reformers, he [Aristotle] said that if the shuttle would weave and the plectrum touch the lyre without a hand to guide them, "chief workmen would not want servants, nor masters slaves." We may doubt, however, whether he yearned for the industrial revolution. The illustration was meant to show the complex nature of the slave as both an instrument of action and a conscious agent who must obey and anticipate his master's will.[65]

The relationship between slave and master was beneficial only to the master. His interests and those of the slave had to be identical because the slave was nothing but a possession, a tool, and in this function an extension of his master's physical nature. The social historian David Brion Davis sums it up succinctly: "The best slave, it would appear, was the one whose humanity had been most nearly effaced."[66] Arendt argued that this situation had come about as a result of the ancients' particularly forceful philosophical-political distinction between freedom and necessity, equality and rulership, speech and silence, action and passivity, work and labor, the public and the private sphere. Historical evidence, in contrast, has suggested that this situation reflected an involved complex of social, economic, and political concerns and developments which would considerably fudge the meanings of such distinctions. Nevertheless, it is important for our context to understand how and why Arendt was so obviously interested in finding, revealing, and preserving such meanings.

In her description of totalitarian enslavement, she had pointed out precisely these characteristics—the literal selflessness, the near-total destruction, in violent coercion,[67] of all that was essentially human: spontaneity in thought, speech, and action, plurality, diversity, and shared interests. In chapter 3 of *The Human Condition* she used the same passage from Aristotle, but gave it a very different interpretation. Paraphrasing Aristotle's own comments on his science fantasy and interspersing quotes from a secondary source supporting her argument,[68] she asserted that the craftsman would indeed no longer need servants. However, household slaves, instruments not of production but of a life process, "which constantly consumes their services," could not be dispensed with.

> It is precisely because from "the instruments of the household noth-
> ing else results except the use of the possession itself" that they
> cannot be replaced by tools and instruments of workmanship "from
> which results something more than the mere use of the instru-
> ment."[69]

In other words, Arendt's concept of household slaves makes them even less human than robots involved in production. Their labor is the least-human occupation because it is totally controlled by necessity and there-fore consumes rather than articulates life-time, not leaving any traces of lived time.

o   5   o

The powerful need to strain against necessity first expressed itself when Arendt asked Rahel to accept as a challenge the accident of her having been born a Jewess. Without such acceptance she would be con-trolled by this accident, unable to develop her potential for diversity and spontaneity, for the new beginning. This need, fed by the experience of total war and holocaust, was the main source of Arendt's distinction be-tween labor and work in *The Human Condition*. In the first chapter, "The Human Condition," she defined as the *vita activa*[70] three "fundamental" human activities—labor, work, and action—each of which corresponds to one of "the basic conditions under which life on earth has been given to man." Labor, in her definition, is the most basic, for it corresponds

> to the biological process of the human body, whose spontaneous
> growth, metabolism, and eventual decay are bound to the vital ne-
> cessities produced and fed into the life process by labor. The human
> condition of labor is life itself.

Work, in contrast, corresponds to the "unnaturalness" of human exis-tence,

> which is not embedded in and whose mortality is not compensated
> by the species' ever-recurring life cycle. Work provides an "artifi-
> cial" world of things, distinctly different from all natural surround-

ings. Within its borders each individual life is housed, while this world itself is meant to outlast and transcend them all. The human condition of work is worldliness.

Action, the only activity that connects men directly, unmediatedly, corre-sponds to the human condition of plurality. It is men, not man, who live on this earth and inhabit, for a time, the world they have made together. And while all aspects of the human condition are in some ways linked with politics, "this plurality is specifically *the* condition—not only the *conditio sine qua non* but the *conditio per quam*—of all political life."[71]

Against human mortality, for which there is no consolation, because it is not compensated by natural cyclicity, is set the comparative endur-ance of human culture. This man-made world houses each individual life because it encloses both its birth and its death. It also expands individual life-time; being housed in it, the individual leaves traces. From the van-tage point of Arendt's definition of the human condition of work as world-liness, it is easier to understand her dismay about the rapid and, to her, often-shoddy rebuilding of German cities, reflecting the Germans' refusal to be inconsolable about the destruction of their cultural artifacts.[72] It was the experienced precariousness of "life itself," instantly consumed in the gas ovens and fires of the war, which made her feel and express so literally the burden of mortality. In some ways similar to Elias Canetti, with whom she shared the secularity and intensity of this feeling,[73] Arendt argued for the protection and extension of life-time, for a relative imperishability of human affairs and a temporary immortality of human existence. This would be achieved by worldliness, a culturally secured quality of life which would defeat the senselessness of past mass destruction of human life and help keep in check the confused rush of mass technocracy into an inhumanly obscure future. The prologue to *The Human Condition* begins with the launching of the first man-made satellite, which then circled the earth in accordance with the same natural laws of gravitation which govern the celestial bodies.

> To be sure, the man-made satellite was no moon or star, no heavenly body which could follow its circling path for a time span that to us mortals, bound by earthly time, lasts from eternity to eternity. Yet, for a time, it managed to stay in the skies; it dwelt and moved in the proximity of the heavenly bodies as though it had been admitted tentatively to their sublime company.[74]

One should be sensitive here to Arendt's emphasis on the tentative proximity of this man-made object, product of human work, to what in human perception are sublime and eternal natural objects. It was an achievement which she thought secondary in importance to no other, because it expanded measurably the reality of human experience in space and time. Important, too, was her interpretation of the reaction to this event: not so much joy, pride, or awe at the astonishing power and mastery of man, but relief about the first "step toward escape from men's imprisonment to the earth." She was disturbed by the desire to escape the human condition, which is inescapably rooted in life on earth:

> Should the emancipation and secularization of the modern age, which began with a turning away . . . from a god who was the father of men in heaven, end with an even more fateful repudiation of an Earth who was the Mother of all living creatures under the sky?[75]

Obviously, Arendt overinterpreted certain aspects of the reaction, which in general was one of joy, pride, and awe. But the point here is that she saw recognition of the importance of a nurturing earth as essential to the quality of human life and that she therefore stressed the need to pose and discuss questions of scientific and technological development in the public sphere of the political and not hide them in the private sphere of the laboratory. It is in this context that she expressed fears about the loss of speech, since the "truths" of modern scientific exploration and mastery of the world can no longer be expressed in "normal"—that is, shared—speech and thought. Science functions in a world in which speech has lost its power:

> And whatever men do or know or experience can make sense only to the extent that it can be spoken about. There may be truths beyond speech, and they may be of great relevance to man in the singular, that is, to man insofar as he is not a political being, whatever else he may be. Men in the plural, that is, men insofar as they live and move and act in this world, can experience meaningfulness only because they can talk with and make sense to each other and to themselves.[76]

The prologue should not be misunderstood as a critique of modern science and technology—the "awesome" achievement of the man-made satellite, "for a time" circling the skies in sublime company, would not have been possible without the highly specialized, largely untranslatable and unsharable communication that is characteristic of modern science. Rather, Arendt wished to stress the implications of scientific and techno- logical mastery for political speech and action. This distinctly, uniquely human mastery over necessity through scientific work, which is deeply satisfying to her, needs the "reality peculiar to the political realm alone"[77] to protect its human significance. The reality of the political realm is one of speech and action, which reveal the "unique distinctness,"[78] the mean- ing of human effort. Moving in "a world where speech has lost its power,"[79] scientists cannot and do not have to answer the "question asked of every newcomer: 'Who are you?'"[80] As scientists, they do not partici- pate in that insertion with word and deed into the human world which Arendt compares to "a second birth," and which is "not forced upon us by necessity, like labor, and . . . is not prompted by utility, like work."[81]

Not to ask the newcomer "Who are you?" means that no answer is expected, no disclosure wanted, no explanation of significance needed. Thus, Jews were not asked who they were by anti-Semites, nor were Communists asked this question by anti-Communists. They were de- fined as the other and thereby deprived, as individuals, of their unique distinctness and, as a group, of their human plurality, which is "the par- adoxical plurality of unique beings."[82] In the case of groups like these, the omission of that question defines their lack of power, emphasizing their encouraged or enforced absence from the political sphere. In the case of scientists it suggests their power to disregard the political sphere.

The connection, which I establish here, exists only by implication, and Arendt's reference to the speechlessness of the world of modern sci- ence, though it dominates the prologue, is not followed up in the main text. Yet it informs the severe critique of the contemporary consumers' mass society which underlies the whole argument of *The Human Con- dition* and occasionally emerges in full force. The conclusion of the chap- ter on labor asserts that the modern mass society of consumers, which has so willfully and irresponsibly disregarded the political sphere, was made possible precisely by a technological mastery over necessity which has gone unquestioned in the political realm. Humans have tried to es- cape from labor because they have wanted to be free from necessity and from efforts that leave "no trace, no monument, no great work worthy of remembrance."[83] But while they have finally succeeded in doing so to a high degree, their willingness and ability to contribute to human world- liness through work that leaves meaningful traces seems sorely dimin- ished.

Arendt did not ask why this was so, because she was not really interested in the attitude of most humans toward labor as she defined it. Humans, in general, have not tried to escape from labor because, in contrast
to work, it leaves "no trace, no monument" worthy of remembrance. Some
who wanted to create such monuments did so; others tried to escape labor
that was particularly unpleasant or boring or limiting, and then it was
indeed slavery—in the fifth and fourth centuries B.C. as well as the nineteenth and twentieth centuries A.D. But by no means have all humans felt
enslaved by all labor; and by no means has all work, as Arendt defined it,
contributed to a worldliness worthy of remembrance. Arendt shared Plato's dilemma of being persuasive to (some) philosophers but not to the
many, and consequently also the age-old temptation to the philosopher or
intellectual to speak *for* instead of *to* the many. In her critique of the mass
culture of a consumers' society she was as normative as Plato was in his
cave allegory. For instance, she praised Marx's concept of *Arbeitskraft*,
labor *power* as central to the achievement of his political thought and
seminal for the modern view of the productivity of all laboring: this productivity lies not in any product of labor but in the human power to labor,
which is the power to create a surplus above and beyond what is needed
for subsistence. But here, too, Arendt forcefully distinguished work from
labor, defining labor as being primarily concerned with "the means of its
own reproduction." Its power (*Kraft*) may not be exhausted with the reproduction of one life process, but it will never produce "anything but
life." [84] It will not contribute, other than in a distinctly limited, subservient
way, to the worldliness achieved by cultural activities.

Is so little meaningful work done in modern consumers' societies
because when all are finally almost freed from labor, they still do not know
anything but labor? In 1850 the workweek averaged 85 hours; in the
early 1990s it may be not only desirable but socially and politically necessary to cut the current average from 40 hours to 35 in order to combat
the increasingly difficult unemployment problem. In a recent essay,[85] Oskar Lafontaine, theorist of the German Social Democratic Party, argues
for a political distinction between *Arbeit* (labor) and *Taetigkeit* (activity)
which is very close to Arendt's distinction between labor and work and
to her view of a central conflict in Marx's concept of labor.[86] Lafontaine
defines *Arbeit* as the other-determined *Erwerbsarbeit* necessary for subsistence, and *Taetigkeit* as self-determined cultural and leisure activity.
But in contrast to Arendt, his understanding of *Taetigkeit* is informed by
the constructive rather than destructive potential of a contemporary social

reality. He, in effect, pleads for more linkage between the private and the public sphere, whereas Arendt wanted a clearer separation. In Lafontaine's view, the concept of *Erwerbsarbeit* and that of the family have to be redefined to be mutually accommodating—above all, in the case of women—and work (labor) within the family has to be seen as socially relevant and rewardable. He also proposes a more flexible concept of what constitutes socially relevant work, a concept based on an already developed widespread interest in broadly conceived and distributed cultural activities that would counteract or balance the perceived negative aspects of the mechanization, fragmentation, and artificialization of factory work. It would have pleased Arendt to know that Lafontaine wants the program of the modern German Social Democratic Party to be centrally informed by these changed and changing ways of looking at different concepts of work and that he views them as a strictly political rather than generally social responsibility.

For Arendt, the danger of what to her was still "future automation" lay less in a "much deplored mechanization and artificialization of natural life" than in the fact that "all human productivity would be sucked into an enormously intensified life process." "The rhythm of machines would magnify and intensify the natural rhythm of life enormously, but it would not change, only make more deadly, life's chief character with respect to the world, which is to wear down durability."[87] Even freed of labor, contemporary technocratic mass society to a large extent remains a "laborers' society," because it is laboring, human or robotic, which, inherently fertile, will provide abundance. Striving for abundance does not create worldliness and does not support the public realm. "The ideals of the *homo faber*, the fabricator of the world, which are permanence, stability and durability, have been sacrificed to abundance, the ideal of the *animal laborans*."[88]

If Arendt had experienced our contemporary situation, thirty years after she wrote this, she would probably have felt more than ever justified in her critique. Popular or mass culture, which she considered a *contradictio in adjecto* and profoundly flawed in its striving for private happiness in abundance,[89] today exhibits many of the characteristics—for instance, the enormous cultural importance of popular music—which she had then only extrapolated from her contemporary situation while constructing her distinctions. But this same construction also caused her perspective on mass culture to be too normatively defined and therefore distorting: undermining the worldliness achieved by the cultural contributions of *homo faber*, the mass culture of *animal laborans* by definition undermines trust in the "permanence and durability of the world which is far superior to that of mortal life."[90] Such a priori devaluation of mass culture shows a disregard for the experience shared by huge majorities in technologically developed mass democracies and in fact sentences them to the voicelessness of oblivion.

o   6   o

In her fascination with the ancients' concept of the "good life" in the visible and thus, for a time, permanent spaces of the public sphere, Arendt stressed the past reality of a peculiarly concrete desire for freedom, because it was seen as anchored in agreed-upon, accepted rules of political activity. The historical realization of this desire, the free coming-together of equals in political speech and action, was a deeply satisfying counterprojection to the radically silenced and immobilized life-in-death under totalitarian rule. It also served to emphasize and clarify the speech-lessness and the deafening noise, the obscuring images, the life-consuming abundance, of technologically developed democratic mass societies after World War II.[91] In its distancing perspective, Arendt's critical conceptualization of post-totalitarian mass culture seems reminiscent of her conceptualization, in *Origins*, of modern masses as the nurturing ground for the rise of totalitarian rule. Here it has, as her admiring and critical reader Kateb put it, "the brilliance that a supremely resourceful creation of character has." "But is the created character truly that of the masses," he asks, "or is it rather a construction divorced in some respects from actuality? This is not a question with an answer, but it is not an idle one either."[92] And indeed it is not, because this question concerns Arendt's interest in the other's experience—even more so in the case of her refusal to see any realization of human potential in the mass culture of technodemocracy. Her indictment is too total—in spite of many fresh and now more than ever relevant observations on the culturally and politically confused, self-consuming conformism of the seemingly so diverse, pluralistic contemporary world. It is as if all her realistic tolerance for such all-too-human wasteful confusion and conformism had been used up by the experience of the total waste of human life-time under totalitarian rule.

Arendt's intense concern with the authority needed to sustain the political life—its clear distinctions and sense of articulated community—had its source in this experience and found affirmation in Greek and Roman culture. Greek political philosophy, however, had not succeeded in

giving a consistent answer to the question "What is authority?" Aristotle
even had to take recourse to examples from the prepolitical sphere of the
private household realm and the experience of a slave economy. It was
exclusively in a political context that he defined man as a political being;
for him the definition did not carry over into other contexts. Arendt, then,
did not find support in Aristotle for her view of a "reality peculiar to the
political realm alone."[93] Moreover, in her view, Greek political philosophy
would not have lost its "inherent utopian character" if it had not been for
the Romans, who in their "indefatigable search for tradition and authority" acknowledged the Greeks as their highest intellectual authority. "But
they were able to accomplish this integration only because both authority
and tradition had already played a decisive role in the political life of the
Roman republic."[94]

The Roman concept of foundation and of the public significance of
the individual was of deep and enduring importance to Arendt because it
enabled that culture to conceive, articulate, and, for a time, anchor a realm
in which human interaction could be fully visible and human speech
could be clearly heard. She thought highly significant the linguistic fact
that the Romans, "perhaps the most political people we have known,"
used synonymously "to live" and "to be among men" (*inter homines esse*)
and "to die" and "to cease to be among men" (*inter homines esse desi-
nere*).[95] To be alive means to share with others, for a time, the earth and
human worldliness; it means to include others—and also be included—
in remembrance. If to be human is to be mortal, different from the im-
mortal gods and the cyclicity of nature, it also means to have a "recognizable life story" from birth to death. Shaped by mortals' "works and deeds
and words," it rises out of biological life to signify the, for Arendt, most
poignantly human ability to leave behind "non-perishable traces."[96]

The Roman "pathos for foundation"[97] carried, in the visible spaces
of public life, the distinct images and sounds of "deeds, and facts and
events and patterns of thoughts or ideas" so that they could be "seen,
heard, and remembered" and then transformed into literature, art, and
other documents of cultural activity. Indeed, the "whole factual world of
human affairs depends for its reality and its continued existence, first,
upon the presence of others who have seen and heard and will remember,
and, second, on the transformation of the intangible into the tangibility
of things."[98] The revolutions of the modern age—the French and the
American—have sought to reclaim these foundations and "to restore,
through founding new political bodies, what for so many centuries had

endowed the affairs of men with some measure of dignity and greatness."
But in this reclamation only the American Revolution has been successful, because the "Founding Fathers" established this new body politic
without resorting to violence and with the help of a, for a time, permanent
Constitution. The conclusion of "What Is Authority?" is curiously ambiguous with regard to this achievement. Authority "as we once knew it,"
that is, as grown out of the "Roman experience of foundation," has "nowhere been re-established." Yet the American Revolution is presented as
the only successful revolution in its distinct emphasis on foundation, because "the framing of the Constitution, falling back on existing charters
and agreements, confirmed and legalized an already existing body politic
rather than made it anew." [99] The new political beginning in eighteenth-
century America was a beginning within the tradition—that is, a fresh
interpretation and use of that tradition. Was it, therefore, closer to reestablishing authority and better equipped to confront "the elementary problems of human living-together?" [100]

These questions are answered in *On Revolution*, published five years
after *The Human Condition* and in the same year as Arendt's report on
the Eichmann trial. The study was stimulated, according to its author, by
a seminar on "The United States and the Revolutionary Spirit" held at
Princeton University in 1959. [101] But Arendt's interest in the role of the
American Constitution goes back to 1951, when she wrote to Jaspers of
her fascination with it—"quite magnificent" [102]—and *On Revolution* is
dedicated "to Gertrud and Karl Jaspers / In reverence—in friendship—
in love." Moreover, both the conceptual construction of distinct cultural
activities in *The Human Condition* and—though here mainly by implication—the analysis of the obscurity of evil in the report on the Eichmann trial have informed her arguments in *On Revolution*.

In her attempt to define the meanings of the American Revolution,
Arendt chose an approach similar to that used in *The Origins of Totalitarianism*, which she had called, in her reply to Voegelin, an "analysis in
terms of history." [103] But the *historein*, the telling of what it was like, is
more firmly shaped, under the influence of *The Human Condition*, into
reconciling stories. As a motto for "Action," chapter 5 of that volume,
Arendt had characteristically chosen a Dinesen quote: "All sorrows can
be borne if you put them into a story or tell a story about them." [104] Taking
the initiative, the actor, as he acts, changes both the world, by acting in
it, and himself, by revealing more than he knew about himself before he
acted. Acting is central to Arendt's concept of the political sphere, espe-

cially in its connection with speech, and both are the stuff of stories. At a 1972 conference on "The Work of Hannah Arendt," Arendt said on the subject of thinking and acting:

> I don't know any other reconciliation but thought. This need is, of course, much stronger in me than it usually is in political theorists, with their need to unite action and thought. Because they want to act, you know. And I think I understood something of action precisely because I looked at it from the outside, more or less.[105]

The question here is not whether Arendt changed, in later years, her personal attitude toward political action. In the forties, her commentary on the German and Palestine questions in some cases affected political behavior and policy—that is, politically she was as active as intellectuals can get. But she had always looked at action "from the outside"—that is, as a phenomenon meriting a reconciling story in addition to conceptual analysis. Her political thought, in spite of its firmly conceptualized basis, could not be contained in a theory or in a philosophy. In its focus on understanding the given as man-made worldliness, it was more concretely engaged and conflicted, and more a process of constructing than a construct. Political thought for Arendt was an activity by which, "in constant change and variation, we come to terms with, reconcile ourselves to reality, that is, try to be at home in the world."[106] Yet though this activity is processual in its revealing, combining, and recombining of distinctions, the distinctions themselves appear with a striking somatic clarity, as if crafted.

In "Labor," chapter 3 of *The Human Condition*, Arendt suggested a surprising connection between thinking and laboring: "underlying [the] tie between the laborer of the hand and the laborer of the head" is the laboring process, because thinking, too, only comes to an end with life itself and leaves no permanent traces, in fact "nothing tangible at all." Working and thinking, then, are two different activities:

> The thinker who wants the world to know the "content" of his thoughts must first of all stop thinking and remember his thoughts. Remembrance in this, as in all other cases, prepares the intangible and the futile for their eventual materialization; it is the beginning of the work process, and like the craftsman's consideration of the model which will guide his work, its most immaterial stage. The work itself then always requires some material upon which it will be performed and which through fabrication, the activity of *homo*

faber, will be transformed into a worldly object. The specific work quality of intellectual work is no less due to the "work of our hands" than any other kind of work.[107]

This description tells us a great deal about Arendt's own intellectual work, with its curiously effective mix of conceptual and fictional strategies that could be called thought-stories. When she said about her friend Walter Benjamin that he "thought poetically," though he was neither a poet nor a philosopher,[108] she could have been referring to herself, too. However, in terms of remembrance her perspective on the world of human affairs differed dramatically from Benjamin's,[109] and her conceptual clarity contrasted sharply with his brilliant confusion.

On Revolution was meant to bring to life—by repeating, in the imagination[110]—a public realm of political speech and action as it had been defined in *The Human Condition*. Of all Arendt's texts, *On Revolution* demonstrates most clearly both the problematic normative eclecticism and the illuminating force of such historiographical thought-storytelling. For she read into the American Revolution a utopian realm of the political as the total opposite of totalitarian domination and the apathetic conformism of mass culture: a mythopoetic projection of political action relinquished and reconquered, of political speech silenced and regained. This construct is not a theoretical statement on the conditions and structures of political speech and action, historical or contemporary. The Jeffersonian "wards," which were so appealing to her as spontaneously established grass-roots democratic structures[111]—somewhat like the *sovjets* in 1905 and 1917 Russia and the *Raete* in 1918/1919 Germany—were never implemented. The life span of such councils has always been extremely brief precisely because such politicization, Arendt's ideal of human interaction, is hard to sustain—it distracts so powerfully from socioeconomic self-interest. But Arendt's too-limited perception of the complex role of self-interest in human interaction prevented her from understanding important aspects of political reality. Significantly articulated individuation in the presence of others is the center of Arendt's concept of the political. Always endangered, in her view, by the isolating selfishness characteristic of the private and social spheres, it is set against the rule of biological necessity. For this reason she praised the American Revolution as the only successful political revolution—namely, a struggle for self-government—in contrast to the social revolution in France, which was caused by poverty and social inequality. The laboring energies of this selfishness, ceaselessly pushing against the political realm, have their source in the political inertia of the social sphere:[112] wealthy eighteenth- and nineteenth-century Berlin Jews who preferred social mobility to political involvement, eighteenth-century Paris crowds clamoring for bread, the rootless, economically desperate mob exploited by totalitarian leaders, beleaguered Zionists in Palestine who imposed on each other the silence of solidarity, the masses of contemporary Western democracies lobotomized by abundance. There is, in Arendt's argument, no acknowledgment of the cultural value of self-interest—in the sciences, in the arts, in industry, in trade. Nor is there recognition of the fact that actors in agonal politics tend to be "absolutistic" rather than "accommodational"; that they are often ruthless in their "urgency to achieve and express individual excellence."[113]

o 7 o

On Revolution, then, should be read as a political fiction with the message of the "good life" among men as political actors engaged in the unconstrained presentation of speech-acts. It is an eloquent plea for civilized behavior, recognizing the foundation of human freedom in articulated human interdependence. The introduction, a discussion of the interrelation of war, violence, and revolution, ends with a juxtaposition that points out clearly the main motivation of Arendt's argument: "The conviction, In the beginning was a crime—for which the phrase 'state of nature' is only a theoretically purified paraphrase—has carried through the centuries no less self-evident plausibility for the state of human affairs than the first sentence of St. John, 'In the beginning was the word,' has possessed for the affairs of salvation."[114]

The "state of nature" as significant location of the original crime was palpably and fearfully real to the refugee from a regime that had manipulated the complex system of a modern mass society in order to destroy the basis of its complexity—namely, its interdependence, plurality, and diversity. "The word," speech, the act of speaking to the other with the intention of being heard and understood, counteracts the silence that supports a totalitarian *utopia*, and is thus the prerequisite for (social-)political salvation. Arendt's concept of political ethics has been articulated, since *The Human Condition*, in the structural description of political speech-acts, which presuppose the speaker's intention to speak to others in order to be understood and which are meaningful only in the realization of this intention. Such acts of speaking responsibly seem to be limited, in her concept, to small, homogeneous, explicitly exclusive groups: the polis, *eutopia*, is predicated on men speaking politically, communally, in the agora while their (economic) self-interests are taken care of at home, in the private sphere, by women and slaves and thus do not have to enter into their public speech-acts. Arendt brackets the voicelessness of women and slaves in the polis in her eagerness to reconstruct examples of communication as concretely related to community. Here speech is an act that intends to be responsive and needs an answer; it is significant only as a politically, communally responsible act carried out in a realm where no responsible speaker will be silenced.

Such acts affirm the promises of a world that is surprising and enriching rather than threatening in its newness. Clearly, Arendt was attracted by the almost graphic quality of the American situation: the need, the challenge, the opportunity, to make a huge continent livable and familiar. Furthermore, livability was understood in familiar (European) terms, avoiding those aspects of the tradition which had threatened the good life and yet being spared a complete break with the tradition. America as the *novus ordo saeclorum* reflected the exhilarating freshness of a new beginning *in* the tradition.

The early Americans, Arendt believed, had not been driven by the search for Utopia as the good place of plenty, but by utopian desires for the good life of unconstrained political interaction. These utopian desires motivated, too, the speech acts so important to the success of the American Revolution. She admired the men who were its agents because, in contrast to the French revolutionaries, they were not caught and then enmeshed in the historical necessity of biological processes. Rather, they succeeded in modifying historical necessity by superimposing on it successfully—that is, intelligibly—their own construct, the Constitution. The achievement of the Constitution cannot be exaggerated. Its formulation and foundation are the locus of the uniquely enduring success of the American Revolution and literally its most profound meaning, and the story of the American Revolution is centered in this uniqueness. In chapter 1 of *On Revolution*, in which she tried to define this uniqueness as the achievement of the Constitution to make possible and to permanently—longer than the individual's lifetime—sustain equality, Arendt relied most clearly on her thought-story of the polis as she had told it in *The Human Condition*. Equality, which "we, following Tocqueville's insights, frequently see as a danger to freedom, was originally almost identical with it." However, equality in antiquity was not one of (individual) condition, "but the equality of those who form a body of peers."[115] The important aspect of this distinction for Arendt's argument is that men, unequal by *nature*, needed an *artificial* institution, the polis, to make them equal—for a time. Equality was possible only in this "specifically political realm, where men met one another as citizens and not as private persons"; that is, it was an attribute of the polis, not of men, who "received their equality by virtue of their citizenship"—as had Arendt in the United States when she became a citizen and remained a Jew.[116]

When Arendt described in this context the concept of freedom in antiquity, she did not so much evaluate it in comparison to freedom in modern terms as present its distinctness. She gave an in many ways narrative (rather than analytical) account of the possible realization of freedom in the Greek polis, and the point of her story was precisely the ancients' insistence on the realization of freedom in appearance. Herodotus's equation of freedom with no-rule rests on the ruler's destruction of the realm of the political, where he could have moved and spoken freely among equals:

> The reason for this insistence on the interconnection of freedom and equality in Greek political thought was that freedom was understood as being manifest in certain, by no means all, human activities, and that these activities could appear and be real only when others saw them, judged them, remembered them. The life of a free man needed the presence of others. Freedom itself needed therefore a place where people could come together—the agora, the market-place, or the *polis*, the political space proper.[117]

Freedom, in the understanding of the ancients, needed to be visible and intelligible. The point of the equation between freedom and equality— and of Arendt's narration—also is to insist on the intelligibility of human affairs removed from the manipulations and distortions of meaning inherent in rulership, be it in the private realm of household favoritism or the social realm of exclusiveness and privilege.

Immediately following this presentation of a situation—at a certain point in time, in a certain man-made space—Arendt argues that "political freedom in modern terms," after the revolutions, did not concern "'life, liberty and property' as such, but their being inalienable rights of man"— namely, civil liberties, "the results of liberation" rather than the "actual content of freedom." The content of freedom is to be found not in the liberation from governments but in the "participation in public affairs, or admission to the public realm."[118] Freedom in the sense of the ancients, then, is not judged better or less good than freedom in the sense of the moderns; rather, the implication of Arendt's evocation of its realization in antiquity is that, like authority, it has been lost in the modern period. The conclusion of section 2 of her argument in chapter 1 of *On Revolution* describes the "revolutionary spirit of the last centuries, that is the eagerness to liberate *and* to build a new house where freedom can dwell," as "unprecedented and unequalled in all prior history."[119] But with the exception of the American Revolution, which ended in the foundation of the Constitution, the admirable utopian energies of this revolutionary spirit remained just that.

The question concerning us here is not that Arendt's perspective on the American Revolution is idiosyncratic, as has been pointed out. She was no doubt a less objectively perceptive observer of American democracy than that amazingly shrewd and open-minded nineteenth-century Hythloday, de Tocqueville. Like her, he understood that the rules governing human intercourse in antiquity were different, relegating strangers, slaves, and women to the status of *barbaroi*. In contrast to her, as a critic points out, "il ne renonce jamais *en fait* a comparer ce qu'il pretend incomparable *en droit*. Il juge par exemple la notion moderne de liberté *plus juste* que l'ancienne."[120] Quite apart from the question of whether de Tocqueville's judgment was by necessity correct, such a comparison was not the issue for Arendt; she wished to define and to distinguish. Using certain historical instances of political interaction as the plot, so to speak, for her political fictions, she deliberately applied a perspective that allowed her not to make such comparisons because she intended these fictions to be, for her purpose, complete. This does not mean, of course, that they ought not to be questioned. But in questioning them, one has to consider their function in the light of their peculiar accessibility. In her historiography, Arendt's use of historical materials was guided by the questions posed in her stories, but these questions were developed out of her historical experience. This is true—to varying degrees—for most historiography that combines narrative strategies with rigorous conceptualization. But Arendt's approach shows a high degree of awareness of the fictional dimension of narration and the model/example character of fiction, which in her case concerns distinctions. Such awareness does not qualify her intention to convince the reader. A model—freedom versus necessity, freedom versus liberty—is presented to the reader for consideration, and in the act of presentation both the author's interest in it and the presentation itself will be clear. This clarity is of the greatest importance to her because she wishes to convince rather than persuade her reader. Her narrative and conceptual strategies indicate that the reader should be able to reproduce and reconsider her argument—that is, be convinced in some cases, not in others, agree and disagree with her spontaneously and critically.

◦ 8 ◦

There is some irony in the fact that the reader of *On Revolution* will be most inclined to contest Arendt's distinctions where she is most clearly intent on presenting her ideal of the political speech-act as the essence of public happiness, and public happiness as the core of man's humanity. In the chapters "The Social Question" and "The Pursuit of Happiness," she strained too much to reenter a place that never existed. It was, she argued, the unusual absence of the predicament of poverty as abject misery from the American scene that accounted for the success of the American Revolution in providing, in the Constitution, that "new house where freedom can dwell," the new artifice that enables temporary equality among peers. Now, in America, too, the laboring poor have to rely on representation, which is indeed indispensable to any democracy outside the confines of very small and homogeneous groups, be they early American townships or revolutionary councils in Hungary. Yet Arendt here, as elsewhere, is deeply ambivalent about representation, which she equates with "mere" self-preservation or self-interest. These, for her, negative safeguards cannot, in any significant way, open the political realm—the agora of the polis—to the many, who therefore cannot distinguish themselves because they are "excluded from the light of the public realm where excellence can shine; they stand in darkness wherever they go." [121] Modern representative mass democracy, focusing on the mediation between numerous conflicts of social (self-) interests, deprives its citizens of significant individuation.

In identifying the public sphere as such a narrowly political space, Arendt relied heavily on John Adams. [122] Given his passion for the political philosophy of antiquity, [123] Adams did not share Madison's and Jefferson's realistic view of representation; and his concept of political action, in contrast to theirs, was agonal rather than accommodational. "Society was not for Adams the hodgepodge of various interests and factions it was for Madison in *The Federalist*, Number 10. The passions may have been varied but there was no doubt in Adams's mind that the interests in the society could be reduced to a duality, the few and the many, those who had attained superiority and those who aspired to it."[124]

More than anything else, wrote a biographer of Adams, he yearned for "solid and lasting fame; not simply the applause that would gratify shallow ambition, but the considered approbation of his society for valuable services rendered. All his life he struggled for greatness—and feared he would miss it."[125] His enduring belief in America's virtue and uniqueness was based on the "differentness" of the country's historical situation and consequently the (potential) moral character of the American people.[126] His concept of virtue, informed by Joseph Butler's *Analogy of Religion* (1740), stressed the public realm in ways that must have delighted Arendt. To Mercy Warren, Adams wrote on April 16, 1776, that public virtue would have to be the foundation of America's new government. There had to be "a positive Passion for the public good, the public Interest, Honour, Power and Glory, established in the Minds of the People," and it had to be "Superiour to all Private Passions." And again: "The only reputable Principle and Doctrine" was that "all Things must give way to the public."[127]

Virtue, in Adams' usage, meant concern for the welfare and nurture of the community rather than of the individual. Jefferson, on the other hand, defined *virtue* as "a love of others, a sense of duty to them, a moral instinct, in short, which prompts us irresistibly to feel and to succor their distresses."[128] For Adams, virtue was Puritan ethics transformed into virtuous republicanism. He asserted that "it was not religion alone, as is commonly supposed, but it was a love of universal liberty [*freedom* in Arendt's usage] that projected, conducted, and accomplished the settlement of America."[129] He wanted the institutions established by the Puritans—schools, militia, congregations, town meetings—to remain the pillars of republican communities. They were needed to restrain the "rascality," "venality," "corruption," "avarice," and "ambition"—human selfishness—that he feared would destroy the revolution. In 1776 he feared that even in America there was not "public virtue enough to support a republic."[130] But ten years later, looking back on the successful revolution, he wrote in his diary:

> It is an Observation of one of the profoundest Inquirers into human Affairs, that a Revolution of Government, successfully conducted and compleated, is the strongest Proof, that can be given, by a

People of their Virtue and good Sense. An Interprize of so much
difficulty can never be planned and carried on without Abilities,
and People without Principle cannot have confidence enough in
each other.[131]

The success of the American Revolution demonstrated to Adams—
and, in a sense, to Arendt—the political virtue of the Americans, their
realized political potential. Arendt set man-made political structures supportive of equality against the experienced fact of natural inequality;
Adams saw republican virtue supported by virtuous institutions. For
Adams, too, the success of the revolution lay in its completion, the Constitution, which was proof positive of the "Virtue and good Sense" of the
people. Arendt shared with Adams a peculiar combination of utopian
beliefs concerning political institutions and a realistic assessment of human limitations. Both believed in the desirability of significant individuation in the public realm. Adams' *spectemur agendi*, "let us be seen in
action," which Arendt quoted,[132] stressed most forcefully the individual's
right to stand out and be recognized. While it is true that distinctiveness,
excellence, needs to be witnessed and communicated, the question remains as to whether and how such communication among the superior
few serves the general political process of persuasion and accommodation: persuasion in the context of conflicting interests, accommodation of
differing opinions. Transferred to eighteenth-century America, Arendt's
perspective, informed by her mythopoetic model of the polis and reaffirmed by John Adams, results in a public realm that is too static, too
unchanging, too unaccommodating to human diversity. The group of political actors she envisioned—the Founding Fathers in Periclean cos-
tume—is homogeneous and stable, also in its absorption of generational
shifts. In their dealings with one another there seem to be no unforesee-
able challenges, no conflicts, no need for spontaneous interaction of any
sort, not to mention negotiation or compromise. In this situation, excellence, the standing out, the distinctiveness itself, assumes a formulaic
quality; it becomes a reliable phenomenon signifying a *status quo*, almost
like successful assimilation to a dominating group of "peers."
    With all of Arendt's interest in and insistence on natality, one detects,
in this portion of her argument, a curious need for security, for the proven.
Her concept of the perfect speech-act synonymous with meaningful political action presupposes a guarantee that the speaker will be able to rely
on being listened to and understood fully according to his stated inten-

tions. Ironically, it is this insistence on being understood fully, this lack of tolerance for any ambiguity, which threatens to undermine understanding. In this ideal model, mutuality seems to be reduced to the individual inviolate in the group, clearly outlined among other individuals, who can be relied on not to question that individual so profoundly as to challenge and thereby compromise his individuality. Constellations within that group may change, but not the fact that they are preestablished.

Referring to Adams as witness and supporter of this meaning of excellence, Arendt quoted one of his illustrations: "If Crusoe on his island had the library of Alexandria, and a certainty that he should never again see the face of man, would he ever open a volume?"[133] The suggested answer is "no." The point of Defoe's novel, however, is the social dimension of the individual, the ineradicable fact of socialization. In what amounts to certainty that he will never see another human face again, Robinson, alone with himself on his island, acts as a social being. Robinson would have read the books written by and about men, because others were part of his socially developed self, and thus reading about them supported his social *and* individual identity. But the social dimension of experience was problematic for Arendt, who therefore emphasized the political realm, which occupies a smaller part of the effects of socialization.

Ever since the Rahel biography, Arendt had been mistrustful of the social sphere, with its ambiguities, hesitations, lacunae, misunderstandings, and, above all, its profoundly unsettling acknowledgment of both human solitariness *and* need for sociableness. In the marketplace of her polis, this disturbing, surprising, conflicted, contradictory, never fully articulated, and therefore disruptive social sphere is subjected to specified forms of political discourse and thus is kept under control. It is this emphasis on the need to manage, to control, to rein in, much more than her bracketing, in setting up her model, the exclusion of women and slaves, that has been disturbing to Arendt's readers. She lamented the obscurity of the unpolitical poor, dependent on representation, and celebrated the excellence of the political rich (propertied, leisured), who can rely on understanding one another. She did not examine the various aspects of obscurity and excellence, privacy and publicity, the many faces of fame; that is, the various individual decisions that go into obscurity, and the various group mechanisms and misunderstandings that operate on excellence.

Arendt's low opinion of representation had its roots in her unwilling-

ness to consider the role of motivations in political decisions, because
they detract from the perfection of the speech-act and can lead to misunderstanding. Representation describes a situation of mutual dependence in terms of self-interest *and* open dialogue. It is true that in such a
situation neither partner can rely on being understood fully according to
his intentions, and that he can rely even less on these intentions being
realized in political action. But the dialogues mediating the different interests are viable performative speech-acts, notwithstanding the compromise nature and ambiguity of negotiation praxis. It is in the social sphere,
which importantly includes the neighborliness of households, an informal
web of relations between people of different sexes, ages, and, at least potentially, socioeconomic status, that mediation between the private and
public realms takes place and where representation is negotiated. Mediation and negotiation develop in the give-and-take of saying "yes" *and* "no"
to the "same" issue, which never seems the same in the different situation
in which each individual continues to find herself in relation to the other
and to the self becoming an other in time.

For Arendt, who is intent on clear distinctions, the social sphere is
that which is corruptible and which corrupts by obscuring the demarcations of both the private and the public sphere. In *The Human Condition*,
she used images of profuse natural growth to describe the peculiarly re-
silient power of the social sphere in pressing against the private and public spheres and creating confusion.[134] As an example, she related the ob-
session with hypocrisy, so striking in the men responsible for the course
of the French Revolution, to the French experience of the vices of the
Court of Versailles, which had been established with the explicit intent
of seducing and corrupting the individual in order to make him unfit for
action in the public realm. It is true that the Versailles principle of promises made and broken, playing on the hopes of men, and kept only out of
fear of men, corrupts private and public speech irrevocably. Yet it is also
true that the concept of political speech as innocent of ambiguity and
deception, a chimeric moment of perfect communication revealing truth
as true community, is in general too remote from the complex life-world
of the individual, which is social.

Significantly, Arendt stressed the prepolitical aspects of the *Rights of
Man* as defined by the French Revolution; they are, she pointed out, the
rights of life and nature—food, dress, reproduction—rather than the
rights of freedom and citizenship.[135] The rights of life and nature are prepolitical because they are tied to the irreducible life basis—that is, to

inequality, conflict, and compromise. Political freedom and citizenship, defined by political speech and, in modern times, a constitution, rise above such ties. They also support modes of speech, action, and identity of which Jews as well as women have been deprived for many centuries. If the modern reader has certain difficulties with Arendt's thought-stories of the polis and the American Revolution, it is not so much because these stories neglect to reject explicitly the past deprivation of participation in the political sphere. Rather, the reason is that Arendt's reconstructions of historically realized political spaces have seemed too clear, too self-sufficient in their reliance on an exclusive purity, stability, reliability, and even predictability of political interaction.

A good case in point is her perspective on the "pursuit of happiness" issue in the Declaration of Independence. In a 1774 Virginia Convention paper, Jefferson had spoken of "a right which nature has given all men, . . . of establishing new societies, under such laws and regulations as to them shall seem most likely to promote public happiness."[136] In her comment, Arendt contrasts this "public happiness" with the "happiness of our people," invoked in royal proclamations, which is limited to the private sphere. "Public happiness," for her, refers to the fun and happiness of the public sphere, with its town assemblies, discussions, deliberations, and decision making. Jefferson may not have had these specific activities in mind at all when he spoke of "public happiness." The Founding Fathers—founding the *covenants* that were to be so important to the founding of the Constitution—had come in groups, united by shared intellectual and emotional needs and concerns and by the common experience of persecution. Jefferson's "public happiness" could very well be understood as reference to a happiness found in the open pursuit of those shared interests and concerns—that is, a happiness that did not have to be experienced in retreat or hiding.

"Public happiness," then, need not be read through Arendt's perspective, where it appears indicative of a distinct separation of the private from the public sphere. Privileging the latter so clearly seems even less convincing. Arendt explicitly does appreciate the fact so familiar to the men involved in the political life of the new state—namely, that involvement in the government of affairs can be experienced as burdensome *and* identity-enhancing. What, after all, is happiness? In the Declaration, to Arendt's chagrin, the attribute "public" is missing. Happiness, Jefferson wrote to Madison on June 9, 1793, is "in the lap and love of my family, in the society of my neighbors and my books, in the wholesome occupation of my farms and affairs."[137] And he would also always stress the great importance of being "a participator in the government of affairs," as he put it in a letter to Joseph C. Cabell on February 2, 1816—a letter from which Arendt quoted repeatedly.[138]

Jefferson was a realist like Madison, who wrote: "If men were angels, no government would be necessary. If angels were to govern men, neither external nor internal controls on government would be necessary."[139] Men are not angels, and so they have to govern themselves, which is a hard job at any time, even if it is exhilarating to some men at some times. Years later, in a letter to John Adams on April 11, 1823, Jefferson speculated, more than half-jokingly, about the possibilities of an afterlife: "May we meet there again, in Congress, with our antient Colleagues, and receive with them the seal of approbation 'Well done, good and faithful servants.'" In this passage Arendt sees "Jefferson's true notion of happiness" come out "very clearly."[140] No one would deny that happiness is experienced in receiving recognition of the significance of one's public work. It is important to note, however, that for Jefferson the realm of happiness was by no means unambiguously, and most certainly not exclusively, located in the public sphere.

Arendt purposely imposed such exclusiveness on Jefferson's statements because, from her experience of German-Jewish history and totalitarian rule, she had come to fear, above all, the consequences of withdrawal into the private sphere away from political speech and action. Thus she lamented the negative influences of Europe's poverty on the development of the American concept of political freedom through the impact of mass immigration on the United States in the nineteenth and twentieth centuries. They caused the American Dream to be removed from the hopes of the American Revolution—to succeed in establishing a solid foundation of freedom—but also from the hopes of the French Revolution—to succeed in contributing significantly to the liberation of men. The American Dream was "unhappily, the dream of a 'promised land' where milk and honey flow."[141] And the rapid development of technology and technocracy in the United States did nothing but serve to realize—that is, reaffirm—that shallow, childish dream.

o   9   o

The first three chapters of *On Revolution* celebrate the public realm and warn of the distractive, seductive power of the private and social spheres. Arendt interpreted John Adams' *spectemur agendi*, "let us be seen in action," to mean the definition and construction of a space where "we are seen and can act," which made even clearer the interdependence between public recognition and action as constituents of identity. This space, in which the good citizen—distinguished from the good man[142]—could be conspicuous, came into conflict with "ruthless and fundamentally antipolitical desires to be rid of all public cares and duties." Ending in the Constitution, the American Revolution was a complete political success. Yet it was always threatened—in fact, undermined—by the growing social desires

> to establish a mechanism of government administration through which men could control their rulers and still enjoy the advantages of monarchal government, to be "ruled without their own agency," to have "time not required for the supervision or choice of the public agents, or the enactment of laws," so that "their attention may be exclusively given to their personal interest."[143]

It is in the second half of the book, which deals with questions related to the Constitution proper, that Arendt's talent for making directly accessible the meanings of political constructs is expressed most effectively. In chapter 4, "Foundation I: *Constitutio Libertatis*," and chapter 5, "Foundation II: *Novus Ordo Saeclorum*," she is able both to draw very clear distinctions and to draw on her own and others' conflicted, ambiguous experience. She looked at the phenomenon of new social-political associations among early American immigrants in the vast wilderness of an unknown land through her own experience of radical dissociation *and* forming new ties in twentieth-century exile. This concrete and peculiarly sympathetic, illuminating perspective was supported by her sharp awareness of the multidirectional potential of cultural change. The trauma of her profoundly ruptured past seems, finally, appeased by the invigorating sense of a new life in a new country—a sense of openness, space, and motion. Yet her sensitivity, almost palpable, to the dangers inherent in such change and new beginnings, to the vulnerability, fragile tenacity, and preciousness of civilized behavior, informs as well her understanding of the early Americans' political realism. Fearing the state of nature, the boundless territory, the unlimited initiative of men bound by no law, they bound themselves together by mutual promise, as the Mayflower Compact said, into a "civil Body Politick" in "the presence of God and one another."[144] Arendt points out how the Pilgrims' covenant, built on reciprocation, broke down precisely that isolation experienced by individuals who are protected in the pursuance of their private goals by a social contract with their ruler. Significantly, the Founding Fathers' concept of covenant was rooted both in the rediscovery of Israel's consent-based covenant with God and in their experience of the actual difficulties in their situation, which they understood *necessitated* association.[145]

It was, in Arendt's view, precisely this *shared, articulated* experience of necessity which supported the thoroughly secular quality of the American Revolution built on these covenants:

> The great good fortune of the American Revolution was that the people of the colonies, prior to their conflict with England, were organized in self-governing bodies, that the Revolution—to speak the language of the eighteenth century—did not throw them into a state of nature, that there never was any serious questioning of the *pouvoir constituant* of those who framed the state constitutions and, eventually, the Constitution of the United States.[146]

The Founding Fathers were perfectly realistic about the undesirable aspects of human nature and they could afford to be so, because "they knew that whatever men might be in their singularity, they could bind themselves into a community which, even though it was composed of 'sinners', need not necessarily reflect this 'sinful' state of human nature."[147] The American version of the perfectibility of man—before it was influenced by Rousseauism during the nineteenth century[148]—was so attractive to Arendt because it

> was not at all based on a semi-religious trust in human nature but, on the contrary, on the possibility of checking human nature in its singularity by virtue of common bonds and mutual promises. The hope for man in his singularity lay in the fact that not man but men inhabit the earth and form a world between them. It is human worldliness that will save men from the pitfalls of human nature.[149]

Worldliness is the public realm of work rather than labor, speech rather than silence, action rather than passivity, visibility rather than darkness, distinctness rather than obscurity, authority rather than coercion, manipulation, or confusion, plurality rather than singularity, articulated community rather than unquestioned solidarity. It is the political space in which the individual living the good life of the citizen can be conspicuous—that is, seen and heard in the presence of others. Humans in their community will act and speak together so that the individual can act and speak communally. In her essay "Civil Disobedience," written twenty-five years after the collapse of Hitler's totalitarian rule, Arendt reflected on the question of justice and the rules of conscience, which "hinge on interest in the self":

> When Socrates stated that it "is better to suffer wrong than to do wrong," he clearly meant that it was better for *him*, just as it was better for him "to be in disagreement with [himself]." Politically, on the contrary, what counts is that a wrong has been done; to the law it is irrelevant who is better off as a result—the doer or the sufferer.[150]

The rules of conscience, she points out rightly, are "entirely negative. They do not say what to do; they say what not to do. They do not spell out certain principles for taking action; they lay down boundaries no act should transgress. They say: Don't do wrong, for then you will have to live together with a wrongdoer."[151]

The problem with these often admirable rules is that they are not self-evident, they cannot be proved, they vary from person to person, and they apply—as it seems from historical evidence—only to a comparatively small minority of humans insofar as they are "thinking beings."[152] And even this small minority seems overburdened with the responsibility of following the rules of conscience in times when the cultural distinction between right and wrong has been seriously shifted or even inverted.[153] Significantly, Arendt uses in this context an example from the 1963/64 Auschwitz trial in Germany of SS men posted at the camp between 1940 and 1945. All of them were charged with murder, but in almost all cases the atrocities committed had nothing to do with the execution of the order for the "final solution." Their crimes were punishable under Nazi law, and in rare cases they were indeed brought to trial under the Nazi government. The defendants had had no other reason to work at an extermination camp than that they had been unfit for military duty: "Hardly any of them had a criminal record of any sort, and none of them a record of sadism and murder. Before they had come to Auschwitz and during the eighteen years they had lived in postwar Germany, they had been respectable and respected citizens, undistinguishable from their neighbors."[154] Whether they had been, before and after the war, "good" men depends on what one means by "goodness"—under the normal circumstances of a more or less functioning democratic system they had been accepted as "good citizens."

It may be disturbing to some readers of this essay that Arendt connects, in her argument, the "merely" individual nature of the rules of
conscience followed occasionally by morally superior individuals under
extremely difficult circumstances with the perverted behavior in such situations of others not so gifted. But in this case more clearly even than in
others, her reason for establishing this connection, which emphasized,
once again, the overriding importance of the political sphere, was indeed
as concrete as it was realistic. She emphatically rejected the suggestion of
a sympathetic reader of her *Eichmann in Jerusalem* that she saw "an Eichmann in each one of us." To say that would be as incorrect and as abstract—that is, contrary to experience—as to say that "Eichmann is in
nobody." Arendt thought there were, in fact, "quite a number of Eich-
manns." [155] But this was not the point she wished to make, for she was
concerned not so much with what people "are" as with what they might
have been or might become under different circumstances. In her view, a
very large majority of people, regardless of any clear innate sense of goodness, are capable of becoming good citizens if they are allowed and encouraged to share the visible spaces of the political realm.

This emphasis on a world shared, a world formed and articulated by
men and women among themselves, was the focus of Arendt's report on
the Eichmann trial. It was the reason, much misunderstood, for her attempt to make her reader consider the communicable secular, rather than
the ultimately not communicable religious, dimension of the Jewish experience. Arendt thought it unwise to stress "the bloodstained road traveled by this people" [156] as if driven by some foreordained mysterious destiny, the fated age-old hostility and separateness of the Gentile world. The
important point for her was that no people ought to have such singularity
imposed on them and consequently embrace its own uniqueness in what
she thought were dangerous ways, socially and politically. [157] The Jewish
people had been sinned against precisely because they had not been allowed to share the earth with other peoples in a significantly political
communal sense, and in reaction they had too unquestioningly invoked
this experience to force denial of community and political silence on other
peoples.

As in all her texts, Arendt's intention in the report on the Eichmann
trial was to reclaim the potential dimension of past political experience
through a thought-story which one could reconcile with that past reality
because it made possible an understanding of it in the present. Her perspective is often unexpected; but seeing things differently, even contro-

versially, she also frequently succeeded in extracting new meanings and a new significance from "previously mute fragments of the past."[158] Such reclamation does not console, precisely because it demonstrates, with the insistency peculiar to Arendt's arguments, what might have been—or might not have been—if humans had been able to act less irresponsibly, if they had been helped to be good citizens. In her 1958 *laudatio* for Karl Jaspers, on the occasion of his being awarded the Peace Prize of the German Book Trade, Arendt described Jaspers' position during the Hitler regime:

> What Jaspers represented then, when he was entirely alone, was not Germany but what was left of *humanitas* in Germany. It was as if he alone in his inviolability could illuminate that space which reason creates and preserves between men, and as if the light and breadth of this space would survive even if only one man were to remain in it. Not that this was actually so or even could have been so. Jaspers has often said: "The individual by himself cannot be reasonable." In this sense he was never alone, nor did he think very highly of such solitude. The *humanitas* whose existence he guaranteed grew from the native region of his thought, and this region was never unpopulated. What distinguishes Jaspers is that he is more at home in this region of reason and freedom, knows his way about it with greater sureness, than others who may be acquainted with it but cannot endure living constantly in it. Because his existence was governed by the passion for light itself, he was able to be like a light in the darkness glowing from some hidden source of luminosity.[159]

I have quoted this passage in full because it contains the central meaning for Arendt of Jaspers the man—that is, the position from which he philosophized. The *laudatio*, in which, following Roman usage, she focused on the greatness and dignity of the individual concerned, enabled her to state publicly what she could not have expressed privately, and the obvious exaggerations of her statements have to be considered in this context. Arendt was fascinated by what she perceived to be Jaspers' capacity to be "inviolable, untemptable, unswayable."[160] It was this capacity, real or imagined, which made particularly important to her the fact that, unlike other thinkers, he shared in his philosophizing her concern for human worldliness. In Jaspers, even more than in—as she read

him—Kant, the conflict between the polis and the philosopher was finally resolved:

> Thinking becomes practical, though not pragmatic; it is a kind of
> practice between men, not a performance of one individual in his
> self-chosen solitude. Jaspers is, as far as I know, the first and the
> only philosopher who has ever protested against solitude, to whom
> solitude has appeared "pernicious" and who has dared to question
> "all thoughts, all experiences, all contents" under this one aspect:
> "What do they signify for communication? Are they such that they
> may help or such that they will prevent communication? Do they
> seduce to solitude or arouse to communication?" Philosophy has
> lost both its humility before theology and its arrogance toward the
> common life of man. It has become *ancilla vitae*.[161]

Eminently a "thinking being," Jaspers had lived according to firm
rules of conscience, but with him these rules, though "self-centered" in
nature, had also become self-evident and needed no proof; they could be
extended into the political community. Writing on questions like German
guilt or the atomic bomb, he did not think in order to act politically, but
his thinking enabled political speech and action. Though Arendt frequently disagreed with Jaspers in the often not unimportant details of an
argument, she clearly looked upon his position, as she perceived and articulated it, as an ideal guiding her own work in the service of common—
that is, shared—human experience. Eichmann's position, which, as she
defined it, totally inhibited thought as well as political speech and action,
was the opposite of this ideal. But the purity of this contrast, which so
strikingly illuminated Arendt's portrayal of Eichmann, also obscured it for
many of her readers, who did not have sufficient access to the conflict, in
her political thought, between the experiential limitation of what can be
asked of humans and the utopian desire to accept only the best. (This
conflict was probably responsible for Arendt's failure, which I cannot discuss here, to make a realistic concept of leadership part of her political
model: there is "the polis," there are the "magnificent" men of the American Revolution, there is the idealized *gestalt* of Jaspers as mediator between the *bios politikos* and the *bios theoretikos*.) Eichmann, whom she
explicitly did not wish to demonize, nevertheless emerges in her portrait
as a monster of commonness, the absolute *corruptio pessima optimi* (the
"optimum" being modern man's intellectual and political potential). This

tension between the literally extraordinary acts of the man and his much remarked-upon general ordinariness was connected with Arendt's unfortunate choice of subtitle for the Eichmann book, *A Report on the Banality of Evil.* Her concept of the political was based on a relational concept of goodness which excludes definitions of wickedness as "banal" or "monstrous." But Eichmann, whom she tried to understand—not for one moment "being understanding"—threatened to collapse the visible spaces of the public realm, and so she made him clearly monstrous in his banality. This construct of a secular monstrosity was centered in her desire to witness, too, the dead Jews' unrealized potential for human worldliness and to preserve it from oblivion. But she had not foreseen that her portrayal of Eichmann, the common man and uncommon murderer, would pose the question of the cultural significance of individual conscience in terms too disturbingly ambiguous for many of her readers and cause profound misunderstanding of her intentions and motivations.

6

The Obscurity of Evil

Listening to Eichmann

This last chapter draws in part on a previously published essay, "The Secularity of Evil: Hannah Arendt and the Eichmann Controversy."[1] In a sense I have written the previous chapters toward this essay, which was prompted as much by Arendt's report on the Eichmann trial as by the overwhelmingly hostile responses to it. The authors of these responses, in their refusal to understand Arendt's intentions and motivations, seemed then largely incomprehensible to me because her argument seemed so accessible: she neither accused nor forgave collectively, nor consoled, nor tried to explain "fully," but instead reclaimed that past space and time in which a figure like Eichmann had been possible—as she had reclaimed in *The Human Condition*, in "What Is Authority?" and in *On Revolution* the space and time in which Eichmann would not have been possible. Such reclaiming challenged my sense of responsibility to look, listen, distinguish, and remember. Few other texts dealing with the uncompleted German-Jewish past had made such concrete claims on my attention in remembrance, and I saw its usefulness precisely in their sustained power.

In the preceding chapters, I have tried to explain how Arendt came to make this claim on herself—and, by extension, on her readers—out of her experience of the German-Jewish past, and how she made it the center of her political historiography. I have also tried to prepare the ground for a more helpful perspective on the misunderstanding between Arendt and readers of her report on the Eichmann trial, a misunderstanding caused, to a large extent, by her approach to historical experience.

Despite their openly selective use of political and philosophical materials and their compelling conceptual compression and direction, the thought-stories she told as a political historiographer have nevertheless retained the conflictedness and ambiguities of historical social-political experience. In the case of her life story of Rahel, her critical essays on political Zionism, the anti-Semitism part of *The Origins of Totalitarianism*, and, above all, the report on the Eichmann trial, this conflictedness has asserted itself all the more forcefully against their strikingly concrete clarity and apparent consistency.[2] Yet the disquieting energy created by this tension—the unexpected, provocative, and controversial direction of her stories—has contributed significantly to a shared process of understanding the German-Jewish past precisely because it has consistently disrupted the status quo of its meaning.

My discussion of Arendt's analysis of the Eichmann trial focuses on the misunderstandings it engendered. These misunderstandings—psychologically motivated deliberate misreadings—are symptomatic of the problems she addressed in her critical discussions of the many different forms of assimilationism—that is, in her terms, loss of the political sphere, worldliness, and critical community. But the point for her and for her sympathetic readers was not that these reactions against her argument were themselves proof positive of its validity. No matter how powerful her desire to convince and how strong its influence on her choice of narrative and conceptual strategies, by intellectual temperament she would not have resorted to the Freudian argument of resistance. She took these reactions seriously and they profoundly surprised and pained her, though they were indeed intimately connected with the position of an exclusive, unquestioning, self-protective solidarity, which she had always considered politically unintelligent and dangerous. They also tended to degenerate into personal attacks that seriously distorted the issues she was trying to clarify. But one must never forget that these bitter rejections came out of an experience which had been so traumatic as to greatly undermine the capacity for trusting the other sufficiently to risk a more flexible, more reflected perspective on the self.

Arendt had shared this experience; yet her reaction was different and quite rare in its consistently independent direction, distinctness, and authorial responsibility. This may be the time to pose a question which so far in this study I have not avoided so much as kept submerged: What was the source, or more realistically one of the main sources, of such independence? Her old friend Hans Jonas spoke of her as "one of the great women of our century. I think I stay in consent with her when I say 'women' and not 'thinkers' (only part of a whole) or 'persons' (a sexless evasion)." Stressing her femininity, he pointed out—rightly, I think— that she considered men the weaker sex, "more removed from the intuitive grasp of reality, more subject to the deception of concept, therefore more prone to illusion and less perceptive of the ambiguity and admixture of shadows in the human equation—thus actually to be protected."[3] On the other hand, working in a field almost totally dominated by men, she has been perceived—and that, of course, was a laudatory perception— to be a "male" thinker.

While in many contemporary feminists' eyes, she would have sinned hugely with her forceful rootedness in an allegedly male "logocentricity"; while she has seen the intellectual position from which she developed her concept of the political as unquestioningly embedded in the "Great" male-dominated Western political-philosophical tradition; while men undoubtedly had the greatest influence over, made the greatest contributions to, her intellectual development; while she thought much of femininity[4] and little of feminism—or of any other "ism" reflecting a position of uncritical intellectual solidarity—Arendt was indeed stronger than many of her male intellectual friends because of her firmer and fuller grasp of reality as a life-world shared with others. She was less subject to the seduction of theories of theory instead of practice, shrewder about the motivations informing her own and others' intellectual positions, and more open to the conflicts and ambiguities of experience.[5]

All these aspects of her intellectual temperament, though not necessarily "feminine," have arguably been strengthened by her cultural experiences as a woman. The acculturation of the woman and the Jew, both of them precarious participants in German culture and (official) history, combined in Arendt's experience to support her particularly focused and flexible perspective on the most difficult, most entangled, most painful, aspect of that culture, the failed German-Jewish symbiosis. Writing in an ostensibly male-dominated tradition of political philosophy, she both accepted and disregarded certain conventions of its discourse. Speaking as a woman among men, she appreciated the authority of a political-philosophical community *and* strained against it. Such a dual attitude toward an intellectual tradition is the basis for all significant intellectual contributions; it is, really, a question of the quality of the tension created and the degree of the illumination sustained by it. In Arendt's case, the tension was increased by her singular position in this tradition as a woman and a Jew, and so was the degree of illumination achieved by her showing the importance of this tradition for the present.

Speaking among men as an equal and as a woman, Arendt brought to her reading of the tradition a characteristic sensitivity to the need for culturally articulated equality, for the spontaneous new beginning in human affairs and relations, for nurturing the self and other, for delight in human plurality and diversity, for tolerance of the other's otherness in appreciation of difference in human relatedness, for a general, nonexclusive human solidarity that would support the relative, temporary permanence of living together on this earth as naturally cultural beings. More concretely, more literally, than many of her male peers in the present and the past, she sought to understand and, with the help of the tradition, express human distinctness. More urgently, perhaps, than they, she wished for it to be preserved in cultural activities that would not be erased inexorably by the rush of life-time but would leave significant traces. The often almost somatic substance of her conceptual definitions, their peculiar accessibility, is connected with her reflecting thought and language against concrete situations. Her thought-stories present political actors so that they can be heard and seen clearly, because they were there and they spoke in the past, and their being there, speaking, was recorded in cultural memory. In Arendt's experience, the responsibility for this memory was a precious and precarious cultural achievement, and for this reason, too, she insisted on the interdependence of worldliness and political community: here are created the visible spaces in which speech and action can become intelligible and their memory can be secure for a time. These intentions, these fears, these hopes, informed the way in which she listened to Eichmann in Jerusalem.

o   2   o

From the Rahel biography on, Arendt looked at the social organism in its complex metabolism involving the individual within the social group within a world shared with other groups. She would agree with her friend Hans Jonas that the power of the living organism to use the world is synonymous with its need to use it. Needs are always directed toward something else, the other, and it is in the direction of the other that the self can develop most fully. Jonas sees the spectrum of needs belonging to an organism as the "measure of the degree of its freedom and individuality."[6] It has been the social and political problem of the Jewish people that the expression of such needs has met with more, as well as more

severe forms of, resistance. In Arendt's view, the experience of this resistance, most extreme, most traumatic in the mass destruction of European
Jewry under the Hitler regime, had informed the creation of the State of
Israel in ways that threatened the realization and defense of diversity,
plurality, and mutuality in social and political interaction. But her critical
analysis of the Eichmann trial, which had been intended to reaffirm the
creation of the State of Israel, was dismissed by most of her Jewish critics
as simply distorted by the apostate's animus.

In her analysis Arendt drew on arguments she had developed in *The
Origins of Totalitarianism* and *The Human Condition*, stressing the fact
that the most important and most difficult issue for the individual as a
member of a mass society in the twentieth century was her ability to act
responsibly out of a context of personal moral convictions reinforced by
other responsible citizens. In a totalitarian system, where almost no such
reinforcement could take place, only an extraordinary person could retain
this ability. In such a system the needs of the social organism are perverted in their total turn against the needs of the other. The individual,
swept up by the energy of this turn, is totally isolated and experiences
great difficulties in trying to think and decide for himself. Bruno Bettelheim, one of the few positive critics of Arendt's Eichmann book, emphasized this fact as one of the most important problems discussed in her
analysis, supporting it with references to his own experience as an inmate
of a concentration camp: the terrible situation in which there were no
voices from the outside giving direction; the silence of totalitarianism
which included Nazis *and* anti-Nazis.[7] In drawing this parallel, in extending the silence to include the victims and the passive and active victimizers, he was, at least implicitly, more understanding of supporters of the
Nazi regime than Arendt was willing to be. Notwithstanding her critics'
complaints to the contrary, she had (and showed most clearly in her report), nothing but contempt for Eichmann. But she saw this contemptible
man caught in a dilemma, which illustrates one of the most dangerous
aspects of modernity:

> Eichmann said he recognized that he had participated in what was
> perhaps one of the greatest crimes in history, but, he insisted, if he
> had not done so, his conscience would have bothered him at the
> time. His conscience and morality were working exactly in reverse.
> This reversal is precisely the moral collapse that took place in Eu-
> rope.[8]

Some people had been able to remain untouched by this reversal, but they were in the very difficult position of having to decide from case to case; no rules existed for the unprecedented, and it is extraordinarily difficult for the individual to arrive at a judgment without being able to rely on a general code established by social agreement at large. Is judgment of the particular possible without reference to a general rule?[9] Discussing the case of Sergeant Anton Schmidt, who over a period of five months had helped Jews in the underground—without payment, as the witness emphasized[10]—and, when caught, had been executed, Arendt stressed the highly important lesson that even under conditions of terror some people will not comply: "Humanly speaking, no more is required, and no more can reasonably be asked, for this planet to remain a place fit for human habitation."[11] Despite her emphasis, this "lesson" remains a rather abstract model. Bettelheim, for instance, is much clearer on the problem of the extraordinariness of such persons. Still, for Arendt, the model served to clarify the human dilemma with which the Eichmann trial, with its underlying metaphysical concept of evil, did not deal. Caught in an inverted system of morals, Eichmann, the "banal" bourgeois, could participate in the causation of events that are still beyond the range of human comprehension. The commonplace man, Arendt said in the chapter entitled "Judgment, Appeal, and Execution," was "no common criminal."[12] The need to comprehend remains all the more urgent.

It was for this reason that Arendt thought anti-Semitism not only a useless factor for the trial but also a positively harmful one. By contrast, the accepted attitude toward this issue is expressed in a 1966 B'nai B'rith–sponsored study:

> The declared purpose of the trial was to bring a criminal to justice, but the trial was also seen as a vehicle for informing public opinion. By recalling the barbaric mass murders engineered by Eichmann and his associates, it would recall to the world the demonic nature of Nazism in particular and anti-Semitism in general, both of which had been countenanced by the German people and, to some extent, by the world at large.[13]

To remind the world "in horrible and painful detail of the consequences that lurk in anti-Semitism" seemed to the authors of this report the trial's successful strategy in its "monumental effort to combat anti-Semitism."[14] Their documentation is contradictory and their findings are inconclusive,[15] but their understanding of the intention behind the trial is correct. In Arendt's view, neither this intention nor the strategy contributed to the attempt at understanding the quality of Eichmann's guilt. She therefore started her report on the trial with the clarification that this case "was built on what Jews had suffered, not on what Eichmann had done."[16] Staged like a play, the whole world its audience, the concern of the trial was the tragedy of Jewry as a whole. Arendt linked the "almost universal hostility in Israel to the mere mention of an international court" to the desire to indict Eichmann exclusively for crimes against the Jewish people instead of, as the international court would have done, for "crimes against mankind committed on the body of the Jewish people."[17]

This distinction was centrally important to Arendt's critique of the trial. Among its many irregularities and abnormalities, the most important was, in her eyes, the charge itself: the crimes committed against the Jewish people.[18] At the root of all the failures and shortcomings of the Jerusalem trial—and, by extension, at the root of some profoundly disturbing conflicts created and suffered by the State of Israel—lay the fact that the catastrophe had been understood not as the "unprecedented crime of genocide," the most recent of crimes, but, because they were thinking "exclusively in terms of their own history," as "the oldest crime they knew and remembered":

> None of the participants ever arrived at a clear understanding of the actual horror of Auschwitz, which is of a different nature from all the atrocities of the past, because it appeared, to the prosecution and judges alike, as not much more than the most horrible pogrom in Jewish history.[19]

The court, then, did not, as did Arendt, define the physical extermination of millions of Jews as a crime against humanity, *Verbrechen gegen die Menschheit*, perpetrated on the body of the Jewish people; nor did it perceive the distinction that "only the choice of victims, not the nature of the crime, could be derived from the long history of Jew-hatred and anti-Semitism."[20] In this context Arendt argued, too, for the importance of the distinction between expulsion and genocide: though both are international crimes, expulsion is an offense against fellow nations, genocide "an attack upon human diversity as such, that is, upon a characteristic of the 'human status' without which the very words 'mankind' and 'humanity' would be devoid of meaning."[21] We are dealing with a "new type of criminal,"[22] she noted, one of the modern state-employed mass-murderers who "must be prosecuted because they violated the order of mankind, and not because they killed millions of people."[23] "Rewriting" the judgment—this alone seemed an act of intolerable arrogance to many of her critics[24]—Arendt addressed Eichmann:

> And just as you supported and carried out a policy of not wanting to share the earth with the Jewish people and the people of a number of other nations—though you and your superiors had no right to determine who should and who should not inhabit the world—we find that no-one, that is, no member of the human race, can be expected to want to share the earth with you. This is the reason and the only reason you must hang.[25]

The mass destruction of Jews—understood as a general Nazi attack on human plurality, diversity, and mutuality rather than as a specific, exclusive attack on the Jewish people—placed the question of Eichmann's crime in the disturbing because potentially ambiguous context of modernity: there were no more completely clear answers regarding the quality of guilt and individual conscience.

Ben-Gurion wanted to make the nations of the world "ashamed," he wanted them and the Jews in the Diaspora to remember how Judaism, "four thousand years old, with its spiritual creations and its ethical strivings, its Messianic aspirations," had always faced "a hostile world."[26] Consequently, the prosecutor Gideon Hausner opened the trial beginning with Pharaoh in Egypt, Haman's "to destroy, to slay and to cause them to perish," and quoting from Ezekiel: "And when I [the Lord] passed by thee, and saw thee polluted in thine own blood, I said unto thee: In thy blood, live." Arendt dismissed this introduction as "bad history and cheap rhetoric" precisely because it was at cross-purposes with putting Eichmann on trial, suggesting, as it did, that there existed some foreordained mysterious destiny, "the bloodstained road traveled by this people."[27] Further, and more important, Ben-Gurion's attempts to use the trial to strengthen Jewish consciousness by emphasizing the age-old hostility of the Gentile world were politically ill-advised,

> for a change in this mentality is actually one of the indispensable prerequisites for Israeli statehood, which by definition has made of the Jews a people among peoples, a nation among nations, a state among states, depending now on a plurality which no longer permits the age-old and, unfortunately, religiously anchored dichotomy of Jews and Gentiles.[28]

Israel needed to look upon itself as a secular, modern state, and it did not make sense for that state to present Eichmann as the demonic incarnation of age-old hostile forces besieging the chosen people. Eichmann was not the Gentile devil to whom the Jew Rudolf Kastner sold his soul when he negotiated with him during the Jewish deportations from Hungary.[29] He was, rather, a perfectly commonplace administrator. What had made him dangerous under the circumstances was indeed the perfection of his normality: "more normal, at any rate, than I am after having examined him," with a "not only normal but most desirable" attitude toward his family and friends, as psychologists have attested.[30] The man Eichmann, as Arendt saw and presented him, was the perfect bourgeois jobholder under a modern totalitarian regime, and thus he was incapable of telling right from wrong. In her opinion, the judges, in not dealing with this crucial fact, "missed the greatest moral and even legal challenge of the whole case."[31] They did not, as did the prosecution, attempt "to try the most abnormal monster the world had ever seen and, at the same time try in him 'many like him,' even the whole Nazi movement and anti-Semitism at large." But they were helpless when confronted with the task of understanding the criminal whom they had to judge.[32] Yet they could not, as for instance Martin Buber did, assume that they had "only in a formal sense a common humanity with those who took part" in the Nazi regime. Rather, their assuming a common humanity with the defendant was a presupposition to their being charged to judge his crime within a legal framework.[33]

○   3   ○

In her report, Arendt's insistence on the secularity of Eichmann's crime and its punishment and on the specificity of his guilt was responsible for the bitter reactions against it, because this perspective prevented the victims, too, from transcending the human condition. In her 1945 essay "Organized Guilt and Universal Responsibility," the first attempt to pose the question of the quality of German guilt, Arendt had marked recognition of what man is capable of as "precondition of any modern political thinking."[34] In her report on the trial she argued from this position, seeing the victims as simply human beings and not as martyrs, pointing out that they, too, had often been deprived of their ability to tell right from wrong, and, more important, that their fate might not have been entirely independent of their actions.

Bettelheim supported Arendt in this view, explaining the reactions to her arguments:

> Arendt is right not to grant the murdered Jews the sainthood of martyrs and to view them simply as men. To those who claim they were martyrs, this is a sacrilegious position, and whoever holds that their actions may have contributed to their fate is accused of trying to assert that the Jews were guilty or that the Nazis were not.[35]

He refers to chapter 7, "The Wannsee Conference, or Pontius Pilatus," in which Arendt discusses the problem of the role of the Jewish leaders in the destruction of their own people, as "undoubtedly the darkest chapter of the whole dark story."[36] Here she sums up her argument on the *Judenraete* in a passage which, as A. Alvarez stated in his lucid review of the Eichmann book, caused an "uproar" in the United States:[37]

> Wherever Jews lived there were recognized Jewish leaders, and this leadership, almost without exception, cooperated in one way or another, for one reason or another, with the Nazis. The whole truth was that if the Jewish people had really been unorganized and leaderless, there would have been chaos and plenty of misery but the total number of victims would hardly have been between four and a half and six million people.[38]

Only a very small part of Arendt's report deals with the problem of Jewish cooperation, as she herself pointed out and as a sympathetic and shrewd reviewer like Alvarez explicitly corroborated.[39] Even if some Jewish groups reacted nervously to her conclusions—the details Arendt relied upon had been published before in Raul Hilberg's *The Destruction of the European Jews* (1961)—and even if their nervousness contributed to the distorted, bitterly angry readings of many reviewers,[40] it is hard to imagine that these few pages of a critical evaluation of *Judenraete* could really have been responsible for such unanimous animosity. The truly provocative element of Arendt's analysis was her insistence that the questions posed by the Eichmann trial had to be dealt with in the context of modern political experience and that Israel should conduct itself—in conducting the trial of Eichmann—as a modern, secular state among other states. In doubting the wisdom of the leaders and, above all, the wisdom of the victims in following them so blindly, Arendt implicitly measured them against a possibly different kind of behavior described by political speech and action. Many of her readers thought such behavior a priori and absolutely impossible, and her implicit expectations unrealistic to a degree which signified the most serious betrayal of her people, even sacrilege. Her characterization of Dr. Leo Baeck, former Chief Rabbi of Berlin, as someone who was "in the eyes of both Jews and Gentiles the 'Jewish Führer,'"[41] was blamed on her appalling, inhuman lack of sensitivity, though in reality it had resulted from her desire to help her readers understand certain important cultural issues. Gershom Scholem, however, complained bitterly:

> In circumstances such as these, would there not have been a place for what I can only describe with that modest German word— "*Herzenstakt*"? You may laugh at the word; although I hope you do not, for I mean it seriously. . . . The use of the Nazi term in this context is sufficiently revealing. You do not speak, say, of the "Jewish leader," which would have been both apt and free of the German word's horrific connotation—you say precisely the thing that is most false and most insulting. For nobody of whom I have heard or read was Leo Baeck—whom we both knew—ever a "Führer" in the sense which you here insinuate to the reader. . . . To speak of all this . . . in so wholly inappropriate a tone—to the benefit of those Germans in condemning whom your book rises to greater eloquence than in mourning the fate of your own people—this is not the way to approach the scene of that tragedy.[42]

In contradistinction to Scholem, however, readers of Arendt's report who were less concerned with unquestioned Jewish solidarity and ineradicable anti-Semitism may very well have been able to understand her motivations in using the word *Führer*. She had intended the usage not for "the benefit of those Germans" whom, if they were guilty, she did indeed condemn, but for the benefit of Jewish readers whom it might have helped to see more clearly that and how the victims had allowed themselves to be led too totally. The crime against humanity committed on the body of the Jewish people does not, in her view, have the dignity of tragedy. Under the total rule of terror there were criminal victimizers and there were victims. Arendt attempted to show that it was in the nature of this particular crime against humanity that the distinction between criminal and victim was not always clear. Scholem simply rejected this attempt with the comment, "What perversity!"[43]

It was, however, important for Arendt's argument to point out that the blurred line between guilty victimizer and innocent victim was particularly problematic in the case of the Jewish leaders' cooperation with the Nazis. Negotiating with a criminal like Eichmann on his never-questioned terms[44] reinforced the perverted system itself, which is the real culprit in the Eichmann case. Acting within this system, sacrificing human beings for the sake of the survival of privileged others, these Jewish leaders were in the shadow of that unprecedented total attack on human diversity, plurality, and mutuality for which Eichmann was to hang. Arendt does not say so explicitly; but the implications are clear and they are deeply disturbing—more so than the fact that there will always be selfish, cruel men and women among every people, and that situations of extreme stress bring out the worst as well as the best in a person. The implications were disquieting because they suggested that the Jewish leaders, too, caught in the totalitarian system, suffered from an impaired moral faculty.

Hugh Trevor-Roper, in a stunningly hostile review of the Eichmann book, accused Arendt of presenting a pious, learned man like Baeck in a way which did serious damage to him and to those who believed in him, and of negating the distance between the murderer and his victim.[45] But he clearly misread what in fact she had said. She had not judged Baeck or anyone else, and she certainly had not negated the distance between him and a murderer. In fact, she was not interested in accusing or judging anyone but Eichmann, but she wanted the judgment to fit his crime. The judgment she sought concerned the relation to a perverted system of total domination, and so she was intent on showing that any cooperation with that system was destructive. So, too, in the case of Leo Baeck, "scholarly, mild-mannered, highly educated, who believed Jewish policemen would be 'more gentle and helpful' and would 'make the ordeal easier' (whereas in fact they were, of course, more brutal and less corruptible, since so much more was at stake for them)."[46] Baeck had not foreseen what a great majority of people, Jewish and non-Jewish, are capable of if they are pressed together by the total rule of terror.

o   4   o

Arendt's critics rejected her findings as based on personal politics of the worst kind,[47] accusing her of almost criminal sympathy for Eichmann,[48] of an unforgivable lack of understanding of the true dimensions of the tragedy: "What is left to the aging sons and daughters of an orphaned people—what is left to us by the *Churban*? Nothing but the certainty of a misfortune that nobody can prepare for," said Manes Sperber, who was accordingly convinced "that we will never succeed in explaining to those who come after us the *Churban*, the Jewish catastrophe of our time."[49]

Arendt did not share such metaphysical certainty. Her argument was based on the assumption that one would be able to prepare, that one would be able to explain, and that precisely the attempt to do so might lead to prevention. She did lack piety and reverence; she emphatically did not share, as Simon lamented, a Jewish "religious concept of history."[50] Nor did she see the "unfathomableness" of Jewish history, "a devotion to the things of this world which is near-demonic" combined with a "fundamental uncertainty of orientation in this world—an uncertainty which must be contrasted with that certainty of the believer concerning which, alas, your book has little to report," Scholem complained.[51] She was not much interested in "that certainty of the believer" in Scholem's sense, which was alien to her as a contemporary of modernity—unless it appeared in its perverted form as ideology, which she analyzed critically. Her experience of totalitarian rule, supported by ideology, made her particularly sensitive to the suggestive evasiveness of concepts like the "unfathomableness" of human history or the "fundamental uncertainty of orientation in this world." What was needed in the aftermath of Nazi rule was not withdrawal into an a priori certainty of the unfathomable depths of Jewish historical experience or of a general fundamental loss of cultural orientation, but rather an attempt to find a human measure by which to judge that history and to establish, for Jews and non-Jews alike, a temporary permanence of human worldliness. It did not help to call the Nazi regime "devilish," "incredibly evil," "demonic," as did Robinson and Simon in their attacks on Arendt's report.[52] If Arendt was certain of anything, it was of the need to understand the social political basis for the moral inversion caused by the Nazi regime—that is, the nature of the profound change it had wrought on the people it enslaved.

This emphasis on rationally accessible explanation was informed neither by "Jewish self-hatred"[53] nor by Jewish self-love. "It can only be understood as a sad result of Diaspora, which we have to look at with surprised disappointment, that a Jewess tries to interpret the tragedy of our people in such a one-sided way," Michaelis-Stern stated in her very negative review in *Das Neue Israel*.[54] In her critique of political Zionism, Arendt had pointed out the expedient and harmful distinction between Galut and Yishuv. Religious certainty that Jewish life in the Galut inevitably declined made it easy for the conscience of the Yishuv, the settlement in Palestine, "to develop its attitude of aloofness. . . . To the puzzling question of how Zionism can serve as an answer to anti-Semitism for the Jews who remain in the Diaspora they cheerfully assert, 'Pan-Semitism is the best answer to anti-Semitism.'"[55] Arendt would have been the first to point out the profound differences between Eichmann's mindless affirmation of a "fateful struggle of the German people" and the implications of Michaelis-Stern's accusation that Arendt did not feel bound to a "fateful Jewish community."[56] Arendt had argued clearly that Eichmann's affirmation of such a bond of "fateful German community" had been used horribly to sustain an atmosphere of "systematic mendacity"[57] pertaining to all social and cultural acts—a uniquely systematic, complete inversion of cultural values and truth. But there were, in her view, some structural similarities. The religious concept of a nationalist Jewish "fateful community" would detract the Jewish people from viewing the issue of peaceful coexistence with the other Mediterranean peoples as a political problem. She did not, as some of her critics claimed, draw any parallel between Eichmann's kind of nationalism and Zionism, but she showed how Eichmann could have found ideas in Zionism that appealed to him—an argument which Scholem rejected out of hand:

> I wish to say only that your description of Eichmann as a "convert to Zionism" could only come from somebody who had a profound dislike of everything to do with Zionism. These passages in your book I find quite impossible to take seriously. They amount to a mockery of Zionism; and I am forced to the conclusion that this was, indeed, your intention.[58]

Her book, he added, had caused "bitterness and shame" regarding its author, who was so shockingly devoid of *Ahavath Yisrael*, love of the people of Israel.[59]

Like Trevor-Roper, who accused Arendt of equating Nazis with Zionists, Scholem chose to misunderstand what she said about Eichmann's professed fascination with Herzl's *The Jewish State* as profoundly as he misjudged her critical attitude toward the State of Israel. Eichmann, as Arendt pointed out in the passages in her book which Scholem found so disturbing,[60] was fascinated by what he called the "idealism" of the Zionists, their ideological priorities, and he agreed with Herzl's concept of a deep and unbridgeable split between the Jews and the Gentiles. He was, then, attracted precisely to those aspects of Zionism which Arendt viewed very critically: Zionist nationalistic exclusiveness, the overemphasis on differences, on borders, on walls against the omnipresent enemy, and the Zionist subjection of the ambiguous, conflict-ridden reality of Jewish interaction with other peoples to the religiously pure certainty of anti-Semitism.

This, of course, did not make Eichmann a Zionist, nor does it suggest that Arendt considered him one when she reported that *he* considered himself converted to Zionism;[61] and of course it did not make a Zionist a Nazi, nor did it suggest Arendt's establishing such an equation. Like the overwhelming majority of Arendt's critics, Scholem proved wrong her expectations regarding the customary intellectual open-mindedness and concentration of educated, liberal readers—even if the text concerned the trial of the man who had prominently participated in the mass destruction of Jews. In her answer to Scholem's letter, Arendt took up the issue of "love of the Jewish people" or *Ahavath Yisrael*:

> I have never in my life "loved" any people or collective—neither the German people, nor the French, nor the American, nor the working class or anything of that sort. . . . the only kind of love I know of and believe in is the love of persons. Secondly, this "love of the Jews" would appear to me, since I am myself Jewish, as something rather suspect. I cannot love myself or anything which I know is part and parcel of my own person. . . . I do not "love" the Jews, nor do I "believe" in them; I merely belong to them as a matter of course, beyond dispute or argument.[62]

On this unquestioned and unquestionable belonging to the group into which one is born is based the responsibility of critical community: Jews, like all other peoples, need to be rebels, as Bernard Lazare said, in their own society, not only in the society of others.[63] Scholem had felt free to define Arendt's position for her—"I regard you wholly as a daughter of our people, and in no other way"—which carried with it the expectation of unquestioning solidarity.[64] Arendt, however, felt free—and expected the same of her readers—to criticize the manner in which Israel presented itself in the trial of Eichmann. In her reply to Scholem, she stated rightly that he had misread her mainly because of her independently critical attitude toward certain aspects of Israeli politics, since her position was reflected in her use of language. He who had dealt with text analysis all his life had been curiously insensitive to Arendt's use of perfectly common stylistic devices because her narrative perspective rejected the assumptions of solidarity:

Public opinion, especially when it has been carefully manipulated, as in this case, is a very powerful thing. Thus, I never made Eichmann out to be a "Zionist." If you missed the irony of the sentence—which was plainly in *oratio obliqua*, reporting Eichmann's own words—I really can't help it. I can only assure you that none of the dozen readers who read the book before publication had ever any doubt about the matter.[65]

Like many of her critics, Scholem reacted above all against Arendt's "tone"—this accusation came up repeatedly in his letter: "It is that heartless, frequently almost sneering and malicious tone with which these matters, touching the very quick of our life, are treated in your book to which I take exception."[66] He lamented her "flippancy," her speaking of terrible tragedy "in so wholly inappropriate a tone";[67] other critics complained about her cold, distant style,[68] her irony. They, too, did not understand the use of *oratio obliqua*, so important to her ironic narrative perspective, which was meant to demonstrate the political importance of language. Only for Eichmann, whom she let speak *through* but not *in* her voice, did she reserve the tone of unmitigated contempt, as the perceptive reader A. Alvarez noted. He found remarkable the focus of her anger on Eichmann's misuse of language: she seemed less interested in the fact that the Nazis had committed those terrible crimes than in the fact that they still did not understand why they should never have done so.[69] This is a most helpful distinction. Arendt's point was that the misuse of language under a totalitarian regime, so clearly demonstrated by Eichmann, had shielded the participants in this regime from understanding the fact and nature of their crimes. The connection of speech and action in politics is of central importance: the almost total perversion of political morals was possible only in the context of a largely corrupt language.

By using the narrative strategy of *oratio obliqua*, Arendt was able to let Eichmann's voice be heard *and* judged through the perspective provided by the context. It was an indirect way of judging, but a very effective one. The reader was admitted into a story which brought together and organized a large number of disparate details, but he was also able to keep a certain distance, to look at different aspects as they evolved, to *not* be overwhelmed. The report was not meant to support ritual mourning; the narrator, showing the inversion of morals, concentrated emotional and intellectual energy on the act of showing, not that of suffering.[70] Like all good storytellers, Arendt was intent on revealing meaning:[71] Eichmann was not an incomprehensible monster; the fact that the events he had helped bring about seemed, and still seem, to be beyond human understanding did not bestow on them the dignity of metaphysical significance. Eichmann was in many ways a normal, insignificant man of negligible intelligence. His "heroic fight with the German language, which invariably defeats him," provided a gold mine for a psychologist—if, as Arendt warned, "he is wise enough to understand that the horrible can be not only ludicrous but outright funny." Eichmann himself admitted at one point that "officialese" (*Amtssprache*) was his only language, and Arendt remarked that he was indeed "genuinely incapable of uttering a single sentence that was not a cliché":

> The longer one listened to him, the more obvious it became that his inability to speak was closely connected with an inability to *think*, namely to think from the standpoint of somebody else. No communication was possible with him, not because he lied but because he was surrounded by the most reliable of all safeguards against the words and the presence of others, and hence against reality as such.[72]

Reality is the presence and words of others. As they were made invisible and silenced, reality—and with it the capacity to judge—was in effect suspended during the Nazi regime.

Arendt's tone of contempt, when she did speak in her own voice *about* Eichmann, was supported by the fact that this dull, unintelligent man had participated so effectively in the exercise of power. When she told about the 1941 plan to evacuate four million Jews to Madagascar, she shifted from direct comment to indirect discourse to a condemning summary evaluation:

> That anybody except Eichmann and some other lesser luminaries ever took the whole thing seriously seems unlikely, for—apart from the fact that the territory was known to be unsuitable, not to mention the fact that it was, after all, a French possession—the plan would have required shipping space for four millions in the midst of a war and at a moment when the British Navy was in control of the Atlantic.[73]

The Madagascar project was inevitably declared "obsolete," and the next step was the "final solution"; but Eichmann did not see the sequence of events in this light. Again I quote Arendt: "Not that Eichmann, the truth-revealer for generations to come, ever suspected the existence of such sinister plans. What brought the Madagascar enterprise to naught was the lack of time and time was wasted through the never-ending interference from other offices."[74] Eichmann was confronted in Jerusalem with two documents concerning a meeting in September 1939 called by Reinhard Heydrich which Eichmann attended; one of them spoke of a "final aim," requiring longer periods of time and top secrecy. Eichmann, reading the documents, was convinced that the phrase "final aim" meant physical extermination, that the men at the top were already thinking in those terms. He could have said it referred to his Madagascar plan, Arendt pointed out. What he did say might have been the truth,

> but then he would have had to admit that the Madagascar project could not have been more than a hoax. Well, he did not; he never changed his Madagascar story, and probably he just could not change it. It was as though this story ran along a different tape in his memory, and it was this taped memory that showed itself to be proof against reason and argument and information and insight of any kind.[75]

It was the narrator's responsibility to the meaning of the story to show, wherever possible, that Eichmann could still react to certain experiences—the problem was that he could not let his actions be informed by them. Arendt reported what Eichmann saw at a death camp in his own words, quoting him—they are simple, certainly inadequate to the horror, but they are not cliché-ridden; he was, indeed, horrified. But all he did was ask to be spared such sights. After letting him speak, she commented:

> He saw just enough to be fully informed of how the destruction machinery worked: that there were two different methods of killing, shooting and gassing; that the shooting was done by the *Einsatzgruppen* and the gassing at the camps, either in the chambers or in mobile vans; and that in the camps elaborate precautions were taken to fool the victims right up to the end.[76]

"Eichmann went to the gallows with great dignity." This observation, too, was misunderstood. "Jewish newspapers stress the fact," wrote Michaelis-Stern, "that the author formulates brilliantly but heartlessly. Clever ideas and intelligent statements must not deceive us as to the failure in terms of human emotions. . . . As an example of her lack of tact I would like to mention that she thinks it necessary to describe the straight posture Eichmann assumed on his way to the gallows—a fact stressed by German newspapers which know the mentality of their readers."[77] Those German newspapers could perhaps be excused if they quoted the sentence out of context, playing up to *some* of their readers' uninformed, cliché-ridden opinions; a serious reviewer could not. Clearly, the context of the paragraph shows that this sort of dignity was Eichmann's idea of impressive self-presentation. Describing how Eichmann walked calmly from his cell to the execution chamber, refusing the black hood, asking to have the bonds loosened so that he could stand straight, Arendt commented: "He was in complete command of himself, nay, he was more: he was completely himself." So were his last words, which she quoted, pointing to their "grotesque silliness":

> "After a short while, gentlemen, we *shall all meet again*. Such is the fate of all men. Long live Germany, long live Argentina, long live Austria. *I shall not forget them.*" In the face of death he had found the cliché used in funeral oratory. . . . It was as though in those last minutes he was summing up the lessons that this long course in human wickedness had taught us—the lesson of the fearsome, word-and-thought defying *banality* of evil.[78]

∘ 5 ∘

In her report on the Eichmann trial, Arendt showed how one quite normal man's inability to think for himself was fed by the moral inversion of totalitarian rule and, in turn, contributed to it until it reached stunning proportions. Most of her critics understood her description of this process to be an attempt to excuse the executioners and accuse the victims. It is this misunderstanding which is amazing, not the anger or the rage. It was caused by her refusal to use anti-Semitism as the main focus in her analysis of the crime and its punishment, which was connected with her insistence on being allowed to tell the story of Eichmann using a storyteller's strategies in negotiating distances and perspectives. Under the circumstances, this seemed intolerable to many of her readers. To Jaspers,[79] Arendt described the attacks on the Eichmann book as organized by the functionaries of Jewish interest groups and by the New York Jewish intelligentsia behaving like a "howling mob"—in notable contrast to academics and students. The Israeli Consul in Chicago had approached her after a lecture and discussed the Eichmann report with her for several hours. "He said repeatedly: Of course, everything you say is true, we know that. But how could you say that as a Jewess in a 'hostile environment'?[80] I said: As far as I know this here is not a hostile environment. And he: But you know that every non-Jewish environment is hostile." She rightly analyzed her transgression: it was unforgivable that she had acknowledged the division of Jews and non-Jews and "even more unforgivable" that she had not made it the center of her narration of Eichmann's crime. She had, of course, argued that Israel's fixation on this division as millennia old and fated had prevented, rather than contributed to, an understanding of the crime. This fixation was fed, as Arendt knew very well, by the age-old status of the Jews as "*odium humani generis* and the terrible age-old fear, which had become virulent again through the experience of Hitler and Auschwitz,"[81] but it profoundly threatened the political future of the State of Israel.

Arendt's report on Eichmann's trial focused on the clear presentation of a crime, the deeds of Eichmann, which were not yet fully understood because they were, in her view, unprecedented. The trial, however, had focused on the presentation of what had been done to the Jews, their sufferings, and, neglecting to really deal with Eichmann's deeds, had further confused the issues.[82] Arendt realized that the issues surrounding the trial were extremely entangled, for they involved the relationship between the Federal Republic of Germany and the State of Israel—that is, the realpolitik of ensuring the reparation payments essential to Israel's survival, the political and emotional question of the uncompleted German-Jewish past,[83] and Israel's position in Palestine. But she wanted to concentrate on what seemed to her to be not only the most important question but also, in spite of the remaining lacunae, the most clearly recognizable question posed by what was, after all, not a game of power but a trial: the quality of Eichmann's guilt.

Whether she was explicitly aware of the link or not, stories as sense-making tools have been used at trials since antiquity because they have made it possible to establish, in relating the different perspectives of different witnesses, the equity needed for the act of judging.[84] In her story of Eichmann in Jerusalem, Arendt sought to articulate and balance the different perspectives as they related to Eichmann's deeds—an undertaking which obviously included Eichmann's own perspective. Admittedly, she was intellectually intrigued with the challenge of understanding the nature of these deeds and being able to judge them.[85] The trial was not, for her, the place or the time for cultural grieving. She was also sharply aware of the very real difficulties of witnessing—both with respect to Eichmann's deeds and to what had been done to his victims.[86] Thus she carefully shaped the stories he told about himself in the process of retelling them so that their meaning would be clear. The emerging portrait of Eichmann, the common man and uncommon murderer, is a rigorously conceptualized literary documentary of the meaning of his deeds and the quality of his crime. Like any text on a certain level of verbal complexity, it accommodates some unresolved psychological conflict and ambiguity, but not confusion of the sort that is reflected in the critical reactions to the portrait.

Irving Howe, a shrewd and sensitive critic of literature and its social energies, was deeply disturbed by the fact that Arendt's report was published in *The New Yorker*, a journal that does not print rebuttals. He was certain that as a consequence of this, a large number of "good middle-class Americans will have learnt that the Jewish leadership in Europe was cowardly, inept and even collaborationist; that the Jewish community helped the Nazis achieve their goal of racial genocide; and that if the Jews had not 'cooperated' with the Nazis, fewer than five to six millions would have been killed." They would receive this information without doubting it, because *The New Yorker*, as Howe remarks, published Arendt's report as literature, and "you don't argue with literature."[87] Now, this was a strange remark coming from a critic like Howe, whose strength has been precisely his arguing with literature. Moreover, and much more important, Arendt's "good middle-class American" readers probably did not read her with the degree of prejudiced inattention to her narrative and conceptual strategies which would have it made possible for them to have "learnt" what Howe said they would have learnt. Arendt was not interested in individual cowardice and ineptitude as elements of her story—unless they were Eichmann's; she separated the problem of cooperation quite distinctly from the problem of individual cowardice, greed, and weakness. She treated cooperation not as an individual error but as a grave political mistake which had its source in the deplorable other-worldliness of the Jewish people. She did not say that there was any possibility of resistance for the Jewish leaders and the Jewish police, but rather that there was the possibility of nonparticipation, as she restated it in a response to her critics:

And in order to do nothing one did not have to be a saint, one needed only to say: I am just a simple Jew and I have no desire to

play any other role. . . . These people still had a certain limited degree of freedom and of action. Just as the SS members, as we now
know, had a limited choice of alternatives.[88]

Whether this observation was correct in the case of Jews—it had
been applied when judging the behavior of members of the SS—is another question, and it may well be that Arendt was not sufficiently realistic. But again, she was not judging Jewish behavior in these, as she very
well knew, extreme, terrible situations; rather, she was explaining its political implications. And she stressed the fact that it was *not* the cooperation of the *Jews* with the *Nazis* that may have increased the number of
victims; it was the cooperation of the Jews with *their leaders* who cooperated with the Nazis. This is a crucial distinction (and is quite clear in
Arendt's account) because it is based on her concept of political action.
This concept largely circumvents the question of leadership because of
its connection, in Arendt's view, with rule and coercion and with political
inequality. However, this concept is not under discussion here; what is
under discussion is the fact that a highly experienced reader like Howe
was unable or unwilling, or both, to recognize a distinction that seemed
perfectly clear to other readers. If Arendt's readers did indeed read her
report as literature to be approached with a certain degree of openness
and concentration, they probably did not need rebuttals to set them
straight as to what Arendt had or had not said. A rebuttal from, for instance, Norman Podhoretz—one of the critical reviewers singled out for
praise by Howe—would not have been helpful to the attempt to understand, and therefore useless to the attempt to judge, what it was that Arendt had said.

In his essay "Hannah Arendt on Eichmann—A Study in the Per-
versity of Brilliance," Podhoretz complained that Arendt had not grasped
the fundamental fact that the Jewish leaders "did what whey did, they
were what they were, and each was a different man. None of it mattered
in the slightest to the final result. Murderers with the power to murder
descended upon a defenseless people and murdered a large part of it.
What else is there to say?"[89] The men who conducted the Eichmann
trial thought differently, and it was important to them—and to Arendt—
what got said. It seems that it was important to Podhoretz, too, in spite
of his impassioned concluding appeal: "The Nazis destroyed a third of
the Jewish people. In the name of all that is humane, will the remnant
never let up on itself?" Arendt, he complained, had not been interested

in a psychological analysis of the Jewish leaders and had not paid enough attention to them: "In stark contrast to the Jews whose behavior in Miss Arendt's version of this story self-evidently explains and condemns itself, the Nazis—or anyway Adolf Eichmann—need the most imaginative attention before they can be intelligently judged."[90]

Arendt's report was about Eichmann's trial—a fact that seemed difficult to accept to a reviewer like Podhoretz, who held "pathological anti-Semitism" on the part of the Nazis and general anti-Semitism on the part of the other nations accountable for all the horrors and saw therein "the justification for Ben-Gurion's statement that one of the purposes of the Eichmann trial was to make the nations of the world ashamed."[91] He rejected Arendt's argument of the inverted moral system under a totalitarian regime, and put the whole world in an adversary position toward the Jewish people: eternally, fatefully persecuted, all that is left to the Jews is grieving over genocide.

Pathological anti-Semitism, Eichmann as a "moral monster" of demonic proportions, were to Arendt answers to the catastrophe of genocide which repressed the questions one needed to ask, and the fact that her argument was misread as anti-Semitic and sympathetic to Eichmann validated her judgment in this matter. Lionel Abel, in his 1963 *Partisan Review* article, "The Aesthetics of Evil—Hannah Arendt on Eichmann and the Jews," accused her of judging both the Jewish councils and Eichmann aesthetically and thus of making Eichmann come off "so much better" than his victims.[92] But this, Mary McCarthy points out in her critique of Abel's critique, "is more a judgment of Abel than of Miss Arendt: reading her book, he liked Eichmann better than the Jews who died in crematoriums. Each to his own taste. It was not my impression."[93] Abel really objected to the fact that Eichmann was presented as commonplace and the moral inversion was described as a secular phenomenon. Referring to Simone de Beauvoir's observation, on the occasion of the trial of Laval, that the criminal on the dock can never be the same person he was when he committed the crime, that the man one wanted to punish has, in a sense, escaped, Abel found Arendt's Eichmann portrait wanting.[94] Eichmann, however, was not Laval, and Arendt was convincing in her analysis of the Eichmann in the dock, who in her clarifying story was such a horribly credible, useful witness to his participation in genocide. It was not—and this was precisely Arendt's point—a question of strength (of Eichmann's being in command) versus weakness (Eichmann pleading not to be executed), of former power versus present impotence. It was a question, then and now, of total loyalty to the wrong set of ideas and to the concept of duty in carrying them out. "Evil in the Third Reich," Arendt said in the conclusion of chapter 7 of her report ("Duties of a Law-Abiding Citizen"), "had lost the quality by which most people recognize it—the quality of temptation." For Eichmann and other law-abiding Nazis, it had become duty, and thus for his victims it had become more evil.

Abel needed to go on believing in the dimension of the monstrous, the ineffable, where a criminal like Eichmann was concerned. Remarking that the anecdotes, told by Arendt to bring out Eichmann's clownishness, rang "true" to him, Abel went to Shakespeare and Kierkegaard for examples of the combined "morally monstrous and the comical."[95] Ironically, he wanted Eichmann to be more interestingly, more profoundly horrible than Arendt thought he was; a more satisfying villain. It would not be very useful to accuse Abel of doing himself what he accused Arendt of—namely, "aestheticizing Eichmann"[96]—but it is true that it was Abel who insisted on Eichmann's being granted the dignity of the profoundly horrible, comical, monstrous villain, criticizing Arendt harshly for regarding Eichmann as "merely a mediocre and comical individual."[97] To Arendt, of course, "merely" is entirely out of place here—she, for one, was intent on showing how and why the mediocre can be ludicrous and horribly dangerous.

Twenty years later, in a review of Young-Bruehl's biography, Abel was remarkably generous to Arendt on her treatment of the question of assimilation,[98] but he had not changed his misreading of the Eichmann book, which he claimed "took back the very insights into totalitarianism which had made the *The Burden of Our Time* an important and probably enduring work."[99] "Most shocking" to Abel, in retrospect, was "the behavior of many members of the intellectual community who supported Miss Arendt in the *Eichmann in Jerusalem* controversy." They had not, he pointed out, supported her in her attitude toward desegregation:[100] "Why did Arendt have to be right when her criticism was directed against the Jews?" Her criticism, however, was directed not against "the Jews" but against certain problematic aspects of the Eichmann trial which had brought out certain problematic aspects of the political self-perception of the State of Israel. Her inquiry had much less to do with certain difficult issues in recent Jewish history—for example, the role of the Jewish councils—than with Israel's attitude toward that history. But these distinctions, though clearly drawn, were not sufficient to calm Abel's fears about a fated, enduring anti-Semitism, and so he professed to being still disturbed, twenty years later, by "the note of anti-Semitism" introduced into the controversy by Arendt's defenders. Jews, he asserted, needed to make an effort to listen to their ancestors, "those my father distinguished for me as not just Jews, but as *the Jews*." [101] However, Arendt's critique of Jewish assimilation in Germany and political Zionism in Palestine, which centrally informed her concept of the political, was based precisely on a rejection of such singularity.

o 6 o

"So far as I know," Mary McCarthy wrote in "The Hue and Cry," "all Miss Arendt's hostile reviews have come from Jews, and those favorable to her from Gentiles, with four exceptions: A. Alvarez, George Lichtheim, Bruno Bettelheim, and Daniel Bell. . . . It is as if *Eichmann in Jerusalem* had required a special pair of Jewish spectacles to make its 'true purport' visible." [102] This is, on the whole, a useful observation, even though, as Dwight Macdonald points out, the exceptions are too many for her claim to be entirely convincing, especially since they include such substantial writers. But Macdonald, too, thought McCarthy's "broader aim" was accurate: "that reactions *in general* divide along Jewish and non-Jewish lines." [103]

The division and the reasons for it appear even clearer now, almost three decades after the controversy, and they are intimately tied up with Arendt's critical analysis of the role of political interaction in Jewish history and the role of Israel's self-perception in contemporary world politics. Her attempt to understand Eichmann, the common man and uncommon murderer, was centered in that critical analysis. The remaining traces of a conflicted "reading" of the criminal Eichmann in her report on his trial were therefore particularly disturbing to those readers who challenged her analysis of the Jewish question in terms of political speech and action. Even worse, one such reaction fed on the other and intensified it.

In spite of the clear distinctions that she brought to her portrait of Eichmann and to her critique of his trial in Jerusalem, Arendt did not fully succeed in penetrating the obscurity of evil in a secular culture. She tried to document clearly what she called the "banality" of the criminal, emphasizing not so much his, under the circumstances, frightening individual psychological normality as its symptomatic signification of the even more frightening moral inversion of a whole culture. She thought the demonization of the criminal harmful to attempts at understanding the mechanisms controlling such inversion and stressed the secular, accessible meanings of the catastrophe. And yet, in her "cool," analytical, "ironical" presentation of the criminal, she rendered monstrous his common inability to think for himself, to reason out of his own experience. If the clearly drawn figure of Eichmann, the perfectly common twentieth-century mass man, emerged as clearly monstrous, was it because of the monstrous consequences of his perfect commonness or because that commonness itself was monstrous? For once, Arendt did not distinguish clearly enough, and so the horror of Eichmann's deeds, of genocide, still seemed in certain ways incongruous to his monstrous commonness. Arendt did not quite succeed, that is, in fitting the crime to the criminal, and it is not clear whether she realized her partial failure. Her distinction between the common man and the uncommon murderer, though useful in the entanglement of issues, alludes to the remaining conflict between her/our enduring inability to fully imagine or grasp the reality of the crime in its true dimensions, and her largely justified sense that she had imagined the reality of Eichmann and understood him.

Understanding in this case meant the opposite of *forgiving*. "Her portrait of Eichmann, far from being lenient, is a masterpiece in rendering the almost unreadably repellent," thought Robert Lowell.[104] But many of Arendt's readers, resisting the commonness of the criminal, did not think so. When she raised questions about the Jewish councils in the sense in which Lazare encouraged the Jew as pariah to be critical of her own people, she encountered resistance even among readers who were sympathetic to her secular cultural-political viewpoint, her multiperspective narrative approach to the problem of evil. "Many of Arendt's strictures are correct," wrote Daniel Bell in the conclusion of his very fair review, "if one can live by a universalistic standard." But in this case Bell insisted on the relevance of "one's identity as a Jew as well as a philosophe." He saw the "agony" of Arendt's book as her taking a stand on the side of "disinterested justice"—that is, her judging both Nazi and Jew. "But abstract justice, as the Talmudic wisdom knew, is sometimes too strong a yardstick to judge the world."[105] Arendt had not judged "both Nazi and Jew"; she had judged Eichmann and had disagreed with the decisions—regarding negotiation with the Nazis—of some Jews. The words *abstract* and *disinterested* were used by Bell with reference to Arendt's own people, but her account of their difficulties was interested—in critical community—and provocatively concrete. In her portrait of Eichmann and in her attempts at clarifying the cultural meaning of his commonness in the situation of totalitarian rule, it was Arendt's concreteness, her realism, which irritated and caused misunderstanding.

Eichmann was an uncommon murderer because he participated in genocide and because he did so without being a murderous person. He was a common man unable to think for himself, and so he conformed to the belief system of a society that exhibited an almost total moral inversion under the rule of terror. But Eichmann clearly conformed more, and more actively, than most other common people. The monstrous quality of his commonness lies precisely in the fact that he is *not* in everyone of us, that his commonness is particular and not general, relational and not absolute. There are different degrees of that inability to think for oneself which Arendt found so prevalent in modern mass society, and there are different degrees of involvement with a criminal regime. There is the question of individual conscience and responsibility even in extreme situations. Arendt did not think this question meaningful to her political analysis. Both her reluctance to deal with it in this context, and her fascination with what she perceived as Jaspers' "inviolable, untemptable, unswayable" attitude during the Nazi regime,[106] were based on her experience of human behavior. She knew that the appeal to individual conscience and consequently responsibility, an article of faith with liberal intellectuals, tended to become extremely difficult when it was put to the test of a difficult reality—unless it was possible to reinforce it by some kind of community.

Arendt, who was indeed more realistic than many of her male intellectual contemporaries, Jewish or non-Jewish, would not have denied the cultural importance of this appeal, but she was less certain that it could be met. It was not a useful question to raise in the context of her report, because the particular quality of Eichmann's guilt was based on a particular and extreme cultural void regarding shared rules of conscience. As the reactions showed, the question of an appeal to rules of conscience could not be quieted, and there was a certain irony in the fact that her compelling—if not, to many readers, convincing—portrait of Eichmann as an uncommonly common man had contributed to its persistence. In their concern for a more stable connection between the criminal, the crime, and the punishment, these readers mistook her reticence to claim the presence of the appeal to individual responsibility, or to lament its absence, for a denial of its validity. Her argument, however, had been based on the *experienced* difficulties inherent in speech and action governed by individual rules of conscience in situations of (almost) totally enforced (almost) total conformism. She had shown in *The Origins of*

Totalitarianism that no human should have such conformism forced upon him, because it made him less than human, a shadow and a slave, silent, passive, and obscure. She had attempted to show in *The Human Condition* that in the visible spaces of the political realm the individual could speak and act as himself precisely because he was in the presence of others, who saw and heard him and would argue and act with *and* against him. From the paradoxes and seemingly impenetrable obscurities of the Jewish condition, which called for the rupture of revealed meaning, she had turned to the visible spaces of antiquity, in which the meaning of the human condition was established by humans as temporarily permanent and consistently accessible.

Would Eichmann, transplanted to those visible spaces from his desk with its memos about "the final solution," have been able to speak among others as a good citizen? Most readers, including those who think Arendt's argument largely convincing, would say "no"; and her emphatic denial of "an Eichmann in each one of us" [107] suggests that she would have agreed with them. No matter how well she understood Eichmann, the uncommon perfection of his commonness could not be separated from what she herself summed up as "the lesson of the fearsome, word-and-thought defying *banality* of evil." [108] It is true that Eichmann's evil commonness had been perfected by the totalitarian regime, but it had also, in turn, contributed to the perfection of totalitarian rule; more, it had made it possible from the beginning. Where, then, did it come from? And what did it mean for mankind, for the Germans, for the Jews? How could it be understood, judged, prevented?

In the spring of 1951, after completing *The Origins of Totalitarianism*, Arendt wrote to Jaspers about the difficulties *and* the challenges of understanding what is the new radical evil in the modern world, in answer to his question about Yahweh's absence from her argument in *Origins*. Whereas Jaspers had implied a need to recognize an anxiety of meaning calling for God to disrupt the flow of time and reveal meaning by showing Himself, Arendt insisted that the crimes of modernity are not dealt with in the Decalogue. Modern radical evil is, according to her definition, making men superfluous *qua* men; [109] it is, then, a transgression not of divinely revealed laws but of human consensus. Thus Arendt focused her judgment of Eichmann's unprecedented crime on his active participation in making men superfluous—that is, on his having carried out the Nazi policy of denying, on principle, certain groups of people the right to share the earth with others. This totalitarian "attack upon human diversity as such, that is, upon a characteristic of the 'human status,'"[110] constituted a violation, heretofore unseen, of "the order of mankind."[111] Eichmann's involvement in this violation, which made him a "new type of criminal,"[112] was the reason for the death sentence—and Arendt stressed that this was the only reason: after such a basic violation, which robbed the "very words 'mankind' and 'humanity'" of their meaning,[113] "no member of the human race" could be expected to share the earth with him.[114]

Arendt's reasoning here was indeed perfectly consistent with her analytical indictment of totalitarianism in *Origins*.[115] Understandably, she did not succeed in lifting a partial obscurity from Eichmann on trial in Jerusalem—that is, from the quality of his guilt—in spite of her stunningly clear portrait of the man's symptomatic commonness and the nature of his crime. But it was this combination of a particular clarity and a particular obscurity to which many readers reacted with hostility, for it had led them to misunderstand, together with the reasons for it, Arendt's motivations and intentions. She had not withdrawn from her people by insisting that Eichmann and his particular guilt be made the center of his trial rather than have that trial focus on Jewish suffering and cultural grieving. She had wanted her people to listen to Eichmann the man, not the devil, and to listen to his victims without ascribing to them an unquestioned, paradisiacal, total innocence, which would once more justify Israel's fortified singular chosenness against the non-Jewish world. Paradise, the promised land, had been predicated on walls and on silence. Arendt had argued for connection rather than withdrawal, communication rather than silence, precisely because she wanted Israel to become a secular state among other states and to outgrow the use of concepts like Diaspora.[116] The story of Eichmann in Jerusalem, then, was told to her readers, Jewish and non-Jewish, in their capacity as citizens who, in agreeing *and* disagreeing with her, would share a common concern for the well-being of the world in which we all live together, for better or for worse.[117]

Notes

Introduction: Thinking in Dark Times

1. The relationship between Jaspers and Arendt is fully articulated in their correspondence, *Hannah Arendt, Karl Jaspers Briefwechsel, 1926–1969*, ed. Lotte Koehler and Hans Saner (Munich: Piper, 1985). All translations of this text are mine.

2. Hannah Arendt, *The Life of the Mind*, vol. 1, *Thinking*, and vol. 2, *Willing* (New York: Harcourt Brace Jovanovich, 1977 and 1978). Elisabeth Young-Bruehl, *Hannah Arendt: For Love of the World* (New Haven: Yale University Press, 1982), makes too much of Arendt's turning to the consolations of philosophy (438–40). I doubt that Arendt longed for the "free air" of philosophy the way Jaspers did. As I will show, her analysis of thinking (*Life of the Mind*, vol. 1) contradicts such acquiescence in the *vita contemplativa*.

3. Arendt, *Thinking*, 3; Hannah Arendt, "Thinking and Moral Considerations: A Lecture," *Social Research* 38 (1971): 417.

4. Arendt, "Thinking and Moral Considerations," 417.

5. Arendt, *Thinking*, 3.

6. See chapter 6 of the present volume.

7. Arendt, *Thinking*, 4 (her emphasis).

8. Ibid.

9. Ibid.; see also Arendt, "Thinking and Moral Considerations," 418.

10. Especially in Arendt's discussion of thinking, Heidegger is explicitly and implicitly present in her arguments. See, however, her critique of his *Identity and Difference*, in *Thinking*, 183–90.

11. Arendt, "Thinking and Moral Considerations," 445.

12. Ibid., 445–46.

13. Midwives are beyond childbearing age.

14. Arendt, "Thinking and Moral Considerations," 432, 435.

15. Arendt here quotes Xenophon quoting Socrates: "The winds themselves are invisible, yet what they do is manifest to us and we somehow feel their approach." She also draws attention to Heidegger's metaphor "storm of thought" ("Thinking and Moral Considerations," 433).

16. Arendt, "Thinking and Moral Considerations," 467–68; idem, *Thinking*, 179.

17. This separation, indicating a questioning of normative political values, is important in view of Arendt's general tendency, beginning with works like "Tradition and the Modern Age" (1954) and *The Human Condition* (1958), to locate her political models in a tradition informed by (meta)political norms formulated in antiquity. In this tendency she shows certain affinities to her fellow exiles and political thinkers Leo Strauss (*Natural Right and History*, 1953) and Eric Voegelin (*The New Science of Politics*, 1952 and *Order and History*, 1956–), from whom she also differs importantly; see chapter 5 of the present volume.

18. Arendt, *Thinking*, 180.

19. Quoted by Arendt, ibid., 181.

20. Arendt, *Thinking*, 181–93.

21. Ibid., 183–85; see also note 10 above.

22. Ibid., 186–87.

23. Ibid., 181–82.

24. Ibid., 192.

25. Ibid., 189. See also Arendt's reference to Kant's maxim: "Always think consistently, in agreement with yourself" (186).

26. Ibid., 190–91.

27. Ibid., 192. The Jaspers quotes are from his *Philosophy*, vol. 2 (1932), trans. E. B. Ashton (Chicago: University of Chicago Press, 1970), 178–79.

28. Martin Jay, in his 1978 *Partisan Review* essay, "The Political Existentialism of Hannah Arendt" (*Permanent Exiles Essays on the Intellectual Migration from Germany to America* [New York: Columbia University Press, 1985], 237–56), remains puzzled by Arendt's "elusive and unpredictable mind" (239) and ranks her among what he calls the "political existentialists," who, for him, include Carl Schmitt, Ernst Juenger, and Alfred Baeumler. He makes here the serious mistake of placing in the company of Juenger and Baeumler the controversial but much more intelligent and complex Carl Schmitt, and this may have contributed to his disregarding the fact that Arendt has proved herself in all her writing since the Rahel biography a writer with deep political concerns. Jay grants her the "tender" rather than "tough" variant of "political existentialism," but maintains that her "political philosophy can justly be situated in the political existentialist tradition of the 1920s" (240). Though he never defines this alleged tradition—Heidegger and Husserl seem to belong to it as well as Jaspers—he accuses her of drawing on it in her, as he puts it, "viewing history as an illegitimate source of constraints on freedom" (243). In this context a critical analysis of Arendt's political thought in its relation to Leo Strauss and Eric Voegelin would have been much more appropriate. It is understandable that Jay does not like Arendt's critique of Marx (245–47), that he criticizes (though distorting the issues) her concept of the polis and her view of the success of the American Revolution (250–53). But it seems the result of a determined misreading to discuss her position so exclu-

sively on the basis of her 1946 *Partisan Review* essay, "What is Existenz Philosophy?" and to see it consistently in terms of her having "succumbed" to "the dangerous charms" of "political existentialism," an "obfuscating ideology in the 1920s, and one not entirely blameless in the rise of fascism" (256).

29. The same passage appears in the essay "Thinking and Moral Considerations," but there it is not so prominent, appearing shortly before the conclusion.

30. Arendt, *Thinking*, 192–93; and idem, "Thinking and Moral Considerations," 446.

31. Ibid., 193.

32. Arendt shares with the majority of Weimar intellectuals the preoccupation with a community/collectivity dichotomy. See my *Weimar Intellectuals and the Threat of Modernity* (Bloomington: Indiana University Press, 1988), pt. 1. In Arendt's analyses, however, the dichotomy is functionally defined.

33. See chapter 1, section 3, of the present volume.

34. See my *Weimar Intellectuals*, pt. 2, chap. 1.

35. See my "The Secularity of Evil: Hannah Arendt and the Eichmann Controversy," *Modern Judaism* 3 (1983): 89–92.

36. Arendt, *Thinking*, 192.

37. See Jay, "The Political Existentialism of Hannah Arendt," 237–38.

38. Ibid., 254.

1. The Quality of Judgment: Arendt and Kant

1. Hannah Arendt, *The Life of the Mind*, vol. 1, *Thinking*, ed. Mary McCarthy (New York: Harcourt Brace Jovanovich, 1977), 217 (editor's postface).

2. "Could I but clear my path at every turning / Of spells, all magic utterly unlearning; / Here I but Man, with Nature for my frame, / The name of human would be worth the claim" (Goethe, *Faust*, pt. 2, lines 11404–8).

3. See Michael Denenny, "The Privilege of Ourselves: Hannah Arendt on Judgment," in *Hannah Arendt: The Recovery of the Public World*, ed. Melvyn A. Hill (New York: St. Martin's Press, 1979), 245–74.

4. Philip Sidney referred to More's *Utopia*, noplace, as "Eutopia," good place: *The Defense of Poesie* (1595), ed. G. E. Woodberry (Boston, 1908), 32.

5. Hannah Arendt, "Isak Dinesen," *Men in Dark Times* (New York: Harcourt, Brace & World, 1968), 104, 105.

6. Hannah Arendt, *Rahel Varnhagen: The Life of a Jewish Woman* (New York: Harcourt Brace Jovanovich, 1974), xv.

7. Arendt, "Isak Dinesen," 105, 106, 109.

8. See John R. Searle, "The Logical Status of Fictional Discourse," in *Expression and Meaning: Studies in the Theory of Speech Acts* (New York: Cambridge University Press, 1979), 58–75.

9. Arendt, *Thinking*, 219 (editor's postface).

10. See Ronald Beiner, ed., *Hannah Arendt Lectures on Kant's Political Philosophy* (Chicago: University of Chicago Press, 1982), Part Two Interpretive Essay.

11. Beiner, who refers to passages that show correspondences between the Kant lectures and *Thinking*, remarks: "In fact, some passages from the latter work are taken, more or less verbatim, from the then unpublished Kant lectures, which must

indicate that she was reasonably satisfied with the understanding of judgment she had already formulated in them. Even more decisive is the fact that the outline of the theory of judgment she offered in a postscript in the *Thinking* volume corresponds very closely to the actual development of the Kant lectures" (ibid., 91).

12. Arendt, *Thinking*, 213.

13. Arendt quotes the Apostle Paul's "early discovery of the will's impotence— 'I do not do what I want, but I do the very thing I hate'"—and "Augustine's insight that what are 'at war' are not the spirit and the flesh but the mind, as will, with itself, man's 'inmost self' with itself" (ibid., 214).

14. Ibid. Important for our context, too, is Arendt's stated intention to trace the history of the will, "whose subject matter is projects, not objects," the will as creator of the person, the will as producer of man's existence. In her view, this "is the last of the metaphysical fallacies, corresponding to the modern age's emphasis on willing as a substitute for thinking" (ibid., 214–15).

15. Ibid., 215. Arendt mentions here "a curious scarcity of sources providing authoritative testimony" to the faculty of judging, Kant's *Critique of Judgment* being the notable exception. See also her annotations of excerpts from Kant's *Critique of Pure Reason* in the early fifties ("Kant," unpublished notebook, Arendt estate), which document her interest in an instinctive, spontaneous (therefore shared) quality of conscience as the locus of moral laws. For example, "Das Gewissen ist ein Instinkt, sich selbst nach moralischen Gesetzen zu richten" (1); or a quote she marked with two crosses: "*Spontaneitaet:* ist 'jenes bewunderungswuerdige Vermoegen, welches mir das Bewusstsein des moralischen Gesetzes allererst offenbart'" (8).

16. Ibid., 215–16. On the connotation "narration" in *historein* see Christian Meier, "Die Entstehung der Historie," in *Geschichte—Ereignis und Erzaehlung*, ed. Reinhart Kosselleck and Wolf-Dieter Stempel (Munich: Wilhelm Fink, 1973), 252.

17. Ibid., 216.

18. Numquam se plus agere quam nihil cum ageret, numquam minus solum esse quam cum solus esset (Never am I less alone than when I am by myself, never am I more active than when I do nothing).

19. Arendt, *Thinking*, 216.

20. See Beiner, *Hannah Arendt Lectures*, 91–92.

21. *Social Research* 38 (1971): 417–46.

22. Beiner, *Hannah Arendt Lectures*, 91.

23. Ibid., 68–69.

24. Arendt, "Isak Dinesen," 109.

25. See Beiner, *Hannah Arendt Lectures*, 68.

26. Arendt, *Thinking*, 216.

27. Hannah Arendt Papers, Library of Congress, container 41, p. 024560; quoted in Beiner, *Hannah Arendt Lectures*, 112.

28. Hannah Arendt, "Basic Moral Propositions," in *Hannah Arendt Lectures*, ed. Beiner, 113.

29. Ibid.

30. Hannah Arendt, *Eichmann in Jerusalem: A Report on the Banality of Evil* (New York: Viking Press, 1963), 256.

31. Ibid., 43–44.

32. Beiner, *Hannah Arendt Lectures*, 70.

33. Quoted in Beiner, *Hannah Arendt Lectures*, 71.

34. Arendt does not comment on this conflict in this context, but she is, in general, aware of it. See her closing statement in "Truth and Politics" on the limitations of the political sphere notwithstanding its "greatness": "It does not encompass the whole of man's and the world's existence. It is limited by those things which men cannot change at will. And it is only by respecting its own borders that this realm, where we are free to act and to change, can remain intact, preserving its integrity and keeping its promises. Conceptually, we may call truth what we cannot change; metaphorically, it is the ground on which we stand and the sky that stretches above us" (Hannah Arendt, "Truth and Politics," *Between Past and Future* (New York: Viking Press, 1961), 264.

35. Ibid.

36. Immanuel Kant, *Critique of Judgment*, no. 40, quoted in Beiner, *Hannah Arendt Lectures*, 71. See also an observation recorded in one of Arendt's unpublished notebooks: "*Verstehen* in der Politik heisst nie, den *anderen* verstehen (nur die weltlose Liebe 'versteht den anderen'), sondern die gemeinsame Welt, so wie sie dem anderen erscheint. Wenn es eine Tugend (Weisheit) des Staatsmanns gibt, so ist es die Faehigkeit, *alle* Seiten einer Sache zu sehen, d.h. sie so zu sehen, wie sie allen Beteiligten erscheint" (unpublished notebook no. 19 [1953], p. 1).

37. See Beiner, *Hannah Arendt Lectures*, 163, n. 155, where he draws attention to that fact. Arendt does not, however, do it as consistently as he states; she let pass "universal rule" in the preceding quote, but "universal standpoint" would have been too clearly in violation of her argument, which stresses the communal associating with the public sphere.

38. Hannah Arendt, "The Crisis in Culture: Its Social and Its Political Significance," in *Between Past and Future*, 197–226. The first part of this essay, with its wholesale rejection of mass culture as entertainment and its rather simplistic analysis of the entertainment industry, reflects the negative reaction to an unfamiliar American mass culture that is so commonly found among European exiles who came to the United States from a very different cultural environment. On the whole, especially where she could see social issues in political terms, Arendt was considerably more circumspect in her views on things American than many of her male fellow European intellectuals.

39. Ibid., 221, 218.

40. Arendt separates the artist from the work of art: the artist, *homo faber*, may be distant to, even mistrustful of, the public realm, but the artist's work takes its place in this realm. The distinction Arendt makes between the social-cultural place of the artist and that of the work of art reflects both her generally conservative taste, informed by high culture, and her specific sympathy for a writer like Brecht.

41. Arendt, "Crisis in Culture," 218.

42. See, e.g., Arendt's travel letters to Jaspers in the fall of 1955; she is particularly impressed by the apparent, palpable articulateness of the Mediterranean world, the surface that does not imply form but is distinctly, visibly formed. About the Greek islands she writes: "Imagine: a *structured* sea" ("Denken Sie: ein gegliedertes Meer").

43. Part 1 of Immanuel Kant's *Critique of Judgment*.

44. Arendt, "Crisis in Culture," 219, 220.

45. Ibid., 221. Beiner (*Hannah Arendt Lectures*, 163, n. 155) draws attention to this passage with respect to Arendt's choice of terms in her reading of Kant; but he does not analyze the passage, nor does he suggest reasons for her translating Kant's *allgemein* as "general" rather than "universal."

46. See Arendt's letters to Heinrich Bluecher from June 18 to August 12, 1941, in which she describes her host family in Winchester, Mass., where she had gone to learn English. She typically misunderstood them to be *kleinbuergerlich* (petit bourgeois), but stressed as very positive their civic-mindedness; she was especially impressed by the wife's father, who held a large number of honorary offices and had "something Prussian" about him. The family, Arendt wrote, spells duty with a very big *d* (Library of Congress; the letters are being prepared for publication in Germany by Lotte Koehler, who kindly made them available to me). Elisabeth Young-Bruehl's account of the stay (*Hannah Arendt: For Love of the World* [New Haven: Yale University Press, 1982], 165–66) is too condescending to the host family—Arendt was touched by their genuine kindness and generosity and might have been troubled by the implications of Young-Bruehl's account, which is based on her misreading of letters written in German. One important misunderstanding concerns the value given here to the adjective *Prussian*, which is clearly positive for Arendt. She thought her hostess, a vegetarian and hiker, who no doubt was a disciplinarian and rather narrow-minded in questions of race, an in many ways brave and impressive woman. A sentence like the following one is totally misleading and unfortunate, in view of Arendt's notable abstention from cultural clichés ("petit bourgeois" being a very European exception): "More Prussian, more *Wandervogel*, than the *Wandervogel* Prussians, Arendt thought, alarmed, that she might have stumbled into a National Socialist home" (165). (The context is Arendt's misunderstanding of her hosts' pacifism.) Young-Bruehl's biography is richly documented and usefully answers many questions, but it does contain many serious errors, and it does not deal well with the European-German part of Arendt, especially not in its relation to her American experience. The result is that Arendt does not really become present intellectually.

47. See Juergen Habermas, "Hannah Arendt's Communications Concept of Power," *Social Research* 44 (1977): 3–24. Bringing up, once more, the issue of Arendt's dichotomy of a public and a private realm, Habermas neglects to consider her clarifications in this respect.

48. Arendt, "Crisis in Culture," 223, 225, 211, 226.

49. See Eric Voegelin, *The New Science of Politics* (Chicago: University of Chicago Press, 1952), 76–80. Arendt, who might have found those passages intellectually congenial, thought the book's direction on the whole "wrong" ("auf dem Holzwege") but important. See letter to Jaspers, Nov. 1, 1952, *Hannah Arendt, Karl Jaspers Briefwechsel, 1926–1969*, ed. Lotte Koehler and Hans Saner (Munich: Piper, 1985), no. 137 (hereafter cited as *Arendt, Jaspers Briefwechsel*). Translations from this correspondence are mine.

50. See Hannah Arendt, "Reflections on Little Rock," *Dissent* 6, no. 1 (Winter 1959): 45–56.

51. Beiner, *Hannah Arendt Lectures*, 134.

52. Arendt, "Crisis in Culture," 221, 223.

53. Beiner, *Hannah Arendt Lectures*, 136. In this context Beiner suggests: "Thus, if we wish to explore other possible sources of a theory of political judgment, one very promising avenue of inquiry is offered by Gadamer's philosophical hermeneutics, which presents a theory of hermeneutical judgment that eschews Kant and appeals to Aristotle's ethics."

54. Ibid., 7.

55. See section 2 of this chapter.

2. Society, Parvenu, and Pariah: The Life Story of a German Jewess

1. Hannah Arendt, *Der Liebesbegriff bei Augustin: Versuch einer philosophischen Interpretation* (Berlin: Julius Springer, 1929). This dissertation was the last to be published in the series.

2. Karl Jaspers to Hannah Arendt, Aug. 4, 1929, *Hannah Arendt, Karl Jaspers Briefwechsel, 1926–1969*, ed. Lotte Koehler and Hans Saner (Munich: Piper, 1985), no. 10; all translations of this source are mine.

3. See Arendt's letters to Bluecher in the fall of 1936, when they were moving toward intimacy, especially those of August 12 and November 26. I would like to express here my gratitude to Lotte Koehler, of New York, for letting me see the Arendt-Bluecher correspondence being prepared by her for publication by Piper, in Munich. The correspondence with Jaspers after the hiatus of World War II (Library of Congress) is centrally informed by such mutual acceptance, and it is difficult to single out individual letters, but see Arendt's letters to him from and about Berkeley, her first real teaching experience, in the spring and summer of 1955.

4. Hannah Arendt, *Rahel Varnhagen: The Life of a Jewish Woman*, trans. Richard Winston and Clara Winston (New York: Harcourt Brace Jovanovich, 1974), xviii. Originally published as *Rahel Varnhagen: Lebensgeschichte einer deutschen Juedin aus der Romantik* (Munich: Piper, 1959); unless otherwise specified, all references are to the 1974 American edition.

5. Letter of April 24, 1816, *Rahel Varnhagen: Briefwechsel*, ed. Friedhelm Kemp, 4 vols. (Munich: Winkler, 1979), 2:393; emphasis Rahel's, translation mine.

6. Hannah Arendt, "Philosophie und Soziologie," *Die Gesellschaft* 7 (1930): 163–76.

7. See my *Weimar Intellectuals and the Threat of Modernity* (Bloomington: Indiana University Press, 1988), pt. 1, sec. 1.

8. Karl Jaspers to Hannah Arendt, April 4, 1946, quoted in Hannah Arendt to Gertrud Jaspers, May 30, 1946, *Arendt, Jaspers Briefwechsel*, no. 39, n. 4.

9. Karl Jaspers to Hannah Arendt, June 27, 1946, *Arendt, Jaspers Briefwechsel*, no. 41.

10. Arendt, *Rahel Varnhagen*, xv.

11. *Arendt, Jaspers Briefwechsel*, no. 21.

12. In later editions the title was changed to *Max Weber: Politiker-Forscher-Philosoph*.

13. *Arendt, Jaspers Briefwechsel*, no. 22.

14. Ibid., no. 23; emphasis mine.

15. This was by no means easy for German-Jewish intellectuals at the end of

the Weimar period; see my *Weimar Intellectuals and the Threat of Modernity*, pt. 3, chap. 1.

16. See Scholem's statistical assessment on the basis of Bruno Blau's 1950 unpublished study, "Development of the Jewish Population in Germany between 1800 and 1945": Gershom Scholem, "On the Social Psychology of the Jews in Germany: 1900–1933," in *Jews and Germans from 1860 to 1933: The Problematic Symbiosis*, ed. David Bronsen (Heidelberg: Carl Winter, 1979), 11–12: "In this context ["the extraordinary strength" of Jewish migration from villages and towns into the cities] the number of foreign-born or first-generation German Jews is also of importance. This figure though by far not as high as anti-Semitic propaganda made it appear, was nevertheless considerable. Before the first World War it amounted to some 15% and by 1930 had increased to 20%, possibly even to 25%, which led to bitter struggles about the franchise of the so-called Eastern Jews within the established Jewish communal organizations. In Berlin the percentage was even higher. Around 1930 almost one-third of the members of the Jewish community were born abroad, or had come to Berlin from territories ceded by Germany under the Versailles convention or were otherwise of foreign nationality. The most extreme case was Saxony—where two-thirds of the Jews were foreign-born."

17. *Arendt, Jaspers Briefwechsel*, no. 24. There is a curious conclusion to Arendt's letter. She, too, is very much preoccupied with Europe's unification, which she can see only under the domination ("Vorherrschaft") of France, for which she cannot wish; such domination, and in this form, would be awful. Arendt's reaction clearly signifies the importance, to her, of a Germany sufficiently strong and whole not to be in need or danger of such domination, even if that would serve the cause of European pacification.

18. Hannah Arendt to Karl Jaspers, Sept. 7, 1952, *Arendt, Jaspers Briefwechsel*, no. 135.

19. Lazare, together with Dreyfus's immediate family and the leading Jewish politician Joseph Reinach, was among the initiators of the Dreyfus campaign; see Stephen Wilson, *Ideology and Experience: Antisemitism in France at the Time of the Dreyfus Affair* (East Brunswick, N.J.: Fairleigh Dickinson University Press, 1982), 83–86.

20. Bernard Lazare, *Job's Dungheap*, ed. Hannah Arendt (New York: Schocken, 1948), 10.

21. The difficulties encountered in this approach are, of course, immense, especially in the German situation, a good example being the "Berliner Antisemitismusstreit" provoked by Heinrich von Treitschke's aggressive demand—that Jews become Germans—in his 1879 "Unsere Aussichten," which was published in *Preussische Jahrbuecher*. The documents relating to this controversy (especially the critical responses of Heinrich Graetz, Hermann Cohen, Ludwig Bamberger, and Theodor Mommsen, and Treitschke's responses to them) are collected in Walter Boehlich, ed., *Der Berliner Antisemitismusstreit* (Frankfurt am Main: Insel, 1965).

22. Theodor Herzl, *The Jewish State* (New York: Herzl Press, 1970), 43–45.

23. Theodor Herzl to Lord Rothschild, Aug. 22, 1902, in *Vision und Politik: Die Tagebuecher Theodor Herzls*, ed. Gisela Brude-Firnau (Frankfurt am Main: Suhrkamp, 1976), 233 (hereafter cited as *Vision und Politik*). Herzl was in the habit

of copying important letters into his diary, and this was one of them. This entry is not, however, contained in *The Diaries of Theodor Herzl*, ed. and trans. Marvin Lowenthal (Gloucester, Mass.: Peter Smith, 1978).

24. Quoted in the editor's postface to *Vision und Politik*, 286; not contained in *The Diaries of Theodor Herzl*.

25. *Vision und Politik*, 232.

26. See Brude-Firnau's informative but too uncritical postface to *Vision und Politik*, 290–95.

27. Arendt, *Rahel Varnhagen*, xv.

28. Ibid., xvii.

29. Ibid., xviii.

30. Ibid., xvii.

31. References to the titles of chapters 1 and 12 of *Rahel Varnhagen*.

32. Hannah Arendt to Heinrich Bluecher, Aug. 12, 1936 (Arendt estate).

33. Hannah Arendt to Heinrich Bluecher, Nov. 24, 1936 (Arendt estate).

34. Hannah Arendt to Heinrich Bluecher, Nov. 26, 1936 (Arendt estate).

35. Arendt, *Rahel Varnhagen*, xiv-xv.

36. Hannah Arendt to Karl Jaspers, Sept. 7, 1952, *Arendt, Jaspers Briefwechsel*, no. 135.

37. Arendt, *Rahel Varnhagen*, 9.

38. Rahel Varnhagen to David Veit, April 2, 1893, *Rahel Varnhagen: Briefwechsel*, 3:20.

39. Arendt, *Rahel Varnhagen*, 199.

40. Ibid., 199–200.

41. Arendt refers here to passages in letters in which Rahel writes about herself in these terms.

42. Arendt, *Rahel Varnhagen*, 201.

43. Ibid.

44. Arendt, *Rahel Varnhagen*, 7. In this context Arendt also mentions the fact of mass baptism among Jews of this generation; see Guido Kisch, *Judentaufen: Eine historisch-biographisch-soziologische Studie besonders fuer Berlin und Koenigsberg* (Berlin: Colloquium Verlag, 1973), chaps. 2 and 3. See also Jacob Katz, *Out of the Ghetto: The Social Background of Jewish Emancipation, 1770–1870* (Cambridge, Mass.: Harvard University Press, 1973), chap. 4.

45. See the discussion of her insistence on the visibility of political space, chapter 1, sections 4 and 5, of the present volume.

46. See the argument in chapter 1, sections 3 and 4, of the present volume.

47. Arendt, *Rahel Varnhagen*, 5.

48. Rahel Varnhagen to Wilhelm von Willisen, Nov. 11, 1825, *Rahel Varnhagen: Briefwechsel*, 4:284–85; Rahel's emphasis.

49. See the discussion of her essays on the problem of exile, written in the forties, in chapter 3 of the present volume.

50. Hannah Arendt to Heinrich Bluecher, Aug. 12, 1936 (Arendt estate).

51. See Arendt's letter to Bluecher, August 24, 1936, in answer to his stories of the miracle-working rabbi ("Wunderrabbi"): The Jews have practiced chasing off the Messiah; "every one of them is the wrong one." By implication: The Jews do not

really want him to come; they do not want a revolutionary change in their own tradition.

52. Ibid.

53. See chapter 1, section 2, of the present volume.

54. Arendt, *Rahel Varnhagen*, xvii.

55. Ibid.

56. Arendt knew this and regretted very much the presumed loss of the manuscript, writing to Bluecher in July 1941 when she heard the news: "I am depressed that Rahel is perdue, and so angry. Darling, you haven't even read it! Sic transit gloria mundi!" Bluecher answers immediately that he had not only read *Rahel* but had been so enchanted by her "that I positively forced you to finish the book." The text, however, was not lost after all, as Arendt found out after the war. See Arendt to Heinrich Bluecher, July 25, 1941, and Heinrich Bluecher to Arendt, July 26, 1941 (Arendt estate).

57. Lotte Koehler, "Rahel Varnhagen," in *Deutsche Dichter der Romantik Ihr Leben und Werk*, ed. Benno von Wiese (Berlin: Erich Schmidt, 1983), 295.

58. Sybille Bedford, "Emancipation and Destiny," *Book Notes*, Dec. 12, 1958, 22, 23.

59. See Arendt's 1957 preface on Varnhagen's editing of those very open letters which he thought offensive to the moral taste of his (rather than Rahel's) readers (Arendt, *Rahel Varnhagen*, xiv).

60. Rahel Varnhagen to Pauline Wiesel, March 12, 1810, printed in the extensive appendix of unedited Rahel letters and diary entries in the 1959 German edition of Arendt's biography of Rahel, *Rahel Varnhagen*, 230.

61. Ibid., 231.

62. Ibid., 230.

63. Rahel Varnhagen to August Varnhagen, March 28, 1814, *Rahel Varnhagen: Briefwechsel*, 2:256; quoted in Arendt, *Rahel Varnhagen*, 6.

64. Ibid.

65. Arendt, *Rahel Varnhagen*, 7: "A political struggle for equal rights might have taken the place of the personal struggle. But that was wholly unknown to this generation of Jews whose representatives even offered to accept mass baptism (David Friedlaender). Jews did not even want to be emancipated as a whole; all they wanted was to escape from Jewishness, as individuals if possible." On the issue of "mass baptism" in the first half of the nineteenth century, see Kisch, *Judentaufen*, 66–67. Kisch does not like the term that was used by the historian of Judaism Heinrich Graetz, who had taken it from a statement made by Rahel. Nevertheless, Kisch agrees to the phenomenon of large-scale conversion at that time in Berlin and Königsberg. On the issue of the struggle for individual social acceptance versus group emancipation, see chapter 3 of the present volume. For the economic-political history of this conflict, see the very thorough documentation in Selma Stern, *Der Preussische Staat und die Juden*, 4 vols. (Tübingen: J. C. B. Mohr, 1962–71). Interesting for our context—Rahel was the daughter of the wealthy Berlin *Schutzjude*, banker, and *Muenzjude* (one of the Jewish businessmen responsible for the quality of coins in the Prussian State and involved in the silver trade)—is Stern's detailed discussion of the situation of Jewish businessmen under the reign of Friedrich Wilhelm I, which ended

the tendency to tolerance and began the combination of control and protection—that is, the strict limitation of Jews as a group and the preferred treatment of favored individual (rich, economically needed or useful) Jews—which characterized the later eighteenth century and informed the Jewish attitude toward social acceptance into the second half of the nineteenth century. For the question of a Prussian identity for Prussian Jews, which is important for Rahel's self-perception, see Stefi Jersch-Wenzel, "Die Herausbildung eines 'preussischen' Judentums, 1671–1815," in *Juden in Preussen—Juden in Hamburg*, ed. Peter Freimark (Hamburg: Hans Christians Verlag, 1983), 20–26. And on the sequence of phases in nineteenth-century Jewish emancipation, see Arno Herzig, "Die Juden in Preussen im 19. Jahrhundert," ibid., 33–37.

66. Rahel Varnhagen to David Veit, Feb. 16, 1805, *Rahel Varnhagen: Briefwechsel*, 3:83: "Ich bin so einzig, als die groesste Erscheinung dieser Erde. Der groesste Kuenstler, Philosoph oder Dichter ist nicht ueber mir. Wir sind vom selben Element. Im selben Rang, und gehoeren zusammen.... Mir aber war das Leben angewiesen." Arendt quotes from Rahel's published letters without giving references, weaving these statements directly into her text; I will provide the references only in those cases where I think it is important to supplement the context of Arendt's text, for my main interest here is *Arendt's* presentation of Rahel's self-presentation. She herself annotates only the quotes from unpublished material contained in the Varnhagen collection of the Manuscript Division of the Prussian State Library, which she had consulted before the war and which she thought had been destroyed during the war. In the late 1970s, however, the Varnhagen archive was discovered preserved, almost completely intact, and catalogued in the Jagellonian Library in Kraków. See Deborah Hertz, "The Varnhagen Collection Is in Kraków," *American Archivist* 44, no. 3 (Summer 1981); and Koehler, "Rahel Varnhagen," 316.

67. Arendt, *Rahel Varnhagen*, xvi.

68. Hannah Arendt to Karl Jaspers, Sept. 7, 1952, *Arendt, Jaspers Briefwechsel*, no. 135.

69. Rahel Varnhagen to Frau von Boye, beginning of July 1800, *Rahel Varnhagen: Briefwechsel*, 1:304.

70. Rahel Varnhagen to Heinrich Karl La Motte-Fouqué, Jan. 30, 1810, in *Rahel: Ein Buch des Andenkens fuer ihre Freunde*, ed. Karl August Varnhagen von Ense, 3 pts. (Berlin, 1934), 1:461.

71. See, for example, Rahel Varnhagen to August Varnhagen, March 15, 1829, in *Buch des Andenkens*, 1:267–68—notwithstanding this letter's (and most of the others') great charm and extraordinary sense of the limitless resources of language.

72. Rahel Varnhagen to Pauline Wiesel, March 12, 1810, *Rahel Varnhagen* (German edition, 1959), appendix, 231.

73. Arendt, *Rahel Varnhagen*, xviii.

74. Diary entry, March 11, 1810, *Rahel Varnhagen* (German edition, 1959), appendix, 230.

75. For examples of Rahel's effect on people, see Koehler, "Rahel Varnhagen," 292–95.

76. Rahel Varnhagen to Heinrich Karl La Motte-Fouqué after the death of Prince Louis, Nov. 29, 1811, *Rahel Varnhagen: Briefwechsel*, 3:309.

77. Friedrich Gentz to Gustav von Brinckmann, quoted in Franz Kobler, *Juden und Judentum in deutschen Briefen aus drei Jahrhunderten* (Vienna, 1935), 149–50; this excerpt is also quoted in Leon Poliakov, *The History of Anti-Semitism*, vol. 3 (originally published in French, 1968; New York: Vanguard Press, 1975), 297.

78. Gentz had followed Rahel's painful affair with the secretary of the Spanish legation, d'Urquijo; see Arendt, *Rahel Varnhagen*, 88–90.

79. See Rahel's letters to Gentz, 1830–32, Arendt, *Rahel Varnhagen* (German edition, 1959), appendix, 271–75.

80. Friedrich von Gentz to Gustav von Brinckmann, Dec. 28, 1803, *Briefe von und an Friedrich von Gentz*, ed. Friedrich Carl Wittichen (Munich, 1910), 2:179.

81. Arendt, *Rahel Varnhagen*, 100–101. Arendt quotes part of the letter in the English edition, but prints the complete letter to Leopold Ranke, June 15, 1832, in the appendix of the German edition, 281.

82. Arendt, *Rahel Varnhagen*, 86–87; Gentz's emphasis.

83. Rahel Varnhagen to Frau von Boye, July 1800, *Rahel Varnhagen: Briefwechsel*, 1:303; Rahel's 1801 diary, in *Buch des Andenkens*, 1:248.

84. Arendt says this, distinguishing Gentz from Rahel (*Rahel Varnhagen*, 88); she published several important letters from Rahel to Pauline in the appendix to the German edition, but she did not draw much on the relationship between the two women.

85. Arendt, *Rahel Varnhagen*, 3.

86. Rahel Varnhagen to David Veit, April 2, 1793, *Rahel Varnhagen: Briefwechsel*, 3:20.

87. Rahel Varnhagen to David Veit, March 22, 1795, ibid., 54.

88. Rahel Varnhagen to Heinrich Karl La Motte-Fouqué, July 26, 1809, *Rahel Varnhagen: Briefwechsel*, 3:295; Rahel Varnhagen to August Varnhagen, Feb. 26, 1809, *Buch des Andenkens*, 1:406.

89. Arendt, *Rahel Varnhagen*, 4.

90. Rahel Varnhagen to her sister Rose, May 13, 1829, *Rahel Varnhagen: Briefwechsel*, 4:314. In her letters to her sister, Rahel writes perceptively about the "Woman Question," which Arendt evidently appreciates. In the appendix of the German edition of *Rahel Varnhagen* (252–53) Arendt includes a letter to Rose of January 22, 1819, which is extraordinarily shrewd in its assessment of the "secondary dependency" syndrome: she warns her sister, who is very much absorbed by caring for a seriously ill husband, about becoming addicted—as women historically have—to the patient's dependency on her, and admonishes her to understand that her "wholeness" and her mobility, her active independent participation in the world, means responsibility to the other too.

91. Arendt, *Rahel Varnhagen*, 13.

92. *Arendt, Jaspers Briefwechsel*, no. 134.

93. See chapter 6, section 4, of the present volume.

94. For understanding the peculiar limitations of this relationship, Arendt really gives as much credit to Marwitz as to Rahel. He did not, she remarks, fall in with the solidarity of two superior outsiders, which Rahel had proposed to him: "Not only because he was, after all, sixteen years her junior and his life was not yet over, but

also because her boundless candor revealed to him that his contempt for the world was something different from her despairing sense of exclusion from it" (Arendt, *Rahel Varnhagen*, 172).

95. Ibid., 12–13.

96. Quoted in Poliakov, *The History of Anti-Semitism*, 3:200–201. Poliakov comments: "Judaism, consolation of their ancestors, was thus becoming the very symbol of sickness and torment for Rahel Levin's generation."

97. Arendt, *Jaspers Briefwechsel*, no. 135.

98. Ibid. In introducing Blumenfeld, she mentions his description of himself as "a Zionist by the grace of Goethe" and Zionism as Germany's gift to the Jews: cultural affinity is seen as liberating from the social problem of assimilation. See, however, George Mosse on Blumenfeld's views in this respect: *German Jews Beyond Judaism* (Bloomington: Indiana University Press, 1985), 14, 76.

99. Hermann Cohen, *Deutschtum und Judentum* (Giessen, 1915). Cohen projected such intimate ("innerlichst") symbiosis in the realization of Kant's idea of an eternal peace. The time of the projection, the first year of World War I, may have influenced Cohen's reliance on the power of the Prussian-German State in bringing it about (47–48). See also the sympathetically critical essay by Steven S. Schwarzschild, "'Germanism and Judaism'—Hermann Cohen's Normative Paradigm of the German-Jewish Symbiosis," in *Jews and Germans from 1860 to 1933*, 129–72.

100. See the first sentence in Lotte Kochler's essay on Rahel: "Zu den deutschen Dichtern [her emphasis] der Romantik gehoert Rahel Varnhagen nicht."

101. See Hermann Greive's thoughtful essay "Minoritaetenstatus und Toleranz," in *Juden in Preussen—Juden in Hamburg*, 110–12. See also Baruch Z. Ophir, "Zur Geschichte der Hamburger Juden 1919–1939," ibid., 81–83, on the "Hamburger System"—that is, for the first time in the history of Jewish communities the separation of state and church, which Ophir thinks contributed to the spirit of tolerance in Hamburg, not only in the relations between Jews, but also in the relations between Jews and non-Jews.

102. Arendt's friend Scholem, who completely misunderstood and was bitterly hurt by her report on the Eichmann trial, gives a highly instructive account of an equally "naive" social exclusion of the Gentile as expression of minority solidarity when he describes as an example of anti-Semitism how his assimilated father was not really accepted socially by his Gentile colleagues, in spite of their obvious respect for his professional competence and liking of his person, and then mentions, without offering an explanation, that the father refused to speak to his Gentile daughter-in-law. See Gershom Scholem, "On the Social Psychology of the Jews in Germany: 1900–1933," in *Jews and Germans from 1860 to 1933*, 18–21.

103. See Arendt, *Rahel Varnhagen*, chaps. 9 and 11.

104. See Arendt's description of Rahel's lovable qualities in Arendt to Jaspers, Sept. 7, 1952, Arendt, *Jaspers Briefwechsel*, no. 135; "love, trees," etc., refers to Rahel's letter to Pauline Wiesel, June 8, 1826, *Rahel Varnhagen* (German edition, 1959), appendix, 263: "Gruenes, Kinder, Liebe, Musik, Wetter."

105. Arendt, *Rahel Varnhagen*, 213.

106. Ibid., 206–8.

107. See the extraordinary letter to Pauline of June 8, 1826, *Rahel Varnhagen* (German edition, 1959), appendix, 263—extraordinary in its mixture of self-deception and insight into her position.

108. Arendt, *Rahel Varnhagen*, 215.

3. The Silence of Exile: Arendt's Critique of Political Zionism

1. "We lost our occupation, which means the confidence that we are of some use in this world. We lost our language, which means the naturalness of reactions, the simplicity of gestures, the unaffected expression of feelings. We left our relatives in the Polish ghettos and our best friends have been killed in concentration camps, and that means the rupture of our private lives." The essay "We Refugees" was published in the January 1943 issue of *Menorah Journal*, and reprinted in Hannah Arendt, *The Jew as Pariah: Jewish Identity and Politics in the Modern Age*, ed. Ron H. Feldman (New York: Grove Press, 1978), 56.

2. Ibid., 55.

3. Ibid., 62–63.

4. Ibid., 63.

5. Ibid., 64.

6. Ibid., 65.

7. Ibid., 66. See also Hannah Arendt, "The Jew as Pariah: A Hidden Tradition," *Jewish Social Studies* 6, no. 2 (1944): 99–122 (reprinted in Arendt, *The Jew as Pariah*, 67–90), where she gives short portraits of "Heinrich Heine: The Schlemihl and Lord of Dreams," "Bernard Lazare: The Conscious Pariah," "Charlie Chaplin: The Suspect," and "Franz Kafka: The Man of Goodwill."

8. See section 6 of this chapter.

9. Michael Denneny, "The Privilege of Ourselves: Hannah Arendt on Judgment," in *Hannah Arendt: The Recovery of the Public World*, ed. Melvyn A. Hill (New York: St. Martin's Press, 1979), 269.

10. Arendt said repeatedly that she had never felt "at home" in any given place or at any given time. This is borne out by her adapting so well to the American intellectual environment. However, she had felt at home in the German cultural tradition, and to be forced into exile by Hitlerism meant a traumatic experience of rupture—as it did for other German-Jewish and German-Gentile exiles—in spite of her admirable adaptation to the American intellectual environment. See my forthcoming *Exile, Modernity, and History*.

11. See Arnold M. Eisen, *Galut: Modern Jewish Reflection on Homelessness and Homecoming* (Bloomington: Indiana University Press, 1986), xi.

12. Ibid., xviii.

13. In the analysis of Arendt's political thought, I have supplied, from the position of hindsight, the terms *her* and *women*. The exclusiveness of the polis—women and slaves, taking care of the economic interests at home, were excluded from the agora—which informed Arendt's political model in *The Human Condition*, is obvious and has often been remarked on; see chapter 5, section 4, of the present volume.

14. Hannah Arendt, "Preface to the First Edition," *The Origins of Totalitarianism* (Cleveland and New York: Meridian Books, 1958), viii. All references are to this edition.

15. Hannah Arendt, "Understanding and Politics," *Partisan Review* 20, no. 4 (1953): 292.

16. Judith N. Shklar, "Hannah Arendt as Pariah," *Partisan Review* 50, no. 1 (1983): 65.

17. Ibid.

18. Jacob Katz, *Out of the Ghetto: The Social Background of Jewish Emancipation, 1770–1870* (Cambridge, Mass.: Harvard University Press, 1973), 80.

19. Fritz Stern, *Gold and Iron. Bismarck, Bleichroeder, and the Building of the German Empire* (New York: Vintage, 1979), 5.

20. Ibid., 462.

21. For examples, see ibid., 475–78. A contemporary observer wrote about Bleichroeder's extremely ostentatious receptions that all of Berlin was divided into two camps: one went to Bleichroeder's parties, enjoyed his fantastic food, and made fun of him, or one made fun of him and did not go (477). There was general praise for Bleichroeder's intelligence and competence, and much, often one-sided criticism of the forms in which he expressed his social ambitions. There is, of course, the general phenomenon of late-nineteenth-century bourgeois ostentatiousness, which Bleichroeder just exaggerated.

22. Ibid., 499; see also Stern's statistical information regarding the distribution of Jews within professional and income groups (ibid.).

23. Arendt prefaces this passage with the well-known joke about the cause of World War I, the Jews and the bicyclists: why the bicyclists—why the Jews?

24. Arendt, *The Origins of Totalitarianism*, 5–6.

25. Stern, *Gold and Iron*, 470.

26. Ibid., 498. See also Arendt, *The Origins of Totalitarianism*, 23.

27. For further discussion of Arendt's distinction between social and political anti-Semitism, see chapter 4, section 4, of the present volume.

28. This essay, originally an address on accepting the Lessing Prize of the Free City of Hamburg in 1959, is included in Hannah Arendt, *Men in Dark Times* (New York: Harcourt, Brace & World, 1968), 3–31.

29. On Gentile-Jewish cooperation in the city of Hamburg, see chapter 2, note 101, of the present volume.

30. For a discussion of the role of friendship in terms of Lessing's famous Enlightenment drama *Nathan the Wise*, which has been included in recent critiques of Enlightenment totalitarian rationalism, see chapter 5, sections 1 and 8, of the present volume.

31. On Arendt's implicit critique of Rousseau see chapter 5, section 7, of the present volume.

32. Arendt, *Men in Dark Times*, 30.

33. Ibid., 12–13.

34. Arendt, *The Jew as Pariah*, 66.

35. For a critical discussion of this view, see chapter 5, section 6.

36. See Hannah Arendt, "Walter Benjamin: 1892–1940," *Men in Dark Times*, 179–82.

37. Richard Lichtheim, *Rueckkehr Lebenserinnerungen aus der Fruehzeit des deutschen Zionismus* (Stuttgart: Deutsche Verlagsanstalt, 1970), 45.

38. See chapters 3 ("The Jewish Company"), 4 ("Local Groups"), and 5 ("Society of Jews and Jewish State") of Theodor Herzl, *The Jewish State* (New York: Herzl Press, 1970). For more on Arendt's "mixed" Zionist position, see sections 6, 7, and 8 of this chapter.

39. See Franz Oppenheimer, "Stammesbewusstsein und Volksbewusstsein," *Die Welt* 14, no. 7 (Feb. 18, 1910): 139–43; reprinted in Jehuda Reinharz, ed., *Dokumente zur Geschichte des Deutschen Zionismus, 1882–1933* (Tübingen: J. C. B. Mohr, 1981), no. 43 (hereafter cited as *Dokumente;* all translations from this source are mine). Oppenheimer, a professor of sociology and economics at Berlin and Frankfurt universities, argues in this essay that the real Zionist idealism is found among Western Jews because they do not, as do the impoverished Eastern Jews, serve their own interests. Rather, they serve an idea: *"Wir Westler sind die Idealisten!"* He makes it clear that Eastern Jews, driven by necessity, have no choice but to be in that sense self-serving. But he wants recognition of the fact that Western Jews as Zionists think and act from choice rather than necessity. They are proud of their noble ancestry, their "Stammesbewusstsein," and at the same time they have the *Volksbewusstsein* of the folk into which they were born (emphasis Oppenheimer's). The German Jew's folk is German, in the present and the future; he is a citizen, not a guest. But he will work for the new creation of a Jewish folk (a term which could be interchangeable with *nation*) in Palestine.

40. See Reinharz's introduction to *Dokumente,* xxx–xxxiv; and Ginat's introduction to Kurt Blumenfeld, *Im Kampf um den Zionismus Briefe aus fuenf Jahrzehnten,* ed. Miriam Sambursky and Jochanan Ginat (Stuttgart: Deutsche Verlagsanstalt, 1976), 12–14 (all translations from this source are mine).

41. See the "streng vertraulich" (classified) guidelines for the founding of a Jewish Wanderbund "Blau-Weiss" Berlin, Nov. 1913 (*Dokumente,* no. 56).

42. Kurt Blumenfeld to Schalom Ben-Chorin, Dec. 12, 1954, in Blumenfeld, *Im Kampf um den Zionismus,* no. 138. Attempting to make clear to Ben-Chorin the specifically German version of Zionism, Blumenfeld pointed out the fact that Jews in Germany had willingly become Germans through civic emancipation and that the great achievement of German Jewry had been the creative "meeting ("Zusammenstoss") of German culture and Jewish nature ("Wesen")." All the "apologetic" literature written by Jews and some Gentiles is based on the assumption that Jews are essentially Germans and that the differences are negligible. This view was shared by the first generation of Zionists. Blumenfeld mentions the lively debate in reaction to Werner Sombart's 1911 lectures on "The Future of the Jews," in which both assimilated Jews and Zionist leaders sharply contradicted Sombart's recommendation that Jews ought not to insist on gaining access to higher positions in society to which they are not suited because of their different race. Sombart argued that it was impossible to recognize the Jews as genuinely part of the German people, and that Jewish nationalism and loyalty to the German nation could not be reconciled. However, a second-generation Zionist, the journalist Julius Becker, defended this position in an article entitled "Sombart und wir," *Juedische Rundschau* 16, no. 50 (Dec. 15, 1911): 589 (*Dokumente,* no. 48). Becker found highly useful Sombart's arguments in support of a "nationaljuedische," Zionist movement, of economic maintenance for Eastern Jews, and a politics of species preservation for Western Jews. But Zionists would

still have to explain to Sombart the real meaning of a "true renaissance of the old Jewish people." Sombart joined the Pro-Palestine Committee and was sympathetic to National Socialism, but in 1939 he rejected Nazi racial theories.

43. In his informative introduction to the Blumenfeld letters (*Briefe*), Ginat stresses too much the ethical value of the *Palaestinozentrism* concept; that is, he makes it too abstract.

44. See *Juedische Rundschau* 34, no. 68 (Aug. 30, 1929): 435–36; *Dokumente*, no. 180.

45. "Denkschrift: An die Zionistische Executive in London," *Dokumente*, no. 183.

46. See *Juedische Rundschau* 37, nos. 73–74 (Sept. 16, 1932): 351–56; *Dokumente*, no. 211.

47. See chapter 4, sections 4 and 6, of the present volume.

48. *Dokumente*, 533.

49. Quoted by Uriel Tal in *Christians and Jews in Germany: Religion, Politics, and Ideology in the Second Reich, 1870–1914* (Ithaca: Cornell University Press, 1975), 156–57.

50. On the punishment of estrangement from the land and the promises of the land, see Eisen, *Galut*, chaps. 1 and 2.

51. Tal, *Christians and Jews*, 157, n. 72.

52. *Kreuzzeitung*, Aug. 13, 1897, supplement to no. 375, quoted in Tal, *Christians and Jews*, 157.

53. Tal, *Christians and Jews*, 158.

54. See chapter 2, note 44, of the present volume.

55. See Arendt, *The Origins of Totalitarianism*, 227–30; see also section 5 of this chapter. Judah L. Magnes, with whom Arendt was to cooperate closely during 1948, had made very similar connections in his *Like All the Nations?* (Jerusalem: Herod's Gate, 1930), 16, 26, 28–29; see section 4 of this chapter.

56. See section 6 of this chapter.

57. *Dokumente*, 537.

58. Arendt's circle of Zionist friends included Robert Weltsch, Siegfried Moses, Georg Landauer, and Salman Schocken (for whom she later worked in New York as an editor). In contrast to non-Zionist Jewish friends like Anne Mendelssohn Weil, she was sensitive to the growing anti-Semitism around her in 1932. Weil remembered a conversation which Arendt ended abruptly with a "You're crazy" because Weil had expressed surprise at her friend's apprehensiveness in this regard. See Elisabeth Young-Bruehl, *Hannah Arendt: For Love of the World* (New Haven: Yale University Press, 1982), 98.

59. Hannah Arendt to Mary McCarthy, Oct. 7, 1967, quoted in Young-Bruehl, *Hannah Arendt*, 139. Arendt habitually used the attribute "aristocratic" when referring to the members of the kibbutzim whose work and attitude she admired; see sections 7 and 8 of this chapter.

60. Quoted in Arthur A. Goren, *Dissenter in Zion: From the Writings of Judah L. Magnes* (Cambridge, Mass.: Harvard University Press, 1982), 29.

61. Ibid., 214 (doc. 41).

62. Ibid., 9–10.

63. Nahum N. Glatzer, ed., *The Judaic Tradition* (Boston: Beacon, Press, 1969), 11.

64. Goren, *Dissenter in Zion*, 213 (doc. 41).

65. Ibid. The context is Ha'am's discussion of the concept of honor in Max Nordau's play *Dr. Kohn*, his rejection of the protagonist's so called heroism in accepting a challenge to a duel.

66. Quoted in Eisen, *Galut*, 72. See also Eisen on Ha'am's admiration for Leo Pinsker's "Auto-Emancipation," on Ha'am's concept of the national spirit ("The National Morality," 1899), and on his critics (70–75). Stuart E. Knee, *The Concept of Zionist Dissent in the American Mind, 1917–1941* (New York: Robert Speller & Sons, 1979), sees in Ha'am's cultural Zionism the source for what he calls the "committed wing" of Jewish "Non-Zionism," among whose "theorists" he counts Magnes (92–95). However, one needs to stress that Magnes was not a theorist but an admirably responsible political activist who from a position of dissent wanted to salvage, as did Arendt, the positive aspects of Zionism; in his case this concerned an extension of cultural Zionism into the political sphere.

67. Journal entry, Sept. 8, 1906, in Goren's *Dissenter in Zion*, 84–85.

68. Judah L. Magnes to Ahad Ha'am, April 1925, ibid., 235.

69. Judah L. Magnes, *Like All the Nations?* (Jerusalem: Herod's Gate, 1930), 14, 16.

70. Ibid., 28–29.

71. The testimony was published as a pamphlet under the same title in London with Victor Gollancz in 1947; it was also published in New York by the Ihud Association of Palestine in 1946, under the title *Palestine: A Bi-National State.* I have quoted from the latter edition, which has an important preface by Magnes.

72. Taking into consideration the Arab desire for independence and fear of Jewish domination and the Jewish desire for immigration and fear of Arab domination, and attempting to find an "honorable compromise," Ihud had suggested the immediate immigration of 100,000 displaced persons—25,000 children; 25,000 parents, relatives, and older persons; 50,000 young people—arguing "that this would bring creative forces into the country and also be an historical act of great mercy" (*Palestine: A Bi-National State*, 12–13).

73. See Arendt's argument in *On Revolution*, as discussed in chapter 5, sections 7 and 8, of the present volume.

74. Judah L. Magnes, "A Solution Through Force?" in *Towards Union in Palestine: Essays on Zionism and Jewish-Arab Cooperation*, ed. Martin Buber, Judah L. Magnes, and Ernst Simon (Jerusalem: Ihud Association, 1947), 14–15.

75. Ibid., 15.

76. Ibid., 18. See also Arendt's argument in *On Revolution*, as discussed in chapter 5, sections 7 and 8 of the present volume.

77. See my *Weimar Intellectuals and the Threat of Modernity* (Bloomington: Indiana University Press, 1988), pt. 1; and my forthcoming article "German Intellectuals: Marginality and the Myth of the Proletariat," in *The Tragedy of German Inwardness*, ed. Hans Schulte, McMaster Series on German Literature, Art, and Thought (New York: UPA, 1989).

78. Magnes, "A Solution Through Force?" 21.

79. Magnes, *Like All the Nations?* 25–27.

80. Hannah Arendt to Kurt Blumenfeld, April 1, 1951, Literatur-Archiv Marbach, 76.929.

81. Hannah Arendt, "To Save the Jewish Homeland: There is Still Time," *Commentary* 5 (May 1948): 398–406; reprinted in Arendt, *The Jew as Pariah*, 178–92 (quote on 180).

82. Young-Bruehl, *Hannah Arendt*, 232, n. 43.

83. *Mitteilungsblatt*, Oct. 12, 1945, quoted in Blumenfeld, *Im Kampf um den Zionismus*, 33.

84. Quoted in Blumenfeld, *Im Kampf um den Zionismus*, 34.

85. Quoted in Young-Bruehl, *Hannah Arendt*, 223.

86. Hannah Arendt, "Zionism Reconsidered," *Menorah Journal* 33 (August 1945): 162–96; reprinted in Arendt, *The Jew as Pariah*, 131–77 (quote on 131).

87. Ibid.

88. Ibid., 133.

89. Ibid., 135.

90. Ibid., 137.

91. Ibid., 137–38. This curiously and instructively echoes the situation described in one of the most thoughtful modern science fiction novels, Ursula Le Guin's *The Dispossessed* (New York: Avon, 1976).

92. Ibid., 138.

93. See Georg Landauer's account "Alijah Chadaschah, 1942–48," criticizing the increasing self-centeredness of Yishuv and the worldlessness of Jewish youth, who seemed not to be interested in anything that happened outside Palestine; Landauer's essay is quoted in Eva Beling, *Die gesellschaftliche Eingliederung der deutschen Einwanderer in Israel: Eine soziologische Untersuchung der Einwanderung aus Deutschland zwischen 1933 and 1945* (Frankfurt: Europaeische Verlagsanstalt, 1967), 136. In Landauer's view, this isolation of Jewish youth would lead to arrogance and precipitous action based on the lack of political awareness. Beling, who did not seem to understand the context of Landauer's remarks, regretted that Landauer, speaking from the position of Alijah Chadaschah, singled out for critique precisely the two most important qualities of youth in the Yishuv: self-confidence and Hebraization.

94. Arendt, "Zionism Reconsidered," 140.

95. In this context Arendt, who was still impetuous in her late thirties, had some very unkind things to say about the level of Zionist "reasoning" about anti-Semitism. This would have increased the danger of her being misunderstood by her readers, as the editors of *Commentary* had feared, but it does not, for the reasonably open-minded reader, devalue her argument.

96. In this part of Arendt's argument, too, her pithy and occasionally elliptical formulations might "turn off" readers who are not predisposed to agree with her: "This Zionist attitude toward antisemitism—which was held to be sound precisely because it was rational, and therefore explained something unexplainable and avoided explaining what could be explained . . ." (Arendt, "Zionism Reconsidered," 147).

97. Ibid., 148.

98. Herzl, quoted by Arendt, ibid.

99. Theodor Herzl, *The Jewish State* (New York: Herzl Press, 1970), 48–49: "I have already referred to our 'assimilation.' I am not saying for a moment that I desire it. Our national character is too famous in history and, despite all degradations, too noble to make its decline desirable. But we might be able to merge with the peoples surrounding us everywhere without leaving a trace if we were only left in peace. But they will not leave us in peace. There seems to be something provoking about our prosperity, because for many centuries the world has been accustomed to regarding us as the most contemptible among the poor. Yet out of ignorance or narrow-mindedness people fail to observe that our prosperity weakens us as Jews and eliminates our peculiarities. Only pressure attaches us to our ancient roots again; [in spite of the Jewish "character . . . too famous in history"?] only the hatred surrounding us turns us into strangers once more.

"Thus, whether we desire it or not, we are and shall remain a historical group of unmistakable solidarity.

"We are a people—our enemies have made us one without our volition, as has always happened in history."

100. Arendt here referred to "Weizmann's dictum during the thirties that 'the upbuilding of Palestine is our answer to antisemitism'—the absurdity of which was to be shown only a few years later, when Rommel's army threatened Palestine Jewry with exactly the same fate as in European countries" (Arendt, "Zionism Reconsidered," 149).

101. Ibid., 150.

102. Ibid.

103. Ibid., 151.

104. Ibid., 160.

105. Ibid., 162–63.

106. Hannah Arendt, "*The Jewish State* Fifty Years After: Where Have Herzl's Politics Led?" *Commentary* 2 (May 1946); reprinted in Arendt, *The Jew as Pariah*, 164–77 (quote on 164).

107. Arendt argued in this context that assimilationist secularization had persuaded "the average de-Judaized Jew that, although he no longer believes in a God who chooses or rejects, he is still a superior being simply because he happened to be born a Jew—the salt of the earth—or the motor of history" ("*The Jewish State* Fifty Years After," 170). Whether it is prudent to generalize like this or not, this observation fits in with the often observed predilection of assimilated Jews for German high culture and the inherent sense of cultural—in contrast to political—superiority associated with it.

108. Ibid., 171.

109. Ibid.

110. For the sake of her argument, which at this stage contrasted Herzl's concept of a sincerely, honestly, simply nationalist anti-Semitism with a new, dishonest anti-Semitism, which would not stop at national borders and wanted to preserve the Jews as political scapegoats, Arendt assumed that Herzl believed in the concept he used. There are indications in his diaries that he had a more complex view; but the arguments he used in favor of Zionism were certainly based on this concept, and Arendt was interested in the political effect and effectiveness of his arguments.

111. Arendt, *"The Jewish State* Fifty Years After," 176.

112. Ibid., 176–77.

113. Martin Rosenblueth had been General Secretary of the Council for the Settlement of German Jews, London, from 1933 to 1940, Director of the Information Division of the Jewish Agency, New York, in 1941, and was to be the representative of Israel's Ministry of Finance in the United States from 1949 to 1961.

114. Blumenfeld, *Im Kampf um den Zionismus,* 197–98.

115. Literatur-Archiv Marbach, 76.961/1: "Mir schreibst Du nie. Ich finde das unrecht. Was schadet es schon, dass Du mich fuer einen kurzsichtigen und engstirnigen Politiker haeltst? Ich bin gern bereit Dir zu erwidern, dass ich viel von dem Liebreiz Deines Wesens, von Deinem geschulten Verstand halte, dass ich aber hinzufuegen muesste, dass unser Verstand an und fuer sich stumpfsinnig ist, und da wir beide wissen, dass Politik keine Wissenschaft, sondern eine Kunst ist, attestiere ich Dir sehr gern, dass Du von der Wissenschaft der Politik viel verstehst."

116. Kurt Blumenfeld to Hannah Arendt, June 26, 1945, in Blumenfeld, *Im Kampf um den Zionismus,* 189–91 (Literatur-Archiv Marbach, 76.960/2). In this letter Blumenfeld is very enthusiastic about his reception in Jerusalem and especially impressed by the young people. There is much he should tell her about Scholem, the university, Buber, questions of education, etc.: "In the meantime I am making propaganda for you here, showing the people your essays and telling them how you have made a position for yourself."

117. Kurt Blumenfeld to Hannah Arendt, Jerusalem, 1945 (no month), Literatur-Archiv Marbach, 76.960/1 (not included in Blumenfeld's *Im Kampf um den Zionismus*).

118. Kurt Blumenfeld to Hannah Arendt, Sept. 19, 1945, Literatur-Archiv Marbach, 76.960/3 (not included in Blumenfeld's *Im Kampf um den Zionismus*).

119. Hannah Arendt to Kurt Blumenfeld, Jan. 14, 1946, Literatur-Archiv Marbach, 76.926/1.

120. Abba Hillel Silver, since 1943 cochairman of the American Zionist Emergency Council and then chairman of the American section of the Jewish Agency. See Judah L. Magnes to Hannah Arendt, July 20, 1948: "I shall be sending you a copy of a letter from Dr. Silver plus comments by Mr. Eban. What they write is exceedingly discouraging, almost as though it was not necessary to plan for tomorrow" (Goren, *Dissenter in Zion,* 505).

121. This is also true of Arendt's analysis of *"The Jewish State:* Fifty Years After," which had not yet appeared when she wrote this letter and which would not help matters between her and Blumenfeld.

122. Arendt, *The Jew as Pariah,* 147.

123. See Hannah Arendt to Karl Jaspers, Sept. 7, 1952, in *Hannah Arendt, Karl Jaspers Briefwechsel, 1926–1969,* ed. Lotte Koehler and Hans Saner (Munich: Piper, 1985), no. 135.

124. Reinharz, *Dokumente,* 535.

125. See chapter 6, section 4, of the present volume.

126. Arendt, *The Jew as Pariah,* 246.

127. See Kurt Blumenfeld to Hannah Arendt, April 20, 1950, evidently in answer to a letter she had written him in an attempt to heal the break between them that

had been created by her activities with Magnes in 1948. Blumenfeld wrote that he should have written her the way she had written him, reaffirming the old friendship, which could sustain even serious disagreements: "Here I am. It's totally irrelevant to me whether you think my current opinions idiotic or correct" and "I have become more and more isolated in the course of the years" (unpublished letter, Literatur-Archiv Marbach, 76.962).

128. See Kurt Blumenfeld to Hannah Arendt, Feb. 22, 1953. Blumenfeld refers here to Arendt's dislike of Zionist literature and her apologies for having concealed this from him for so long: "You will be surprised that I have known it for a long time. There is no Zionist literature [this sentence was cut from the published version in Blumenfeld's *Im Kampf um den Zionismus*, 245]. We just have different opinions about Herzl, his significance, and his writing. So what! ["Nu wenn schon!"]" (Literatur-Archiv Marbach, 76.965/1).

129. Blumenfeld, *Im Kampf um den Zionismus*, 197–98. Blumenfeld authorized Rosenblueth to inform Arendt of his reaction.

130. See his remark in the January 17, 1946, letter to Martin Rosenblueth (ibid., 198): "Sie haette ihren Weg, den Weg einer 'revolutionary expediency,' allein gehen sollen." (The implication is: without Zionism.) In the context of the Eichmann controversy, Scholem mistakenly ascribed to Arendt a position on the left (see chapter 6, section 4, of the present volume).

131. *Dokumente*, 513.

132. Goren, *Dissenter in Zion*, 462; see Magnes's journal entries concerning his interviews with Secretary of State Marshall and President Truman, documents 129 and 130 in this collection.

133. Ibid., 463; see document 132 in this collection.

134. On the occasion of Magnes's death, Arendt wrote to Jaspers on October 31, 1948, how much she admired him and that the fact of his illness had contributed to her decision to accept the chairmanship of the political committee of Magnes's small American organization (*Arendt, Jaspers Briefwechsel*, no. 73).

135. Hannah Arendt, "To Save the Jewish Homeland: There Is Still Time," reprinted in Arendt, *The Jew as Pariah*, 178–92 (quote on 182).

136. The United Nations resolution had been based on the illusionary—to Arendt, highly apolitical—assumption that such partitioning and the founding of a Jewish state could be brought about without outside intervention. In view of Arab discontent, and impressed by the arguments of Jewish groups like Magnes's, the United States reversed its stand on the resolution, proposing instead a trusteeship for Palestine, but this was rejected by both the Arab Higher Committee and the Jewish Agency. The Jews wanted to adhere to the U.N. decision; the Arabs wanted a Palestine ruled by its present majority, with minority rights granted to the Jews. In her article Arendt stated the fact that the Jewish Agency "announced the proclamation of a Jewish state for May 16, regardless of any United Nations decision. It remains a fact, meanwhile, that trusteeship, like partition, would have to be enforced by an outside power" (Arendt, "To Save the Jewish Homeland," 178).

137. Ibid., 179.

138. Only Soviet Russia and its satellites had been clear and consistent in the

last turbulent months in their support for partition and the immediate proclamation of a Jewish state.

139. Arendt, "To Save the Jewish Homeland," 181.

140. Ibid.

141. Here Arendt quotes from a December 1947 essay in the *New Leader* by Benjamin Halpern, who proclaimed the new Jew to be the Israeli soldier. He attacked "To Save the Jewish Homeland" in the August 1948 issue of *Jewish Frontier*, accusing Arendt of suffering from an "enfant-terrible complex" which caused her to discredit successful Zionists like Herzl, Weizmann, and Ben-Gurion, and labeling her a "collaborationist."

142. Arendt, "To Save the Jewish Homeland," 185.

143. Ibid.

144. Arendt explicitly does not speak of a new type of Jew here, in contrast to Halpern; see note 141 above.

145. Arendt, "To Save the Jewish Homeland," 185–86.

146. Ibid., 192.

147. See the correspondence between Arendt and Magnes from July to October 1948 concerning the presentation of proposals for the confederation plan (Goren, *Dissenter in Zion*). Arendt, for instance, collaborated with Magnes on his reply to Abba Eban's "The Future of Arab-Jewish Relations" (*Commentary* 6 [Sept. 1948]: 199–206), which was published in the October issue of *Commentary* (Judah L. Magnes to Hannah Arendt, Aug. 31, 1948, in Goren, *Dissenter in Zion*, doc. 136).

148. Hannah Arendt, "Peace or Armistice in the Near East?" *Review of Politics*, Jan. 1950; reprinted in Arendt, *The Jew as Pariah*, 193–222 (for quote, see 193n).

149. See Judah L. Magnes to Hannah Arendt, July 20, 1948, in Goren, *Dissenter in Zion*, doc. 133, written in answer to Arendt's letter of July 14 containing a statement of the history and purpose of Ihud, which Magnes thought would be useful not only in the United States but also in Jerusalem. Magnes wrote that he was particularly impressed by Arendt's "analysis of the reasons why the Zionist leadership did not more actively pursue a policy of peace and understanding."

150. Hannah Arendt to Judah L. Magnes, Oct. 3, 1948, Library of Congress; quoted in Young-Bruehl, *Hannah Arendt*, 233.

151. Hannah Arendt, "The Mission of Bernadotte," *New Leader*, Oct. 23, 1948, 8, 15.

152. Hannah Arendt to Judah L. Magnes, Sept. 17, 1948, Library of Congress; quoted in Young-Bruehl, *Hannah Arendt*, 232.

153. Goren, *Dissenter in Zion*, doc. 138. See also Magnes's Diploma Day address, "Rebellion," Dec. 6, 1945 (pamphlet, Hoover Institution, Stanford), in which he admonished the "Doctors, Graduates and Comrades" to look at rebellion circumspectly: "The question before us is: Have we reached such a desperate position that nothing is to be hoped from the public opinion of the world and that there is no other way before us except desperate acts? In my humble opinion the answer is No. . . . If you despair completely of all the other peoples of the world and you feel that there is no longer any morality in the world, then all is indeed lost for you and even the most successful of rebellions would not succeed" (3).

154. Goren, *Dissenter in Zion*, doc. 139.

155. Hannah Arendt to Hans Kohn, Nov. 12, 1948, Library of Congress; quoted in Young-Bruehl, *Hannah Arendt*, 232.

156. To Elliott Cohen she wrote in November 1948 that she was not qualified for "direct political work": "I do not enjoy to be confronted with the mob, am much too easily disgusted, have not enough patience for maneuvering, and not enough intelligence to maintain a certain necessary aloofness." She thought that appeals to combat terrorism in Israel might be made through the synagogues or through trained lecturers who had been taught to handle hostile crowds. See Hannah Arendt to Elliott Cohen, Nov. 24, 1948, Library of Congress; quoted in Young-Bruehl, *Hannah Arendt*, 233, 513.

157. Arendt, "Peace or Armistice?" 194.

158. Ibid. Magnes saw very clearly the magnitude—in human and political terms—of this problem. In his last diary entry, five days before his death, he contemplated the idea of a "Marshall Plan for the Middle East." "Maybe through economic aid some chance of peace," he wrote; "otherwise war and hatred for decades" (Goren, *Dissenter in Zion*, doc. 140).

159. Arendt, "Peace or Armistice?" 196–97; certain parallels to Nazi Germany are clearly intended in this argument.

160. Ibid., 199.

161. Ibid.

162. Ibid., 200–201.

163. Ibid., 201. Arendt mentions here the fact that "the few exceptions, such as common export organizations of Jewish and Arab orange growers or a few factories that employed both Jewish and Arab labor, only confirmed the rule" (ibid.). Magnes, Buber, and Moses Smilanski, in their 1946 "Testimony before the Anglo-American Inquiry Commission for the Ihud (Union) Association," pointed out that the personal relations between Arabs and Jews were "still fair," that there existed "no deep racial animosity between these two related Semitic peoples," "no present religious animosity," that there was a certain amount of economic cooperation in the cities and a "large measure of cooperation between villages in the farming districts" (*Palestine: A Bi-National State*, 8). These observations are meant to point out the dichotomy between spontaneous cooperation on a daily practical basis and planned, orchestrated national animosity—a situation that requires political structures.

164. Arendt, "Peace or Armistice?" 202–5. Because she was trying to show the solidity, as it were, of the separation between Jews and Arabs, Arendt stressed here the fact that also those socially progressive groups—for instance, members of the kibbutzim—who had not come to Palestine as nationalists had become convinced by the situation "that it was impossible to come to terms with the Arabs without committing national and social suicide."

165. Ibid., 206.

166. Ibid., 207.

167. Ibid.

168. Ibid., 214.

169. Ibid., 207–8.

170. Ibid., 209.

171. See chapter 5, sections 4 and 5, of the present volume.

172. Hannah Arendt to Judah L. Magnes, Oct. 3, 1948, Library of Congress; quoted in Young-Bruehl, *Hannah Arendt*, 233.

173. Arendt, "Peace or Armistice," 209–13.

174. Ibid., 211.

175. Ibid., 210.

176. See Arendt's discussion of the economic advantages of war for Israel in its dependence on help from American Jewry, ibid., 220–21: "Charity money can be mobilized in great quantities only in emergencies, such as in the recent catastrophe in Europe or in the Arab-Jewish war; if the Israeli government cannot win its economic independence from such money it will soon find itself in the unenviable position of being forced to create emergencies, that is, forced into a policy of aggressiveness and expansion. The extremists understand this situation very well when they propagate an artificial prolongation of the war which, according to them, never should have ended before the whole of Palestine and Transjordan are conquered."

177. Ibid., 211.

4. The Quality of Guilt: The Trial of the Germans

1. Hannah Arendt to Kurt Blumenfeld, July 17, 1946, Literatur-Archiv Marbach, 76.926/2. A friend going to Palestine, presumably to see Blumenfeld, too, had not come by to see Arendt before he left, because he knew about their disagreement regarding Zionism and the future of Palestine. Arendt was dismayed that friendship and personal loyalty, which she thought all-important, counted for so little, and declared her enduring fondness for Blumenfeld with the generous enthusiasm that was so characteristic of her letters to him.

2. Ibid.: "Wenn Du sehr viel Zeit hast, und sehr viel Ruhe (aerztlich vorgeschriebene) und sehr viel Lust, mal was Gutes und auch Erstaunliches zu lesen, dann lies den Tod des Vergil von Hermann Broch. (Und sag nicht, Du hast schon mal was von ihm gelesen; denn alles was er vorher geschrieben hat, zaehlt wirklich nicht.)"

3. Kurt Blumenfeld, *Im Kampf um den Zionismus*, ed. Miriam Sambursky and Jochanan Ginat (Stuttgart: Deutsche Verlagsanstalt, 1976), 204–6.

4. Hannah Arendt to Kurt Blumenfeld, July 19, 1947, Literatur-Archiv Marbach, 76.928.

5. For critical responses to Arendt's concept of totalitarianism, see sections 4 and 8 of this chapter.

6. Hannah Arendt, "Organized Guilt and Universal Responsibility" (1945), reprinted in Hannah Arendt, *The Jew as Pariah: Jewish Identity and Politics in the Modern Age*, ed. Ron H. Feldman (New York: Grove Press, 1978), 229.

7. Karl Jaspers, *The Question of German Guilt* (New York: Dial Press, 1947).

8. There are some parallels to Friedrich Meinecke's argument in his 1946 *The German Catastrophe: Reflections and Recollections* (Boston: Beacon Press, 1963), chap. 15: "The areas in which we must spiritually establish ourselves again are marked out for us. These areas are the religion and the culture of the German people" (112). In order to win back a "spiritual contact with the other occidental countries,"

Meinecke emphasized in 1946, when his book was published in Germany, "the cultivation of our own peculiarly individual German spiritual life" by establishing "Goethe Communities" in "every German city and larger village" (117–21). On Jaspers' suggestions as to how to deal with the problem of "moral guilt"—the guilt that interests him most and on which he gives the most detailed advice, see section 7 of this chapter.

9. Jaspers, *The Question of German Guilt*, 31–32.

10. Richard A. Wasserstrom, "Conduct and Responsibility in War," in *Philosophy and Social Issues* (Notre Dame, Ind.: University of Notre Dame Press, 1980), 181.

11. Quoted in Telford Taylor, *Nuremberg and Vietnam: An American Tragedy* (Chicago: Quadrangle Books, 1970), 41.

12. Wasserstrom refers to Article 23(e) of the Annex to the Hague Convention of 1907, which prohibits weapons "calculated to cause unnecessary suffering," and argues that the doctrine of "military necessity" makes it "virtually impossible for the soldier to determine from his limited perspective whether an ostensible war crime in fact comes under this exemption" (Wasserstrom, "Conduct and Responsibility in War," 174) See also the detailed discussion of "defense" and "self-preservation" in combat situations in Paul Woodruff, "Justification or Excuse: Saving Soldiers at the Expense of Civilians," *Canadian Journal of Philosophy*, supplementary volume 8 (1982): 159–76.

13. Wasserstrom, "Conduct and Responsibility in War," 176.

14. Ibid., 185.

15. See Michael Walzer, "Moral Judgment in Time of War," in *War and Morality*, ed. Richard A. Wasserstrom (Belmont, Calif.: Wadsworth Publishing, 1970), 61, for qualifications regarding the responsibility of officers in the field, in the situation of combat, to uphold the limits of brutality regardless of considerations of legality: "But it may be the case that only some act of brutality against the enemy will save the lives of the soldiers under their command, to whom they have an even clearer responsibility. . . . Whatever one thinks of such acts, when they are literally incidents, they are at least understandable. And when the exigencies of each incidence are taken into account, they are possibly justifiable: here the end may justify the means. But it is something else again when brutality becomes a settled policy. Then it is probably true that officers ought to disobey, or at least to protest, the commands which follow from that policy (and which are unrelated to the exigencies of some particular situation). They ought to do so even if they still approve of the ends for which the war is being fought. Protest and disobedience are now the necessary consequences of their judgments, the only way they have to 'humanize' the struggle."

16. On this distinction see Woodruff, "Justification or Excuse," 164–67.

17. See the reservations stated in note 15. They constitute an extremely important moral desideratum, but they may be too unrealistic in certain situations because they are defined by a particular kind of society and army, and a particular kind of war.

18. Taylor, *Nuremberg and Vietnam*, 42–43; see also note 15 above.

19. Ibid., 44; see also 209, n. 3, for more examples.

20. Taylor quotes Justice Story's 1827 statement: "While subordinate officers

are pausing to consider whether they ought to obey, or are scrupulously weighing the evidence of the facts upon which the commander-in-chief exercises the right to demand their services, the hostile enterprise may be accomplished" (*Nuremberg and Vietnam*, 44–45). See also note 21 below.

21. Taylor quotes Justice Curtis, whose opinion twenty-five years after Justice Story's, in his eyes, "made much the same point": "I do not think the defendant was bound to go behind the order, apparently lawful, and satisfy himself by inquiry that his commanding officer proceeded upon sufficient grounds. To require this would be destructive of military discipline and of the necessary promptness and efficiency of the service" (*Nuremberg and Vietnam*, 45). However, there is the important difference that Justice Curtis's opinion explicitly mentions the apparent lawfulness of the order—that is, it at least refers to the problem of knowledge.

22. Quoted by Taylor, ibid., 47.

23. Ibid.

24. The provision in the British manual states that soldiers are "bound to obey lawful orders only," though in combat conditions they could not "be expected to weigh scrupulously the merits of the order received," yet they also could not "escape liability if, in obedience to a command, they commit acts which both violate unchallenged rules of warfare and outrage the general sentiment of humanity." The American provision says that violation of the laws of war may be punished, but that the fact of having obeyed the "order of a superior or a government sanction" may be taken into consideration when determining culpability (quoted by Taylor, ibid., 48–49).

25. The distinction between "war crimes" and "crimes against humanity" was not drawn clearly at the Nuremberg trials, because of the nature of that particular war, especially on the eastern front, and of the regime in whose name it was fought. See Michael Musmanno, *The Eichmann Kommandos* (Philadelphia: Macrae Smith Co., 1961), chaps. 1 and 2.

26. In his *Nazi Doctors: Medical Killing and the Psychology of Genocide* (New York: Basic Books, 1986), Robert Jay Lifton analyzes the Nazi concept of "genocide as a means of national and racial healing" (xii), which he thinks unique in the context of involving physicians in genocide and responsible for the "healing-killing paradox" he found in many Nazi doctors.

27. For an instructive use of the war argument in the extreme situation of "coping" with participating, under orders, in the mass destruction of human life in the camps, see a piece of anecdotal evidence in Lifton's *Nazi Doctors* (394): Eduard Wirths, Chief Auschwitz Doctor, whom Lifton discusses in detail as an example of the "healing-killing conflict," repeatedly threatened subordinate physicians who showed reluctance to participate in the selection of victims for gassing or in the removal of gold fillings from corpses with the principles of "Fuehrer order," as if frontline duty and the danger of desertion were involved, the argument being that such reluctance was incredible "during the fifth year of the war!"

28. Arendt, "Organized Guilt and Universal Responsibility," 229.

29. Ibid., 229–30.

30. *The Judgment of the International Tribunal at Nuremberg* (Washington, D.C.: Government Printing Office, 1947), 3–4. Significantly, the tribunal's definition

of "War crimes" specifies "Namely, violations of the laws or customs of war," thereby pointing to the fluid, imprecise nature of the concept of "laws" in the context of warfare.

31. Arendt, "Organized Guilt and Universal Responsibility," 231; Arendt's emphasis.

32. Ibid.

33. See note 24 above. Taylor (*Nuremberg and Vietnam*, 48) quotes from an article Goebbels wrote for the *Deutsche Allgemeine Zeitung* (May 28, 1944), in which he condemned the Allies' bombing of German cities: "No international law of warfare is in existence which provides that a soldier who has committed a mean crime can escape punishment by pleading as his defense that he followed the commands of his superiors. This holds particularly true if those commands are contrary to all human ethics and opposed to the well-established usage of warfare."

34. See chapter 1, section 2, of the present volume.

35. See chapter 1, note 7, above.

36. See the useful distinction between "Eigenerfahrung" and "Fremderfahrung" in memory and the relation of the experience of "Lebenszeit" and of "Weltzeit" in Hans Blumenberg, *Lebenszeit und Weltzeit*, 92–98.

37. See chapter 6, section 4, of the present volume. See also Hans Kohn, "Zion and the Jewish National Idea," *Menorah Journal* 46, nos. 1–2 (1958), reprinted in Michael Selzer, ed., *Zionism Reconsidered: The Rejection of Jewish Normalcy* (New York: Macmillan, 1970), 175–212.

38. See Albert Speer, *Inside the Third Reich* (New York: Avon, 1971).

39. Arendt, "Organized Guilt and Universal Responsibility," 230.

40. Hannah Arendt, "Understanding and Politics," *Partisan Review* 20, no. 4 (1953): 377.

41. Ibid.

42. Ibid., 381.

43. I will not, in this context, address the question, much discussed in the fifties and echoed in the recent *Historikerstreit*, of the validity of an argument based on the assumption of profound analogies between Hitlerism and Stalinism. See Carl J. Friedrich, "The Evolving Theory and Practice of Totalitarian Regimes," in Carl J. Friedrich, Michael Curtis, and Benjamin R. Barber, *Totalitarianism in Perspective: Three Views* (New York: Praeger, 1969), 123–64, especially n. 33.

44. Arendt, "Understanding and Politics," 388–89.

45. For the sake of this beginning, too, Arendt was very disappointed with the unwillingness of many Germans to face the reality of the "aftermath of Nazi rule." See section 7 of this chapter.

46. The uncritical acceptance of a position of cultural-political distance from which to judge others makes the notes taken by the Nuremberg prison psychologist G. M. Gilbert in *Nuremberg Diary* (New York: Basic Books, 1947) an in many ways disappointing document. Gilbert, with his knowledge of German and his free access to the Nazi leaders on trial for war crimes and crimes against humanity, allowed his own sympathies and antipathies to color his attempts at understanding what it was like to be Goering, Streicher, Funk, Papen, etc. Finding some of the men and their reactions more acceptable than others (notably Fritzsche and Speer), he did not try

to sort out the meanings of the different mechanisms of blaming or not blaming what had happened on Hitler and Himmler, of denial and admission, obedience and disobedience, and, above all, denial and contrition (see especially 46–49: the reactions to the showing of Nazi atrocity films). Gilbert was interested exclusively in their psychological (rather than also in their sociopolitical) pathology and thus in evaluating/judging rather than understanding them. The negative implications of this limited perspective can be seen even more clearly in Florence R. Miale and Michael Selzer's detailed interpretation of the Rorschach tests administered by Gilbert (see his introduction to the volume) in *The Nuremberg Mind: The Psychology of the Nazi Leaders* (New York: Quadrangle/New York Times Book Co., 1975). In contrast to Gilbert's Nuremberg diary notes written in 1945–46, this interpretation of his records almost three decades later reflects one long series of hermeneutic fallacies. See also Miale and Selzer's misunderstanding or misinterpretation of Arendt's position in her report on the Eichmann trial (6–8).

47. See chapter 1, section 3, of the present volume.

48. Arendt, "Understanding and Politics," 387; Arendt's emphasis.

49. On Arendt's equation of totalitarian rule with terror, see Benjamin R. Barber, "Conceptual Foundations of Totalitarianism," in Friedrich, Curtis, and Barber, *Totalitarianism in Perspective*, 3–52, especially n. 37.

50. Hannah Arendt, *The Origins of Totalitarianism* (Cleveland and New York: Meridian Books, 1958), 466; all references to this source are to this edition.

51. See Reinhart Koselleck, "Perspective and Temporality: A Contribution to the Historiographical Exposure of the Historical World," *Futures Past: On the Semantics of Historical Time* (Cambridge, Mass.: MIT Press, 1987), 130–55, especially 136–40.

52. See the highly emotional *"Historikerstreit:" Die Dokumentation der Kontroverse um die Einzigartigkeit der nationalsozialistischen Judenvernichtung*, texts by Rudolf Augstein, Karl Dietrich Bracher, Martin Broszat, Micha Brumlik, Walter Euchner, Joachim Fest, Helmut Fleischer, Immanuel Geiss, Juergen Habermas, Hanno Helbling, Klaus Hildebrand, Andreas Hillgruber, Eberhard Jaeckel, Juergen Kocka, Robert Leicht, Richard Loewenthal, Christian Meier, Horst Moeller, Hans Mommsen, Wolfgang J. Mommsen, Thomas Nipperdey, Ernst Nolte, Joachim Perels, Hagen Schulze, Kurt Sontheimer, Michael Stuermer, Heinrich August Winkler (Munich: Piper, 1987). (No one seems to have wanted the responsibility of serving as editor for these texts, which reflect apparently irreconcilable opposing positions.) This documentation of the bitter, highly polarized debate, in the second half of the eighties, of the Nazi genocide of Jews as a historically unique event shows very clearly the difficulties faced by the historiographer of the recent past in maintaining such a self-questioning position. See the contribution to this collection by Christian Meier, "Verurteilen und Verstehen" (48–61), which is based on a lecture given in Tel Aviv in January 1986.

53. Arendt, "Organized Guilt and Universal Responsibility," 232.

54. The political importance of the economic chaos is stressed by everyone who lived in Germany during those years; see notes 74 and 97 below.

55. Lifton tends to see the problem too clearly in terms of a general German cultural-generational situation, and then interprets his interviewees' remarks either too

freely in Freudian analytical terms or, if he agrees with them, accepts them too easily at face value. See, for example, his case history of a psychiatrist who worked for a month at a killing center, managed to leave, but then continued to work for the regime on relatively harmless tasks. His children, he told Lifton, asked him, "Why didn't you leave sooner?" "His answer, sadly put to me and undoubtedly to them as well, was, 'We simply didn't ask questions at the time.' He stressed with approval the difference between his and his contemporaries' unquestioning belief in Hitler and the new generation's insistence on questioning everything" (Lifton, *The Nazi Doctors*, 109). Stanley Milgram, in *Obedience to Authority: An Experimental View* (New York: Harper Colophon Books, 1974), reports on his experimental research in 1960–63 into the quality of obedience and authority. He seems to question the assumption of profound generational and/or cultural differences/changes, arguing instead that unquestioning obedience to authority depends on individual temperament and, much more importantly, on the immediate pressures of a given situation. He also partly corroborates some of Arendt's conclusions in her report on the Eichmann trial, and his findings are in certain ways applicable to her arguments in "Organized Guilt and Universal Responsibility" and *The Origins of Totalitarianism*. See sections 7 and 8 of this chapter; and Fred I. Greenstein, *Personality and Politics* (Chicago: Markham, 1969), chaps. 4 and 5.

56. Arendt, "Organized Guilt and Universal Responsibility," 234.

57. Ibid., 235.

58. George Kateb, *Hannah Arendt: Politics, Conscience, Evil* (Oxford: Martin Robertson, 1983), 85. For a detailed discussion of this issue in connection with Arendt's reading of John Adams, see chapter 5, section 8, of the present volume.

59. Arendt, "Understanding and Politics," 377. See also Milgram, *Obedience to Authority*, 6: "Even when the destructive effects of their work become patently clear, and they are asked to carry out actions incompatible with fundamental standards of morality, relatively few people have the resources needed to resist authority. A variety of inhibitions against disobeying come into play and successfully keep the person in his place."

60. Hannah Arendt, "The Aftermath of Nazi Rule," *Commentary* 34 (1950): 342–53. See also her reports on her experiences in Germany to her friend Hilde Fraenkel in New York: "the Germans are working themselves dumb and stupid" (Dec. 20, 1949), and "About Germany one could write a book, but I will write only an article" (Feb. 4, 1950), both in the Library of Congress.

61. Arendt, "The Aftermath of Nazi Rule," 342.

62. Ibid., 353.

63. Elisabeth Young-Bruehl, *Hannah Arendt: For Love of the World* (New Haven: Yale University Press, 1982), 245.

64. Arendt, "The Aftermath of Nazi Rule," 342.

65. Ibid., 343. Note the European intellectual's characteristic anti-bourgeois, anti–mass culture bias: "Ugly little one-story structures that might have been imported from some Main Street in America spring up on some of the great avenues to conceal fragmentarily the grimness of the landscape, and to offer an abundance of provincial elegance in super-modern display windows."

66. See Alexander and Margarete Mitscherlich, *The Inability to Mourn: Prin-*

ciples of Collective Behavior (1967; New York: Grove Press, 1975). See also section 5 of this chapter and note 129.

67. Arendt, "The Aftermath of Nazi Rule," 348.

68. See my *Weimar Intellectuals and the Threat of Modernity* (Bloomington: Indiana University Press, 1988), chap. 5.

69. Consider the massive "suppression" of the participation in crimes against humanity by physicians involved in medical experiments with camp inmates under the guise of scientific interest and progress (see Lifton, *The Nazi Doctors*). The membership of physicians in the NSDAP was very high (about 45 percent, in contrast to 22 percent of Germany's teachers). Curiously, in this professional elite, in dramatic contrast to the conventional common-sense understanding of their professed professional standards, the highly formalized, ritualized procedural conditions of modern medical technology made it easier to blunt an individual-professional sense of the physician's responsibility to his patients. On the professional difficulties encountered by physicians trying to open a discussion of these problems, see the recent report "Aerzte unter Hitler: 'Mission verraten,'" *Spiegel* 42, no. 3 (Jan. 18, 1988): 76–80.

70. Gilbert, *Nuremberg Diary*, 48. Most of the defendants at the first Nuremberg trial showed (and verbalized) strong emotional disturbance and disbelief, which Gilbert, who was intent on finding or eliciting contrition, recorded (46–49); Speer, in accordance with his usually calm demeanor, "showed no outward emotional effects."

71. Ibid., 47.

72. Fritzsche was to be acquitted by the tribunal, though the German courts treated him more sternly; see Eugene Davidson, *The Trial of the Germans* (New York: Macmillan, 1966), 532–52.

73. Gilbert, *Nuremberg Diary*, 306.

74. The question of the importance of the charismatic leader for the functioning of the Third Reich remains open, in spite of new research tendencies in the historiography of the recent past which stress the role of power conflicts on the national and local levels and the role of elites (see section 7 of this chapter). There are many witnesses for Hitler's importance in the initial consolidation of the Reich. See, for example, Hans Staudinger, *The Inner Nazi: A Critical Analysis of "Mein Kampf"* (Baton Rouge: Louisiana State University Press, 1981), who emphasizes Hitler's importance under the conditions in which the German middle class found itself: "I cannot sufficiently stress the social and economic conditions and the foreign political situation of Germany after the war and during the following inflation that created an atmosphere favorable for quacks and faith healers. It was the hopelessness, the incertitude of great numbers of the middle class and of the agricultural population throughout the twenties and culminating in the depression that led them into following a 'leader.' Furthermore, Hitler's personality cannot be overrated as a factor in building the Nazi movement" (19). For an excellent account of the distribution and execution of power during the first years of Hitler's rule, see Martin Broszat, *The Hitler State: The Foundation and Development of the Internal Structure of the Third Reich* (London: Longman, 1981) (originally published in German in 1969 under the title *Der Staat Hitlers*).

75. Davidson points out that the "French prosecution, alone among the four

victorious powers, made no distinction between the Nazis and the rest of the nation" (*The Trial of the Germans*, 7).

76. Ibid., 8.

77. Rainer C. Baum, *The Holocaust and the German Elite: Genocide and National Suicide in Germany, 1871-1945* (Totowa, N.J.: Rowman and Littlefield, 1981), viii. On Baum's discussion of Arendt's concept of a "banality of evil" and his indebtedness, in his discussion of the role of elites, to her analysis in *Origins* of "destratification of social inequalities," see section 7 of this chapter.

78. Davidson, *The Trial of the Germans*, 8. Davidson also speaks about the "surrealistic" quality of the brutality in the camps (9), and especially the medical "scientific" imagination does indeed seem surrealistic in the manner of atavistic modern science fiction. For an early warning of precisely this kind of combination, see H. G. Wells, *The Island of Dr. Moreau* (1896).

79. On the question of knowledge of the mass destruction among the German population, see Baum, *The Holocaust and the German Elite*, 10; see also Heinz Boberach, *Meldungen aus dem Reich: Meldungen aus den Geheimen Lageberichten des Sicherheitsdienstes der SS* (Dusseldorf: Luchterhand, 1965). It is an extremely difficult question to pose and answer from the perspective of hindsight; it is also an extremely important cultural question.

80. Davidson, *The Trial of the Germans*, 7.

81. Robert H. Abzug, *Inside the Vicious Heart: Americans and the Liberation of the Nazi Concentration Camps* (New York: Oxford University Press, 1985), 120: "It could almost be seen and hung over the camp like a fog of death."

82. Davidson, *The Trial of the Germans*, 7. Davidson's example of such a demonstration is an essay by Karl Jaspers, "The Significance of the Nuremberg Trials for Germany and the World," *Notre Dame Lawyer* 22 (Jan. 1947). See, however, the discussion of Jaspers' arguments later in this chapter.

83. See, however, Taylor's argument in *Nuremberg and Vietnam*, 42-45.

84. Jaspers, *The Question of German Guilt*, 51-52.

85. Ibid., 2.

86. Ibid., 53-55.

87. Ibid., 9-20. Again and again Jaspers insisted that it was up to the individual to recognize moral guilt and responsibility.

88. Ibid., 39.

89. Ibid., 49.

90. Ibid., 79-81. However, on the question of national character, Jaspers is quite sensibly skeptical (88).

91. Ibid., 81: "By our feeling of collective guilt we feel the entire task of renewing human existence from its origin—the task which is given to all men on earth but which appears more urgently, more perceptibly, as decisively as all existence, when its own guilt brings a people face to face with nothingness." With this notion of a somehow spiritually superior if now problematic Germanness, Jaspers is curiously close to Thomas Mann's questionable position in *Doctor Faustus*, with its easy access to the proverbial higher meaning of a cultural-political catastrophe. See Karl Jaspers to Hannah Arendt, Dec. 10, 1945, *Hannah Arendt, Karl Jaspers Briefwechsel, 1926-1969*, ed. Lotte Koehler and Hans Saner (Munich: Piper, 1985), no. 32.

92. Hannah Arendt to Karl Jaspers, Aug. 17, 1946, *Arendt, Jaspers Briefwechsel,* no. 43.

93. Karl Jaspers to Hannah Arendt, Oct. 19, 1946, ibid., no. 46.

94. See the editors' remarks, ibid., no. 46, n. 7; see also my "The Secularity of Evil: Hannah Arendt and the Eichmann Controversy," *Modern Judaism* 3 (1983): 75–94.

95. Hannah Arendt, *Sechs Essays* (Heidelberg: Schneider, 1948).

96. For a thoughtful, helpfully balanced attempt to describe the situation in the early thirties, see Wilhelm Roepke, *The Solution of the German Problem* (New York: G. P. Putnam's Sons, 1947), 49: "It was indeed a sort of terrible mass epidemic, rapidly spreading and every day making fresh victims, even in quarters one had always supposed to be immune. And against this Nazi plague nothing seemed to avail, neither the appeal to common sense nor the moral appeal, while on the other hand it was furthered by every possible circumstance and chance happening [Roepke had discussed before the economical and political chaos], in a way which made one feel that is was indeed the march of destiny. All classes were dosed with the poison in the most effective quantity and strength in each case, and everywhere every class was brought down, clerks and mechanics with their employers, peasants and aristocrats, professors, officers, industrialists, bankers, civil servants. The friend of yesterday turned overnight into one possessed, with whom it was no longer possible to argue, and the more the movement succeeded the more the nervous, the cynical, and the ambitious joined the genuinely convinced fanatics, the crazy, and the moral perverts, and the more the will power of those responsible for the administration of the state was crippled."

97. Hannah Arendt to Gertrud Jaspers, May 30, 1946, in *Arendt, Jaspers Briefwechsel,* no. 39. Mrs. Jaspers had complained that it was not possible to speak about "'our' problem," with German friends, only with American friends: "Die grenzenlose Not ueberall in Deutschland ist gewiss eine Entschuldigung, aber fuer mich vertieft dieser Mangel an Herzensguete den Bruch" (quoted in no. 39, n. 4). Arendt answered that the Jewish question was front-page news in the United States, but that this did not make the situation any better: "'Our' problem today is our dead," Arendt wrote. She could not live in an environment in which they were not mentioned, and she was certain that it would be much better if there were more talk about that problem in Germany.

98. Significantly, Arendt thought one of the most immediately urgent actions ought to be the dissolving of the camps and the ending of the particularly destructive *Staatenlosigkeit* of the DP's—that is, their politically unreal state of not being citizens, not having a voice in any state (Hannah Arendt to Karl Jaspers, Aug. 17, 1946, ibid., no. 43).

99. See note 52 above.

100. Hannah Arendt to Karl Jaspers, Aug. 17, 1946, *Arendt, Jaspers Briefwechsel,* no. 43: Bluecher, she wrote, had said the same thing to her a year ago.

101. As Jaspers wrote, "fuehle ich mich zum ersten Mal unbefangen als Deutscher." Whether he remembered their exchange in 1933 (see *Arendt, Jaspers Briefwechsel,* nos. 22 and 23; and chapter 2, section 1, of the present volume) about the subtitle *Deutsches Wesen* for his Weber book or not, he mentioned here that he

used the subtitle only after having overcome an inner resistance and in the situation that prevailed at that time.

102. Hannah Arendt to Karl Jaspers, July 9, 1946, Arendt, Jaspers Briefwechsel, no. 42.

103. Gerhard Ritter, "The German Professor in the Third Reich," Review of Politics 8, no. 2 (April 1946): 242–54. Ritter was Ordinarius for German History at Freiburg University until 1956. His explanation for the German catastrophe was that Germany had been too democratic and that the army had not played any part at all in the coming to power of the Nazis; see his "The Fault of Mass Democracy" (1955) and "The Military and Politics in Germany" (1957), both reprinted in The Nazi Revolution: Germany's Guilt or Germany's Fate? ed. John L. Snell (Boston: D. C. Heath and Co., 1959), 76–84 and 73–76, respectively. For a good short and critical overview of postwar German historiography on the German question, see the introduction by George Iggers to the collection edited by him, The Social History of Politics: Critical Perspectives in West German Historical Writing since 1945 (Dover, N.H.: Berg, 1985), 1–48.

104. Hannah Arendt, "What Is Existenz Philosophy?" Partisan Review 8, no. 1 (Winter 1946): 50.

105. Jacques Taminiaux, "Heidegger et Arendt lecteurs d'Aristote," Hannah Arendt: Confrontations, Les Cahiers de Philosophie 4 (1987): 49–52. Taminiaux shows how Arendt, in contrast to Heidegger, stressed the aspect of plurality in Aristotle's concept of the polis.

106. Arendt, "What Is Existenz Philosophy?" 50.

107. Ibid., 51.

108. See the still-authoritative Christian von Krockow, Die Entscheidung Eine Untersuchung ueber Ernst Juenger, Carl Schmitt, Martin Heidegger (Stuttgart: Ferdinand Enke, 1958).

109. The question here is not whether Arendt was doing justice to Heidegger's importance as one of the most enduringly provocative and influential twentieth-century philosophers, or whether she presented her argument against him clumsily. Her critical distance to him was unambiguous and she continued to be intrigued by his thought: see Young-Bruehl, Hannah Arendt, 246–48. Arendt analyzed her intellectual attraction and repulsion very well in her letter to Jaspers on September 29, 1949 (Arendt, Jaspers Briefwechsel, no. 93), in which she asserted that Heidegger did not have any character, not even a particularly bad one, that he was a compulsive liar and escapist, that his attitude toward the modern world was cheaply self-deceptive—and yet, she admitted, she continued to be moved by his intellectual passion and, to her, seductive use of language.

110. Arendt, The Origins of Totalitarianism, 314.

111. Reinhard Hoehn, Reichsgemeinschaft und Volksgemeinschaft (Hamburg, 1935), 83; quoted in Arendt, The Origins of Totalitarianism, 363, n. 59.

112. Arendt, The Origins of Totalitarianism, 315. For a useful, clear summary of Arendt's argument in chapters 10 and 11 of that work, see Baum, The Holocaust and the German Elite, 28–31.

113. Baum, The Holocaust and the German Elite, 30.

114. Arendt, The Origins of Totalitarianism, 315.

115. Arendt's argument here (ibid., 326–29: "The Temporary Alliance Between the Mob and the Elite") has many stimulating insights about the attitude of intellectual elites, on which she concentrates her discussion. There are, however, many examples which do not fit her argument and her distinction between mob and mass is not always convincing.

116. On the left, the body of the folk was the party. Though many of Arendt's general observations on the similarities between right-wing and left-wing totalitarianism are questionable, her analysis of similar attraction to the intellectuals is useful. A very good example is Brecht. She admired much of his work but was never taken in by his unreflected "Marxism," seen at its worst in his mindless celebration of party solidarity in his teaching dramas.

117. See Baum, *The Holocaust and the German Elite*, 3.

118. Hannah Arendt to Karl Jaspers, Aug. 17, 1946, *Arendt, Jaspers Briefwechsel*, no. 23.

119. Karl Jaspers to Hannah Arendt, June 27, 1946, ibid., no. 41.

120. Jaspers, *The Question of German Guilt*, 90.

121. Jaspers here discusses in some detail "the political acts of the victorious powers since 1918, and their inactivity while Hitler Germany was organizing itself" (ibid., 91–93).

122. Ibid., 95–96.

123. Ibid., 97.

124. Ibid.

125. Wilhelm Roepke, *Die deutsche Frage* (Erlenbach-Zurich: Eugen Rentsch, 1945).

126. Quoted in Jaspers, *The Question of German Guilt*, 95.

127. Kurt Blumenfeld to Hannah Arendt, Nov. 5, 1954, *Im Kampf um den Zionismus*, 253–58. (Jaspers refers to Arendt's argument in "Organized Guilt and Universal Responsibility" in *The Question of German Guilt*, 84.) See also Ben Halpern, "Guilty, But Not Answerable," *Jewish Frontier*, April 1948, 41–60. Jaspers had written Arendt (Nov. 9, 1948, *Arendt, Jaspers Briefwechsel*, no. 75) that Halpern had sent him a copy of his article with an accompanying letter which he had not answered because Halpern's critique of Jaspers' *Question of German Guilt* had been dictated by an "a priori hatred." On the other hand, Jaspers conceded that hatred might have made Halpern see more clearly, and that he himself might do well to reflect on Halpern's accusations. Arendt answered (Nov. 19, 1948, *Arendt, Jaspers Briefwechsel*, no. 76) that Halpern unfortunately belonged to that group of Jews who believe that every non-Jew is by definition an anti-Semite, a theory which he had tried to explain to Bluecher. Halpern wanted her or Jaspers to answer, which she promised to do should the article find an echo. This does not seem to have been the case. Only 276 copies of the American translation of Jaspers' *Schuldfrage* were sold in 1948. He commented on January 13, 1949 (Karl Jaspers to Hannah Arendt, *Arendt, Jaspers Briefwechsel*, no. 81) that the book had come out too late in the United States, at a time when the issue was no longer current.

128. Kurt Blumenfeld to Hannah Arendt, Nov. 5, 1954, *Im Kampf um den Zionismus*, 256; see also Kurt Blumenfeld to Immo von Hattingberg, Jan. 17, 1955, ibid., 264–67, where he again quotes the Jaspers passage concerning German anti-

Semitism and credits Jaspers with a pure heart and total lack of realism.

129. Jaspers' moral authority in Germany during the first postwar years was very great. His loosely structured, conceptually sometimes opaque, and redundant discussion of German guilt had, right after the war, a much better chance to help develop this ability than had the Mitscherlichs' magisterial psychological-historical *The Inability to Mourn*, published in German in 1967, because Jaspers, notwithstanding the problematic transhistorical, transpolitical aspects of his argument, refrained from prescriptions and (Freudian) categorizations.

130. "There is no denying the fact that Germans as such bear a legal responsibility for the damage done by the government that acted in their name. . . . We might equally speak of a collective responsibility of the Germans in the sense of a historical responsibility for the faulty development of the German Reich since the time of Bismarck, and we have every reason to wish that the Germans felt this responsibility as intensely as possible.

"It is quite a different thing, however, to establish a collective responsibility of all Germans in the sense of a real partnership in a punishable crime for which we assume them to be guilty because they happen to have this passport and this domicile. Let us stress most emphatically that this is simply a barbaric notion that would lead us back to the darkest periods of mankind when group responsibility still took the place of personal responsibility. As Christians we ought to know that it is nonsense to speak of 'collective guilt,' because guilt is always personal" (Roepke, *The Solution of the German Problem*, 85).

131. Ibid., 50. For Roepke's lengthy indictment of the intellectuals, his own group, see 51–81.

132. On the importance of a composite perspective in this situation, see ibid., vi. See also the introduction and part 1 of my *Weimar Intellectuals*.

133. Hannah Arendt, "Ideology and Terror: A Novel Form of Government," *Review of Politics* 15, no. 3 (July 1953): 303–27; and idem, "Totalitarian Imperialism: Reflections on the Hungarian Revolution," *Journal of Politics* 20, no. 1 (Feb. 1958): 5–43.

134. David Riesman to Hannah Arendt, Aug. 26, 1949, Library of Congress, quoted in Young-Bruehl, *Hannah Arendt*, 255.

135. Young-Bruehl (*Hannah Arendt*, 253) seems too positive in her evaluation of this review as "thoughtful." Voegelin did have praise for part 1 of *Origins* and for the wealth of material that went into the book. But he declared immediately that Arendt's way of dealing with totalitarianism was not the best one and that the "spiritual disease of agnosticism" was the "peculiar problem of the modern masses"—a view of the problem which Arendt did not think important for her treatment of the materials (Eric Voegelin, "The Origins of Totalitarianism," *Review of Politics*, 73).

136. Arendt, *The Origins of Totalitarianism*, 458, quoted in Voegelin, "The Origins of Totalitarianism," 74.

137. Arendt, *The Origins of Totalitarianism*, 459, quoted in Voegelin, "The Origins of Totalitarianism," 74.

138. Voegelin, "The Origins of Totalitarianism," 75.

139. Ibid., 76 and 75.

140. Significantly, Voegelin, in quoting, left out the part of Arendt's sentence

which contains the phrase "nihilistic banality" (see note 138 above).

141. Arendt, *The Origins of Totalitarianism*, 427, 459.

142. Ibid., 451, 457.

143. Ibid., 459.

144. Ibid.

145. On Hitler's notorious plans for the suicide of the German people, National Socialist or not, should the war be lost, see Sebastian Haffner, *The Meaning of Hitler* (New York: Macmillan, 1979), 149–65; and Speer, *Inside the Third Reich*, 460–62, 502–4. Speer quotes Hitler: "If the German nation is now defeated in this struggle, it has been too weak. That will mean it has not withstood the test of history and was destined for nothing but doom" (502).

146. Arendt, *The Origins of Totalitarianism*, 478–79.

147. Ibid., 427, 457.

148. Hannah Arendt, "A Reply to Eric Voegelin," *Review of Politics* 15 (Jan. 1953): 77.

149. Ibid., 78. The book, she says in this context, "does not really deal with the 'origins' of totalitarianism—as its title unfortunately claims."

150. Arendt refers here to Kant's concept of *Einbildungskraft*, and, to make sure she would not be misunderstood, she distinguished imagination (too) clearly from "fictional ability" (ibid., 79). See, however, chapter 1, sections 1 and 3, of the present volume.

151. Arendt, "Reply to Eric Voegelin" 80 (Arendt's emphasis).

152. Ibid. After his visit with Jaspers, Blumenfeld wrote Arendt that Jaspers thought of her primarily as a historian, whereas for him "Hannah is above all a great thinker" (Kurt Blumenfeld to Hannah Arendt, Nov. 5, 1954, *Im Kampf um den Zionismus*, 256).

153. Arendt, "Reply to Eric Voegelin," 81. She addressed only briefly (80) the question of equating liberalism—she was not a liberal, she insisted—with totalitarianism, since Voegelin's argument was clearly not meant to make (common) sense.

154. Ibid., 81. See also Baum (*The Holocaust and the German Elite*, 30) on the politically destructive "selflessness" of these masses, their lack of selfish interests.

155. See Elias Canetti's poetic-anthropological description of crowds and the exercise of power in his 1960 *Masse und Macht* (*Crowds and Power*, 1962). See also my "Doubting Death: On Elias Canetti's Drama 'The Deadlined,'" *Mosaic* 7, no. 2 (1974): 1–23.

156. In this context (part 1 of chapter 10 of *Origins*), Arendt tries to establish a similar total "incorporation" of the individual into the movement also for Soviet rule, though she acknowledges the in some ways different situation. This attempt is not successful; but her observations are borne out in the case of Nazi ideology by other observers of Hitler's relationship with the masses. See Speer, *Inside the Third Reich*, chaps. 5, 10, 11, 13; and Elias Canetti, "Hitler, According to Speer," and "The Arch of Triumph," in *The Conscience of Words* (New York: Seabury, 1979), 145–52 and 153–70.

157. Arendt, *The Origins of Totalitarianism*, 323. Arendt deals with totalitarian organization in chapter 12; she is (relatively) insufficiently interested in the phenomenon of the totalitarian state (see chap. 12, sec. 1).

158. Arendt, *The Origins of Totalitarianism*, 438. One of the problems of Lifton's *Nazi Doctors* concerns his limited understanding of the implications of Nazi ideology for the context in which the doctors who were loyal to National Socialism functioned. He rather too simply treats all the cases he discusses, including the physicians who had agreed to be interviewed, as deeply disturbed patients whose illness had been their total perverting of the Hippocratic oath—healing as killing.

159. Arendt, "Reply to Eric Voegelin," 82. Arendt is quite explicit about the negativity of this connection: "Those who conclude from the frightening events of our times that we have got to go back to religion and faith for political reasons seem to me to show just as much lack of faith in God as their opponents" (ibid.).

160. Ibid., 83. See Hannah Arendt to Karl Jaspers, Nov. 1, 1952, *Arendt, Jaspers Briefwechsel*, no. 137, in which she comments on *The New Science of Politics* as wrong, "auf dem Holzwege," but important.

161. Arendt, "Reply to Eric Voegelin," 84.

5. Visible Spaces: Good Men and Good Citizens

1. "Weder dem Vergangenen anheimfallen noch dem Zukuenftigen. Es kommt darauf an, ganz gegenwaertig zu sein."

2. Hannah Arendt to Karl Jaspers, March 4, 1951, *Hannah Arendt, Karl Jaspers Briefwechsel, 1926–1969*, ed. Lotte Koehler and Hans Saner (Munich: Piper, 1985), no. 109; all quotations from this text are in my translation.

3. Karl Jaspers to Hannah Arendt, Feb. 15, 1951, ibid., no. 108: "herrlich in der Forderung." Arendt was to change the ending, which was indeed too hopefully uplifting and seems to have been influenced by her friend Hermann Broch's equally uplifting conclusion to his tetralogy *The Sleepwalkers*. On this see my *Weimar Intellectuals and the Threat of Modernity* (Bloomington: Indiana University Press, 1988), chap. 6.

4. Hannah Arendt, *The Origins of Totalitarianism*, enl. ed. (New York: Meridian Books, 1958), 496.

5. Ibid., 500.

6. Ibid., 497, 499.

7. Arendt even introduces in her short discussion of the councils here the issue of an (overly) clear distinction between the economic and the political. She is dealing only with the revolutionary councils and the political situation, explicitly leaving open the question of whether factories can be run under the ownership and management of the workers. And then, in parentheses, she makes what is to her a crucial distinction: "(As a matter of fact, it is quite doubtful whether the political principle of equality and self-rule can be applied to the economic sphere of life as well. It may be that ancient political theory, which held that economics, since it was bound up with the necessities of life, needed the rule of masters to function well, was not so wrong after all. For it is somehow, albeit paradoxically, supported by the fact that whenever the modern age has believed that history is primarily the result of economic forces, it has come to the conviction that man is not free and that history is subject to necessity.)" Ibid., 498.

8. Hannah Arendt to Karl Jaspers, Sept. 28, 1951, *Arendt, Jaspers Briefwechsel*,

no. 113. She uses here the untranslatable expression "es ist ihnen in Fleisch und Blut uebergegangen."

9. See Elisabeth Young-Bruehl, *Hannah Arendt: For Love of the World* (New Haven: Yale University Press, 1982), 237.

10. Hannah Arendt to Karl Jaspers, Sept. 28, 1951, *Arendt, Jaspers Briefwechsel*, no. 113: "Ich bin immer wieder dankbar, hierher verschlagen worden zu sein."

11. Hannah Arendt to Karl Jaspers, May 13, 1953, ibid., no. 142.

12. Here Arendt singled out Sidney Hook, who had attacked her.

13. Hannah Arendt to Karl Jaspers, Oct. 6, 1954, *Arendt, Jaspers Briefwechsel*, no. 160.

14. "It is fantastic [*herrlichst*] here. Jaspers next door, very lively, always ready for discussions. Always criticizing me with enormous kindness and in friendship, in real solidarity" (Hannah Arendt to Kurt Blumenfeld, Aug. 6, 1952, Literatur-Archiv Marbach, 76.930/1; all quotations from these letters are in my translation).

15. Hannah Arendt to Kurt Blumenfeld, Oct. 14, 1952, Literatur-Archiv Marbach, 76.930/2.

16. Hannah Arendt to Kurt Blumenfeld, Feb. 2, 1953, Literatur-Archiv Marbach, 76.931/1.

17. Arendt's phrase.

18. Hannah Arendt to Kurt Blumenfeld, Nov. 16, 1953, Literatur-Archiv Marbach, 76.931/4.

19. See Arendt's letter to Karl Jaspers, Oct. 6, 1954, about McCarthyism and anti-Semitism, in answer to Jaspers' letter of Aug. 29, 1954 (*Arendt, Jaspers Briefwechsel*, nos. 160 and 159). In the latter, Jaspers had told her about Blumenfeld's visit in the most positive manner, stressing very much their shared Germanness, *das gemeinsame Deutsche*. Blumenfeld was as German as Hannah Arendt, he insisted, referring, at the same time, to the "alienness" of Blumenfeld's Russian-Jewish wife, a sense which Arendt shared. Blumenfeld had come away from the visit with more ambivalent feelings; see his letter to Arendt, Nov. 5, 1954 (Kurt Blumenfeld, *Im Kampf um den Zionismus: Briefe aus fuenf Jahrzehnten*, ed. Miriam Sambursky and Jochanan Ginat [Stuttgart: Deutsche Verlagsanstalt, 1976], no. 136), and chapter 4, notes 126 and 127, of the present volume. In the same context, Jaspers quoted Blumenfeld, to whom "a very prominent" American Jew had written that it was going to be dangerous (*brenzlich*) for American Jews now. Arendt explained the proportionally large number of Jewish-American intellectuals (see text above) and asserted that there had never been as little anti-Semitism in America before. Notwithstanding his profound loyalty to German high culture, Blumenfeld was much more sensitive about possible anti-Semitism than was Arendt, and especially in later years, when he was in ill health, he may occasionally have overreacted. Besides, Jaspers' description of him, no matter how kind and understanding, reflected quite clearly Jaspers' inability to let go of his pet illusions about the German-Jewish past—an inability which Arendt alludes to very gently in her answering letter.

On the other hand, Blumenfeld was also sensitive to what he perceived to be exaggerated eastern Jewish solidarity. In his letter to Arendt on Dec. 12, 1955 (Literatur-Archiv Marbach, 76.967/7), he expressed his gratitude to her for dedicating to him the first part of *The Origins of Totalitarianism*, "Antisemitism," which was published separately in the German edition of *Origins*. (She had asked him about the dedication on March 29, 1953 [Literatur-Archiv Marbach, 76.931/2], afraid that it might cause him unpleasantness.) He also complained about their old friend Scholem's apodictic attitude toward the Jewish question, noting that his wife, Fanja, had turned her Galician background into a program: German Jews "luckily lack this kind of sham solidarity" ("fehlt zum Glueck diese Art von unechter Solidaritaet")—a sentiment shared by Arendt. Blumenfeld repeatedly expressed his regret that the Jewish encounter with German culture, which had brought about a "period of the highest intellectual and human achievement," was known only to a small, albeit important, group in Israel (see his letter to Arendt of Nov. 22, 1956, Literatur-Archiv Marbach, 76.968/6). See here as well Michael K. Nathan's balanced account of the role of the eastern Jewish experience in Israel's self-perception, "Israel—ein Juedischer Staat?" *Der Spiegel*, 1988, no. 3: 106–7.

20. In her letter to Blumenfeld on Nov. 16, 1953 (Literatur-Archiv Marbach, 76.931/4), Arendt described the snobbish exclusiveness that was characteristic of Princeton as "naive."

21. See the long quote from this proposal in Young-Bruehl, *Hannah Arendt*, 276. Overstating the results of Arendt's study of Marxism, Young-Bruehl calls it "a strenuous critique of the whole great Western tradition. Her project for a study of the totalitarian elements of Marxism turned into a plan for laying the foundations of a new science of politics" (277). Arendt certainly searched for and provided a new reading of the tradition, but it was not a "strenuous" critique of the tradition, nor could it have been meant, in her self-consciously specific, concrete focus on the human condition, to lay the foundations of a new science of politics.

22. Quoted by Young-Bruehl, ibid., 277–78.

23. Young-Bruehl (ibid., 278) mistakenly claims that this essay was added to *Origins* as an epilogue. Rather, the epilogue was an optimistic analysis of the implications of the Hungarian revolution.

24. Quoted by Young-Bruehl, ibid., 279.

25. Hannah Arendt to Kurt Blumenfeld, Oct. 14, 1952, Literatur-Archiv Marbach, 76.930/32.

26. Arendt introduces the chapter "Labor" with a statement which is typical of her eclectic and, in a curiously literal way, responsive dealing with the tradition: "In the following chapter, Karl Marx will be criticized. This is unfortunate at a time when so many writers who once made their living by explicit or tacit borrowing from the great wealth of Marxian ideas and insights have decided to become professional anti-Marxists, in the process of which one of them even discovered that Karl Marx himself was unable to make a living, forgetting for the moment the generations of authors whom he has 'supported'" (Hannah Arendt, *The Human Condition* [Garden City, N.Y.: Doubleday, 1959], 71). See also Arendt's letter to Karl Jaspers, June 3, 1949, *Arendt, Jaspers Briefwechsel*, no. 90, about the current intellectual climate, in which every "little idiot" believed in his right and duty to look down on Marx, when a few years earlier it had taken courage to say that Marx had not solved all the puzzles of the world.

27. Hannah Arendt, "Tradition and the Modern Age," *Between Past and Future* (New York: Viking Press, 1961), 17–40, especially 17.

28. Ibid., 18.

29. Ibid., 20.

30. Ibid., 21.

31. Ibid., 23. In this context, Arendt reminds her readers that it was "against the time-consuming political life of an average full-fledged citizen of the Greek polis that the philosophers, especially Aristotle, established their ideal of *skhole*, of leisure time, which in antiquity never meant freedom from ordinary labor, a matter of course anyhow, but time free from political activity and the business of the state" (20).

32. Ibid., 24.

33. Ibid., 25.

34. Ibid., 18.

35. Arendt here defines the modern age as emerging with the scientific revolution of the seventeenth century, climaxing politically in the revolutions of the eighteenth century, and spreading socially with the Industrial Revolution of the nineteenth century (Arendt, "Tradition and the Modern Age," 27).

36. Ibid.

37. Ibid., 26.

38. In section 3 of "Tradition and the Modern Age," Arendt gives examples of this revolt-bondage relationship; she seems especially interested in Nietzsche's devaluation of values and his rejection, important to her, of a "value-free" science (*wertfreie Wissenschaft*), which she distinguishes sharply from the Roman historian's attitude of *sine ira et studio* (ibid., 34).

39. Ibid., 29.

40. Ibid.

41. Ibid., 40.

42. When the essay was reprinted in *Between Past and Future*, Arendt changed the title to "What Is Authority?" but on the first page drew attention to the all-important fact of its having vanished from our contemporary world (Hannah Arendt, "What Is Authority?" *Between Past and Future*, 91–141; subsequent references in this chapter are to this edition).

43. Ibid., 93.

44. Ibid., 94.

45. The essay was first published in *Authority*, ed. Carl J. Friedrich (Cambridge, Mass.: Harvard University Press, 1959). A German version, "Was ist Autoritaet?" appeared in *Der Monat* 8, no. 89 (Feb. 1956): 29–44.

46. Arendt, "What Is Authority?" 92.

47. Ibid., 97.

48. Ibid., 98.

49. Ibid., 100.

50. Functionalism is calling communism a "new religion" because, in spite of its declared atheism, it fulfills, in some social-psychological aspects, the same function as did and does traditional religion: "It is as though I had the right to call the heel of my shoe a hammer because I, like most women, use it to drive nails into the wall" (ibid., 102).

51. In this context Arendt was particularly critical of the political conservatives, who, she believed, had quite a good chance of being heard in the late fifties. She was convinced that if society followed their recommendations, "we shall not find it hard to produce such substitutes, . . . we shall use violence and pretend to have restored authority" (ibid., 103).

52. Ibid., 104.

53. Arendt, *The Origins of Totalitarianism*, 466; see also chapter 4, section 8, of the present volume.

54. Arendt, "What Is Authority?" 104.

55. Ibid., 107.

56. Ibid., 110.

57. Responding to the 1956 essay "Was ist Autoritaet?" Jaspers rejected Arendt's interpretation of the *Republic*, arguing that Plato had not intended to establish a program but had projected "staatliches Tun," activities carried out and authorized by the state, the truth of which could not be subsumed under the general concept of truth. Plato was speaking of an "Abbild des Urbilds in schwebender Verfassung," an image of the archimage which could not be pinned down to mean merely an image (Karl Jaspers to Hannah Arendt, April 12, 1956, *Arendt, Jaspers Briefwechsel*, no. 184). Arendt, not at all persuaded by these fanciful (untranslatable) obfuscations, insisted that Heidegger's reading of Plato, with its distinction between *Richtigkeit* ("correctness") and *Wahrheit* ("truth") ("Vom Wesen der Wahrheit" 1942/43) was right: the cave allegory changes truth into correctness; the ideas become norms (Hannah Arendt to Karl Jaspers, July 1, 1956, *Arendt, Jaspers Briefwechsel*, no. 187).

58. Arendt, "What Is Authority?" 110–13. In this context, Arendt argues that the idea of the good, which is the source of the philosopher's claim to domination, is found only in the explicitly political parts of the *Republic*. In the first books the philosopher is still defined as a lover of beauty, and the original function of the ideas was not to rule or control the chaos of human affairs but to illuminate their darkness: "It seems that Plato was the first to take exception to the political irrelevance of his new teaching, and he tried to modify the doctrine of ideas so it would become useful for a theory of politics" (Arendt, "What Is Authority?" 113). This observation could serve as a useful comment on the sterile, but bitter and highly polarizing debate of theory versus praxis in German intellectual Marxist circles in the twenties and again in the late sixties and seventies.

59. See my discussion of this issue in the introduction to this volume.

60. Arendt, "What Is Authority?" 116.

61. Ibid., 117. In *The Human Condition*, chap. 2, Arendt draws attention to the sharp distinction in every Greek citizen's life between what was his own (*idion*) and what was communal (*koinon*): "[It was] a simple historical fact that the foundation of the polis was preceded by the destruction of all organized units resting on kinship, such as the *phratria* and the *phyle*" (25).

62. Arendt, *The Human Condition*, 74. See also ibid., 27–34, where Arendt explains in some detail the role of the household in coping with necessity, which ruled over all its activities: "What all Greek philosophers, no matter how opposed to *polis* life, took for granted is that freedom is exclusively located in the political realm, that necessity is primarily a prepolitical phenomenon, characteristic of the private

household organization, and that force and violence are justified in that sphere because they are the only means to master necessity—for instance, by ruling over
slaves—and to become free" (29–30).

63. See David Brion Davis, *The Problem of Slavery in Western Culture* (Ithaca:
Cornell University Press, 1966), chap. 3. Davis points out that Aristotle, in contrast
to Plato's harsher position, saw no reason why the master should not converse with
the slave in a friendly manner; in his view, the relationship, based on natural differences body/soul, animals/men—was mutually beneficial (70).

64. See the thoughtfully consistent critical exploration of Arendt's concept of the
political in George Kateb, *Hannah Arendt: Politics, Conscience, Evil* (Oxford: Martin
Robertson, 1984), chap. 1.

65. Davis, *The Problem of Slavery*, 70.

66. Ibid., 71.

67. Ibid., 30: "Because all human beings are subject to necessity, they are entitled to violence toward others; violence is the prepolitical act of liberating oneself
from the necessity of life for the freedom of world. This freedom is the essential
condition of what the Greeks called felicity, eudaimonia, which was an objective
status depending first of all upon wealth and health."

68. Winston Ashley, "The Theory of Natural Slavery, according to Aristotle and
St. Thomas" (Ph.D. diss., University of Notre Dame, 1941), chap. 5.

69. Arendt, *The Human Condition*, 106.

70. Arendt had first intended to use *vita activa* as the title for the book which
became *The Human Condition*. In her letter to Jaspers on April 7, 1956 (*Arendt,
Jaspers Briefwechsel*, no. 183), she referred to the manuscript as *Vita Activa*, treating
essentially the political implications of labor, work, and action. The title of the 1960
German translation of *The Human Condition* was *Vita Activa oder vom taetigen Leben*.

71. Arendt, *The Human Condition*, 9–10.

72. See Hannah Arendt, "The Aftermath of Nazi Rule," *Commentary* 34
(1950): 342–53.

73. See my "Doubting Death: On Elias Canetti's Drama *The Deadlined*," *Mosaic* 7 (1974): 1–23.

74. Arendt, *The Human Condition*, 1.

75. Ibid., 1–2.

76. Ibid., 4.

77. Arendt, "What Is Authority?" 93.

78. Arendt, *The Human Condition*, 156.

79. Ibid., 4.

80. This disclosure, Arendt says in this context, "of who somebody is, is implicit
in both his words and his deeds; yet obviously the affinity between speech and revelation is much closer than that between act and revelation" (ibid., 158).

81. Ibid., 157.

82. Ibid., 156.

83. Ibid., 73.

84. Ibid., 77.

85. Oskar Lafontaine, "Arbeitslosen-oder Freizeitgesellschaft? Ueber Reform-

politik in einer veraenderten Welt," *Der Spiegel*, 1988, no. 7: 34–41. This essay sums up the argument of Lafontaine's book-length study, *Die Gesellschaft der Zukunft* (Hamburg: Hoffmann & Campe, 1988).

86. See Arendt, "Tradition and the Modern Age," 24–25; and idem, *The Human Condition*, 90 (where she quotes herself from that earlier essay: "Such fundamental and flagrant contradictions rarely occur in second-rate writers; in the work of the great authors they lead into the very center of their work") and 113.

87. Arendt, *The Human Condition*, 114.

88. Ibid., 110. Arendt did not think much of the cultural and leisure activities that Lafontaine would like to see supported politically: "Marx predicted correctly, though with an unjustified glee, 'the withering away' of the public realm under conditions of unhampered development of the 'productive forces of society,' and he was equally right, that is, consistent with his conception of man as an *animal laborans*, when he foresaw that 'socialized men' would spend their freedom from laboring in those strictly private and essentially worldless activities that we now call 'hobbies'" (101).

89. Ibid., 115. For more on the concept of private versus public happiness, see section 8 of this chapter.

90. Arendt, *The Human Condition*, 104.

91. See ibid., 4–6.

92. Kateb, *Hannah Arendt*, 70–71.

93. Arendt, "What Is Authority?" 93.

94. Ibid., 120.

95. Arendt, *The Human Condition*, 10.

96. Ibid., 19 and 304, n. 19.

97. Arendt, "What Is Authority?" 140.

98. Arendt, *The Human Condition*, 83.

99. Arendt, "What Is Authority?" 141, 140.

100. Ibid., 141. These are the last words of the essay.

101. Hannah Arendt, *On Revolution* (New York: Viking Press, 1963), "Acknowledgements." See also Hannah Arendt to Karl Jaspers, Nov. 16, 1958, *Arendt, Jaspers Briefwechsel*, no. 233: "I am in the middle of American history preparing my Princeton lectures on the concept of revolution. . . . It is breathtakingly exciting and magnificent, namely the American Revolution, the founding of the republic, the Constitution. Madison, Hamilton, Jefferson, John Adams—what great men. And if one looks at the situation today—what decline."

102. See section 1 of this chapter.

103. See chapter 4, section 8, of the present volume.

104. Arendt, *The Human Condition*, 155. On Arendt's interest in Dinesen's concept and art of storytelling, see chapter 1, section 1, of the present volume.

105. Hannah Arendt, "On Hannah Arendt," in *Hannah Arendt: The Recovery of the Public World*, ed. Melvyn A. Hill (New York: St. Martin's Press, 1979), 303.

106. Hannah Arendt, "Understanding and Politics," *Partisan Review* 20, no. 4 (1953): 377.

107. Arendt, *The Human Condition*, 79.

108. Hannah Arendt, "Walter Benjamin: 1892–1940," *Men in Dark Times* (New York: Harcourt, Brace and World, 1968), 156.

109. Arendt's emphasis on remembrance may have been influenced by Benjamin, for whom it was central; see my *Weimar Intellectuals*, chap. 4.

110. See chapter 1, section 1, of the present volume.

111. See Hannah Arendt to Karl Jaspers, Feb. 19, 1965, *Arendt, Jaspers Briefwechsel*, no. 369. In the context of describing to Jaspers the Berkeley students movement as "something really genuine" coming out of the civil rights movement, she agrees with Jefferson on the desirability of the "*Ward-* oder Raete-System der Klein-Republiken."

112. On Arendt's disagreement with Thomas Paine in this respect, see Kateb, *Hannah Arendt*, 124–26; and section 8 of this chapter.

113. Peter Fuss, "Hannah Arendt's Conception of Political Community," in *Hannah Arendt: The Recovery of the Public World*, 173. See Young-Bruehl, *Hannah Arendt*, 398–401, on critical reactions to *On Revolution*. Robert Nisbet, "Hannah Arendt and the American Revolution," *Social Research* 44 (1977): 63–79, rightly points out Arendt's "omission of regard for the existence of 'the social question' in the American colonies and later in the American states which the Constitution brought officially into existence" (65). Juergen Habermas, "Hannah Arendt's Communications Concept of Power," *Social Research* 44 (1977): 3–24, is uncritical of Arendt's concept of power as "the ability to agree upon a common cause of action in unconstrained communication" (3). He is not disturbed, then, by the absence of social-psychological considerations and sees certain weaknesses not so much in the normative aspects of the concept as in Arendt's ("conservative") dependence on the polis as a model. Dolf Sternberger, "The Sunken City: Hannah Arendt's Idea of Politics," *Social Research* 44 (1977): 132–46, is not explicitly critical of this dependence or of the fact that "psychological suspicions did not burden, did not even bother her" (135), but he rightly points out that in her "brilliant phenomenological description of action" the "inherent goal of all political action" (namely, power) "remains oddly obscure" (145). In other words, he understandably minds the fact that we are never really told what this unconstrained political communication in action and speech is about.

114. Arendt, *On Revolution*, 11.

115. Ibid., 23. See Jean-Michel Chaumont, "Individualisme et Modernité chez Tocqueville et Arendt," *Hannah Arendt: Confrontations, Les Cahiers de Philosophie* 4 (1987): 115–46. Chaumont sees Arendt in an implicit confrontation with de Tocqueville in *On Revolution*; I, in contrast, see a fairly consistent attempt on her part to read de Tocqueville for affirmation of her own argument.

116. Arendt, *On Revolution*, 23.

117. Ibid., 24.

118. Ibid., 25. "If revolution had aimed only at the guarantee of civil rights, then it would not have aimed at freedom but at liberation from governments which had over-stepped their powers and infringed upon old and well-established rights" (ibid.).

119. Ibid., 28.

120. Chaumont, "Individualisme," 140 (his emphasis).

121. Arendt, *On Revolution*, 63.

122. Jaspers (Karl Jaspers to Hannah Arendt, Dec. 31, 1958, *Arendt, Jaspers Briefwechsel*, no. 234), in response to Arendt's enthusiastic remarks on the men of the American Revolution (Hannah Arendt to Karl Jaspers, Nov. 16, 1956, ibid., no. 233), remembered Hamilton as most admirable, a risk-taking aristocrat, a statesman without illusions, in contrast to the prototypically American Jefferson, well-meaning, average, not without cunning or illusions. Arendt, in her answer (Hannah Arendt to Karl Jaspers, Jan. 31, 1959, ibid., no. 235), disagreed: Jefferson was better than Jaspers remembered, and the greatest figure among all of them was John Adams.

123. Adams read widely in history and philosophy and admired particularly the Stoics. See the *Catalogue of the John Adams Library in the Public Library of the City of Boston* (Boston, 1917).

124. Gordon S. Wood, *The Creation of the American Republic, 1776–1787* (New York: Viking Press, 1972), 576.

125. John R. Howe, Jr., *The Changing Political Thought of John Adams* (Princeton: Princeton University Press, 1966), 23.

126. Ibid., 30.

127. Quoted by Howe, ibid., 31–32.

128. Thomas Jefferson to Thomas Law, June 13, 1814; quoted by Howe, ibid., 31.

129. Quoted by Merrill D. Peterson in *Adams and Jefferson: A Revolutionary Dialogue* (New York: Oxford University Press, 1978), 6.

130. Quoted by Peterson, ibid.

131. Diary entry, July 16, 1786, quoted by Howe, ibid., 57.

132. Arendt, *On Revolution*, 64.

133. Quoted by Arendt, ibid., 64.

134. Arendt, *The Human Condition*, 43–44: "The social realm, where the life process has established its own public domain, has let loose an unnatural growth, so to speak, of the natural; and it is against this growth, not merely against society but against a constantly growing social realm, that the private and intimate, on the one hand, and the political (in the narrower sense of the word), on the other, have proved incapable of defending themselves."

135. Arendt, *On Revolution*, 104–9.

136. Quoted by Arendt, ibid., 124.

137. Jefferson wrote this at the age of fifty. The sentence preceding the quote reads: "The motion of my blood no longer keeps time with the tumult of the world. It leads me to seek for happiness in the lap and love of my family . . ." (Thomas Jefferson, *Writings*, ed. Merrill D. Peterson [New York: Library of America, 1984], 1010).

138. See Arendt, *On Revolution*, 124. The context of the phrase quoted by Arendt is: "Where every man is a sharer in the direction of his ward-republic, or of some of the higher ones, and feels that he is a participator in the government of affairs, not merely at an election one day in the year, but every day; when there shall not be a man in the State who will not be a member of some one of its councils, great or

small, he will let the heart be torn out of his body sooner than this power be wrested from him by a Caesar or Bonaparte" (Jefferson, *Writings*, 1380).

139. James Madison, *The Federalist* 51 (Feb. 6, 1788), in *The Papers of James Madison*, ed. Robert A. Rutland (Chicago: University of Chicago Press, 1977), x, 477.

140. Quote and comment in Arendt, *On Revolution*, 127.

141. Ibid., 138.

142. This distinction, Aristotelian in origin, is basic to Arendt's political thought. See section 5 of this chapter; and Hannah Arendt, "Civil Disobedience," *Crises of the Republic* (New York: Harcourt Brace Jovanovich, 1972), 65.

143. Arendt, *On Revolution*, 133.

144. Ibid., 166–67.

145. Ibid., 173 (emphasis mine).

146. Ibid., 164.

147. Ibid., 166.

148. See the discussion of Arendt's distinguishing Lessing's concept of friendship between peers from Rousseau's concept of compassion and solidarity in fraternity in chapter 3, section 2, notes 30 and 31, of the present volume. See also Patrice Canivez, "Le Sentiment et Le Politique," *Hannah Arendt: Confrontations, Les Cahiers de Philosophie* 4 (1987): 53–80, a usefully qualifying account of Arendt's linking Rousseau's concept of pity as political passion to the *terreur* stage of the French Revolution with the equations "unlimited pity equals pitiless" and "*terreur* equals totalitarianism." Canivez argues that compassion in Rousseau is not unlimited and faceless, as Arendt understands it, but limited and visible: *voisinage, famille, face en face* (63). Less convincing is his own linkage of compassion with *l'amour de soi*—in contrast to *l'amour-propre*—in the direction of *l'amour d'autrui* and *communauté* (64).

149. Arendt, *On Revolution*, 174.

150. Arendt, "Civil Disobedience," 62–63. For a discussion of Arendt's use of this quote from *Gorgias* in another context, see the introduction to the present volume.

151. Ibid.

152. Arendt, "Civil Disobedience," 63.

153. For a discussion of the difficulties involved in remaining a moral person in extreme situations—battle, totalitarian rule—see chapter 4, section 2, of the present volume.

154. Arendt, "Civil Disobedience," 71, n. 35.

155. Arendt, "On Hannah Arendt," 308.

156. Hannah Arendt, *Eichmann in Jerusalem: A Report on the Banality of Evil* (New York: Viking Press, 1963), 16.

157. See Noam Chomsky, "Israel and the Palestinian," *Towards a New Cold War: Essay on the Current Crisis and How We Got There* (New York: Pantheon, 1982), 230–98.

158. James Miller, "The Pathos of Novelty: Hannah Arendt's Image of Freedom in the Modern World," in *Hannah Arendt: The Recovery of the Public World*, 203.

159. Hannah Arendt, "Karl Jaspers: A Laudatio," *Men in Dark Times*, 76.

160. Ibid., 76–77.

161. Hannah Arendt, "Karl Jaspers: Citizen of the World?" ibid., 86; the quote within this quote is from Jaspers' "Ueber meine Philosophie."

6. The Obscurity of Evil: Listening to Eichmann

1. Dagmar Barnouw, "The Secularity of Evil: Hannah Arendt and the Eichmann Controversy," *Modern Judaism* 3 (1983): 75–94.

2. This, of course, is more true for some groups of readers than for others. Black readers, as a group, might be less inclined to tolerate Arendt's bracketing of the slavery question in *The Human Condition* than white readers.

3. Hans Jonas, "Acting, Knowing, Thinking: Gleanings from Hannah Arendt's Philosophical Work," *Social Research* 44 (1977): 25–26.

4. Elisabeth Young-Bruehl, *Hannah Arendt: For Love of the World* (New Haven: Yale University Press, 1982), 239–44.

5. See Arendt's essays on Hermann Broch, Walter Benjamin, and Bertolt Brecht, in Hannah Arendt, *Men in Dark Times* (New York: Harcourt Brace Jovanovich, 1968).

6. Hans Jonas, "Biological Foundations of Individuality," *Philosophical Essays: From Ancient Creed to Technological Man* (Englewood Cliffs, N.J.: Prentice-Hall, 1974), 196.

7. Bruno Bettelheim, "Eichmann, the System, the Victims," *New Republic* 148, no. 4 (1963): 23–33; reprinted in *Die Kontroverse Hannah Arendt: Eichmann und die Juden*, ed. F. A. Krummacher (Munich: Nymphenburger Verlagshandlung, 1964), 91–113. See also H. G. Adler, *Der Verwaltete Mensch Studien zur Deportation der Juden aus Deutschland* (Tübingen: Mohr, 1974).

8. Michael Denneny, "The Privilege of Ourselves: Hannah Arendt on Judgment," in *Hannah Arendt: The Recovery of the Public World*, ed. Melvyn A. Hill (New York: St. Martin's Press, 1979), 255; Denneny quotes from his notes on Arendt's lectures.

9. Ibid.

10. Hannah Arendt, *Eichmann in Jerusalem: A Report on the Banality of Evil* (New York: Viking Press, 1963), 209. Arendt made a large number of small changes for the 1964 German edition and the 1965 revised second American edition. These changes reflected her desire to remove or change passages that could too easily be misunderstood/misconstrued as hostility toward Israel or insufficient respect for the difficulties of Jewish history.

11. Ibid., 212. See also Arendt's exchange with Hans Jonas, in *Hannah Arendt: The Recovery of the Public World*, 311–15.

12. Arendt, *Eichmann in Jerusalem*, 224.

13. Charles Y. Glock, Gertrude J. Selznick, and Joe L. Spaeth, *The Apathetic Majority: A Study Based on Public Responses to the Eichmann Trial* (New York: Harper and Row, 1966), 1.

14. Ibid., 5.

15. Ibid., 129–31.

16. Arendt, *Eichmann in Jerusalem*, 4. See also Hannah Arendt to Heinrich Bluecher, May 6, 1961, in which she describes the trial as "a real show trial"—more

importantly, as a trial that has little to do with Eichmann and everything to do with the sufferings of the Jews (Library of Congress).

17. Arendt, *Eichmann in Jerusalem*, 5.

18. Ibid., 233.

19. Ibid., 245–46.

20. Ibid., 247. See Hannah Arendt to Karl Jaspers, Feb. 5, 1961 (*Hannah Arendt, Karl Jaspers Briefwechsel, 1926–1969*, ed. Lotte Koehler and Hans Saner [Munich: Piper, 1985], no. 277), in which she tries to arrive at a definition of Eichmann's crime before the beginning of the trial: "One will probably have to use the concept of *hostis humani generis*—whatever way you translate that, but not: crime against humaneness (*Menschlichkeit*) but humanity (*Menschheit*)." It was decisive, she thought, to understand that although the Jews had been the main victims, one had to define the crime in broader terms.

21. Ibid.

22. Ibid., 253.

23. Ibid., 249.

24. See Golo Mann, "Der verdrehte Eichmann," in *Die Kontroverse Hannah Arendt*, 190–98; and Hugh Trevor-Roper, "How Innocent was Eichmann?" *New York Times*, Sunday, Oct. 13, 1963, reprinted in *Die Kontroverse Hannah Arendt*, 182–89.

25. Arendt, *Eichmann in Jerusalem*, 256.

26. Ibid., 7.

27. Ibid., 16.

28. Ibid., 8; see also Arendt's 1950 essay "Peace or Armistice in the Near East?" in Hannah Arendt, *The Jew as Pariah: Jewish Identity and Politics in the Modern Age*, ed. Ron H. Feldman (New York: Grove Press, 1978), 193–96.

29. Arendt, *Eichmann in Jerusalem*, 37–38.

30. Ibid., 22.

31. Ibid., 23.

32. Ibid., 253.

33. Ibid., 230. Martin Buber's "Eine Anmerkung," in *Die Kontroverse Hannah Arendt*, 233–34, does not deal with the point Arendt raises; see also Mann's blatant misreading of her text, "Der verdrehte Eichmann," 192–93.

34. Hannah Arendt, "Organized Guilt and Universal Responsibility," in *The Jew as Pariah*, 236.

35. Bettelheim, "Eichmann, the System, the Victims," 24–25 (*Die Kontroverse Hannah Arendt*, 95).

36. Arendt, *Eichmann in Jerusalem*, 104.

37. A. Alvarez, "It Did Not Happen Everywhere," *New Statesman* 66 (Oct. 11, 1963): 488; reprinted *Die Kontroverse Hannah Arendt*, 178.

38. Arendt, *Eichmann in Jerusalem*, 111.

39. Alvarez, "It Did Not Happen Everywhere," 488. In her reply (Hannah Arendt, "The Formidable Dr. Robinson," in *The Jew as Pariah*, 260–76) to Walter Laqueur's review of Jacob Robinson's *And the Crooked Shall Be Made Straight: The Jewish Catastrophe and Hannah Arendt's Narrative* (1965) (Walter Laqueur, "Footnotes to the Holocaust," in *The Jew as Pariah*, 252–59), Arendt pointed out correctly

that she had only touched on the issue marginally and that it had been the concerted attacks on her book which had centered on that issue and indeed had succeeded in trumpeting it all over the world. Laqueur, in his reply to her reply, acknowledged that officers of Jewish interest groups had indeed tried to "monopolize the historiography of the catastrophe in their own hands; they did valuable work in collecting source material but discouraged all 'outsiders' and all the more ambitious projects to write the history of the period in one of the world's main languages; they failed to enlist younger historians and make them partners in their work. (Mr. Robinson's book was apparently meant to be the final word on the subject—at least for the time being.) This was a mistaken policy and it has resulted in a serious crisis" (Arendt, *The Jew as Pariah*, 278–79). See also Walter Laqueur, *The Terrible Secret: Suppression of the Truth about Hitler's "Final Solution"* (Boston: Little, Brown, 1981), especially chap. 6.

40. See, for instance, Ernst Simon, "Hannah Arendt—Eine Analyse," in *Die Kontroverse Hannah Arendt*, 39–77.

41. Arendt, *Eichmann in Jerusalem*, 105.

42. Gersholm Scholem, "Brief an Hannah Arendt," reprinted in *Die Kontroverse Hannah Arendt*, 208, 209; English version in Arendt, *The Jew as Pariah*, 242.

43. Scholem, "Brief an Hannah Arendt," 210 (Arendt, *The Jew as Pariah*, 243).

44. See Arendt, *Eichmann in Jerusalem*, 116: "Nobody . . . came to me and reproached me for anything in the performance of my duties."

45. Trevor-Roper, "How Innocent was Eichmann?"

46. Arendt, *Eichmann in Jerusalem*, 105.

47. Trevor-Roper, "How Innocent was Eichmann?" Scholem, "Brief an Hannah Arendt," quoted by Arendt in *The Jew as Pariah*, 243–44.

48. Simon, "Hannah Arendt—Eine Analyse," 57; Michael A. Musmanno, "Der Mann mit dem unbefleckten Gewissen," in *Die Kontroverse Hannah Arendt*, 86; Hans Tramer, "Ein tragisches Fehlurteil," ibid., 161; Eva Michaelis-Stern, "Tragt ihn mit Stolz, den gelben Fleck!" ibid., 159.

49. Manes Sperber, "Churban oder die unfassbare Gewissheit," in *Die Kontroverse Hannah Arendt*, 9, 32.

50. Simon, "Hannah Arendt—Eine Analyse," 68.

51. Scholem, "Brief an Hannah Arendt," 240–41.

52. Jacob Robinson, "Juedische 'Kooperation,'" in *Die Kontroverse Hannah Arendt*, 232; Simon, "Hannah Arendt—Eine Analyse," 51.

53. Michaelis-Stern, "Tragt ihn mit Stolz," 153.

54. Ibid., 160.

55. Arendt, *The Jew as Pariah*, 151.

56. Michaelis-Stern, "Tragt ihn mit Stolz," 153.

57. Arendt, *Eichmann in Jerusalem*, 47.

58. Scholem, "Brief an Hannah Arendt," 244–45.

59. Ibid., 241.

60. Arendt, *Eichmann in Jerusalem*, 36–38.

61. Ibid., 36.

62. Arendt, *The Jew as Pariah*, 246–47. See also the passage that I omitted in the quote, a clarifying reference to "a conversation I had in Israel with a prominent

political personality who was defending the—in my opinion disastrous—non-separation of religion and state in Israel. What he said—I am not sure of the exact words anymore—ran something like this: 'You will understand that, as a Socialist, I, of course, do not believe in God; I believe in the Jewish people.' I found this a shocking statement." The "political personality" was Golda Meir—at Scholem's request Arendt had agreed to leave out name and feminine pronoun—and Arendt reported on their conversation to Heinrich Bluecher on April 26, 1961: "Yesterday I was invited to a party together with Golda Meir and we argued (*streiten*) till one o'clock at night—but, as she is, after all, an American, we did not really fight (*zerstreiten*), in the end it was almost like friendship. The subjects themselves—essentially the question of the constitution, the separation of state and church, the prohibition of mixed marriages, respectively the still existing Nuremberg laws—in part quite horrendous" (Library of Congress; all translations from this correspondence are mine).

63. Arendt, *The Jew as Pariah*, 129.

64. Scholem, "Brief an Hannah Arendt," 242.

65. Arendt, *The Jew as Pariah*, 248.

66. Scholem, "Brief an Hannah Arendt," 241.

67. Ibid., 242.

68. See Robert Rie's silly "Literarisches Nachspiel zum Eichmann-Prozess," in *Die Kontroverse Hannah Arendt*, 33–38; Simon, "Hannah Arendt—Eine Analyse," 41; Michaelis-Stern, "Tragt ihn mit Stolz," 159; Mann, "Der verdrehte Eichmann," 190.

69. Alvarez, "It Did Not Happen Everywhere," in *Die Kontroverse Hannah Arendt*, 179–80.

70. See the instructive account of the trial by Harold Rosenberg, "The Trial and Eichmann," *Commentary* 34 (Nov. 1961), reprinted in *The Commentary Reader*, ed. Norman Podhoretz (New York: Athenaeum, 1966), 99–100, 106–9.

71. See Arendt, *Men in Dark Times*, 104: "The story reveals the meaning of what otherwise would remain an unbearable sequence of sheer happenings."

72. Arendt, *Eichmann in Jerusalem*, 43–44.

73. Ibid., 71.

74. Ibid., 72.

75. Ibid.

76. Ibid., 84.

77. Michaelis-Stern, "Tragt ihn mit Stolz," 159.

78. Arendt, *Eichmann in Jerusalem*, 231 (her emphasis).

79. Hannah Arendt to Karl Jaspers, Nov. 24, 1963, *Hannah Arendt, Karl Jaspers Briefwechsel, 1926–1969*, ed. Lotte Koehler and Hans Saner (Munich: Piper, 1985), no. 343.

80. This phrase appears in English in the original.

81. Hannah Arendt to Karl Jaspers, Nov. 24, 1963, *Arendt, Jaspers Briefwechsel*, no. 343.

82. Arendt made this distinction in her letter to Heinrich Bluecher of May 6, 1961 (Library of Congress).

83. In all her private communications, Arendt was highly critical of postwar Germans (politically to the right or left) and postwar Germany—though she had

praise for the Federal Republic's reliability regarding the reparation payments. In a long letter to Jaspers on March 14, 1965 (*Arendt, Jaspers Briefwechsel*, no. 371), she asserted collusion between Adenauer and Ben-Gurion regarding the direction of the Eichmann trial: Israel was not going to embarrass the current West German government, which had not encouraged cultural witnessing of the troubled past, because it relied on the reparation payments. In the same letter she praised Jaspers' *Der Spiegel* interview with Rudolf Augstein, "There Is No Statute of Limitations for Genocide" (March 10, 1965). In her letters from Jerusalem to Bluecher and Jaspers, she complained, rather harshly, about the many Germans who had come to observe the trial, suffering from a bad case of philo-Semitism, "Israelitis," and theatrical emotionalism. See especially the letter to Jaspers of April 13, 1961 (*Arendt, Jaspers Briefwechsel*, no. 285). In this letter she was also harshly critical of the "oriental mob" at the trial; the Galician prosecution—in contrast to the judges, to whom she referred as "bestes deutsches Judentum"—and the police, in control of all organization, whom she disliked because they spoke only Hebrew and looked Arabic; and, quite emphatically, the orthodox Jews, "who make life impossible for all sensible people." She was depressed by the great poverty she saw everywhere, and disturbed by the reality of what seemed to her a tremendous cultural difference. For her, too, as for most intellectuals, it had been far easier to celebrate human diversity than to experience it on a daily basis. Her cultural prejudices, quite outspoken in her letters to friends and family, should not be kept secret, because they were part of her acculturation and her temperament, both of which are reflected in her political thought. But they also ought not to be thought of as detracting from the validity and usefulness of her critical analyses of the trial. See also Arendt's letter to Heinrich Bluecher, April 15, 1961 (Library of Congress). In both letters she stressed the lack of real interest in the trial among the local population, asserting that it had to be artificially provoked.

84. See Kathy Eden, "Poetry and Equity: Aristotle's Defense of Fiction," *Traditio* 38 (1982): 17–43.

85. Working on the Eichmann book in the summer of 1962, Arendt wrote to Jaspers that she could not deny having fun with it: ". . . obwohl ich nicht leugnen kann, dass die Eichmanngeschichte mir Spass macht" (Hannah Arendt to Karl Jaspers, July/August 1962, *Arendt, Jaspers Briefwechsel*, no. 311).

86. See Arendt's introduction to Bernd Naumann, *Auschwitz* (New York: Praeger, 1966), xi–xxx. This introduction to a report on the Auschwitz trials, which began in December 1963 and December 1965, respectively, complements usefully the argument of her Eichmann report. Arendt started the introduction with an explicit critique of the German "climate of public opinion" (xii), which had enabled the defendants to lead normal lives under their own names for many years before they were indicted—a fact which influenced the trial and which she herself referred to as in some ways mitigating in her later essay "Civil Disobedience" (see chapter 5, section 9, of the present volume). She pointed out that "the local courts—with the exception of Frankfurt, where the state's attorney's office was under Dr. Fritz Bauer, a German Jew—had not been eager to prosecute, and German witnesses were notoriously unwilling to cooperate." But then she analyzed the stories of witnesses who did cooperate, stories which often indicted other inmates for being "asocial," "beasts in human form," mentioning that "the Galician Jews were highly undisciplined" and that the

German witnesses, who did not indulge in this kind of emotional presentation, were often unwilling to repeat in court what they had said in pretrial hearings on camera for fear of being accused of lack of solidarity (xiii). The weak link in the evidence of the trial were the witnesses, Arendt asserted. Expressing her horror in the face of the accounts of brutalities, she spoke about the intolerable guilt of the victimizers, but she also tried to show the accidentality of survival and the determination to survive which created impossible dilemmas in impossible situations (xxx). She analyzed the different cultural pressures brought to bear on the witnesses as well as the substance of their stories: in the case of some Jewish witnesses, the expected emotional inten-sity, which obscured the information; in the case of German witnesses, their orienting themselves toward public opinion—that was why the public climate in Germany in the sixties was so important—and still not thinking for themselves.

87. Irving Howe, "The New Yorker and Hannah Arendt," *Commentary* 36 (April 1963): 319.

88. Hannah Arendt, "Personal Responsibility under Dictatorship," *The Listener*, Aug. 6, 1964, 207.

89. Norman Podhoretz, "Hannah Arendt on Eichmann—A Study on the Per-versity of Brilliance," *Commentary* 36, no. 3 (1963): 205; reprinted in *Die Kontro-verse Hannah Arendt*, 119–35.

90. Podhoretz, "Hannah Arendt on Eichmann," 205.

91. Ibid., 207, 208.

92. Lionel Abel, "The Aesthetics of Evil—Hannah Arendt on Eichmann and the Jews," *Partisan Review* 30, no. 2 (Summer 1963): 219. Howe praises this essay highly.

93. Mary McCarthy, "The Hue and Cry," *Partisan Review* 31, no. 1 (Winter 1964): 84.

94. Abel, "The Aesthetics of Evil," 220.

95. Ibid., 225–26. See McCarthy's critique of this argument, "The Hue and Cry," 88.

96. Abel, "The Aesthetics of Evil," 219.

97. Ibid., 228–29.

98. Lionel Abel, "Jews without 'the Jews,'" *This World*, Winter 1983, 11.

99. Ibid., 14; Abel's reference is to the title of the British edition of *The Origins of Totalitarianism*.

100. Abel was referring here to the reaction to Arendt's problematic and pecu-liarly confused "Reflections on Little Rock," *Dissent* 6, no. 1 (Winter 1959): 45–56; some of these critical responses are included in this same issue of *Dissent*.

101. Abel, "Jews without 'the Jews,'" 18–19. See also Walter Laqueur's contin-ued misreading of the Eichmann report and bitterly hostile attitude toward Arendt (*The Terrible Secret*). In chapter 6 of that work, he came to conclusions about the usefulness of the Jewish councils which echoed what Arendt had said in her Eich-mann report and for which he had attacked her so fiercely. He did not, of course, think it necessary now to qualify his former attacks. Rather, in his contribution to a symposium on the fortieth anniversary of *Kristallnacht*, "Hannah Arendt in Jerusa-lem: The Controversy Revisited," he used the same arguments—obvious distortions of her statements, personal attacks—he had used in his original critique of the book,

starting with the following assertion: "It is difficult to think of a book in living memory that stirred up as much controversy as Hannah Arendt's *Eichmann in Jerusalem*.
Miss Arendt still has her angry detractors and fanatical supporters." This was a curious evaluation of the responses to the book, which were extraordinarily aggressive in
the negative "camp" and calm and circumspect in the positive one (*Western Society
after the Holocaust*, ed. Lyman H. Legters [Boulder, Colo.: Westview Press, 1983],
107–20).

102. McCarthy, "The Hue and Cry," 82.

103. Dwight Macdonald, "Arguments: More on Eichmann," *Partisan Review*
31, no. 2 (Spring 1964): 265–66. William Phillips, writing to Mary McCarthy about
her critique of Abel's piece, tries to be fair—by expressing appreciation for both positions: McCarthy is "above all out to defend Hannah" (ibid., 278); Abel is "trying
to convict Hannah" (ibid., 280). However, it seems to me that McCarthy is mainly
trying to clear the way to Arendt's argument. Phillips complains about Arendt's
"snide" tone, her irony, when talking about organized Jewry; she uses, he says, the
same irony and coldness when talking about the complicity of the German people,
"but, obviously, most of our friends are less sensitive to her anti-Germanism" (ibid.,
281). Arendt would have denied any such anti-ism, and insisted on the "privilege of
ourselves," the independent position from which she spoke (see note 8 above).

104. Ibid., 261.

105. Daniel Bell, "The Alphabet of Justice: Reflections on *Eichmann in Jerusalem*," *Partisan Review* 30, no. 3 (Fall 1963): 417–29.

106. See Hannah Arendt, "Karl Jaspers: A Laudatio," *Men in Dark Times*, 76–
77.

107. Hannah Arendt, "On Hannah Arendt," in *Hannah Arendt: The Recovery
of the Public World*, 308.

108. Arendt, *Eichmann in Jerusalem*, 231.

109. Hannah Arendt to Karl Jaspers, March 4, 1951, *Arendt, Jaspers Briefwechsel*, no. 109.

110. Arendt, *Eichmann in Jerusalem*, 247.

111. Ibid., 249.

112. Ibid., 253.

113. Ibid., 247.

114. Ibid., 256.

115. If Abel complained that Arendt had taken back in her Eichmann report
"the very insights into totalitarianism" which had made *Origins* such an important
book, he had failed to understand her argument; see Abel, "Jews without 'the
Jews,'" 14.

116. It is important to note here a significant accident: in 1963, the year the
report on the Eichmann trial appeared in book form, Arendt published her study of
the American Revolution.

117. Macdonald insists on the importance of a "universalistic" yardstick in this
context ("Arguments," 269). See also Melvyn A. Hill, "The Fictions of Mankind and
the Stories of Men," in *Hannah Arendt: The Recovery of the Public World*, 275–300;
and Stephen J. Whitfield, "'A Life 'Ennobled by Thought and Enriched by Love,'"
Patterns of Prejudice 16, no. 4 (1982): 55–58, who argues, on the occasion of the

Eichmann book, that it "may thus be considered a vindication of the role to which many Jews have been attracted—that of the non-partisan intellectual, who notices the strangeness of the familiar and seeks to clarify the senselessness of modern history" (58).

Index

Mendelssohn, Moses (*continued*)
  Enlightenment tolerance, 68; *Jerusalem oder ueber religioese Macht und Judentum,* 66
Miale, Florence R., 280 n. 46
Michaelis-Stern, Eva, 235–36, 240
Milgram, Stanley, 281 n. 55, 282 n. 59
Military law, 142; domestic, 144, 147
Military necessity, 140–42
Military Penal Code, German (1872), 142
Misch, Georg, 63
Mitscherlich, Alexander and Margarete: *The Inability to Mourn,* 282 n. 66, 288 n. 129
Mitteilungsblatt, 103
Modernity, 15, 186, 187, 196–97, 208, 227, 229, 231, 254 n. 17, 293 n. 35
Mommsen, Theodor, 260 n. 21
Monster, 221–22, 230, 239, 245, 248–49
More, Thomas: *Utopia,* 255 n. 4
Mortality, 194–95, 200–201
Moses, Siegfried, 269 n. 58
Musmanno, Michael, 279 n. 25, 302 n. 48

Naphtali, Fritz, 88
Narrative perspective, 237–38, 243, 248
Natality, 128–29, 136, 165, 173, 176–77, 188, 211
Nathan, Michael K., 291 n. 19
Nationalism: German, 86–88, 90, 91, 93, 94; Zionist, 89–90, 103, 109
Naumann, Bernd, 304 n. 86
Nazi regime, 128, 136, 140, 143, 146, 148–49, 155, 158, 160, 162, 165, 167, 169, 171, 173–74, 218, chap. 6 passim, 280 n. 46, 290 n. 158; demonic nature of, 228, 235
Necessity, 179, 192–94, 197, 204, 206, 208, 217, 290 n. 7, 294 n. 62, 295 n. 67
Neue Freie Presse, 39
New beginning, 1, 10, 128, 148–49, 154–55, 170, 173, 176, 179, 186–87, 202, 206, 216, 226

Nietzsche, Friedrich, 28, 181, 184, 186, 293 n. 38
Nisbet, Robert, 297 n. 113
Nixon, Richard, 181
Nordau, Max, 270 n. 65
Nuremberg laws, 89, 302 n. 62
Nuremberg trial, first, 142, 144, 156–58, 279 n. 25, 283 n. 70

Obedience, chap. 4 passim
Ophir, Baruch Z., 265 n. 101
Oppenheimer, Franz, 268 n. 39
Order, chap. 4 passim
Oriental Jews, 113, 303 n. 83

Paine, Thomas, 297 n. 112
Palaestinozentrismus, 86–87
Palestinian Jews, 89, 109, 122–23, 128, 272 n. 100
Palestinian partition, 119, 121, 124, 136
Palestinian question, 105, 111, 132–33, 203
Panama scandal, 39
Pan-Semitism, 109, 236
Pariah, 39, 42, 44–46, 67, 70–71, 75, 78–79, 81, 83–84, 107, 119
Parvenu, 43–45, 67, 70, 75, 78, 82–84
Paul (the apostle), 256 n. 13
Permanence, 28, 199–200, 206, 226, 235, 250
Phillips, William, 306 n. 103
Philosopher-king, 191
Pinsker, Leo, 270 n. 66
Plato, 4–5, 28, 181, 183–87, 190–91, 193, 198, 294 nn. 57 and 58; *Gorgias,* 5
Plurality, 5, 24, 84, 173, 175–78, 184, 193–94, 196, 197, 200, 205, 217, 226, 229, 233
Podhoretz, Norman, 244–45
Poliakov, Leon, 55
Polis, 4, 13, 24, 132, 152, 190, 192–93, 206–7, 209, 211–12, 214, 221, 293 n. 31, 294 n. 61
Prepolitical phenomena, 213, 294 n. 62, 295 n. 67

Wilson, Stephen, 260 n. 19
Wirths, Eduard, 279 n. 27
Witnessing, 157, 243, 304 n. 86
Wolff, Jona, 135
"Woman Question," 42, 50–51, 264 n. 90
Woodruff, Paul, 278 n. 12
Worldlessness, 79, 82–83, 271 n. 93, 296
 n. 88
Worldliness, 32, 195, 197–99, 201, 217,
 220, 222, 224, 226, 235
World Zionist Organization, 86, 88, 104–
 5
Wrede, Prince Friedrich von, 40

Xenophon, 254 n. 15

Yishuv, 101–2, 107, 109–10, 113, 117–
 18, 122–23, 129–31, 133, 136, 235,
 271 n. 93
Young-Bruehl, Elisabeth, ix, x, 154, 246,
 253 n. 2, 258 n. 46, 288 n. 135
Youth Aliyah, 95

Zevi, Sabbatai, 119
Zionism, 38, 40, chap. 3 passim, 238,
 268 n. 39; ideology of, 86, 110, 131;
 political, ix, x, 89, 91, 96, 112, 135–
 36, 145, 224, 235, 247; revisionist,
 103–5, 119; spiritual-cultural, 97, 99
Zionistische Vereinigung fuer Deutschland (ZVfD), 38, 86–89, 94–95

Designed by Martha Farlow

Composed by Graphic Composition, Inc., in Eldorado and Bernhard Modern Bold

Printed by Thomson-Shore, Inc., on 50-lb. Glatfelter B-16 and bound in
Holliston Roxite A with Multicolor endsheets

DAGMAR BARNOUW is professor of German and comparative literature at the University of Southern California. She is the author of *Weimar Intellectuals and the Threat to Modernity*.